HH

Hans Holbein the Younger

Painter at the Court of Henry VIII

Essays by Stephanie Buck and Jochen Sander

Thames & Hudson

This book has been published to accompany the exhibition
Hans Holbein 1497/98–1543. The Mauritshuis, The Hague. 16 August – 16 November 2003
The exhibition was sponsored by Rabobank and Unilever

Lenders to the exhibition

Her Majesty Queen Elizabeth II
Her Majesty Queen Beatrix
His Royal Highness Moritz Landgraf von Hessen-Darmstadt

Staatliche Museen zu Berlin, Gemäldegalerie, Berlin
Herzog Anton Ulrich-Museum, Kunstmuseum des Landes Niedersachsen, Braunschweig
Hessische Hausstiftung, Darmstadt
Staatliche Kunstsammlungen, Gemäldegalerie Alte Meister, Dresden
National Gallery of Scotland, Edinburgh
Galleria degli Uffizi, Florence
Städelsches Kunstinstitut, Frankfurt am Main
The House of Orange-Nassau Historic Collection Trust, The Hague
Niedersächsische Landesgalerie, Hannover
The National Gallery, London
The Royal Collection, London
The Metropolitan Museum of Art, New York
Musée du Louvre, Paris
The Saint Louis Art Museum, Saint Louis
Kunsthistorisches Museum, Gemäldegalerie, Vienna
National Gallery of Art, Washington

Page 9: Hans Holbein the Younger, *Selfportrait*, *c.* 1542/43. Florence, Galleria degli Uffizi

Translated from the German by Rachel Esner
Catalogue, foreword and appendices translated from the Dutch by Beverley Jackson

First published in the United Kingdom in 2003 by Thames & Hudson Ltd, 181A High Holborn, London WC1V 7QX

www.thamesandhudson.com

First published in hard cover in the United States of America in 2004 by Thames & Hudson Inc., 500 Fifth Avenue, New York, New York 10110

thamesandhudsonusa.com

British Library Cataloguing-in-Publication Data
A catalogue record for this book is available from the British Library

ISBN 0-500-09318-0

Printed and bound in The Netherlands by Waanders Printers, Zwolle

Contents

Foreword

Around 1700, stadholder-king William III (1650-1702) had over thirty paintings from the British royal collections transferred to the Netherlands, to decorate his recently renovated hunting lodge Het Loo, near Apeldoorn. After William's unexpected death in 1702, Britain claimed them back in the name of Queen Anne, who had succeeded him on the throne, but the States-General decided not to accede to this request, and the British did not press the matter. So part of this collection remained in the stadholder's family throughout the eighteenth century. In 1816 William I, the first king of Holland, donated it along with the stadholder's remaining paintings to the Dutch state for inclusion in the Royal Cabinet of Paintings founded that year, which moved into its permanent premises in the Mauritshuis in 1822.

◂ Five of the paintings from Britain were attributed in 1700 to Hans Holbein the Younger. Three of them ended up in the Mauritshuis. In addition to a portrait of Jane Seymour, today attributed to the artist's studio, these were Holbein's masterful *Portrait of Robert Cheseman* and *Nobleman with a hawk*. Both these men are depicted with birds of prey perching on one hand, and it is fair to assume that this was why William III chose them for his hunting lodge. Whatever the case may be, the significance of his decision becomes clear when we realise that these two portraits are the only paintings by Holbein belonging to Dutch public collections.

◂ The staff of the Mauritshuis had long cherished the ambition of devoting an exhibition to Hans Holbein. We were fully aware, however, that it would be extremely hard to arrange for the loan of the paintings and drawings, which are almost five hundred years old and therefore very fragile. But Britain's royal collections again played a key role. At an early stage we were offered an extremely generous loan: fifteen drawings, three paintings and a miniature, all of them important works in the artist's oeuvre. This offer secured the nucleus we needed, enabling us to persuade others from whom we sought loans of the importance of the exhibition, the first ever to be devoted to this artist in the Netherlands. The result is a selection of almost forty paintings and drawings dating from almost every year from 1523 until Holbein's death in 1543.

◂ Hans Holbein was a versatile artist who excelled in a variety of genres and techniques. In the first few years of his career he worked as a decorative painter in Basel, made woodcuts for use as book illustrations, and painted a number of impressive Biblical scenes and altarpieces. As his career progressed, he focused increasingly on portraiture. It is this part of his oeuvre, above all, that earned him great fame during his lifetime. Many of his portraits, drawings as well as paintings, exhibit an astounding mastery of technique and an almost unparalleled ability to convey the character of those he depicted.

◂ Many of Holbein's portraits are of prominent contemporaries — great intellectuals as well as statesmen and military commanders. His appointment as court painter to King Henry VIII of England around 1536 led to a series of portraits of royalty and courtiers. Before then he had depicted some of his fellow countrymen in London, the Steelyard merchants, producing portraits of remarkable openness and spontaneity. And in 1523, while working in Basel, he made several portraits of Desiderius Erasmus that still largely determine the scholar's image today: the frail figure with noble features, seated in his study and holding a book, or depicted in profile, committing his thoughts to paper in rapt attention. The exhibition contains some superb examples of each of these types. We also consider ourselves most fortunate to have secured loans of the preliminary drawings for some of the painted portraits, thus creating a unique opportunity to subject the master's working methods to close scrutiny.

◂ The exhibition focuses primarily on the portraits that Holbein produced in England in the years 1526–1528 and 1532–1543, when he was in the foremost ranks of society and his artistic star shone brightest. But work from his Basel period has also been selected. Aside from the portrait of Erasmus already mentioned, from the

Louvre, this includes the *Darmstadt Madonna* from the collection of the Hessische Hausstiftung. This portrait of the Basel burgomaster Jakob Meyer and his family grouped around an image of the Virgin Mary is perhaps Holbein's most brilliant painting. It had no longer been provided on loan for many years, but an exception was made for this exhibition.

As the above account makes clear, this show could never have been achieved without the kind willingness of many people to entrust their precious property to us for a period of time. In the first place we are enormously grateful to Her Majesty Queen Elizabeth II, without whose generous gesture the exhibition would have been impossible. The loans from the Royal Collection make up the heart of the exhibition. We are also much indebted to Her Majesty Queen Beatrix for making available one of Holbein's rare miniatures. His Royal Highness Moritz, landgrave of Hessen-Darmstadt, also merits a separate mention for his willingness to allow the magnificent *Darmstadt Madonna* to return to this country temporarily after more than 300 years. Our special thanks are also due to Sir Hugh Roberts, Lady Jane Roberts and Sir Christopher Lloyd for their enduring and patient support of this project. Isabel, duchess of Ratibor, Count Jan de Marchant et d'Ansembourg and John Somerville all mediated to help procure loans.

Numerous members of staff at museums and others working in the field have laboured with true dedication to make loans possible or to provide us with information. I should particularly like to thank Maryan Ainsworth, Herbert Beck, Brent R. Benjamin, Michael Clarke, Timothy Clifford, Jean-Pierre Cuzin, Alan Donnithorne, Everett Fahy, Susan Foister, Silke Gatenbröcker, Heide Grape-Albers, John Hand, David Jaffé, Jan Kelch, Walter Liedtke, Julia Lloyd Williams, Henri Loyrette, Jochen Luckhardt, Neil MacGregor, Judith Mann, Harald Marx, Philippe de Montebello, Larry Nichols, Earl A. Powell III, Martin Roth, Charles Saumarez Smith, Karl Schütz, Wilfried Seipel, Bert Treffers, Annamaria Petrioli Tofani, Meinolf Trudzinski, Arthur K. Wheelock Jr, Marieke de Winkel and Bernard Woelderink.

The catalogue gains enormously from the articles by Stephanie Buck and Jochen Sander, who were willing to impart their fund of knowledge on Holbein's work. The catalogue texts were written by Ariane van Suchtelen, Quentin Buvelot and Peter van der Ploeg, while the appendices were provided by Epco Runia and Bieke van der Mark. The essays were translated into English by Rachel Esner, and the entries by Beverley Jackson. Victor de Leeuw designed the catalogue for the publisher.

Two paintings were restored especially for this exhibition. For the restoration of the *Portrait of Jane Seymour* from the Kunsthistorisches Museum in Vienna, I should like to thank Karl Schütz and restorer Monika Strolz. Johnny van Haeften provided the funding that made the restoration of Holbein's *Portrait of Robert Cheseman* financially possible. Petria Noble at the Mauritshuis was responsible for the difficult task of the actual restoration work.

An immensely costly exhibition such as Hans Holbein 1497/98–1543 is heavily reliant upon financial support from third parties. We are grateful to the Rabobank and to Unilever for their willingness to sponsor this project. The Mauritshuis has collaborated closely with both these companies in the recent past, on the Johannes Vermeer and Paulus Potter exhibitions. Many will share our pleasure that we were able to appeal to their generosity once again. In addition, the museum again received considerable financial assistance from the Friends of the Mauritshuis.

In conclusion, I should like to thank all the staff at the Mauritshuis for their exemplary dedication, creativity, and determination in helping to bring this exhibition about. The outstanding cooperation between the different departments during the long and sometimes complicated preparations is worthy of special mention.

The reputation of the Mauritshuis is based on its Dutch Masters of the Golden Age. It should not be forgotten, however, that the gallery's collection is far more comprehensive than this. Besides the well-known masterpieces by Rembrandt and Vermeer and their contemporaries, the Mauritshuis boasts Dutch paintings from the eighteenth century, Flemish Masters from the fifteenth, sixteenth and seventeenth centuries, and a number of German paintings from the sixteenth century, including the works by Holbein already mentioned. The present exhibition seeks to highlight this latter, less well-known aspect of the collection. The Mauritshuis is delighted that thanks to the kind cooperation of so many people from home and abroad, it is able to present this superb overview of the work of one of the world's greatest artists. I hope that many art lovers will derive inspiration from the paintings, drawings and miniatures of the extraordinarily accomplished Hans Holbein the Younger.

Frederik J. Duparc
Director

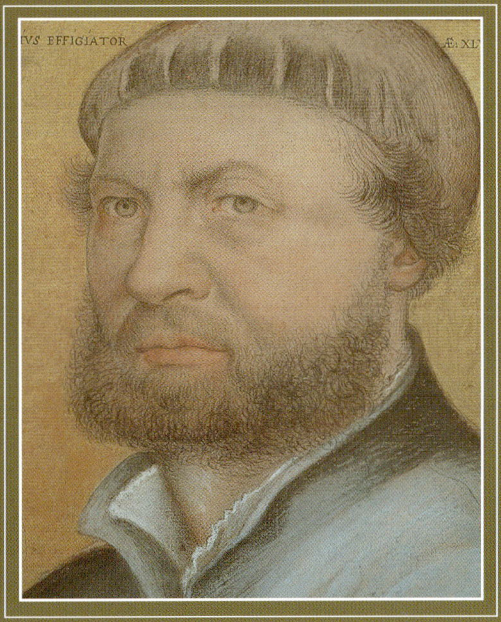
IVS EFFIGIATOR
Æ. XL

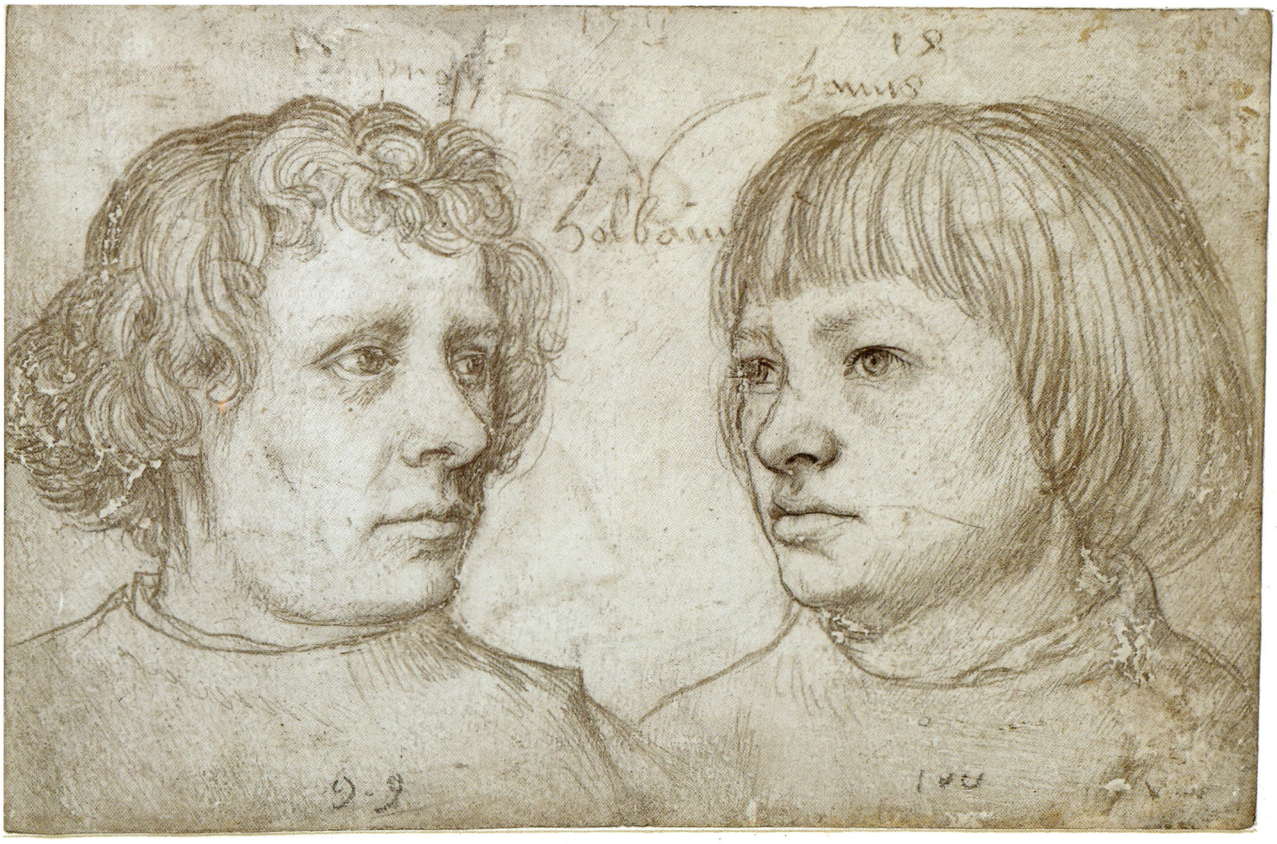

fig. 1
Hans Holbein the Elder, *Portrait of Ambrosius and Hans Holbein*, 1511.
Silverpoint on white-coated paper, 103 x 155 mm.
Berlin, Staatliche Museen zu Berlin, Kupferstichkabinett

Hans Holbein the Younger

Portraitist of the Renaissance

Stephanie Buck

As almost no other period in European history, the Renaissance was characterised by its internationality. Although during the Middle Ages the ubiquity of Latin had already helped facilitate the exchange of ideas among scholars, Gutenberg's invention of printing around the middle of the fifteenth century accelerated the wide and accurate diffusion of thoughts and discoveries in all areas of the humanities. Thanks to their judicious policies of intermarriage, many of Europe's ruling houses were closely linked, while trade joined the countries north and south of the Alps at the economic level.

This was the period in which today's western understanding of humanity was formed: the humanists regarded man as an independent being, capable of rational thought and assuming responsibility within the Christian world view; he was at the centre of their thought. In the north, this laid the foundation for the profound social and religious changes of the Reformation. At around the same time, the Anglican Church split from the Roman Catholic, and the English king declared himself the sole religious leader.

Hans Holbein occupies an important place in these developments in two respects. On the one hand, his portraits —already praised during his lifetime— provide us with likenesses of the major figures of the political and intellectual life of the period. In them, contemporaries such as Erasmus of Rotterdam (c. 1466/69–1536), Thomas More (1478–1535) and Henry VIII (1491–1547) appear as if alive, so that the epoch takes on a concrete, individual face. This can partly be explained by the fact that the various functions of these portraits and the attitudes of the sitters towards their own representation, as well as the works' owners can be reconstructed. At the same time, the artist's life and work are deeply marked by the developments briefly outlined above, so that his oeuvre as a whole and his biography —or at least what can be gleaned of it from the few details we know— appear as a mirror, reflecting the essential features of his age. This is especially true of the internationality that characterises Holbein's artistic profile. By focusing on his portraiture in particular, we can sketch this profile in some detail.

Early years in Augsburg

Hans Holbein the Younger was born in the flourishing commercial centre of Augsburg. He was the second son of Hans Holbein the Elder (c. 1460/65–1524), one of the most renowned panel painters of the Late Gothic period, who devoted himself not only to the traditional field of religious painting, but also to portraiture.[1] A large number of small silverpoint drawings, partly preserved in their original sketchbook context, bear witness to his extraordinary abilities as a portraitist, and his (not merely technical) affiliation with the Netherlandish art of the mid to late fifteenth century[2] he had probably encountered on a journey to the Netherlands.[3] The double portrait of the artist's sons (fig. 1), Ambrosius (c. 1493–1519?), the eldest, and the younger Hans,[4] is striking in its intimacy, and is the

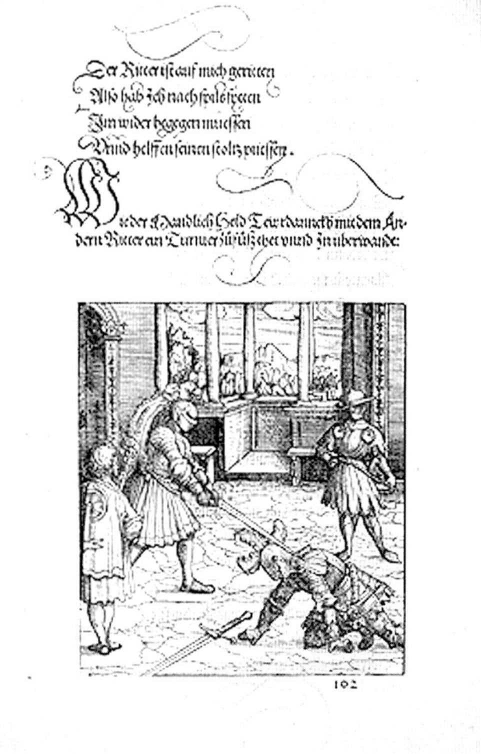

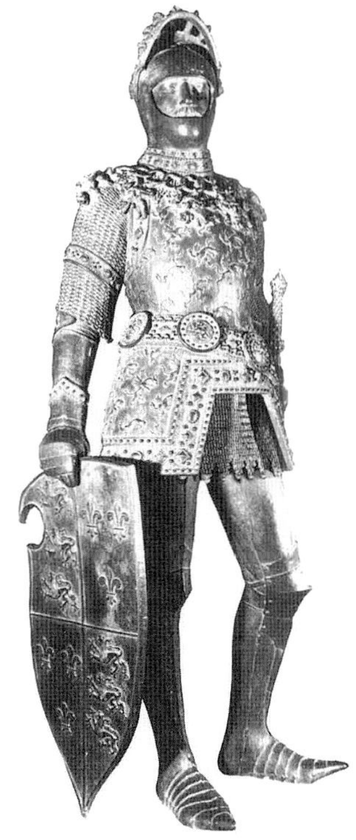

fig. 2
Hans Burgkmair, *Theuerdank defeats a knight*, woodcut from *Theuerdank*, 1517

fig. 3
Peter Vischer, after a design by Albrecht Dürer, *King Arthur*, 1513

only document of the brothers' years of birth: as indicated, Hans was fourteen at the time, meaning he was born at the end of 1497 or the beginning of 1498; Ambrosius appears to be about five years older; the numbers above his head cannot be deciphered, however.

‹ Few primary sources pertaining to the life of Hans Holbein the Younger have survived.[5] The Netherlandish artists' biographer Carel van Mander (1548–1606) was the first to publish an account of his life in his *Schilder-boeck* of 1604.[6] Researched around half a century after Holbein's death, however, it is neither reliable nor particularly detailed, so that to this day we have only the vaguest picture of how the artist may have lived and worked. It is generally assumed that the elder Holbein trained both his sons as painters. In addition to such practises as combining silverpoint and red chalk in a single drawing, transferring pattern drawings to panel using pouncing techniques (see cat. nos. 14–15),[7] or painting in oil glazes on a white ground — a process perfected by the early Netherlandish artists and used throughout Europe around 1500 — the young Holbein would also have learned to compose perspectively convincing spaces and three-dimensional figures.

‹ It was Hans Burgkmair (1473–1531), whom art historians today consider — next to the elder Holbein — the most important of the more than 20 artists active in Augsburg between 1490 and 1515,[8] who introduced another important feature into Augsburg art, namely the ornaments, architectural forms and figural types of the Italian Renaissance, which he had come to know on a journey to northern Italy in 1506/07. Burgkmair followed in the footsteps of the Nuremberg painter Albrecht Dürer (1471–1528), who had spent time in Venice in 1495/96 and again in 1505–1507. Italian ornamental prints and small sculptures also arrived in the city thanks to the trade of the local Fugger family, who were among the wealthiest merchants and bankers of the Holy Roman Empire. Their chapel at the Church of St Anne, the tomb of Jakob, Ulrich and Georg Fugger — perhaps designed by Dürer, constructed under the supervision of Hans Hieber (c. 1480–1521/22) and consecrated in 1518 — introduced Augsburg, and thus Germany, to the architectural style of the early Italian Renaissance.[9] This made it possible even for artists who could not travel across the Alps, such as Hans Holbein the Elder, to become acquainted with this important new vocabulary.[10]

‹ In addition to these Italian forms, with which the younger Hans Holbein was undoubtedly acquainted from an early age, it was likely Burgkmair as well who introduced him to the woodcut as a source of income and potential field for technical experiment. While Holbein's own father apparently hardly worked in the medium, Burgkmair belonged to a group of artists engaged in a number of large-scale graphic projects for Maximilian I (1459–1519), whose range and aspiration overshadowed everything previously achieved in this domain. In the so-called *Triumphal arch*, completed in 1515, and the *Triumphal procession*, left unfinished at Maximilian's death — the German emperor sought to promulgate his fame and that of the House of Habsburg.[11] Already in the years 1509–1512, when the younger Holbein was still living in Augsburg, Burgkmair designed woodcuts for a Habsburg genealogy and illustrations for Maximilian's autobiographical *Theuerdank* (fig. 2). Woodcuts would be important for both Ambrosius and Hans.

◂ It is difficult to judge the exact nature and extent of Albrecht Dürer's impact on the younger Holbein. It may be taken for granted that his famous woodcuts and engravings were known in Augsburg at the time.[12] Moreover, several sculptures based on his designs could be found in the city: the bronze statues of the Goth king Theoderich (*c.* 455–526) and the legendary King Arthur (fig. 3), cast by Peter Vischer (*c.* 1460–1529) in Nuremberg in early 1513 and destined for the monumental tomb of Maximilian I,[13] and the epitaphs of the Fugger brothers in the Church of St Anne, executed by the workshop of the Augsburg sculptor-family Daucher on the basis of Dürer's drawings from 1510.[14] In addition, Hans Schäufelein (*c.* 1482–1539/40), who probably entered Dürer's studio as a fully trained painter in 1503 and remained there until 1507, worked with Holbein the Elder in Augsburg around 1509.[15] It seems likely, then, that the younger Hans had studied Dürer's art during his apprenticeship.

—

In humanist Basel

Evidence of Holbein's interest in Dürer is found in his earliest surviving work: the marginal illustrations to Erasmus of Rotterdam's *In praise of Folly*, executed in Basel in 1515, when he was only seventeen or eighteen years of age (figs. 5-8).[16] It remains unclear exactly when and why Holbein left Augsburg, but it seems likely he came to the city in the Upper Rhine Valley in the course of his journeyman's travels. Here, he once again met up with his brother, who had already left Augsburg some time before. In this period, no one could predict that neither of the two young painters would ever return permanently to their native town: Ambrosius appears to have died at an early age — in any case there is no mention of him after 1519.[17] That same year, Hans was admitted to the painters' guild 'Zum Himmel'; he married the widow Elsbeth Binzenstock (p. 26, fig. 23), and became a burgher of Basel in 1520.

◂ Even before Martin Schongauer worked at nearby Colmar, the Upper Rhine Valley had been one of the most artistically fertile and innovative areas in Germany, attracting painters from other regions.[18] Having completed his training, Dürer, too, had travelled to Colmar, where he intended to meet Schongauer. Finding the master had died in 1491, he continued on to Basel, which, as a town with a university (opened in 1460), was already an important centre for book printing.[19] Like Holbein a generation later, the young Dürer worked for the printers, creating woodcut illustrations for, among others, Sebastian Brant's (1457–1521) *Narrenschiff* (*The ship of fools*), published in 1494 by Johann Bergmann von Olpe. Written in German, it was an extraordinary popular success.[20] In it, life is interpreted as a thoughtless voyage with an uncertain outcome, and all sorts of human weaknesses and sins are expounded on and denounced as foolish (fig. 4).

◂ Erasmus's *In praise of Folly* — in which *moria* (Folly) herself is the narrator — also exposes man's inanity, but in an ironical, reflective and ambiguous manner that paradoxically blurs the boundaries between foolishness and wisdom.[21] Erasmus had written this astute and multi-layered text in London in 1509, at the house of his friend Thomas More (see cat. no. 3), to whom it is also dedicated. It was first published in Paris and Strasburg in 1511, and over 40 editions, in the original Latin as well as in French and German, had appeared by the time of Erasmus's death in 1536. In 1515, Johannes Froben (*c.* 1460–1527) published a reprint with commentary by the Utrecht humanist Gerardus Listrius. A copy of this edition belonged to the Basel schoolmaster and classical scholar Oswald Geisshüsler (1488–1552), known as Myconius, who is thought to have taught Hans and Ambrosius Holbein to read and write, and may even have instructed them in Latin. It is illustrated with 82 pen-and-ink drawings; a note by Myconius on the title page indicates that they were executed within ten days.[22] Although it is difficult to be certain of the attribution of each individual drawing, most of them can, in fact, be ascribed to the young Hans Holbein, who drew with verve.

◂ Among the latter is undoubtedly the introductory drawing, which de-

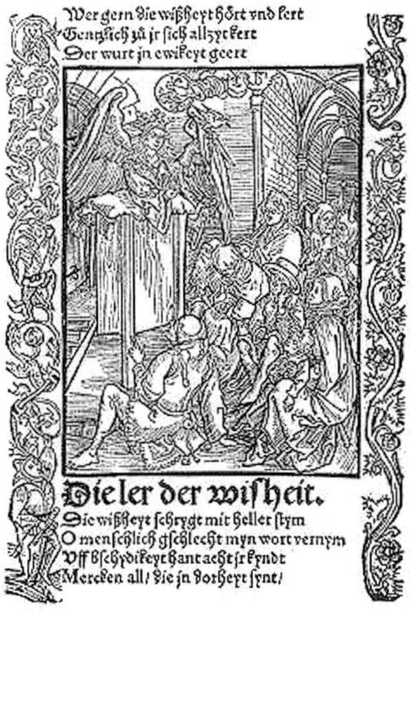

fig. 4
Albrecht Dürer,
The teaching of wisdom,
woodcut from
The ship of fools,
Basel 1494

picts Folly as a fashionable, pointy-nosed young woman at a pulpit, preaching with eloquent gestures to her congregation (fig. 5).[23] The columns and vaulting in the background indicate the scene takes place in the side aisle of a church. This is confirmed by a comparison with the Dürer woodcut that served as Holbein's model: *The teaching of wisdom* from the *Ship of fools* (fig. 4).[24] The scene takes place in a church with a view into a side aisle with ribbed vaulting, where Wisdom stands on a pulpit preaching; in contrast to Holbein's drawing, only some members of her audience wear the jester's cap. In Dürer's illustration to Brant's text, Wisdom is winged and crowned, and thus clearly identifiable as the direct instrument of the hand of God; in Erasmus and Holbein, Folly, with her cap and bells, takes over this role — an ironic figure, who imparts wisdom only in a roundabout way.

◂ In the text, Folly mocks many different groups and social classes. Accompanying Erasmus's description of the way princes always seem to prefer pleasantries from the mouths of fools to the truths spoken by the wise, is a depiction of Maximilian I —easily recognisable by his prominent nose, jutting chin and straight, shoulder-length hair—with a court jester (fig. 6).[25] It is not clear whether Holbein based the likeness on a portrait of the emperor, or if he had actually seen the sovereign with his own eyes in Augsburg, enabling him to draw his features from memory.[26] The drawing is remarkable on two counts. First, for the confidence with which Holbein has defined the profile without needing to correct himself. This already reveals the economical, linear style that would later characterise his portraits, where the sitter's face is captured with a few precise lines. Then there is the simple fact that Holbein included a representation of the reigning German emperor in this context, thereby concretising Erasmus's critique, although the author mentions no names. By 1515 Holbein certainly would have been aware of the fact that Maximilian was given to glorifying himself and his house through works of art to an extraordinary degree. His personification of the rank of princes —who 'in the midst of all their prosperity [...] seem to me most unfortunate, because, having no one to tell them truth, they are forced to receive flatterers for friends'[27]— thus takes on a caustic edge. Myconius, as the owner of the book, must have accepted this, and very likely even derived a particular pleasure from it.[28]

◂ The marginal illustrations to *In praise of Folly* show that even as a young man, Holbein entered into the world of satire and double entendre. That he actively reflected and commented on his personal circumstances in his art is further demonstrated by a black-ink drawing accompanying the passage in which Erasmus writes that powerful statesmen like Julius Caesar treat wise men like Brutus with suspicion, while failing to fear drunks like Anthony (fig. 7).[29] It depicts a bearded old man gazing at a youth wearing a crown and a fool, who face each other. The mature gentleman is unmistakably Holbein's father; the boy with the crown is Ambrosius, while Hans himself identifies with the jester.[30] It is difficult to interpret the drawing in relation to the text. Quite apart from this, however, Holbein's empathy with the fool clearly reveals something of his self-understanding and ambition as a painter: like the author Erasmus, he adopts the guise of moria in order to analyse human nature and behaviour with both acuity and irony.[31]

◂ Even before he became his patron, then, Holbein was acquainted with Erasmus's work. The latter was probably already aware of the young painter by 1515, as Myconius notes that the drawings should please him.[32] This appears to have been the case. Above the drawing of a scholar writing in his study (fig. 8) —inscribed (perhaps by Myconius himself) 'Erasmus'[33]— a remark of the humanist is recorded that reads: 'Oh, if only Erasmus looked like that, he would surely take himself a wife'.[34]

◂ There is some debate as to whether or not this is, in fact, a likeness of Erasmus.[35] A comparison with Holbein's 1523 half-length profile portraits (cat. no. 1 and p. 16, fig. 11) reveals only a vague physiognomic resemblance. The man in the drawing appears much younger and, sticking out his head and craning his neck, more lively and less reserved than the noble scholar-prince in the painting, sitting bolt upright, his eyes lowered, almost closed. As with the depiction of Maximilian I, the drawing is certainly not based on a life study of the individual in question; nonetheless, there can be little doubt that Holbein intended it as a representation of Erasmus, as it appears next to a passage in which Folly mentions the scholar by name.[36] Moreover, Myconius's annotation clearly indicates that the humanist himself identified with the figure. Evidently, Erasmus —who was 46 years old in 1515— was flattered by this youthful image, although he simultaneously sought to distance himself from it with his ironical statement that if he still looked like that he would take himself a wife. Of course, as a priest —he was ordained in 1492— this would have been prohibited anyway.[37]

◂ It is conceivable, however, that Holbein did know some-

▸
fig. 5
Hans Holbein
the Younger,
Folly at the pulpit,
1515.
Drawing from
Myconius's copy
of Erasmus's
In praise of Folly.
Basel, Öffentliche
Kunstsammlung,
Kupferstichkabinett

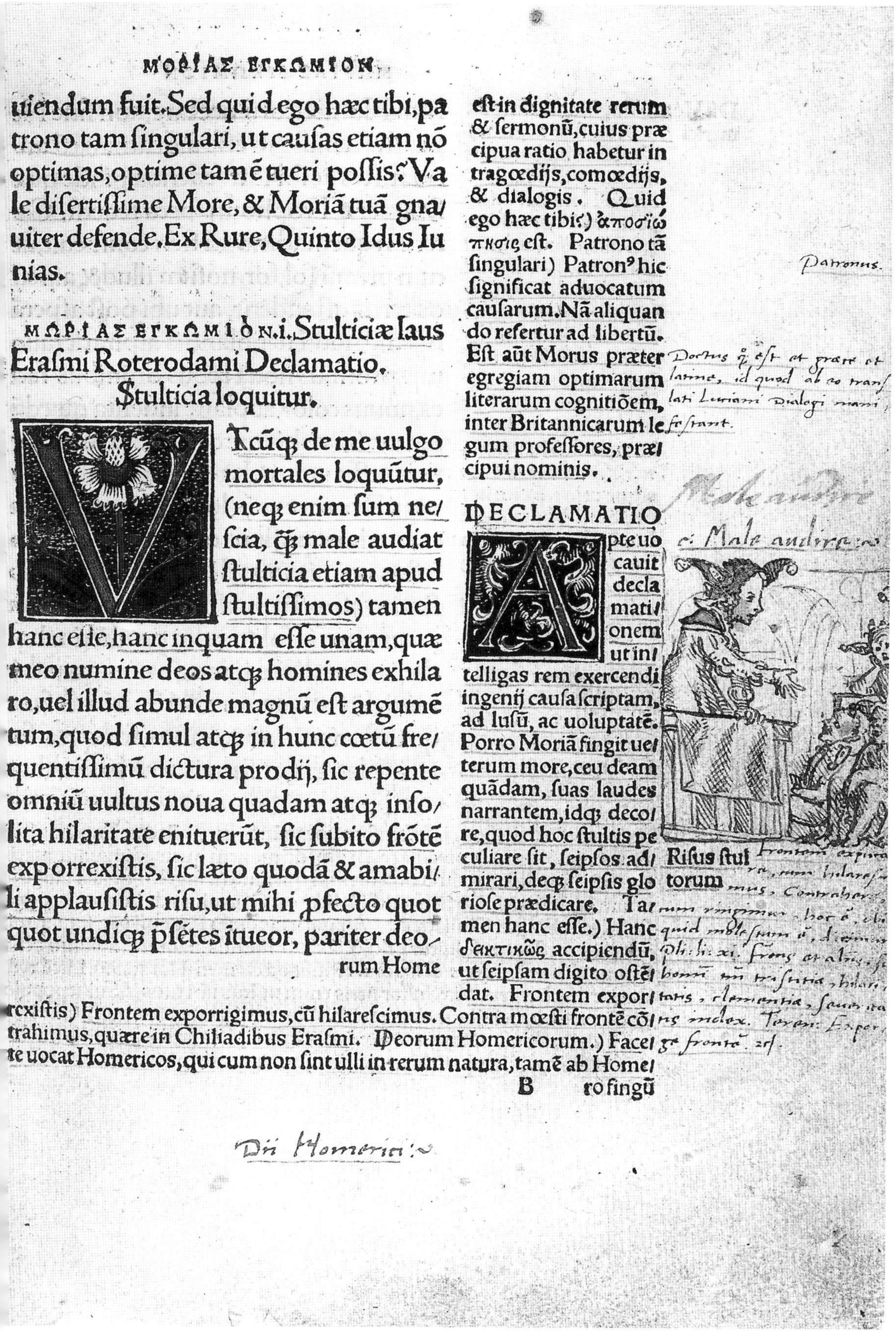

ΜΩΡΙΑΣ ΕΓΚΩΜΙΟΝ.

uendum fuit. Sed quid ego hæc tibi, patrono tam singulari, ut causas etiam nō optimas, optime tamē tueri possis? Vale disertissime More, & Moriā tuā gnauiter defende. Ex Rure, Quinto Idus Iunias.

ΜΩΡΙΑΣ ΕΓΚΩΜΙΟΝ.i. Stulticiæ laus Erasmi Roterodami Declamatio.

Stulticia loquitur.

Vtcūq; de me uulgo mortales loquūtur, (neq; enim sum nescia, q̄ male audiat stulticia etiam apud stultissimos) tamen hanc esse, hanc inquam esse unam, quæ meo numine deos atq; homines exhilaro, uel illud abunde magnū est argumētum, quod simul atq; in hunc cœtū frequentissimū dictura prodij, sic repente omniū uultus noua quadam atq; insolita hilaritate enituerūt, sic subito frōtē exporrexistis, sic læto quodā & amabili applausistis risu, ut mihi ꝑfecto quot quot undiq; ꝑsētes ītueor, pariter deorum Home

est in dignitate rerum & sermonū, cuius præcipua ratio habetur in tragœdijs, comœdijs, & dialogis. Quid ego hæc tibi?) ἀποσιώπησις est. Patrono tā singulari) Patron⁹ hic significat aduocatum causarum. Nā aliquando refertur ad libertū. Est aūt Morus præter egregiam optimarum literarum cognitiōem, inter Britannicarum legum professores, præcipui nominis.

DECLAMATIO) Apteuocauit declamationem ut intelligas rem exercendi ingenij causa scriptam, ad lusū, ac uoluptatē. Porro Moriā fingit ueterum more, ceu deam quādam, suas laudes narrantem, idq; decore, quod hoc stultis peculiare sit, seipsos admirari, deq; seipsis gloriose prædicare. Tamen hanc esse.) Hanc δεικτικῶς accipiendū, ut seipsam digito ostēdat. Frontem exporrexistis) Frontem exporrigimus, cū hilarescimus. Contra mœsti frontē cōtrahimus, quære in Chiliadibus Erasmi. Deorum Homericorum.) Facete uocat Homericos, qui cum non sint ulli in rerum natura, tamē ab Homero fingū

Risus stultorum

B

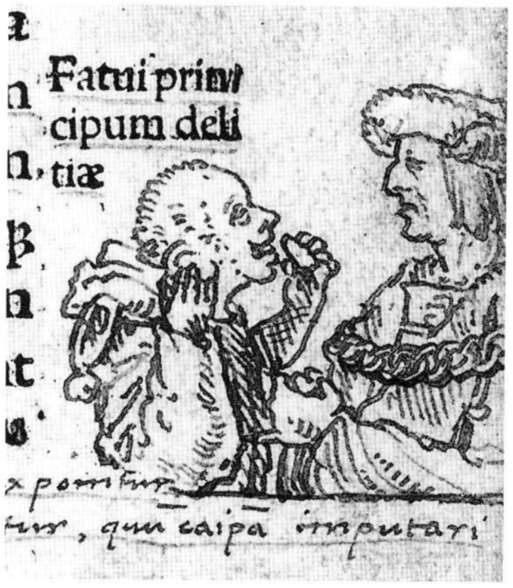

fig. 6
Hans Holbein
the Younger,
Emperor Maximiliaan I with a fool, 1515.
Drawing from
Myconius's copy
of Erasmus's
In praise of Folly.
Basel, Öffentliche
Kunstsammlung,
Kupferstichkabinett

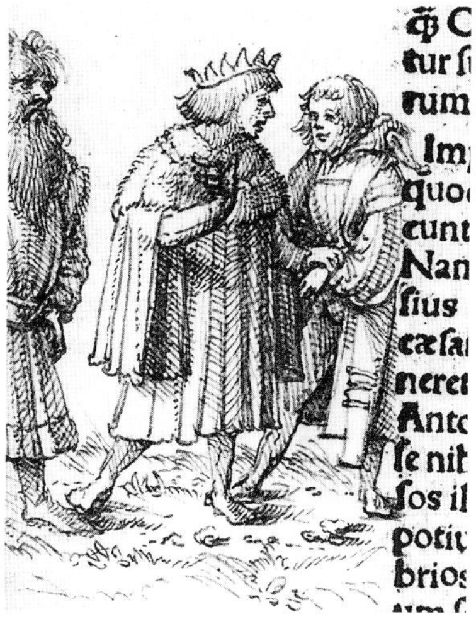

fig. 7
Hans Holbein
the Younger,
An old man with a beard, a young man with a crown, and a fool, 1515.
Drawing from
Myconius's copy
of Erasmus's
In praise of Folly.
Basel, Öffentliche
Kunstsammlung,
Kupferstichkabinett

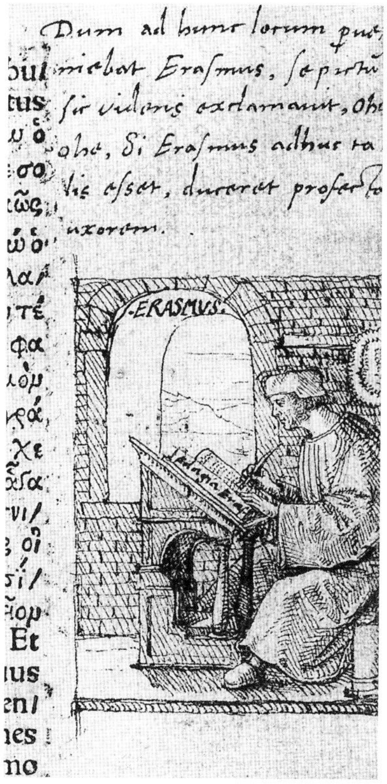

fig. 8
Hans Holbein
the Younger,
The diligent scholar,
1515. Drawing from
Myconius's copy
of Erasmus's
In praise of Folly.
Basel, Öffentliche
Kunstsammlung,
Kupferstichkabinett

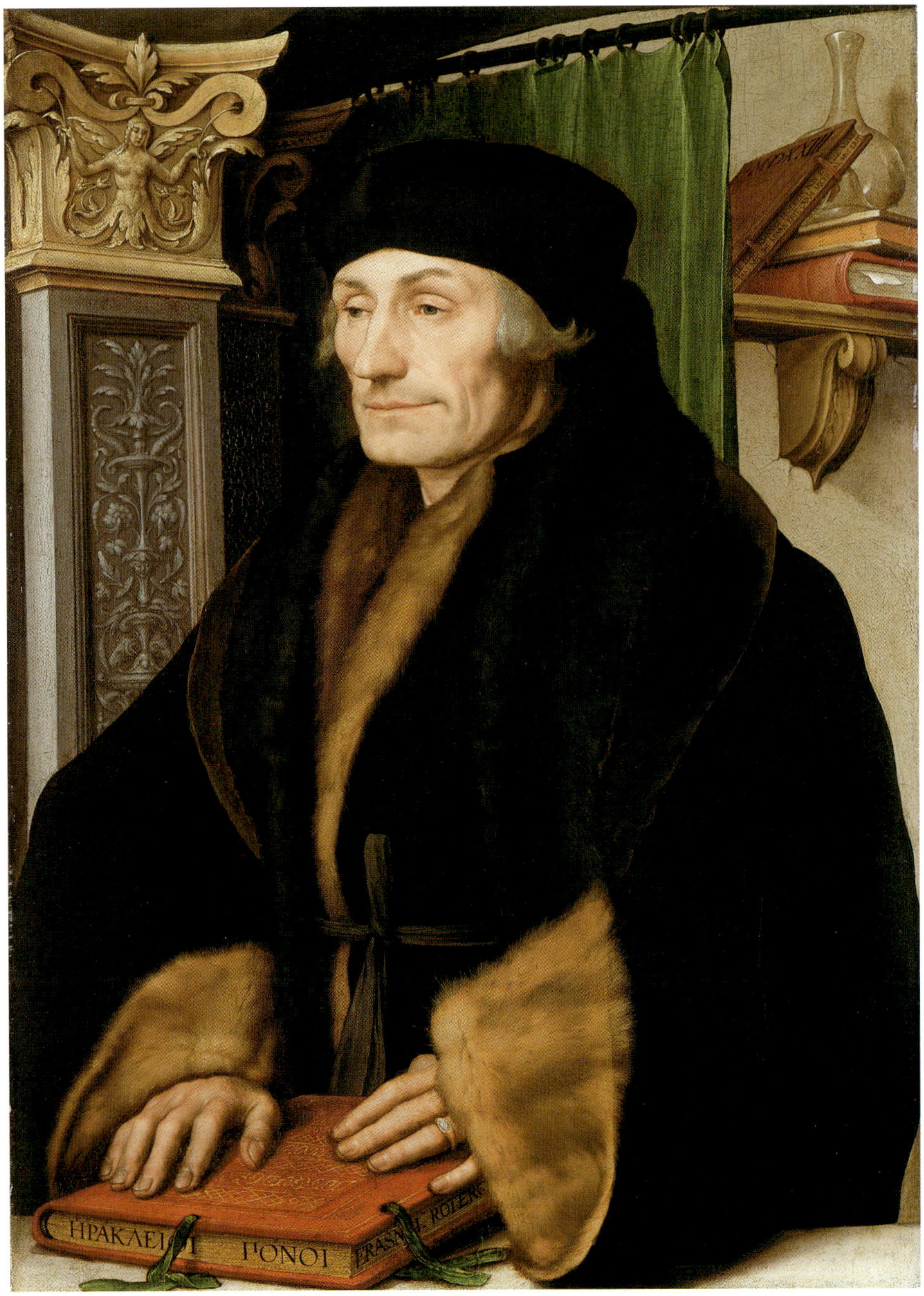

fig. 10
Hans Holbein the Younger, *Portrait of Desiderius Erasmus*, 1523. Panel, 73.6 x 51.4 cm. London, The National Gallery (on loan from a private collection)

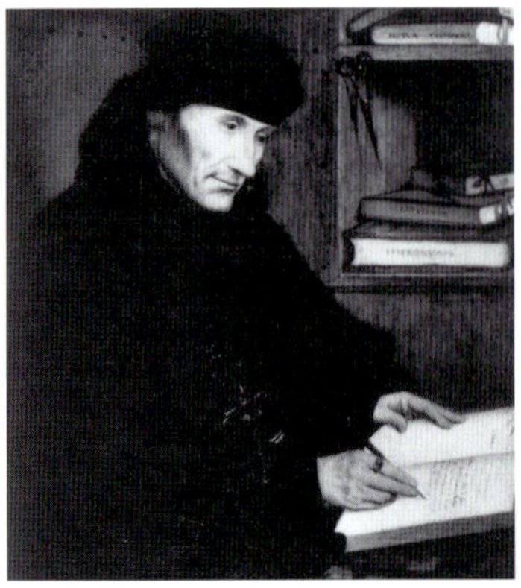

fig. 9
Quentin Massys, *Portrait of Desiderius Erasmus*, 1517. Panel, 50.3 x 45 cm. London, The Royal Collection

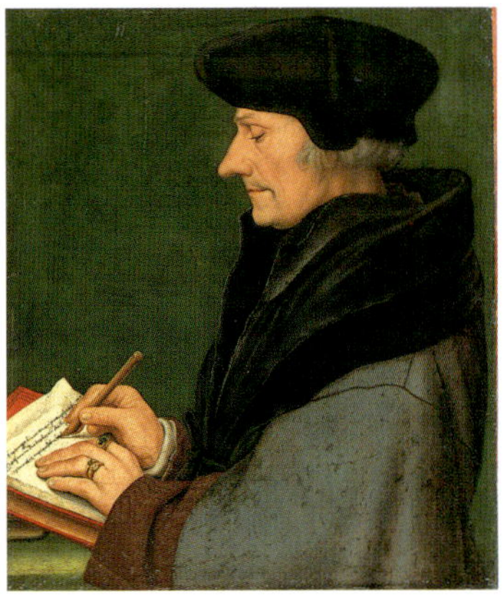

fig. 11
Hans Holbein the Younger, *Portrait of Desiderius Erasmus*, 1523. Paper, glued on panel, 36.8 x 30.5 cm. Basel, Öffentliche Kunstsammlung

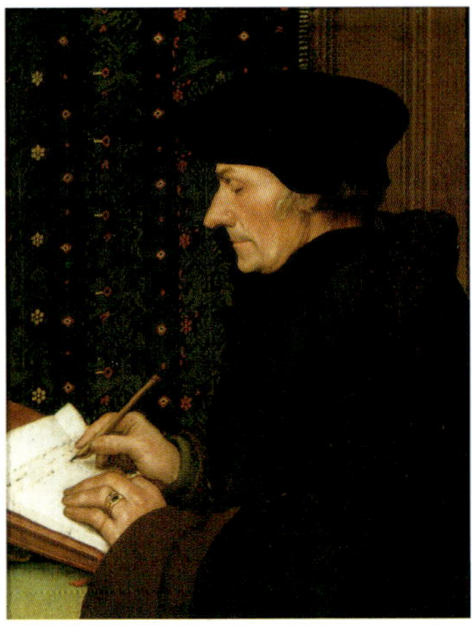

cat.no. 1
Hans Holbein the Younger, *Portrait of Desiderius Erasmus*, 1523. Paris, Musée du Louvre

thing of the humanist's appearance already in this period, as beginning in 1514 Erasmus spent just under two years in Basel, before settling there for the longer period 1521-1529. Holbein probably did not base his drawing on a pre-existing likeness, as the earliest documented Erasmus portrait was painted only in 1517, by Quentin Massys (*c.* 1465/66 – 1530) (fig. 9); the panel formed one wing of a diptych intended for Erasmus's friend, the humanist Thomas More, with the other depicting the Antwerp town clerk Pieter Gillis, called Aegidius (*c.* 1486–1533).[38] Holbein's 1523 portraits — the one in London with the Renaissance pilaster (fig. 10),[39] which shows the scholar in three-quarters profile, as well as the two closely associated likenesses in Paris (cat. no. 1) and Basel (fig. 11)[40] — were his first to be based on one or more actual sittings. During these sessions, the artist presumably made a number of drawings, which in turn served as bases for the paintings.[41]

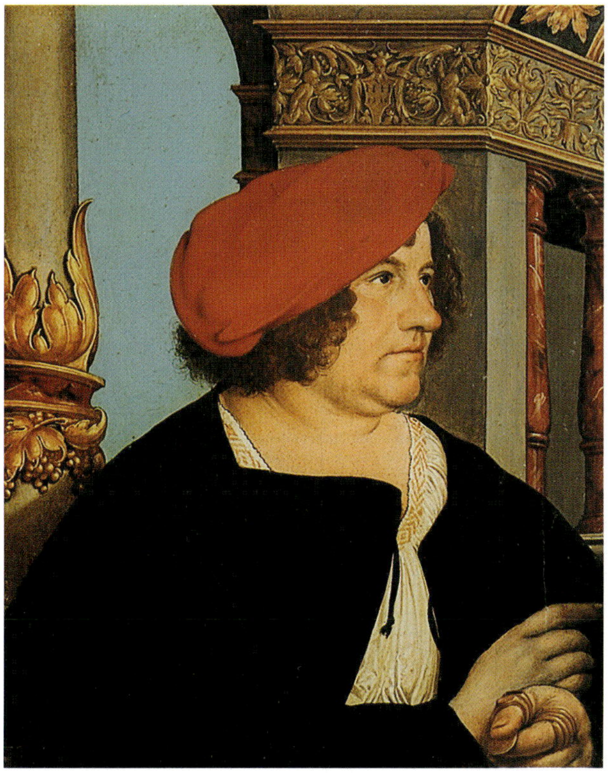

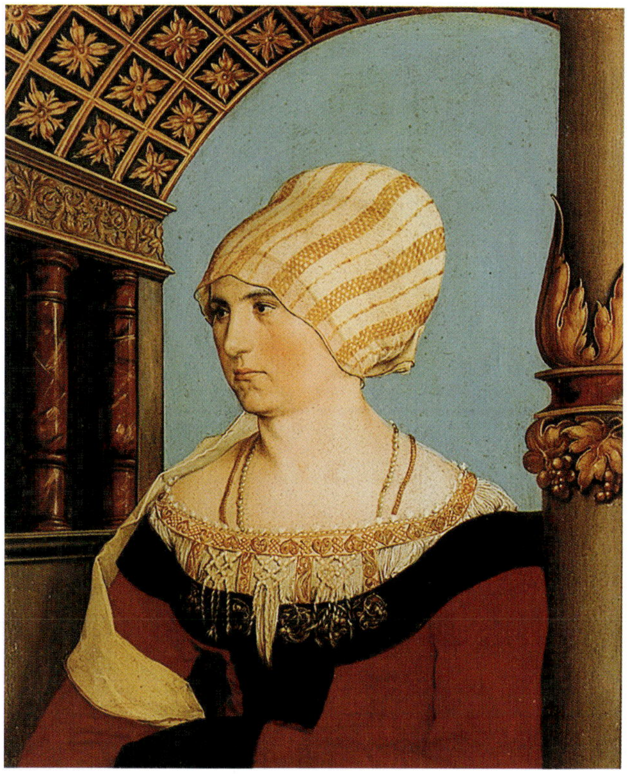

fig. 12-13
Hans Holbein
the Younger,
Pendant portraits of Jakob Meyer zum Hasen, burgomaster of Basel, and his wife Dorothea Kannengießer,
1516. Panel,
each 38.5 x 31 cm.
Basel, Öffentliche
Kunstsammlung

This working method is documented by Holbein's earliest surviving portrait panels, likenesses of the burgomaster Jakob Meyer and his wife Dorothea Kannengießer (figs. 12, 13), dated 1516, which the artist prepared in detailed silverpoint drawings.[42]

◂ The Paris and Basel Erasmus portraits 'quote' not only the profile view found in the drawing of the scholar in *In praise of Folly*, but also the pose of the hands, placed close together on the sheet on which he is writing. This correspondence was hardly a coincidence and one may even surmise that the favourable impression made by the drawing played a role in the commission for the portrait series of 1523, at least subliminally. Of greater importance, however, was probably the fact that by this time Holbein had made something of a name for himself as a portraitist in Basel, in particular with such innovative and lifelike works as the 1519 portrait of the young Bonifacius Amerbach (1495–1562) (fig. 14), Erasmus's friend and sole heir.[43] In addition, Holbein was already Basel's most important religious painter, and with the decoration of the Great Council Chamber of the town hall he received the most important commission offered by the city in the 1520s.

◂ Given the number of surviving images, it seems that at this juncture portrait painting, which would later come to dominate Holbein's career, was not yet at the centre of his work. As no contracts or receipts of payments for panel paintings have survived, and one can only speculate about the working hours invested, it is difficult to gauge which of the various genres he practiced was the most lucrative. An important source of income was presumably the woodcuts, many of which have been preserved.[44]

Intermezzi: in France and England

Despite his obvious success in Basel, Holbein does not appear to have been particularly well off. He was only able to purchase a house in 1528 — and this was probably due to the resounding financial success of his first sojourn in England. He set out on the journey in 1526, like Dürer in 1520/21 stopping first in Antwerp. He carried with him a letter of introduction, written by Erasmus to his friend Petrus Aegidius.[45] It is dated 29 August 1526 and asks the latter to have someone show Holbein the house of Quentin Massys, and adds that Holbein could also act as a courier if necessary. Clearly, Holbein hoped for some sort of exchange with his Netherlandish colleague, but we know neither whether the two actually met nor how Holbein was received in Antwerp — five years previously, Dürer had been feted like a prince.[46] The main reason for the trip, however, appears to have been financial: Erasmus states in his letter that the arts were 'freezing' in Basel, and that Holbein hoped to earn some money while in England.

Holbein had already left Basel once before, namely in 1524, on that occasion travelling to France, probably also in search of work. Once again, it is thanks to Erasmus's correspondence that we know something of the journey: on 3 June 1524, he wrote to the Nuremberg humanist Willibald Pirckheimer (1470–1530) that he had sent two portraits 'by a rather skilful artist' to England, and that the same artist had taken another with him to France.[47] The latter appears to have been one of the two profile portraits of Erasmus at his writing desk, probably the Basel version (fig. 11), which is painted on paper and was therefore easier to transport. It also depicts the scholar composing the first lines of his commentary on the Gospel of St Mark, written in 1523 and published the following year by Froben, with a dedication to the French king.[48] François I (1494–1547) was very interested in bringing Erasmus to France, promising him the position of treasurer of the city of Tours, which would have guaranteed his financial security.[49] Although Erasmus seriously considered taking up the appointment, his notorious poor health and the uncertain military situation in France at the time led him to decide against it. Given this background, Holbein may have hoped the portrait would attract the attention of the monarch, who had employed Leonardo da Vinci (1452–1519) as court painter from 1517 until his death, and win him as a patron.[50] He was apparently unsuccessful in this endeavour,[51] and returned to Basel, where he is once again mentioned in the sources on 3 March 1526, when he was paid for painting several coats of arms.[52]

The exact length and route of Holbein's journey to France is uncertain, although we do know he stopped at Bourges, where he visited the burial chapel of the ducal palace and made drawings (fig. 15, 16) after Jean de Cambrai's (died 1438) polychrome portrait sculptures (after 1416) of Jean de Berry (1340–1416) and his wife Jeanne de Boulogne (born 1377).[53] Here, for the first time, Holbein used yellow chalk in addition to the

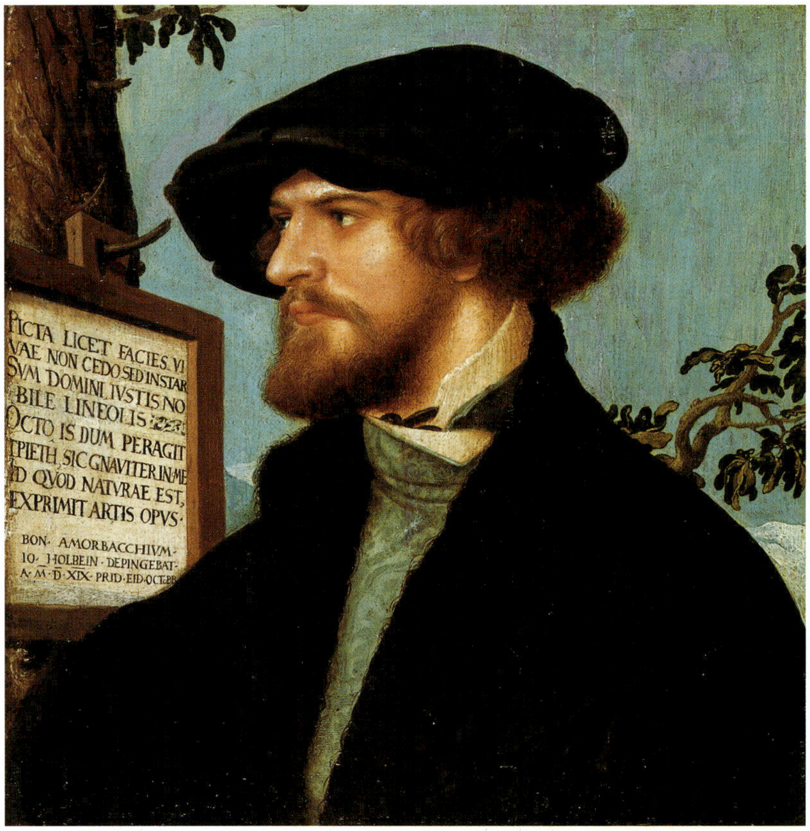

fig. 14
Hans Holbein the Younger, *Portrait of Bonifacius Amerbach*, 1519. Panel, 28.5 x 27.5 cm. Basel, Öffentliche Kunstsammlung

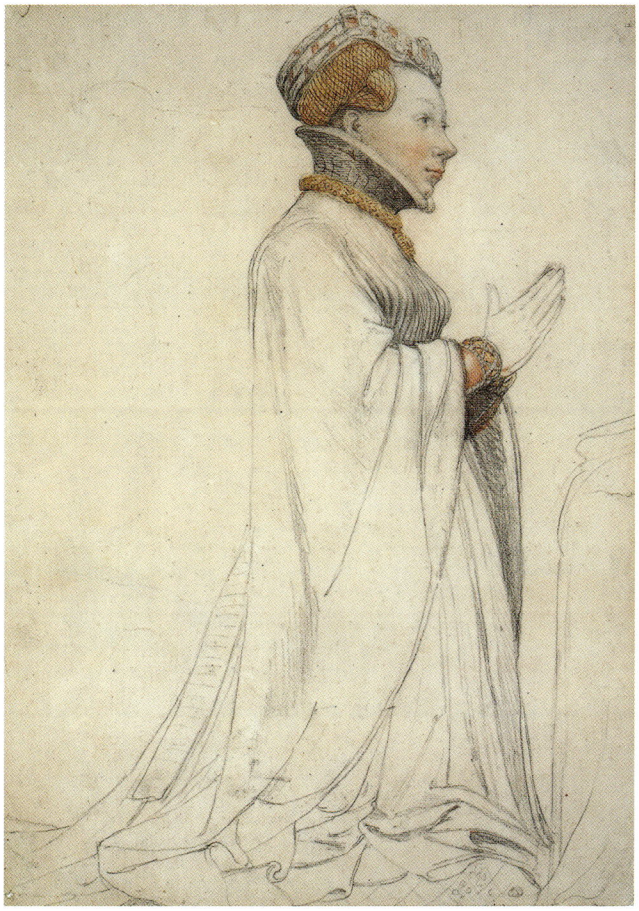

fig. 15
Hans Holbein the Younger, *Portrait of Jeanne de Boulogne, duchess of Berry*, 1524. Black and coloured chalk on paper, 396 x 275 mm. Basel, Öffentliche Kunstsammlung, Kupferstichkabinett

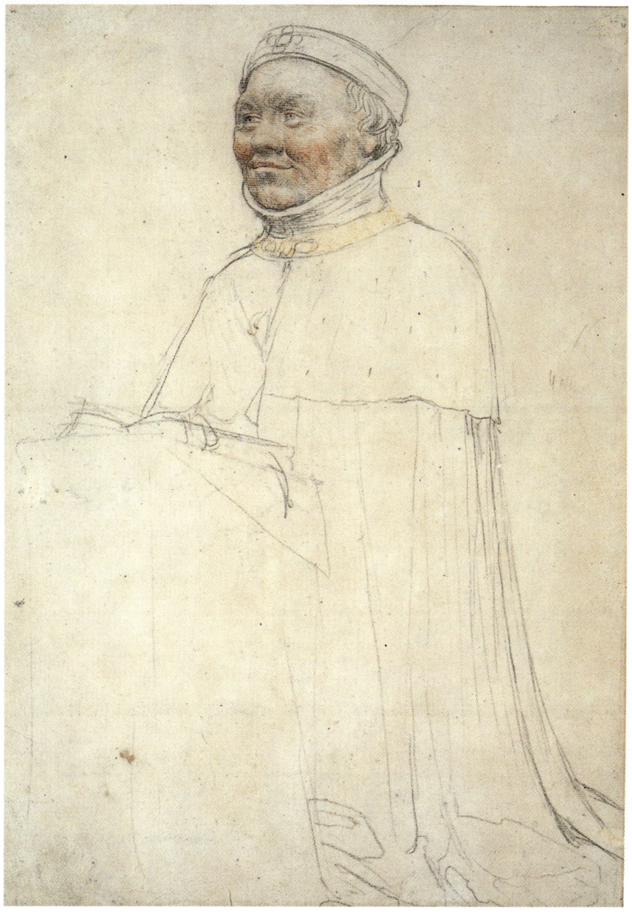

fig. 16
Hans Holbein the Younger, *Portrait of Jean de France, duke of Berry*, 1524. Black and coloured chalk on paper, 396 x 275 mm. Basel, Öffentliche Kunstsammlung, Kupferstichkabinett

usual black and red, thereby achieving a hitherto unknown painterly effect. This technique, first documented in France in the work of Jean Fouquet (*c.* 1415/20–1481),[54] obviously appealed to him, as he would use it repeatedly in his portrait studies in the years to come, for example in the 1527 series of members of the family of Thomas More.

◂ By the time he arrived in England in 1526, Holbein was presumably already familiar with Thomas More's *Utopia*: this treatise on political philosophy, with its underlying wit, had first been published by Dirk Martens in 1516 in Louvain; two years later it was reprinted by Froben in Basel, illustrated with two woodcuts attributed to Ambrosius Holbein (fig. 17).[55] Although Erasmus's letter introducing Holbein to his London friend has not survived, it most certainly once existed, as on 18 December 1526 More responded: 'Your painter, dear Erasmus, is a wonderful artist,

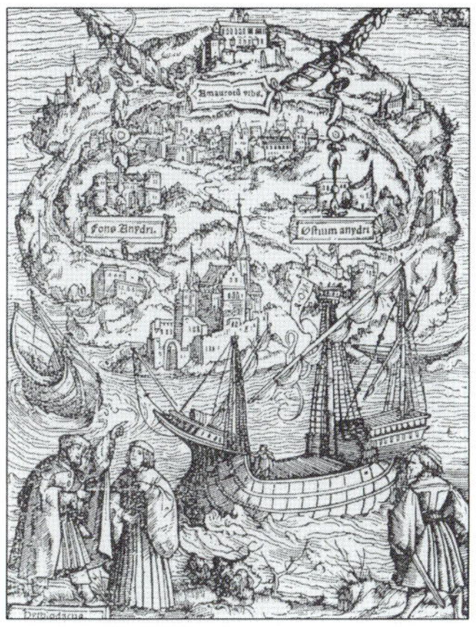

fig. 17
Attributed to Ambrosius Holbein, *The isle of Utopia*, woodcut for Thomas More's *Utopia*, Basel 1518

but I'm afraid he won't find England as fruitful and lucrative as he had hoped. But I will do my best to ensure that it is not a complete waste of time'.[56]

◂ More kept his word. As van Mander reports, he took Holbein into his home in Chelsea and commissioned at least two paintings from him: a half-length portrait (fig. 18)[57] and a group portrait of the More family, shown united in study and prayer. The latter is lost, and is now known only from a preliminary drawing (fig. 19) and in copies.[58] As the first family portrait in which the figures are grouped informally and shown in a domestic setting, this composition is extremely important for the history of the genre north of the Alps. Flanked by his ageing father and his son John, the *paterfamilias* is shown seated in the centre. The picture eloquently illustrates the notion of equality in the education for both daughters and sons, still unusual at this

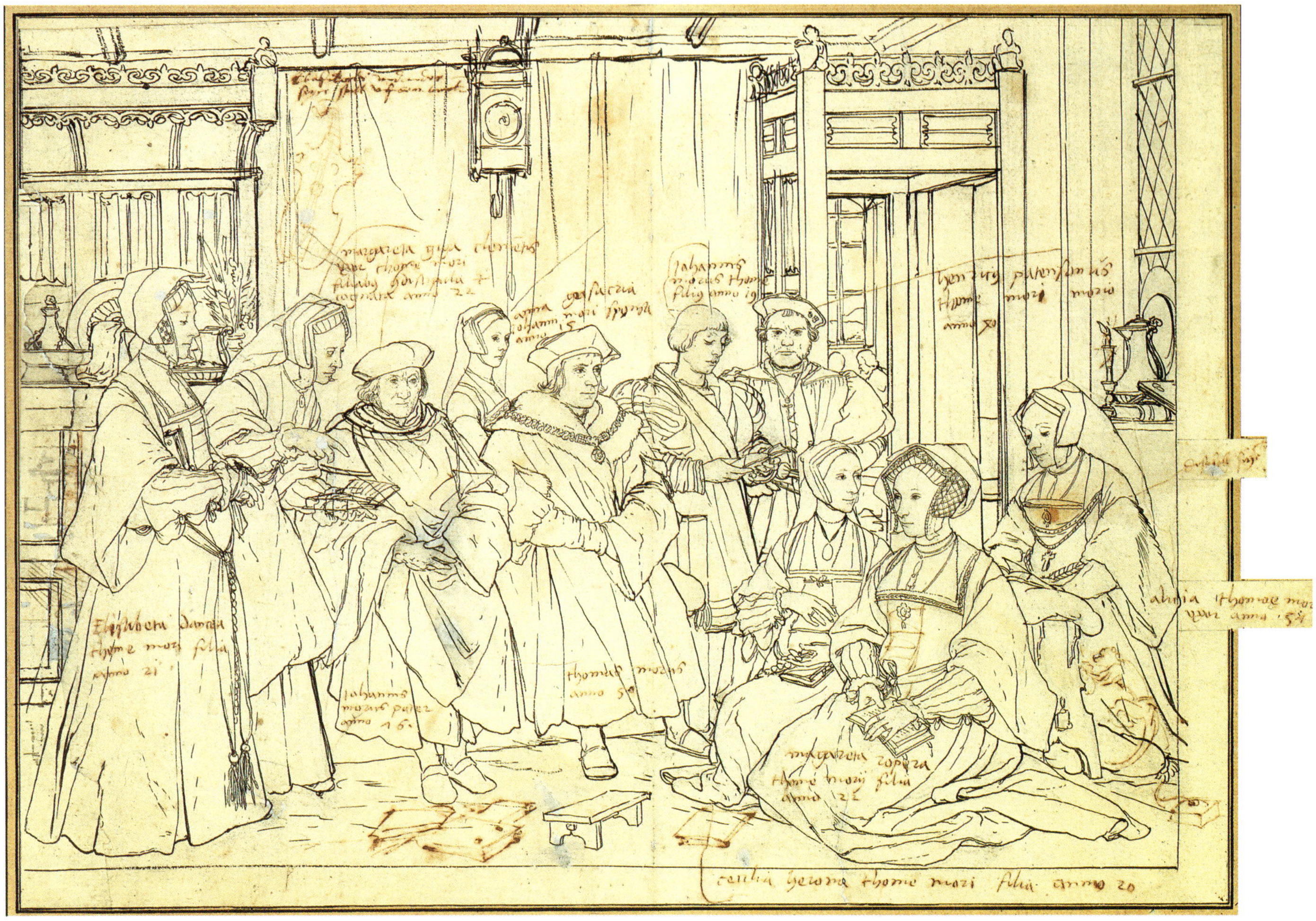

fig. 19
Hans Holbein the Younger, *Study for the portrait of Sir Thomas More and his family*, 1527. Pen and black ink on paper, 385 x 525 mm. Basel, Öffentliche Kunstsammlung, Kupferstichkabinett

time. This clearly demonstrates that More followed the principles expounded in his own *Utopia*.[59]

◂ As with the studies of individual figures, this purely linear pen drawing, with its strong emphasis on contour, was not meant as an autonomous work of art, but was rather a preparatory study — as indicated by Holbein's notations of the changes to be made, probably at More's request. For example, he added a few extra books strewn about the floor and recorded that Lady Alice was to be shown seated and not, as here, kneeling in prayer. In addition to the corrections written in the artist's hand, the Bavarian court astronomer and tutor to More's children, Nikolaus Kratzer (*c.*1487–1550), whose likeness Holbein would paint in 1528 (fig. 20),[60] added the names and ages of the figures in Latin.

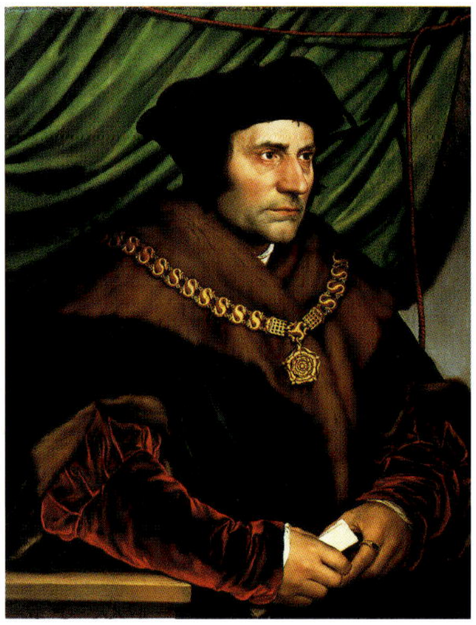

fig. 18
Hans Holbein the Younger, *Portrait of Sir Thomas More*, 1527. Panel, 74.2 x 59 cm. New York, The Frick Collection

◂ These annotations are also found on the copy of the painted version executed by Rowland Lockey (*c.*1565/67–1616) in the last decade of the sixteenth century (fig. 21), which also incorporates a large number of Holbein's changes — Alice More (1471–*after* 1534), for example, is here depicted sitting. Not included, however, are the books on the floor, which so well characterised the intellectual atmosphere of the humanist's household. Instead, a small dog occupies the foreground. Hinz and Müller have quite plausibly interpreted this as a sign that by de-emphasising the private character of the original, Lockey's copy was meant to shift the focus of the work to its more dynastical aspect.[61]

It was precisely the work's intimacy, however, that impressed and touched Erasmus when Holbein, on his return to Basel, presented him with a version of the group portrait traditionally identified with the compositional drawing discussed above, which comes from the 'Amerbach-Cabinett' and is thus documented as present in the city since the late sixteenth century.[62] In a thank-you letter of 6 September 1529, addressed to More's eldest daughter, Margaret Roper (1505–1544), Erasmus writes that the 'Painter Olpeius' had captured the family so perfectly that even had he been there himself he 'would hardly have been able to see more'.[63] In the same letter, and in another to More himself, he longingly expressed his wish to see his beloved friends in person once more before he died.[64]

This points to an important function of the portrait in this period, one that photography would assume at a later date, namely: to provide those far away with an image of the people they love. The illusion of nearness to the portrait subject assuages the pain of separation while simultaneously exacerbating it. Such an effect can only be achieved with a 'naturalistic' representation, one that reproduces the sitter's physiognomy accurately, and can be enhanced by depicting the person in his or her characteristic surroundings and engaged in everyday activities. No other northern European artist before Holbein had sought to capture a similar context, so that Erasmus's praise is both understandable and more than a mere topos.[65]

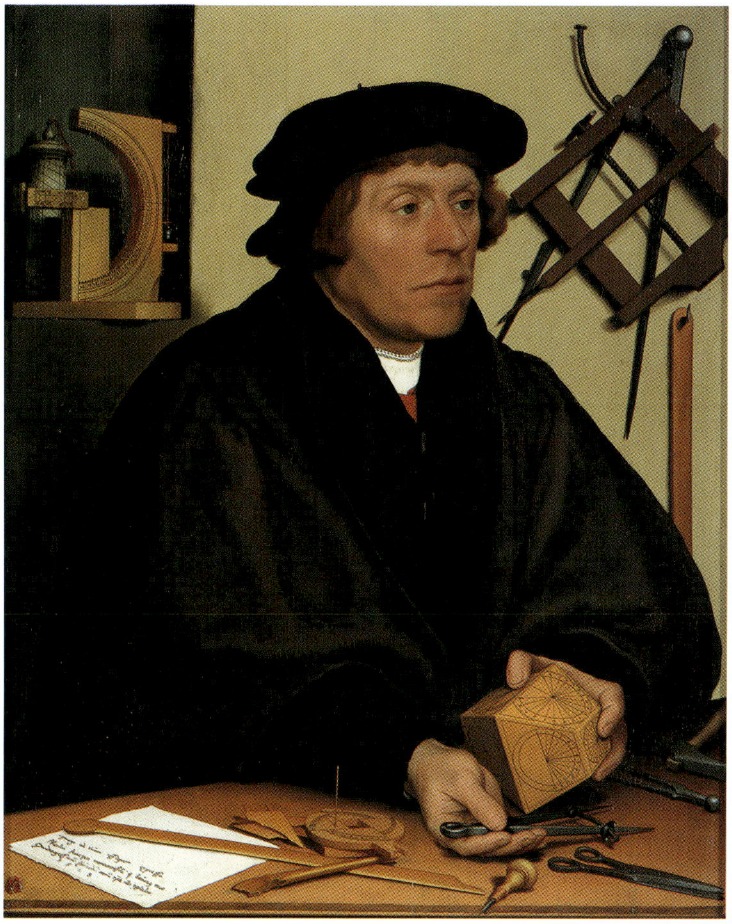

fig. 20
Hans Holbein the Younger, *Portrait of Nicolaus Kratzer*, 1528.
Panel, 83 x 67 cm.
Paris, Musée du Louvre

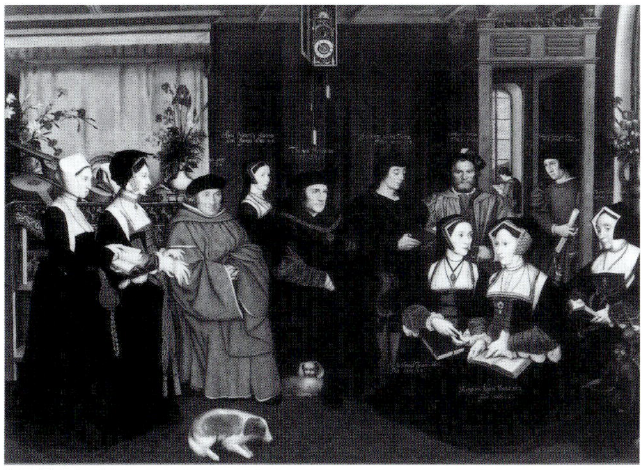

fig. 21
Rowland Lockey, copy after Hans Holbein the Younger, *Portrait of Sir Thomas More and his family*.
Canvas, 250.2 x 303.1 cm.
Wakefield, Nostell Priory

A further function of Holbein's portraits can be gleaned from a letter written by Erasmus to the archbishop of Canterbury, William Warham (c.1456–1532), on 4 September 1524. Warham was an important benefactor and had provided Erasmus with financial support since at least 1509.[66] In his missive, Erasmus expresses his hope that the bishop had by now received his likeness, so that he would have something to remember him by. The work in question was very likely the portrait now in London with the Renaissance pilaster (fig. 10) — one of the two pictures mentioned in the letter to Pirckheimer of 3 June 1524. The gift was designed to strengthen Warham's ties to the scholar while the latter was alive, and to serve as a reminder after his death. The medallion Erasmus commissioned from Massys in 1519 served the same purpose: it could be cast in either bronze or lead, depending on the status of the particular recipient.[67]

Warham's answer has not been preserved, but he must have been deeply impressed by Holbein's portrait, as he requested his own likeness from him in 1527, while the painter was working in London (fig. 22).[68] In his biography of the bishop in

De Antiquitate Britannicae, published in 1572, Matthew Parker notes that Warham had two versions made, one for himself and one as a gift for Erasmus.[69] The work now in Paris is the only one of these Holbein originals to have survived. It shows the archbishop in a pose similar to that of Erasmus in the portrait with the pilaster, giving visual form to his sympathy and admiration for his protégé.[70] The link between the works is not limited to the pose alone, but also has a deeper dimension: in his own portrait, Erasmus appears as an author having completed his work. The book lying in front of him is offered to the viewer —and thus primarily to Warham himself. He is meant to read it— as indicated by the loosened ribbons holding the cover together. Written along the fore edge, partially covered by Erasmus's sleeve, are the words 'ERASMI ROTERO'; on the text block, written in Greek, we find 'The labours of Hercules' — equating the superhuman achievement of the author Erasmus with the deeds of the antique demigod. While Hercules was the embodiment of physical power, the frail humanist is the incarnation of intellectual strength. The fruits of his labours, sponsored by Warham, now lie before him; Erasmus appears to present them to his benefactor as a form of thanks. By taking up Erasmus's stance in his own portrait, but here empty handed —the prayer book that should occupy the brocaded cushion has been pushed aside— Warham may be indicating his readiness to receive Erasmus's gift and to benevolently accept the scholar's gratitude. At the same time, he pays homage to Erasmus by adopting his pose.[71]

◂ Should such a structure in fact underlie the two pictures, it would place the notion of *dialogue* at their very heart — despite the fact that the figures themselves are mute. Given that the humanists cultivated discourse through their written correspondence, and attached great importance to it in the cognitive process, the portraits would thus engage with a fundamental aspect of humanistic thought.[72] In addition, Holbein could be seen as implicitly taking up a position within the paragone debate, asserting the primacy of painting over poetry.

◂ Holbein would certainly have recommended himself in England with such finely tuned portraits, so appropriate to the flexible spirit of the humanists — all the more as in contrast to the Continent the country had no established painting tradition against which he could be measured. Native artists such as 'Serjeant Painter' John Brown (died 1532) or his successor Andrew Wright (died 1543)[73] were far less of a challenge to Holbein than the scores of Netherlandish painters active at the time, in particular the miniature painters of the Horenbout family.[74] Gerard Horenbout (before 1465–1541?) was among the outstanding masters of his craft, and his son Lucas (1490/95–1544) was court painter to Henry VIII from 1525 until his death and also a renowned painter of portrait miniatures —a field Holbein would enter in the 1530s (cat. nos. 32, 35). Italians such as Vincent Volpe (died 1536) and Bartolommeo Penni (1491–*c.* 1553)—brother of Raphael's pupil Giovan Francesco Penni (*c.* 1496–1528) and of Luca Penni (*c.* 1500/04–1557)— who, like Nicholas Bellin da Modena (*c.* 1490–1569), had worked for François I in Fontainebleau, were active in England as well,[75] although on the evidence of the surviving works not as portraitists.

◂ It seems safe to assume there was some form of contact between these artists: in 1527 Holbein worked with Volpe on the ephemeral decorations for the new Banqueting House in Greenwich.[76] Among the numerous artists involved, it was a certain 'Master Hans' —who can be identified with Holbein— who was the highest paid. Thus, only a few months after his arrival in England he had managed to become a successful painter. His links to the English humanists, in particular to Thomas More, with his connections to politics and thus to the court, were pivotal.

—

In Reformation Basel

Possibly due to previous agreements with the city council, Holbein returned to Basel in 1528, after an absence of two years. On 29 August he purchased his house.[77] On 28 March 1531 he bought the building next door; this was probably made possible by the commission he had received in 1530 to paint the last remaining wall of the Council Chamber.[78] Almost no panel paintings have survived from the years before 1532, when he left Basel once again and settled permanently in England. In this period he reworked and completed the Darmstadt Madonna (see essay Jochen Sander and cat. no. 2), executed for Jakob Meyer already in 1526, before the first England journey. He also painted a portrait of his own wife and two children, Philip and Catherine (fig. 23),[79] and probably another of Erasmus, this time in tondo,[80] and several

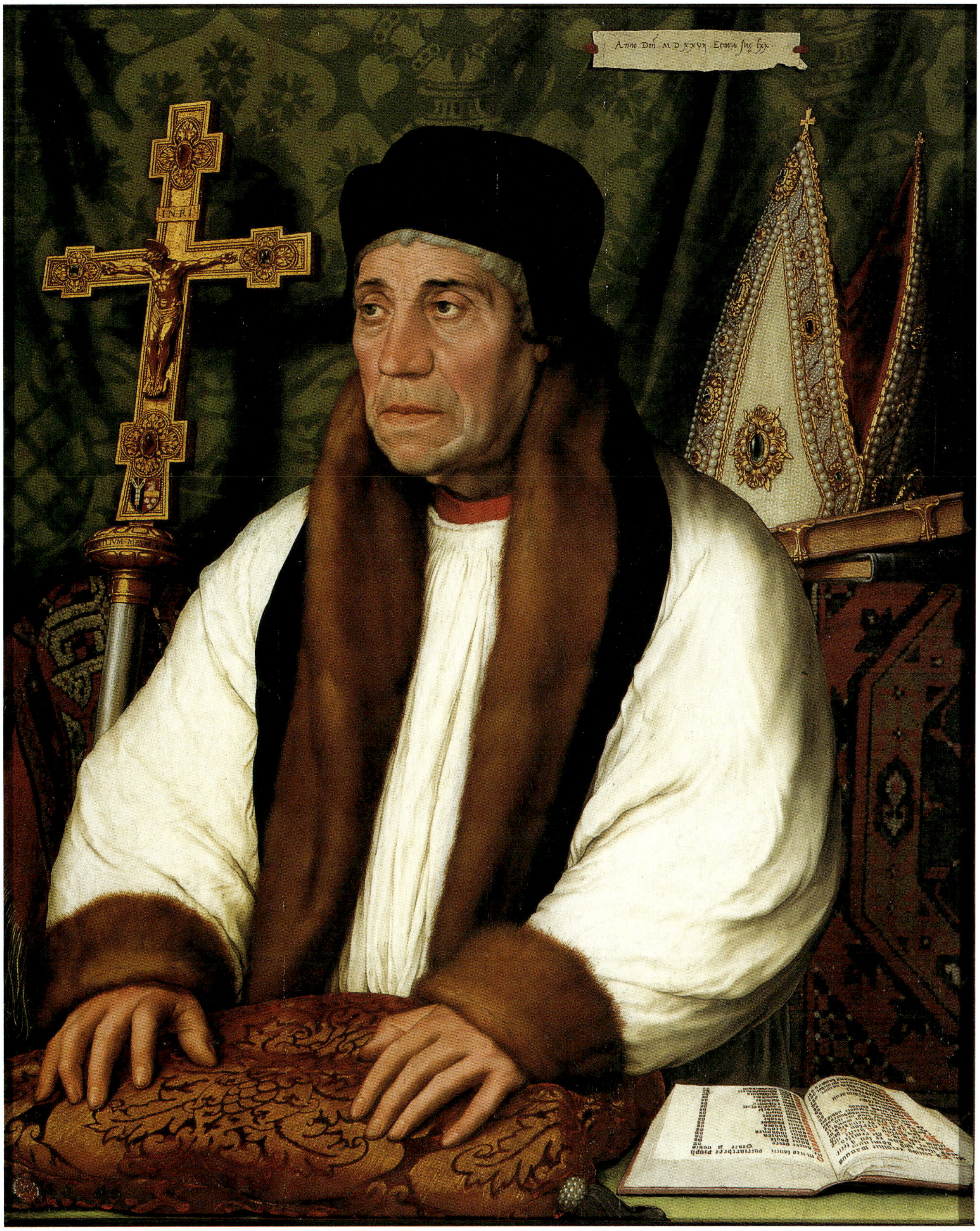

fig. 22 Hans Holbein the Younger, *Portrait of William Warham, archbishop of Canterbury*, 1527. Panel, 82 x 67 cm. Paris, Musée du Louvre

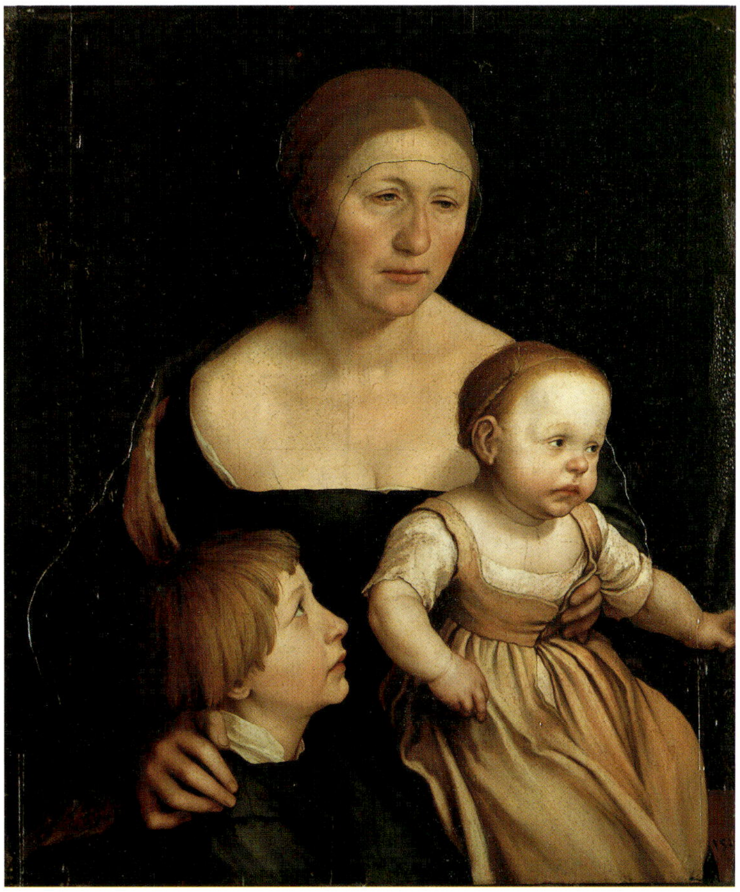

fig. 23
Hans Holbein the Younger, *Portrait of Elsbeth Binzenstock, the artist's wife, and her two children Philip and Catherine*, c. 1520. Four sheets of paper, glued to panel, 77 x 64 cm. Basel, Öffentliche Kunstsammlung

grisailles for the wings of the organ in Basel Cathedral, which seem to have been the last large-scale commission for a religious work he received.

The attitude of the Church towards religious art had changed fundamentally in the course of the Reformation. The frequent, almost blind veneration of images, intermingled with elements of superstition, and the splendour of church interiors with their numerous artworks were harshly criticised. Works of art began to be removed from Basel's churches in April 1528, and on 9 and 10 February 1529 iconoclast riots broke out. On 1 April, finally, the city officially declared itself on the side of the Reformation.[81] It was during these violent events that Erasmus —who had denounced the shortcomings of the Church, but was nonetheless critical of Martin Luther (1483–1546) and remained a Catholic to the end of his life— left Basel for Freiburg.

As with many German masters of the early sixteenth century, Holbein's attitude towards these changes is not easily defined. With the disappearance of religious painting as a possible source of income, he may well have regarded his future as rather sombre. It would also seem that he was not a particularly committed partisan of the Reformation, as he was required to explain to his guild on 18 June 1530 why he had failed to take part in the Reformed Communion, as had been ordered. He replied that before he could go 'he needed a better explanation of the table', i.e. the Reformed Last Supper.[82] Given that his declaration was crossed out using the same ink with which it was written, we can only assume that he got his explanation and accepted it. This image of the painter as rather indifferent to political and theological problems is only reinforced by Holbein's later career in England, at the court of Henry VIII.

—

Holbein at the Court of Henry VIII

In 1532 Holbein again set out for London, once more with letters of introduction from Erasmus in hand. He had, however, required the help of Bonifacius Amerbach in acquiring them, as we learn from Erasmus's correspondence. In it, the scholar claims Holbein has used Amerbach to 'extort letters for England' from him, had then remained more than a month in Antwerp, 'and would have stayed longer if he had found someone stupid enough [to take him in], and in England deceived those to whom he had been commended'.[83] It remains unclear whether this devastating verdict was connected with Erasmus's disapproval of Holbein's all-too-compliant attitude towards the reformers in Basel. It is also unclear to whom he was recommended in England, and who it was that he deceived.

Upon his arrival in London, Holbein found himself confronted with an entirely new situation: William Warham died in August 1532; Thomas More had resigned as chancellor to Henry VIII in the spring of that year and was in difficult financial straits. The king's policies were responsible for these latter developments.[84] Henry, who at seventeen had ascended the throne in 1509, following the death of his father, Henry VII, founder of the Tudor dynasty, was much admired among the humanists for his culture, virtue and appearance. His first marriage was to Catherine of Aragon (1485–1536), the widow of his brother Arthur, who had died at an early age. As the aunt of Charles V, who would succeed Maximilian as German emperor in 1519, she was closely allied with the Habsburgs. She became pregnant several times, but the sons she bore failed to survive, leaving the king without the heir he so desired.

◂ Having fallen in love with the charming and spirited Anne Boleyn (c. 1501–1536) Henry sought to divorce Catherine, who was now in her early forties. Initially, he requested an annulment, but this was denied. Political considerations undoubtedly played an important role in the pope's decision, as Charles V (1500–1558) disapproved of the dissolution of his aunt's marriage. In 1533, Henry VIII —to whom the pope had granted the title 'defender of the faith' in 1521 for a treatise he had written in opposition to Martin Luther— married the now-pregnant Anne in secret, without papal permission. Five months later, Thomas Cranmer (1489–1556), successor to William Warham as archbishop of Canterbury, declared Henry's first marriage invalid. Catherine was banished from court. Through a variety of new laws, the king declared himself head of the Church of England, and demanded that his subjects recognise this with an oath. Thomas More, who had been against the divorce and was a passionate champion of the Catholic faith and persecutor of heretics, had already withdrawn from politics when he resigned his post as chancellor on 16 May 1532, a day after the clergy had been forced to submit to the new rulings. In 1534 he refused to swear the Oath of Supremacy, as prescribed by the Act of Succession passed in March of that year. On 17 April he was imprisoned in the Tower of London and was executed for treason on 6 July 1535.[85]

◂ In 1532, then, Holbein could no longer count on More's help. Instead, he won Anne Boleyn as a patroness,[86] and shortly after his arrival painted a portrait of Thomas Cromwell (c. 1485–1540), More's successor as lord chancellor (fig. 24).[87] Erasmus may well have known early on about these new-found contacts, and this may in part explain his disparaging comments. From a moral perspective, Holbein may have revealed himself as an opportunist; from an economic point of view, however, his actions are quite understandable, particularly if we assume he understood portraiture not only as an intellectually ambitious means of creating penetrating interpretations of man in the humanist sense, but also as a craft and a way of earning a living, which did not require taking any particular stance on the political and religious debates of the day. This seems to be how Erasmus viewed him as well, for he refers to Dürer, not Holbein, as the new Apelles —the greatest painter of antiquity— and in fact rarely mentions Holbein by name.[88]

◂ In any event Holbein again managed to adapt to the new circumstances during his second visit to England. The appeal sent by the Basel burgomaster Jakob Meyer zum Hirtzen on 2 September 1532 to 'Master Hans Holbein the painter, now in England' remained unsuccessful: on the condition that he return to the city as soon as possible, Holbein was promised 30 guilders a year so that he could stay at home and take care of his wife and children.[89]

◂ Already in 1532, Holbein was able to develop an important new clientele among the economically powerful German

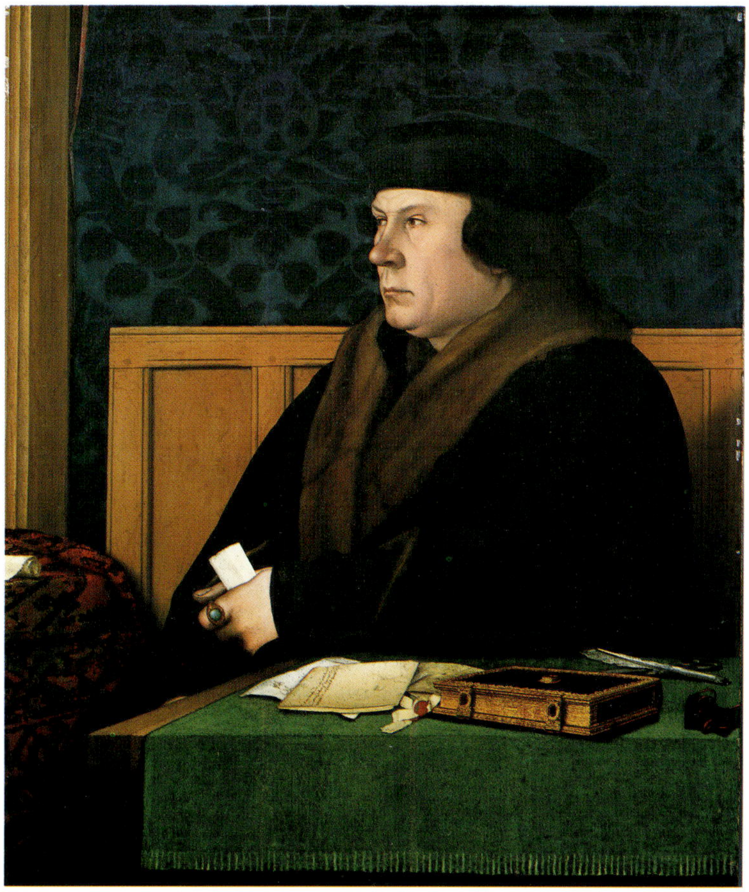

fig. 24
Hans Holbein the Younger (workshop?), *Portrait of Thomas Cromwell*, c. 1533.
Panel, 76 x 61 cm.
New York, The Frick Collection

merchants of the *Stahlhof* (Steelyard), the London branch of the Hanseatic League (see cat. no. 12), who —like his earlier English patrons— were interested in having their portraits painted (cat. nos. 12, 17, 18).[90] Wilson has suggested that tensions between the Catholic More family and these tradesmen from Lutheran Germany had prevented Holbein from making contact with them during his previous stay in England.[91] If this was the case, the fact that he was now taking on their commissions would provide further evidence of the artist's rejection of his former benefactor.

◂ The series of 'Steelyard portraits' opens with the comparatively large and extraordinarily skilful and elaborate likeness of Georg Gisze (1497–1562) (fig. 25),[92] with which the artist hoped to recommend himself for further commissions from the merchants. Holbein here shows off his skills to their best advantage, depicting the various objects surrounding the model —posed behind a table in what appears to be his office— with such naturalism and material specificity that they seem entirely real and tangible. However, Holbein's portrait in fact questions the very reality it seems initially to so mimetically reproduce: the perspective is distorted —the walls do not meet at a right angle— and the table, covered with a magnificent carpet, is not perfectly rectangular. The lower right-hand corner is missing, and the artist even goes so far as to highlight this area, first by allowing a pen to stick out over the edge, and then by depicting the pewter writing set from a higher point of view than the table itself, so that it appears about to slide off. Unstable, too, is the seal dangling from the plank at the upper left: the chain could not possibly have been slung so loosely around the corner of the shelf without the weight of the seal dragging it down. The gold balance suspended nearby —the very epitome of stability and equipoise— is also lopsided. Holbein has hung it right beside Gisze's motto, 'No joy without sorrow', thereby suggesting that the equilibrium of the sitter's life referred to in the text has somehow become unsettled, or perhaps even disappeared altogether.[93] The opulently painted world of the merchant Gisze is thus in no way as secure as it first appears. The specific arrangement of details thwarts the viewer's expectations of finding in the painting a faithful likeness of reality, forcing him to reflect on them and hence, thanks to the painter's interpretation, to come to a deeper understanding of the person depicted. Thus, Holbein's portrait points to something beyond the tangible world, although at first glance it appears purely objective.

◂ In an even more obvious manner, Holbein's great masterpiece of the early 1530s, the so-called *Ambassadors* (fig. 26),[94] questions the reality he so perfectly captures and, simultaneously, the reality of painting itself, which reproduces three dimensional spaces and bodies on a two-dimensional panel. At the left is the picture's patron, Jean de Dinteville (*c.* 1503–1555), who was sent by the French king François I to monitor Henry VIII's divorce proceedings and would act in his sovereign's name as godfather to Anne and Henry's daughter, born on 7 September 1533. At the right is Bishop Georges de Selve (*c.* 1508–1541), who had come to

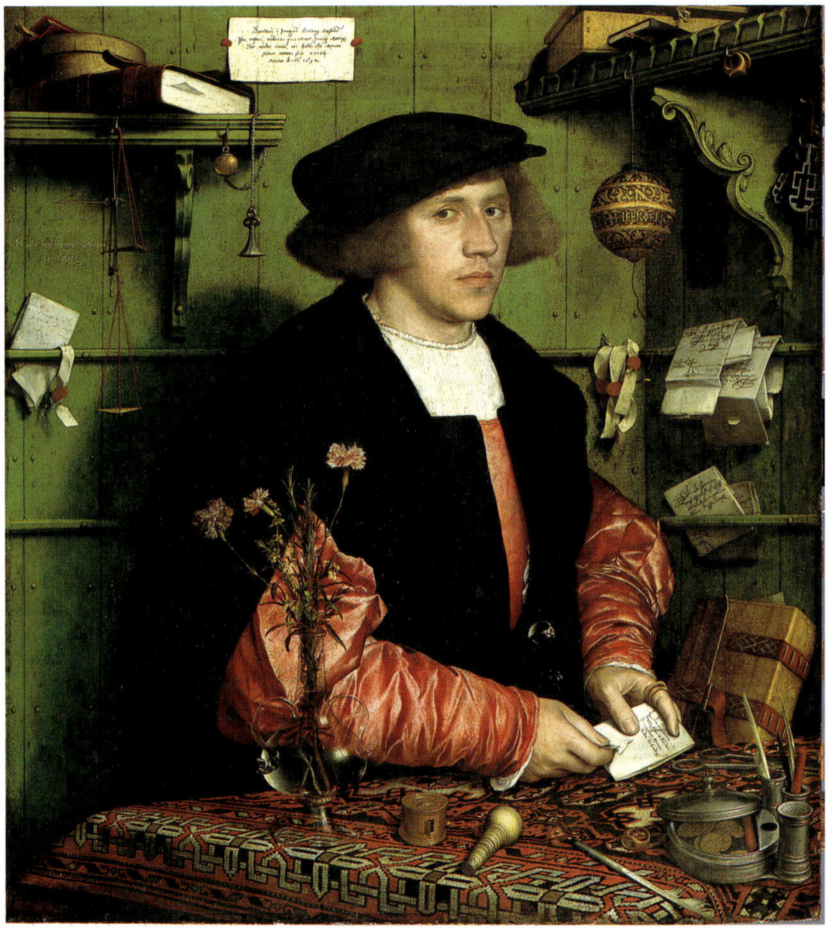

fig. 25
Hans Holbein
the Younger,
Portrait of
Georg Gisze, 1532.
Panel, 96.3 x 85.7 cm.
Berlin, Staatliche
Museen zu Berlin,
Gemäldegalerie

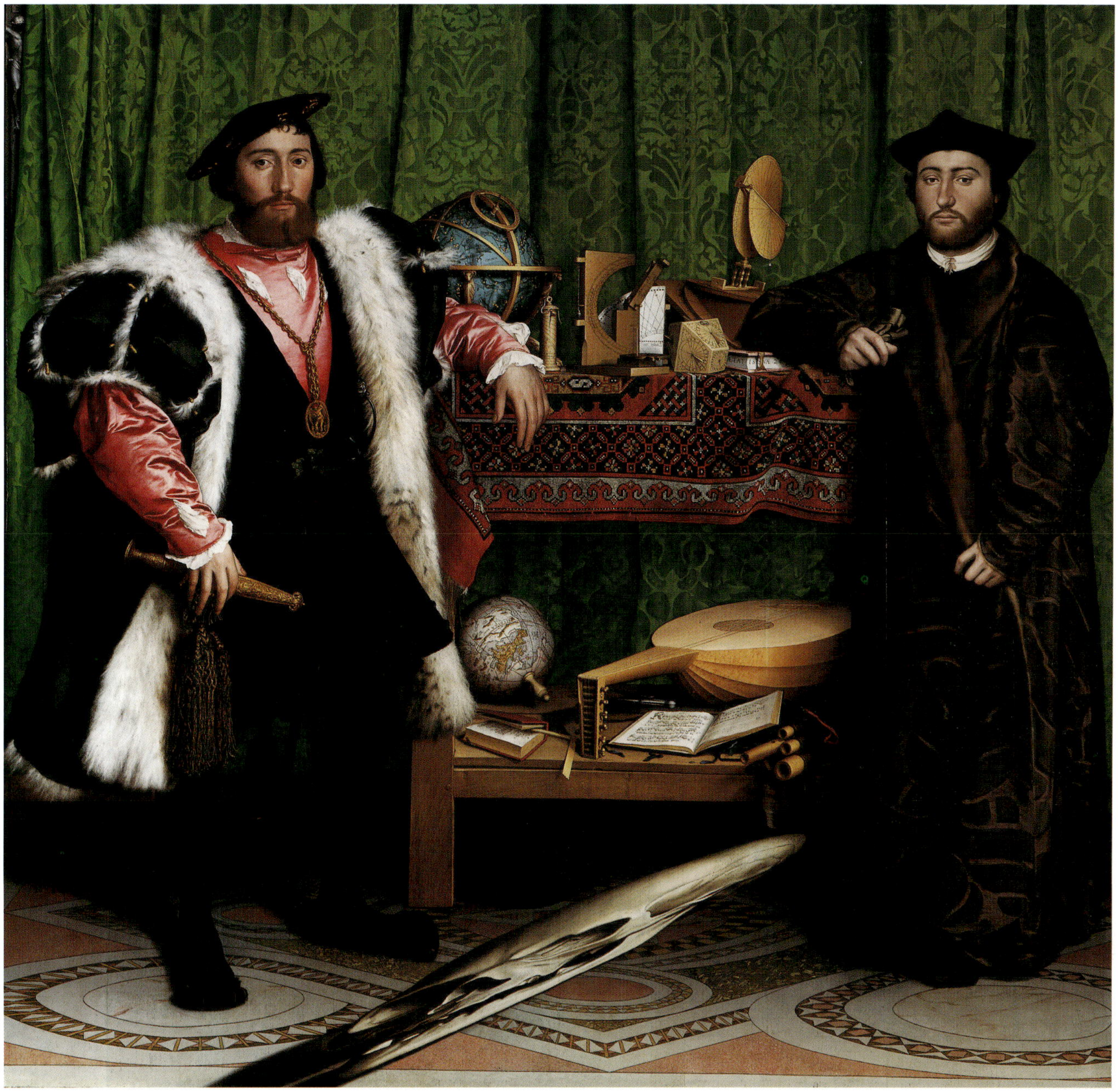

fig. 26
Hans Holbein the Younger, *Double portrait of Jean de Dinteville and Georges de Selve, known as 'The ambassadors'*, 1533. Panel, 207 x 209.5 cm. London, The National Gallery

England on a secret mission in May 1533. Floating before them in the central foreground is a skull. As a *memento mori*, it clearly refers to the transience of all earthly things, not simply to the mortality of the two men portrayed, but also to that of all the objects so splendidly and realistically reproduced on the *étagère* between them. Holbein shows the skull in distorted perspective, as an anamorphosis. From a frontal position, the image is unreadable. Observed from an extreme oblique angle, however, the fantastical shape is transformed into a human skull, while the figures themselves and everything around them becomes deformed and unreal. Thus death is always present, even if we sometimes fail to recognise it, and, once acknowledged, life becomes unrecognisable and all beautiful things are turned into nothing but fleeting illusions.

◂ These were the portraits that helped make Holbein's reputation in London. He did numerous likenesses of the members of the Steelyard, using smaller panels than for the Gisze portrait, posing the sitters against a neutral background and

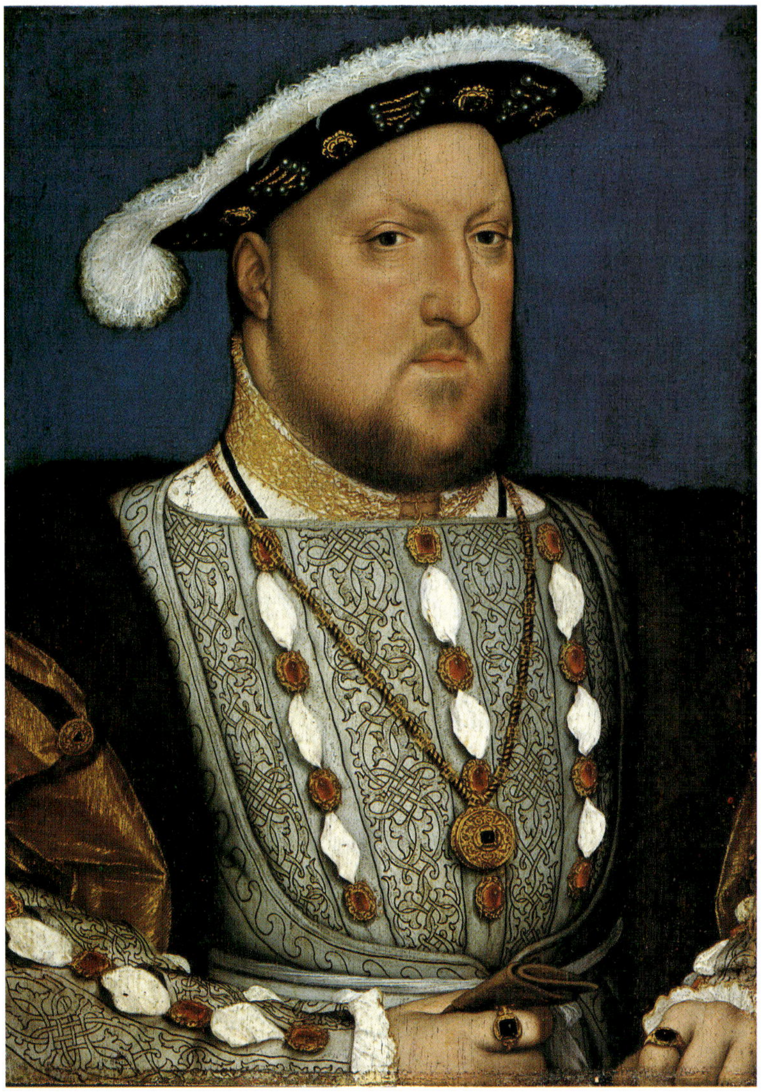

fig. 27
Hans Holbein the Younger, *Portrait of Henry VIII, king of England*, c. 1536/37. Panel, 27.5 x 17.5 cm. Madrid, Museo Thyssen-Bornemisza

inscribing most of the works with their names and age (cat. nos. 12, 17, 18). He also greatly reduced the number of objects surrounding the sitter. It therefore seems likely these clients were charged at a lower rate. But this reduction of means in the later portraits is also stylistically significant, as particularly in the preparatory drawings —which often served as cartoons for the final works[95]— Holbein developed an extraordinarily precise manner of drawing, reducing the sitter's physiognomy to its bare essentials. While the portrait drawings of the 1520s aimed for a more painterly effect and are remarkable for their vitality and spontaneity, it is the concentration and accuracy of their characterisations and the balanced economy of their compositions that distinguish the later sheets. That the neutral background and minimal accessories found in these portraits cannot always be linked to the price of the painting is demonstrated, finally, by the various likenesses of the family of the king (cat. nos. 27, 33), Holbein's most important patron.

‹ By 1536 at the latest Holbein was court painter to Henry VIII, receiving a regular salary. This can be gleaned from a letter by the French poet Nicolas Bourbon (*c.* 1503 – *c.* 1550), who had fled to England in 1535, was fostered by Anne Boleyn and, following her fall the next year, returned to his native country. Writing to Thomas Soulemant —Henry VIII's French secretary— on 5 September 1536 he sent Holbein his greetings, referring to him explicitly as the king's painter.[96] When exactly he had attained this position remains unclear, however, as the *Accounts of the Treasurer of the Chamber* for the years 1532–1537 have been lost.[97] In addition to designs for decorative art and jewellery, Holbein supplied a number of portraits, among them the strikingly small bust-length portrait of Henry VIII (fig. 27)[98] and the half-length likeness of Jane Seymour (*c.* 1508/09–1537), who became the king's third wife immediately following the execution of Anne Boleyn and finally bore him the male heir he so desired (cat. no. 27). In both these portraits, the sitters appear against plain backgrounds.

‹ Holbein used costly ultramarine for his portrait of the king. In 1539, the artist also portrayed the heir to the throne, Edward (1537–1553), against a neutral background (cat. no. 33), originally a cobalt blue. The smalt pigment employed —made from finely ground blue glass and in Holbein's time presumably still expensive— was not light-fast, however, so that today it appears as a brownish grey.[99] The likeness seems to have been Holbein's New Year's gift to the sovereign; in return he received a gold cup.[100]

‹ In all three portraits the garments are accented with powdered gold and also with silver, giving them a particularly luxurious appearance. By renouncing the spatially defined surroundings that would have served to localise them, by instead setting them against a flat plane of colour, Holbein —like his early Netherlandish predecessors Jan van Eyck and Rogier van der Weyden— lifts his sitters out of the temporal dimension. This sense of timelessness is enhanced by the fact that in

Holbein's later portraits, and particularly in the likeness of Henry VIII, in which the body casts no shadows, the figure is bound to the surface by an emphasis on contour and thus appears highly stylised. At the same time, the extraordinarily subtle modelling of the face and body makes the sitter seem life-like and extant. In this way, Holbein created portraits of individuals that strike the viewer as perpetually present, reconciling the paradox between the here-and-now and eternity.

This same quality can also be found in the portraits of Christina of Denmark (fig. 28)[101] and Anne of Cleves (fig. 29).[102] Jane Seymour had died in childbirth in 1537, leaving Thomas Cromwell to search for a new wife for the monarch among the higher ranks of Europe's nobility. Holbein was sent to a number of these candidates in order to paint their portraits.[103] It was in this context that he executed his likeness of the Danish princess Christina (1522–1590), then just sixteen years of age. Following the death of her husband, the duke of Milan, Francesco Maria Sforza (1492–1535), she was then living in Brussels at the court of her aunt, Maria of Hungary (1505–1558). Thanks to a report written by the English ambassador John Hutton to Cromwell on 14 March 1538, we know something of the circumstances of the sitting.[104] According to him, the courtier Philipp Hobby arrived in Brussels on 10 March, accompanied by a servant of His Royal Highness known as Mr Hans, i.e. Holbein. The ambassador arranged for a painting session on 12 March at 1 p.m., which lasted three hours. In this brief period, Holbein undoubtedly made only sketches; nonetheless, Hobby claimed that a perfect portrait was created. The artist was already back in London on 18 March. Henry VIII was shown the portrait and must have fallen instantly in love, for it is recorded that he was in such an excellent mood that he had musicians play for him the entire day.

It was on the basis of these preparatory drawings, now lost, that Holbein created the

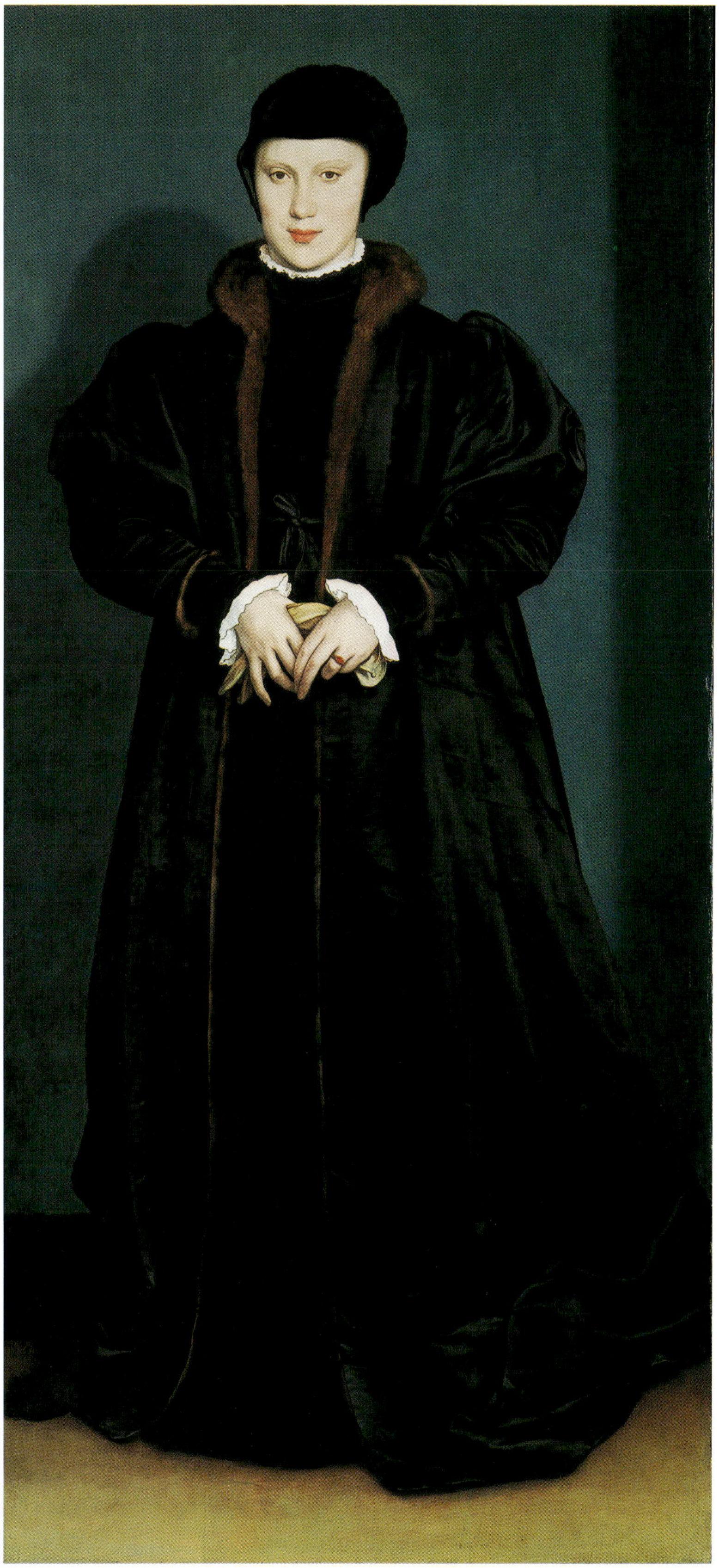

fig. 28
Hans Holbein
the Younger,
Portrait of Christina of Denmark, duchess of Milan,
c. 1538. Panel,
179.1 x 82.6 cm.
London, The National Gallery

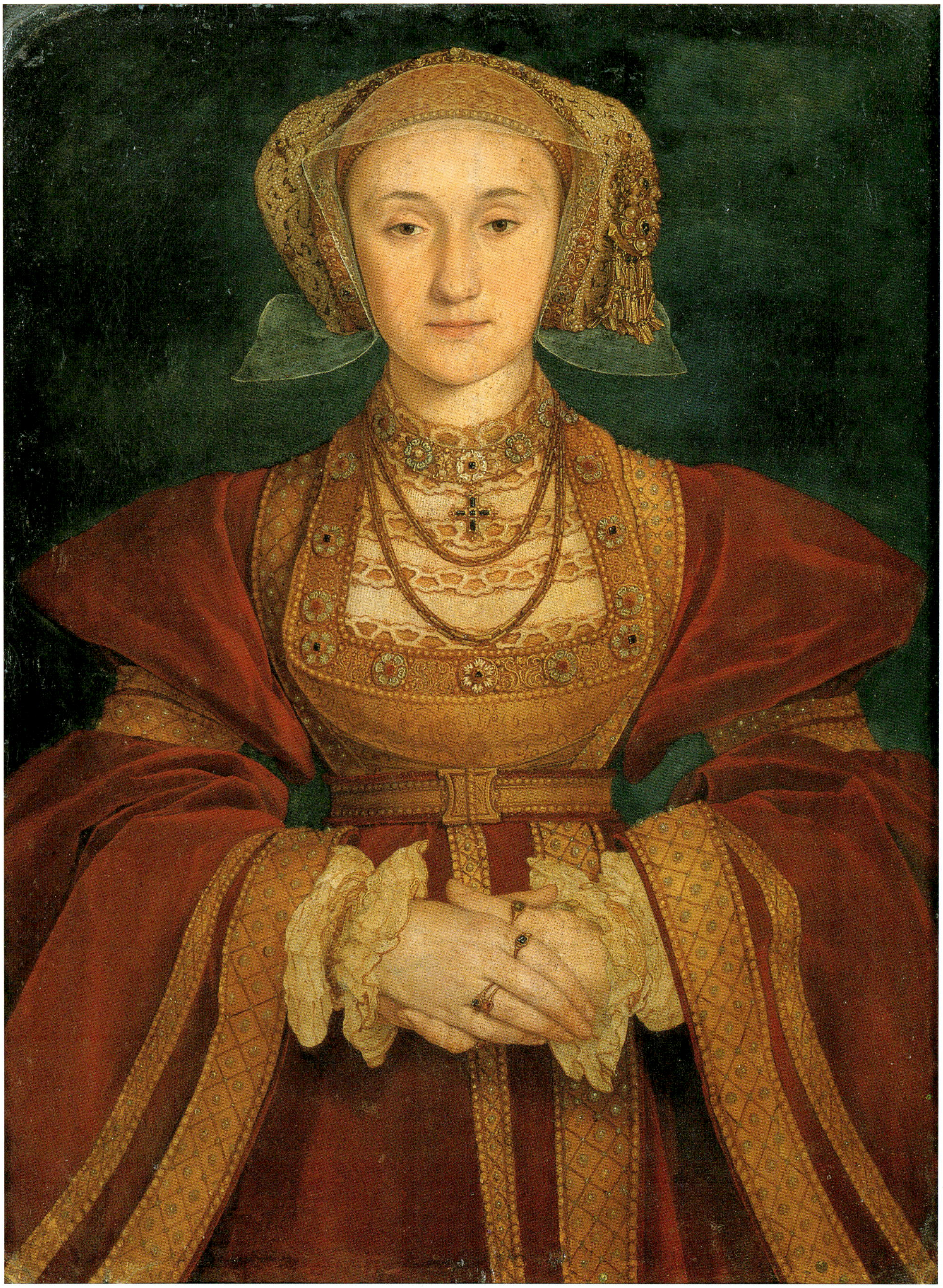

fig. 29
Hans Holbein
the Younger,
Portrait of
Anne of Cleves,
c. 1539.
Parchment,
glued to canvas,
65 x 48 cm.
Paris, Musée
du Louvre

surviving full-length panel painting (fig. 28). The elegant portrait depicts the young lady in her black widow's garb. Holbein's masterly arrangement of the tall, imposing figure and painterly perfection are striking: deliberately simple in composition, the portrait comes alive in the colour contrast between the brilliantly executed black garments, the radiant, porcelain-like flesh and the unusual blue-green background, on which both figure and frame cast noticeable shadows. These create a vague suggestion of space, out of which the duchess seems to emerge — her left shoulder and the hem of her skirt at the right appear to come slightly forward, creating an impression of graceful motion. Both her body language and facial expression reveal a self-confident, even wilful personality: her gaze seems almost to challenge the viewer, without, however, relinquishing anything of her inborn noble reserve. In this portrait, the artist stresses the figure's unmediated presence, and thus the work's topicality. Still, it is no 'snapshot', which would have made her beauty seem ephemeral: the ambiguity of the background releases Christina from the restrictions of time and space, so that she strikes one as eternally youthful.

Probably for both personal and political reasons, Henry failed in his attempts to gain Christina's hand in marriage. Having examined a number of other candidates, his choice finally fell on Anne of Cleves (1515–1557), whom Holbein painted in July or August 1539 in Düren (fig. 29).[105] As had been the case with Christina of Denmark, portraits of the proposed bride had been sent to England beforehand, but Henry regarded them as unsatisfactory, as Anne's face was shrouded by what he called a 'monstrous' veil. He clearly found her attractive in Holbein's likeness, as wedding plans were soon made. But when she arrived in England on 27 December 1539, his illusions, based on Holbein's portrait, were shattered. Henry was revolted by 'this Flemish mare', declared himself incapable of consummating the marriage, which had taken place on 6 January 1540, and had the bond annulled already on 9 July of the same year.[106]

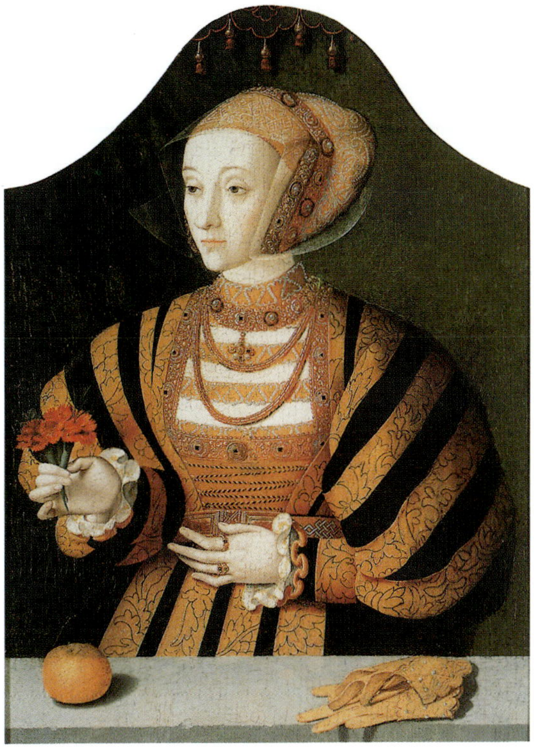

fig. 30 Circle of Bartel Bruyn the Elder, *Portrait of Anne of Cleves.* Panel. Oxford, St. John's College

In the case of the marriage portrait, Henry certainly expected Holbein to deliver him a 'genuine' likeness of his future wife, one that neither stylised nor idealised nature. In fact, however, Holbein did not produce such a 'document', as demonstrated by a comparison with a second portrait of Anne, attributed to a painter from the circle of Bartel Bruyn the Elder (fig. 30).[107] Here, the artist shows the sitter in three-quarters profile. In contrast to Holbein's *en face* depiction, her features appear far less regular — her face is longer, her chin sharper and her mouth smaller. She thus lacks that majestic, restrained nobility that Henry VIII, feeling well disposed towards it, must have initially found in the Holbein portrait. For such a viewer, the somewhat absent gaze might well give the sitter an additional aura of mystery. If, however, one regards Holbein's likeness critically, this same expression could be interpreted as simple-minded or vacuous. Without actually falsifying, Holbein created a portrait that leaves room for individual interpretation. Henry VIII seems to have been unaware of this. At least in this instance, Holbein failed to meet the expectations of his patron, who was apparently incapable of differentiating between art and nature, and their respective realities.

Holbein certainly did not disappoint in the most prestigious commission Henry had bestowed on him in 1536/37, while Jane Seymour was queen: the imposing mural at Whitehall Palace, probably a decoration for the so-called Privy Chamber, the king's private quarters, where only his closest associates were received.[108] Before the palace burned down in 1698 the Flemish painter Remigius van Leemput (1607–1675) made a copy of the mural —much praised by van Mander— for Charles II (1630-1685) (fig. 31).[109] It shows Henry VIII and Jane Seymour, as well as the king's deceased parents and founders

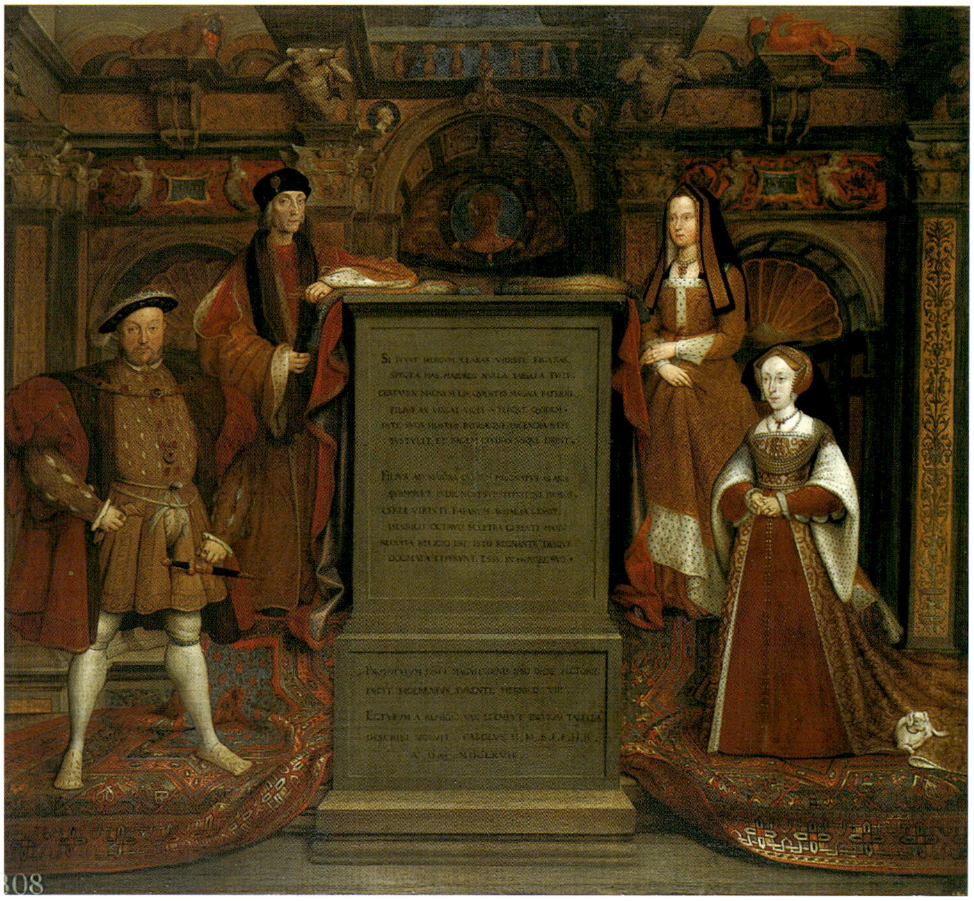

fig. 31
Remigius van Leemput, copy after Hans Holbein the Younger, *Group portrait of Henry VII, Elizabeth of York, Henry VIII and Jane Seymour*, 1667. Canvas, 88.9 x 98.7 cm. London, The Royal Collection

of the Tudor dynasty, Henry VII (1457–1509) and Elizabeth of York (1465–1503). They are depicted life-size and set against an architectural backdrop reminiscent of a triumphal arch. An inscription praises the Tudor monarchs, whereby the son's fame is ranked higher than that of his father.[110] This message is also conveyed by the figure of Henry VIII, standing with his legs spread wide, his huge physical presence comparable only to that of the powerful bronze funerary statue of Maximilian I that Holbein may have seen as a youth in Augsburg.[111] Like the German emperor with his monumental *Triumphal arch* and tomb, both of which aimed to praise and immortalise the house of Habsburg through art, Henry VIII sought to create a permanent glorification of the Tudor dynasty, whose continuation was now assured thanks to the birth of a male heir. At the same time, the king had Holbein portray him as both the strongest and most elegant of all rulers. Just as a generation earlier Burgkmair and Dürer had created what would become the lasting image of the German emperor, so Holbein cast that of the English king.

◂ Holbein appears to have been happy with his life in England. He never went back to Basel, although on 16 October 1538 the city council drew up a contract granting him a number of unusual concessions in order to persuade him to return.[112] During a brief visit to the town in the autumn of 1538 he praised the general circumstances in England, as recorded in a letter of 12 September from the Basel student Rudolf Gwalther to the Swiss Protestant reformer Heinrich Bullinger (1504–1575) in Zurich.[113] We do not know whether the far-reaching consequences of the failed portrait of Anne of Cleves had an effect on Holbein's relationship with the king, which might have dampened his enthusiasm for his adopted land. In any case, he was not held directly responsible for the repercussions of his work: it was not Holbein but rather Cromwell, who had arranged the marriage, who fell from grace. The official reason for his execution was treason, but the unfortunate marriage had strained the relationship between the king and his minister, so that Henry readily gave heed to the recriminations of Cromwell's opponents, led by Thomas Howard, Duke of Norfolk (1473–1554). Holbein, on the other hand, survived Henry's divorce unscathed. Although we know of no commissions after 1539, the artist continued to receive a salary until his death, indicating he had not entirely fallen out of favour.

'Stranger, you wish to see pictures that perfectly resemble life? Behold this work by Holbein's noble hand'[114]

Unlike Dürer, who left the strongest mark on German Renaissance art, Holbein was no theoretician who sought to clarify the fundamental questions of art and nature.[115] His medium of expression was the painted image, not the written word. This was likely the reason that Erasmus thought more highly of Dürer —a good friend of the eminent humanist Willibald Pirckheimer— than of Holbein,[116] although he was undoubtedly happy with the latter's work, as the number of portraits he commissioned indicates.

Because no printed treatises, private letters or notes have come down to us, Holbein the man has remained largely unknown, like so many late medieval artists whose ideas and motivations can only be gleaned from an analysis of their works. He appears to have understood painting in the traditional sense, as a craft rather than as one of the liberal arts. This is also indicated by that fact that Holbein —in contrast to Dürer, but also to Hans Baldung Grien (*c.*1484/85–1545) and Albrecht Altdorfer (*c.*1480–1538)— rarely signed his drawings. Despite their extraordinary independent aesthetic value for today's viewer, he apparently did not regard them —at least in most cases— as autonomous works of art. Rather, he viewed them as tools with a specific purpose, as working material in the production of paintings, and thereby composed pragmatically and economically by varying and reusing his motifs. This was the case, for example, with the portraits of Erasmus writing, and in the Whitehall mural, whose figures reappear in the same poses in the individual panel portraits of Henry VIII and Jane Seymour (p. 28, fig. 27 and cat. nos. 26-28).

Holbein reveals himself only indirectly in his art, whereby in the case of the portraits his interpretation often seems to be a concealed and witty commentary on the sitters themselves. This produces a kind of hidden tension with the primary naturalistic effect — a result of Holbein's extraordinary painterly skill, which is striking for its stupendous realism and makes the figures seem truly present, as if reality were reproduced exactly. This tension between the evocation of reality and an indirect commenting and relativisation reveals Holbein's character as quite similar to that of Erasmus. This quality made him the ideal portraitist of both the humanists and the court.

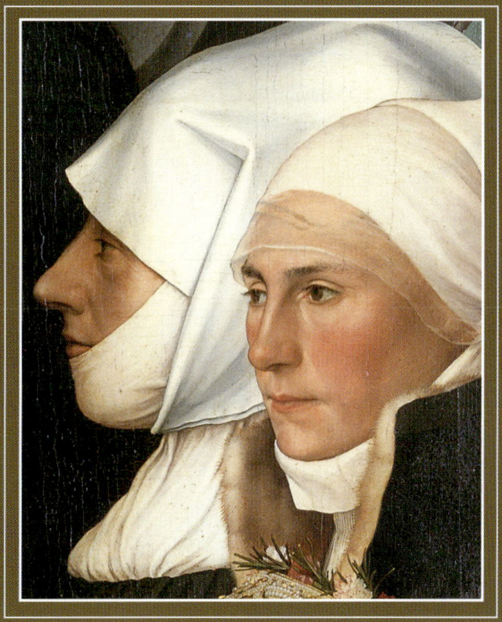

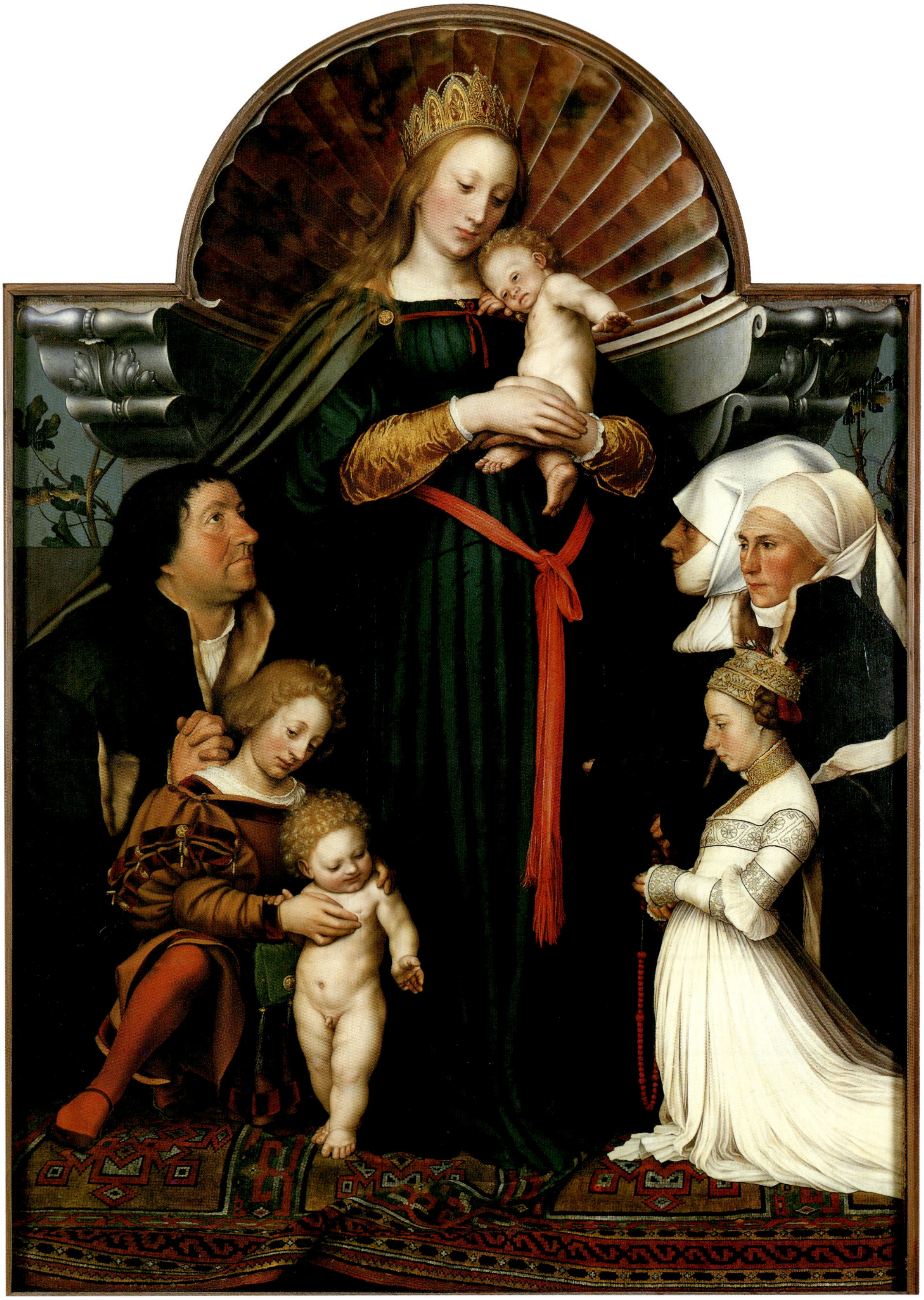

fig 1 Hans Holbein the Younger, *Darmstadt Madonna*, c. 1525/26 and 1528/29. Panel, 146.5 x 102 cm. Courtesy of the Hessische Hausstiftung

The Darmstadt Madonna

On the genesis and development of Holbein's panel for Jakob Meyer zum Hasen

Jochen Sander

The *Darmstadt Madonna* (fig. 1 and cat. no. 2), named after its present location, the Schloßmuseum in Darmstadt, is one of the few surviving religious works of Holbein's Basel period.[1] As so often in the artist's oeuvre, the composition has a monumentality surprising for its relatively small size: the panel, rounded at the top, is a mere 146.5 x 102 centimetres. The now-lost frame, which undoubtedly echoed the scalloped niche with projecting consoles that surrounds the figures, would have served to underline this grand effect. A masterpiece that draws on both the religious painting of Italy and on the detailed realism of Early Netherlandish portraiture, the *Darmstadt Madonna* is not only one of Hans Holbein's most important works, but also a major contribution to European painting of the sixteenth century.

—

A family portrait

The *Darmstadt Madonna* depicts the Virgin with the Christ Child in her arms; she stands on a raised socle covered with a carpet, backed by a tabernacle-like niche. As in images of the Virgin of Pity (*Madonna della Misericordia* or *Schutzmantelmadonna*, see also cat. no. 2), her cloak spreads out behind the kneeling figures to either side. To her right, in a pose of pious veneration, is the former Basel burgomaster Jakob Meyer zum Hasen; beside him is a fashionably dressed youth, looking in the direction of the viewer. He tenderly embraces a little boy standing nude in the foreground, whose gesture and gaze likewise point beyond the picture frame.[2] At the left of the Virgin kneel three female members of the donor's family, each holding a string of prayer beads: closest to the Virgin and almost entirely obscured by her cap, chinband and mantle, is probably Meyer's first wife, Magdalena Baer, who had died already in 1511. His second wife, Dorothea Kannengießer, is shown in the middle, next to the couple's daughter, Anna. While their caps and guimpes characterise the wives as married women, Anna is shown as a marriageable young lady, her hair tucked up under a so-called *Jungfernschapel*, decorated with carnations and sprigs of rosemary. Backing the figures is a shoulder-high wall, above which vines are visible against a blue sky.[3]

Unlike so many, the name of the donor of the *Darmstadt Madonna* has never fallen into obscurity, thanks in part to the fact that the painting stayed in the family's possession until the early seventeenth century, and also to Holbein's portraits of the burgomaster and his wife, painted already in 1516 (p. 17, figs. 12-13). These pendant portraits have always remained in

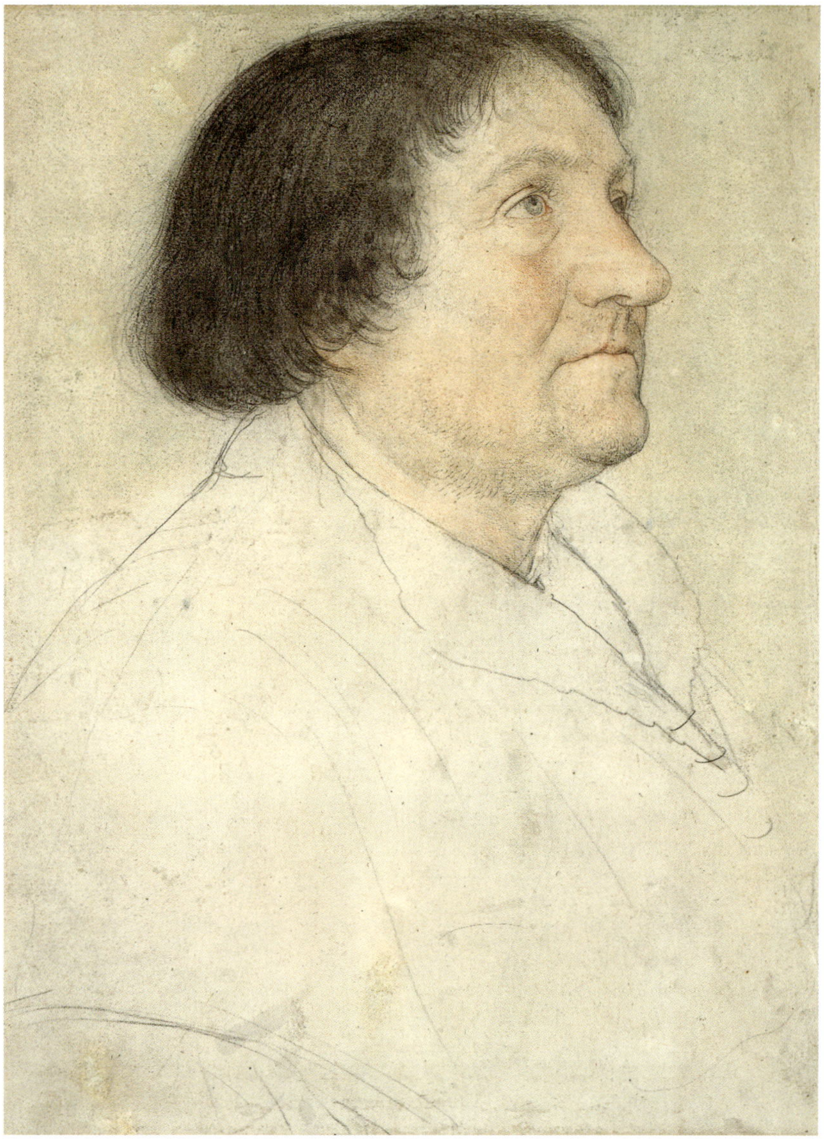

fig. 2
Hans Holbein the Younger, *Portrait of Jakob Meyer zum Hasen*, c. 1526. Black and coloured chalk on paper, 383 x 275 mm. Basel, Kunstmuseum, Kupferstichkabinett

Basel and now hang in the city's Kunstmuseum. When the portraits were painted, the prosperous merchant and money-changer Jakob Meyer had just been elected burgomaster from the ranks of the guilds. Re-elected every two years, he would remain in this post until 1521. In October of that year, however, he was accused of corruption and relieved of office; he was later put on trial and even briefly imprisoned. He never regained his political influence, although he was considered a leader of the Catholic cause until the triumph of the Reformation in Basel in 1529. He died in 1531, having remained true to his faith.[4]

◂ The *Darmstadt Madonna* was commissioned several years after Meyer's disgrace, probably in 1525/26, as indicated by the original portrayal of his daughter Anna. Ageing has caused the paint to become transparent in places, revealing under the headgear that her hair once hung loose about her shoulders. She is depicted with just this hairstyle —typical for young girls— in one of the three portrait drawings in black and coloured chalk that served as studies for the *Darmstadt Madonna* (figs. 2–4), now in the Kupferstichkabinett in Basel. Although we do not know exactly when Anna Meyer was born, it was certainly after her parents' marriage, which took place at the earliest in 1511. This would mean that she was about 13 or 14 years old at the time of the drawings, and thus of the earlier version of the *Darmstadt Madonna*.

◂ When one considers that Holbein left for his first trip to England in mid-1526, and would not return to Basel until the second half of 1528, one can assume the reasons for the changes undertaken: Anna had now reached a marriageable age and was already engaged to her future husband, Nikolaus Irmy. This shift in Anna's social status was apparently so important to Meyer that he wished to see it reflected in his painting.[5] Given the economic situation that faced Holbein on his return to the city, shortly before the iconoclasm brought on by the Reformation, he was undoubtedly more than happy to fulfil Meyer's request.

◂ We can only speculate on the original location and function of the *Darmstadt Madonna*. The fact that the painting survived the iconoclastic riots of 1529 unscathed —in contrast, for example, to the now-fragmentary *Last supper* in Basel — could indicate that it was initially kept in a place inaccessible to the public. Often mentioned in this context is the small moated castle at Groß-Gundeldingen, just outside the city walls, which served as Meyer zum Hasen's country seat.[6] There is, however, no concrete evidence of this. One cannot entirely rule out that the work originally hung in one of Basel's many churches, as the removal of paintings took place in phases and, at least in the early stages, in an orderly fashion. The town clerk Johannes Gerster, for example, donor of the so-called *Solothurn Madonna* (fig. 5), which hung in the parish church of St Martin, apparently had his painting returned to him undamaged in April 1528, when this church and others were emptied.[7]

◂ Until around 1606, the *Darmstadt Madonna* was the property of the direct descendants of Jakob Meyer zum Hasen, and remained in its city of origin, Basel, until sometime in the mid-1630s. It was then purchased by the Amsterdam engraver and art dealer Michel LeBlon, who had it copied by a German-born painter active in the Netherlands, Bartolomäus Sarburgh (*c.* 1590– *after* 1637) (fig. 6). He eventually sold both works on the international market. The widow of the French king, Maria de' Medici, purchased the copy, while the Amsterdam banker Jacob Loskaert became the lucky owner of the original. Notwithstanding that both the *Darmstadt Madonna* and its copy thus disappeared for many years from public view, the praises the work received in the art literature (beginning already in the early seventeenth century) meant Holbein's painting was not forgotten.[8] While Sarburgh's version reappeared in a Venetian collection in the early 1720s and in 1744 entered the Gemäldegalerie in Dresden, where it still hangs today, Holbein's original was only rediscovered in the 1820s, on the Paris art market. Acquired in 1822 by Prince Wilhelm of Prussia for his wife, Princess Marianne von Hesse-Homburg, in 1852 it became the inherited property of the grand dukes of Hesse and bei Rhein, and in 1997 of the Hessische Hausstiftung. Previously kept in Berlin's Stadtschloß, the painting has thus been housed at the Residenzschloß in Darmstadt since the mid-nineteenth century.

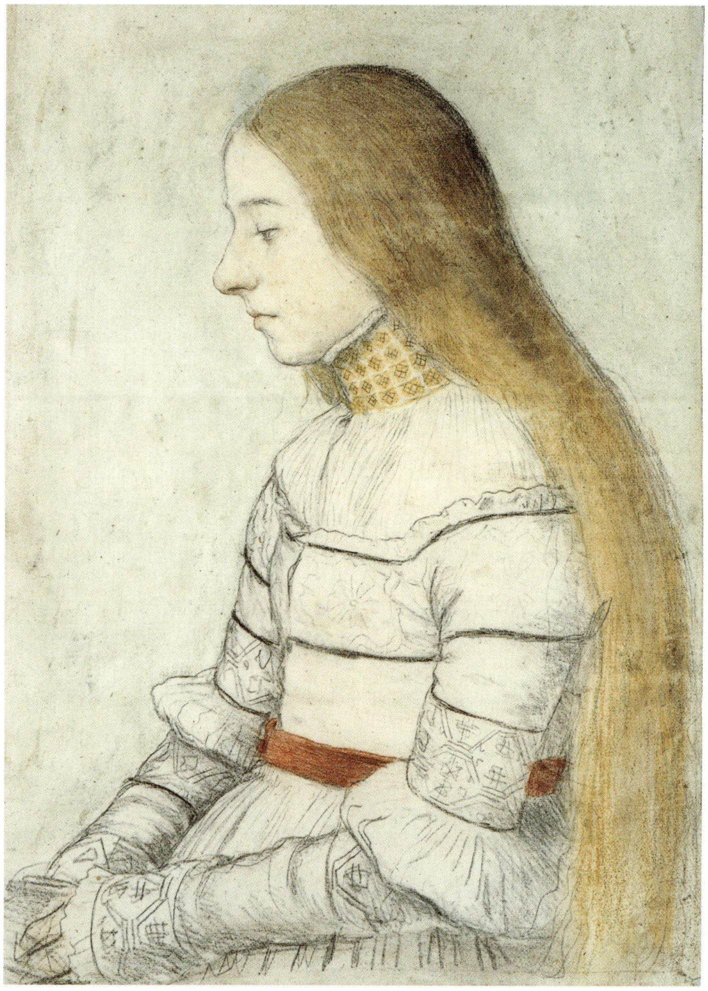

fig. 4
Hans Holbein the Younger, *Portrait of Anna Meyer*, *c.* 1526.
Black and coloured chalk on paper, 391 x 275 cm.
Basel, Kunstmuseum, Kupferstichkabinett

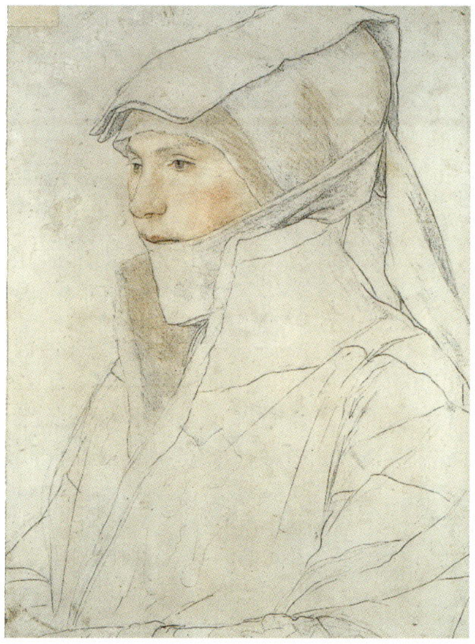

fig. 3
Hans Holbein the Younger, *Portrait of Dorothea Kannengießer*, *c.* 1526.
Black and coloured chalk on paper, 395 x 281 mm.
Basel, Kunstmuseum, Kupferstichkabinett

The 'Holbein controversy'

The *Darmstadt Madonna* only became known to a wider audience following its transfer to its present location. This did not mean, however, that it was immediately and generally accepted as the Holbein original. Since its rediscovery in the eighteenth century, this honour had been given to Sarburgh's copy. Already celebrated in the older literature and long part of the magnificent Dresden collection, the painting reached the peak of its fame in the early 1800s. It was not only considered Hans Holbein the Younger's most important work, it was also the basis for his reputation as the 'Raphael of the North' — a notion underlined in the programmatic hanging of the picture across from the equally famous *Sistine Madonna*. In the

1870s, the question of the attribution of the Dresden and Darmstadt works became the focus of a controversy that would have far-reaching methodological consequences for the relatively new discipline of academic art history.[9] In addition to the seniority of its claim to be the Holbein original, the partisans of the Dresden picture (interestingly enough, mainly artists) continually made reference to its supposedly superior 'beauty'. Their arguments, so clearly marked by the taste of the period, were dismissed by the champions of the Darmstadt picture (mostly art historians), who pointed to the changes made to the heads of both Dorothea Kannengießer and Anna Meyer, visible in the Darmstadt but not in the Dresden version. While the former initially followed the drawings preserved in Basel's Kupferstichkabinett and was then altered by the artist at a slightly later date, the painter of the latter had only the final painting to work from. The maker of the copy, Bartolomäus Sarburgh, was clearly also influenced by the aesthetics of his own time, 'correcting' not only what he must have felt was Holbein's rather cramped composition by enlarging it, but also 'modernising' both the figural and facial types, and even in some instances the colouration.

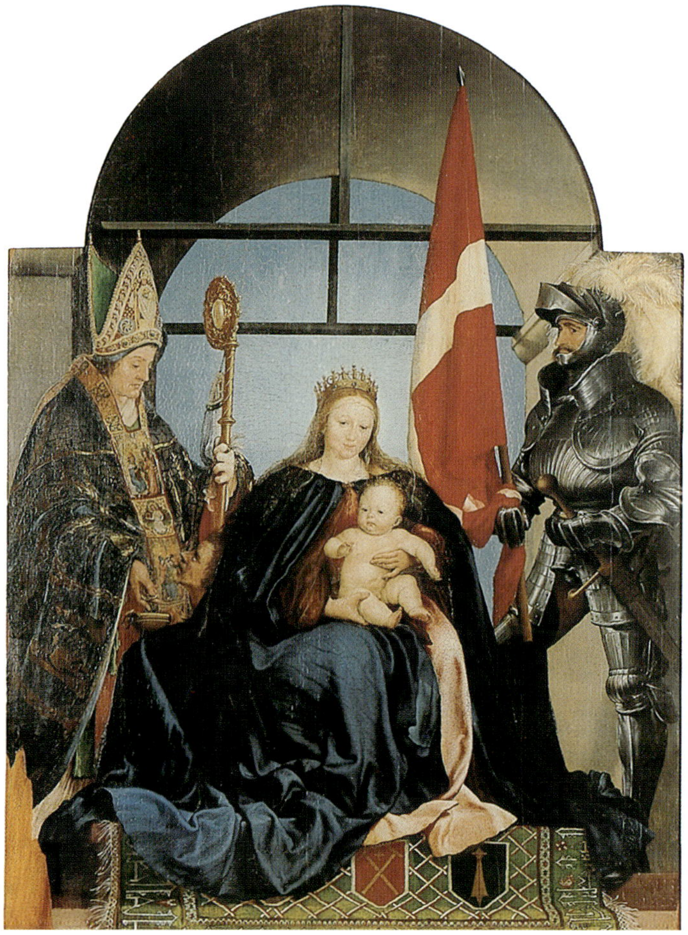

fig. 5
Hans Holbein the Younger, *Solothurn Madonna*, 1522. Panel, 140.5 x 102 cm. Solothurn, Kunstmuseum

Genesis and development

Observations and reflections on the genesis of the *Darmstadt Madonna* were important not only within the framework of the 'Holbein controversy' of the nineteenth century; they would continue to play an important role in all examinations of the picture up to our own day. In the decade following the Second World War, the painting was on long-term loan to the Kunstmuseum in Basel, where it was subjected to a thoroughgoing technical analysis. The x-ray photographs made on this occasion revealed a number of alterations that had hitherto remained invisible to the naked eye, particularly in the heads of the female members of the donor's family (fig. 7). Until recently, Hans Reinhardt's interpretation of this evidence was generally accepted.[10] Reinhardt believed he had discovered that Meyer's first wife, Magdalena Baer, was not included in the initial colour lay-in of the composition. She was added only later, he thought, after Holbein's return from England in 1528, when Meyer asked him to change Anna's hairstyle and the cap and chinband originally worn by Dorothea Kannengießer. The trigger for these extensive modifications was presumed to be the death of the donor's two sons, whom Reinhardt (and traditional Holbein scholars in general) identified with the boys at the left. By adding a likeness of his first wife, who had died already in 1511, according to Reinhardt, Meyer thus belatedly transformed the *Darmstadt Madonna* into a kind of memorial.

◂ This assumption, however, is countered not only by the complete absence of any mention in the sources of two Meyer sons who had allegedly died in childhood (not to mention the lack of portrait studies similar to those of the donor, his wife and daughter), but also by the naked little boy himself, who is clearly the young John the Baptist. As Hans Ost has demonstrated, the *Darmstadt Madonna* follows in the tradition not only of the Virgin of Pity, but also of images of the Madonna and Child with St John the Baptist, popular above all in Italy.[11] Only recently has Stephanie Buck shown that Reinhardt's sweeping conclusions, generally accepted even among scholars today, are based on a misreading of the x-ray photographs,[12] and her standpoint has now been confirmed with the help of infrared reflectography.[13] This examination revealed not only that the figure of Magdalena Baer was part of Holbein's composition from the very beginning, but also provided some insight into the picture's genesis (as far as the paint layers are penetrable by long-wave light), which turns out to be far more complex than had previously been thought. Perhaps the most surprising discovery was that the three portrait studies of the donor and his family in the Basel Kupferstichkabinett (figs. 2-4), always believed to have formed the *basis* for the *Darmstadt Madonna*, were not in fact preliminary studies at all, but rather executed in the course of the painting process.

◂ The underdrawing, applied with a brush in several phases, is purely linear and schematic, with no hatching whatsoever to indicate the surface relief. In the case of the Madonna and the Christ Child (fig. 8), as well as of the two boys (fig. 9), there is little difference between the final painted forms and the underdrawing. This is quite typical of Holbein's working method. Quite the opposite is true of the members of the donor's family. Initially, the three women were all depicted in strict profile (fig. 10): while Magdalena Baer looked straight up at the Virgin, Anna's head was slightly bent forward, her eyes focused on the ground; Dorothea Kannengießer, finally, looked directly left towards her husband. The colour lay-in already introduced several substantial changes to the figures of the adult women. Magdalena's head was set more or less as we see it today, although slightly to the right; this is indicated by the neck or chin cloth clearly visible in the x-ray (fig. 7). Dorothea's head (placed somewhat to the right of where it is now), on the other hand, was turned to create a three-quarter profile, so that the nose no longer overlaps the left side of her face — in other words, was given the same bearing, although not the same position, as we see today. In the case of Anna Meyer, the initial lay-in followed the underdrawing, as demonstrated in the infrared and x-ray photographs of Dorothea Kannengießer's white cap band (later painted over), which once extended to just below her present nose. The girl's dress —at least the upper portion— had a slightly different pattern than it does now: the infrared examination revealed a dark, narrow zone under the broad embroidered band, perhaps some kind of braiding or trim. In accordance with her slightly different pose, Anna's dress did not always spread out as widely across the carpet as it does now, nor trail so far behind her.

◂ Infrared reflectography also revealed major differences between the underdrawing and the lay-in of the figure of the donor himself (fig. 11). In the former, it seems, Meyer's head was farther to the right, as indicated by the strands of hair in

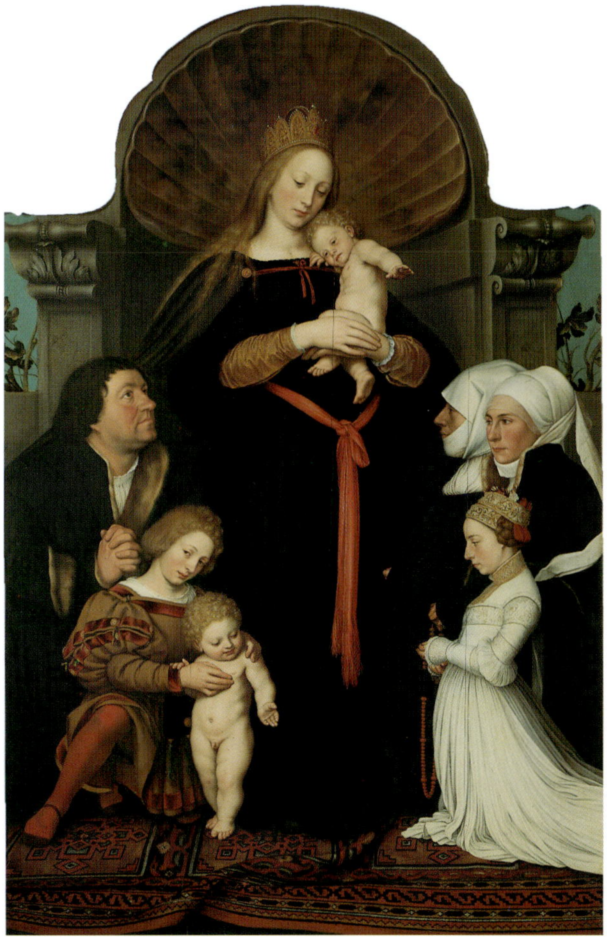

fig. 6
Bartholomäus Sarburgh,
Copy after Holbein's Darmstadt Madonna, c. 1635/37.
Panel, 159 x 103 cm.
Dresden, Staatliche Kunstsammlung, Gemäldegalerie

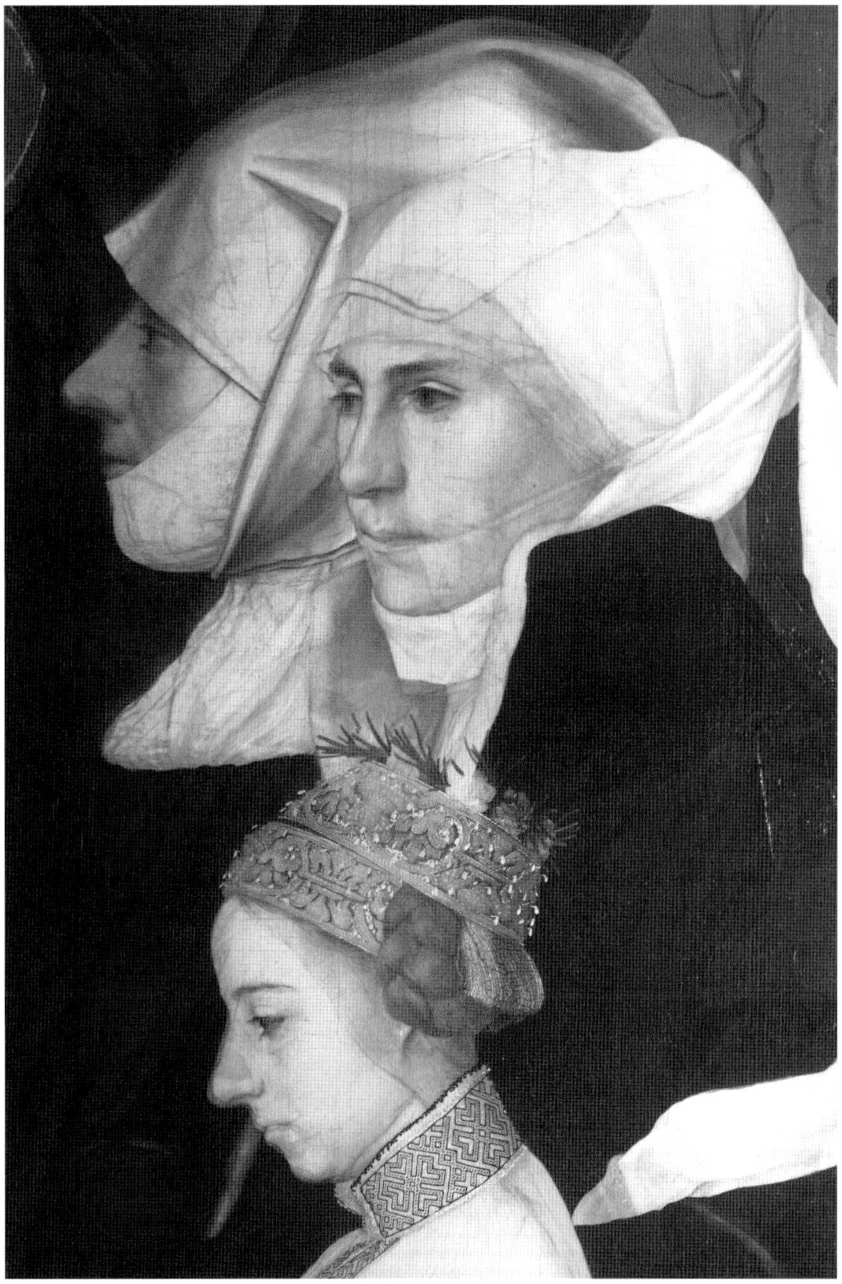

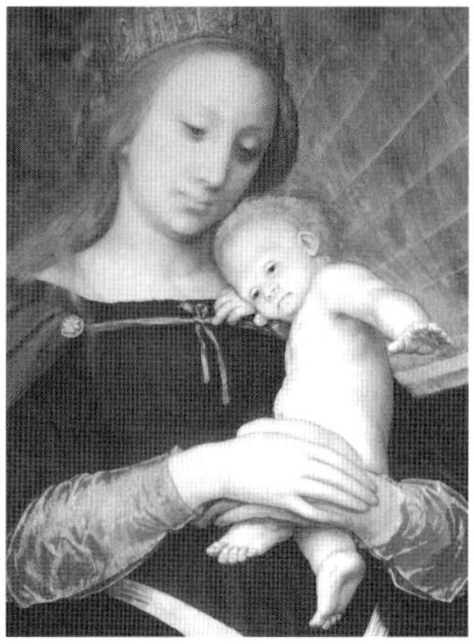

fig. 8
Darmstadt Madonna. Infrared image of the Virgin and Child. (Photograph courtesy of the author)

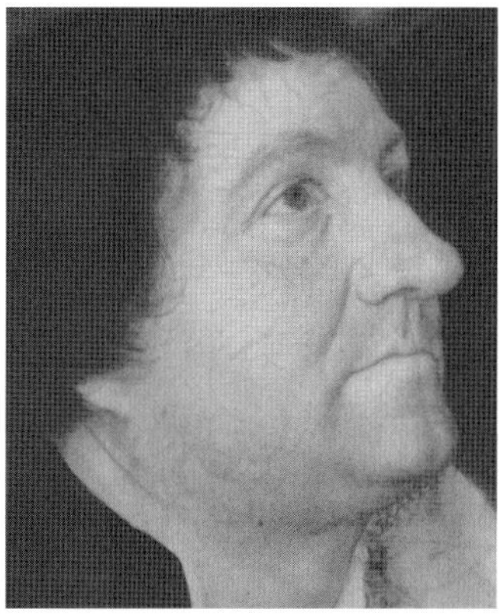

fig. 10
Darmstadt Madonna. Infrared image of the female members of the donor's family. (Photograph courtesy of the author)

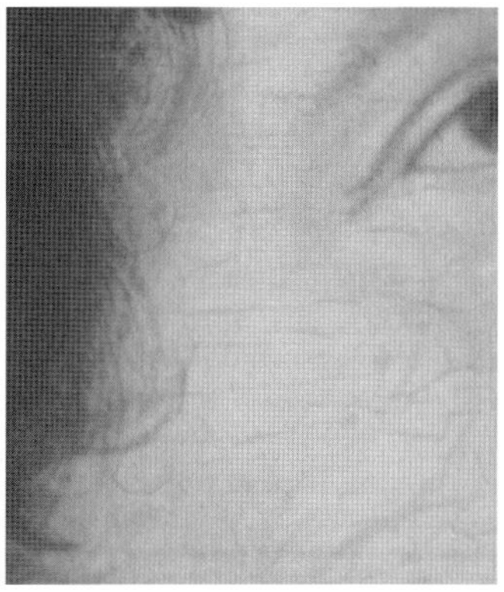

fig. 11
Darmstadt Madonna. Infrared image of the head of Jacob Meyer. (Photograph courtesy of the author)

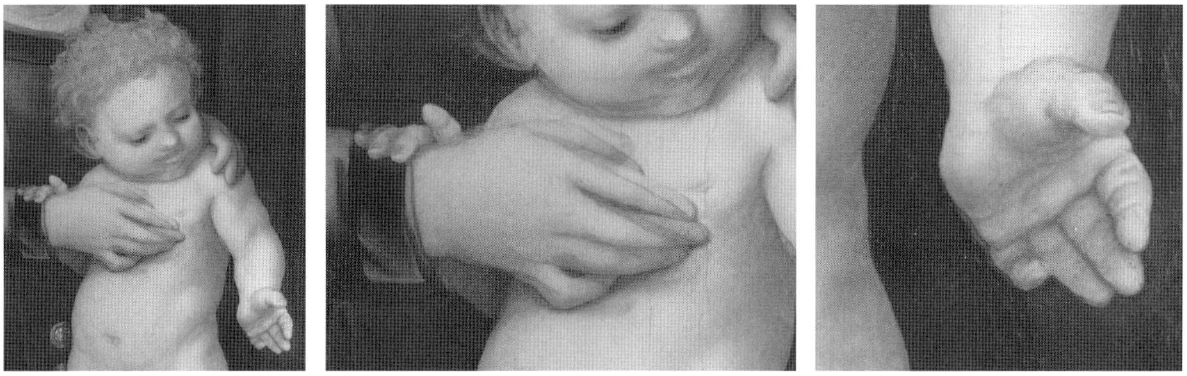

fig. 9
Darmstadt Madonna. Infrared image of the nude boy (Photograph courtesy of the author)

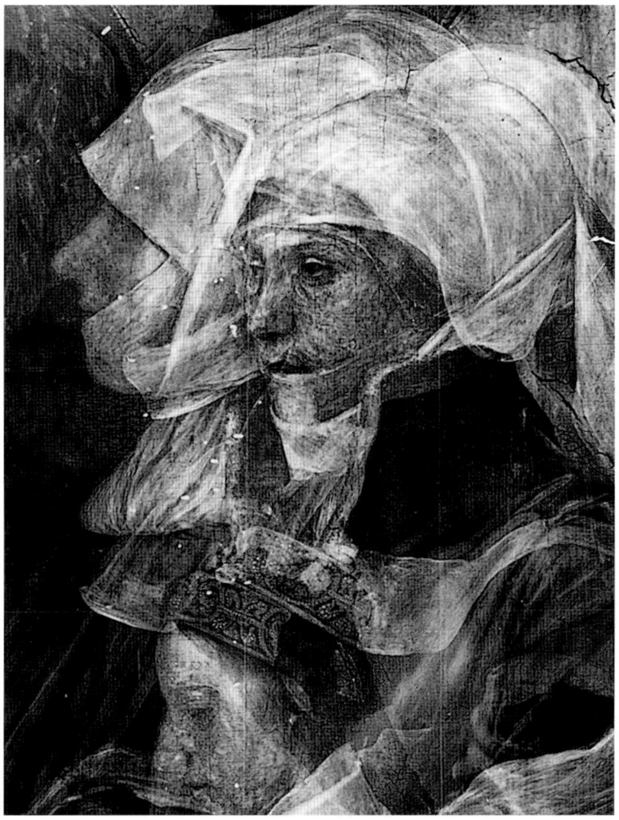

fig. 7
Hans Holbein
the Younger,
Darmstadt Madonna.
X-ray image of
the heads of the
female members
of the donor's family.
(Photograph courtesy
of the Kunstmuseum
Basel)

the area of his present cheek. In the initial lay-in, his head was probably already much in the position it occupies today, whereby the shirt and gown were once again altered at the neckline in the course of painting.

It was only at this stage in the execution of the *Darmstadt Madonna* that the Basel portrait drawings were carried out. Meyer was evidently pleased with Holbein's composition as a whole —the group of the Virgin and Child remained unchanged[14]— but not with the individual donor figures. The discrepancies between painter and patron were apparently so great that Holbein chose to present his client with the series of portraits studies, fully worked up in black and coloured chalk, and comparable in size to the heads as they would appear in the final painting. Meyer must have been satisfied with these, as Holbein used them to make a new underdrawing over the already extant faces of Jakob, his daughter and Dorothea Kannengießer. The traces of graphite and the press lines found in all three Basel drawings indicate that the sheets were used to mechanically transfer the motifs to the (partially re-prepared) panel, as for the first time Maryan Ainsworth and Molly Faries have shown was the case for the 1527 portrait of Lady Guildford in The Saint Louis Art Museum (cat. no. 6).[15] During a recent re-examination of the Basel drawings, Christian Müller discovered that the versos of all three show traces of a mechanical transfer of the drawing to the support or —more likely— to some kind of intermediary cartoon.[16]

The final likenesses in the *Darmstadt Madonna* would follow these new underdrawings to the letter. Appropriate to its function, Holbein's figures are somewhat more dignified and solemn in the painting than in the drawings. This is particularly the case with Meyer himself, who in the portrait study appears unshaven but in the finished work has been relieved of all vestiges of stubble. Here, the immediacy and intimacy of the drawings —aspects that qualify them as independent works of art— are abandoned in favour of an official, even ceremonial character. Still, the genesis of the picture was not yet at an end, as it was only with the implementation of the changes demanded by the patron only after Holbein's return from England that it came to the final and well-known alterations to the women's heads.

The Catholic pictorial tradition

Commissioned just three years before the triumph of the Reformation in Basel, and reworked a mere year before the iconoclastic riots, the *Darmstadt Madonna* is an unequivocal expression of Jakob Meyer's commitment to the old faith. Mary is not simply the Mother of God, but also the Queen of Heaven: while the form of her diadem is an explicit reference to the crown of the Holy Roman Empire,[17] the scalloped niche appears as a kind of monumental halo. In addition, she is the Virgin of Pity, into whose hands Meyer and his family have given themselves, whereby the inclusion of the donor's first wife, Magdalena Baer, gives the scene from the very beginning the character of an epitaph. An essential element of the highly Catholic iconographic programme is, of course, the young John the Baptist at the Virgin's feet. His pointing gesture could be read as an allusion to the words spoken shortly before Christ's baptism in the river Jordan: "Ecce Agnus Dei" — "Behold, the Lamb of God" (John 1:29). Should the *Darmstadt*

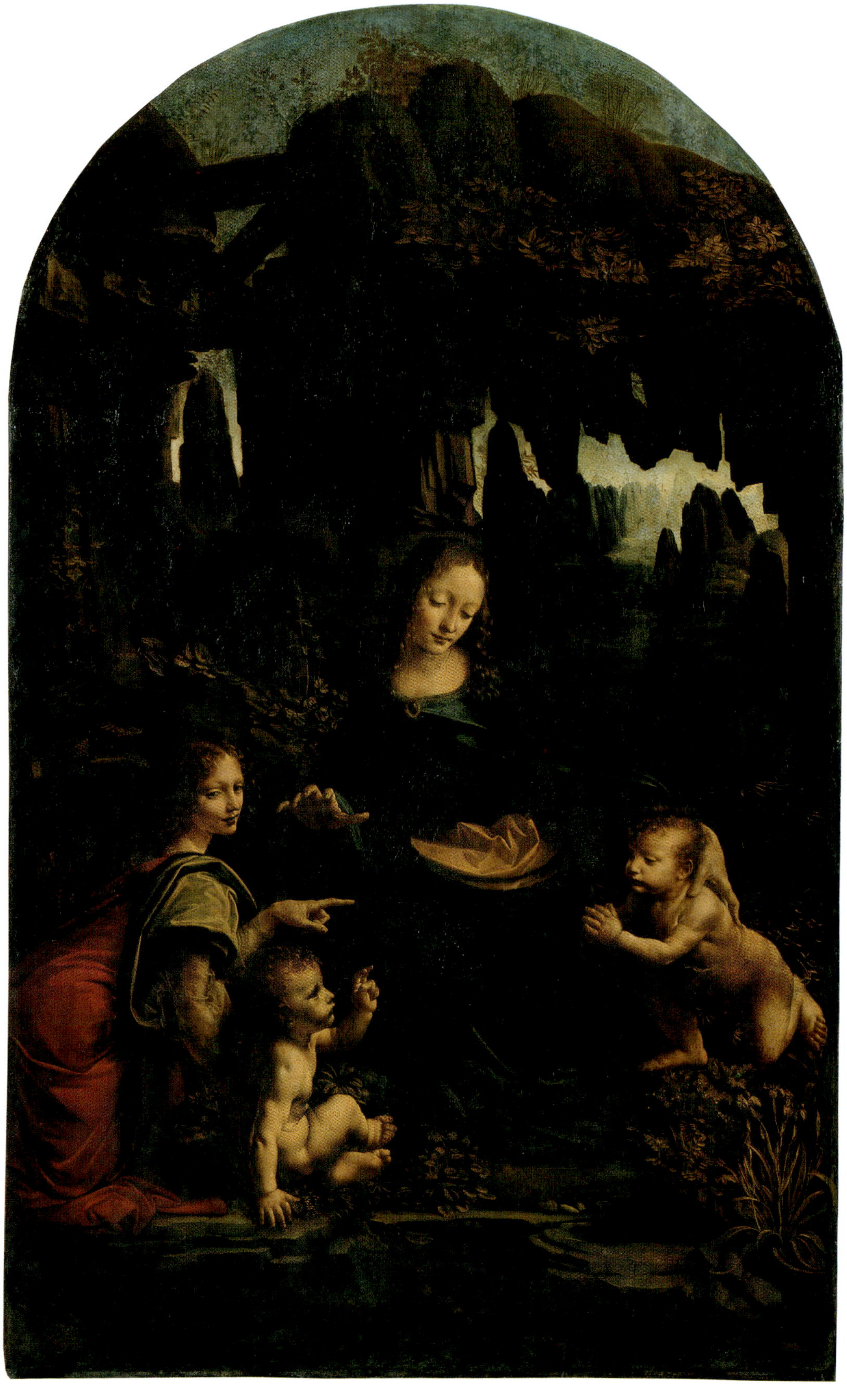

fig. 12 Leonardo da Vinci, *Madonna of the Rocks*, c. 1483-1506. Canvas, 199 x 122 cm. Paris, Musée du Louvre

Madonna have originally hung above an altar, it would have created a link to the Eucharist, which rests on the altar during the celebration of mass.

◂ Like the Virgin and Child, the naked little boy's idealised form and the use of the *sfumato* made popular in the works of Leonardo da Vinci identify him as extraneous to the donor's family. The same is true of the youth, whose face, moreover, resembles that of the Madonna — almost like a younger brother — and who is also depicted in a manner quite outside the more realistic conventions governing the likenesses of the donors. The figure is very likely a direct borrowing from Leonardo's *Madonna of the Rocks* (fig. 12).[18] Holbein must have seen one of the two surviving versions of this composition (or one of the many copies after it) at the court of François I, during his trip to France in 1523/24. It was the source not only for the generally 'smoky' characterisation of the holy figures and the head-types of both the Madonna and Child, but also of the motif of the foreshortened left hand — in Leonardo it is the Virgin's, in Holbein Jesus'. The angel supporting the Christ Child in the Leonardo painting was very likely the inspiration for the figure group of the two boys: the pose of the angel and the youth are almost identical, as is the gaze directed out of the picture towards the viewer; here, however, the pointing gesture has wandered from the angel to John the Baptist, who is shown standing.

◂ In the Holbein, Leonardo's angel — clearly marked as such by the wings — has been transformed into a fashionably dressed youth. He is given one striking accessory, which may provide a clue to his identity — the pouch hanging from his belt, which is a symbol of St James (in German: Jakob), the patron saint of pilgrims.[19] It is typical of Holbein's equally uninhibited and creative treatment of pictorial tradition that one cannot be entirely certain whether this youthful 'Jakob' is a kind of secularised patron saint of the donor, or if he is meant as an idealised representation of a son of Meyer, not mentioned in the sources and dead before the commission was given, and who, like his father, bore that name. Keeping in mind the audacity of Holbein's transformation of the theme of the Entombment (fig. 13), his inventive treatment of new subject matter — as in the portrait of the family of Thomas More (p. 20, fig. 19) or the portrait of his own wife and children (p. 24, fig. 23) — and his reformulation of established pictorial motifs and secularisation of religious conventions of representation, this striking depiction of the older boy, who corresponds so little to the visual norm, may perhaps appear somewhat less unusual.

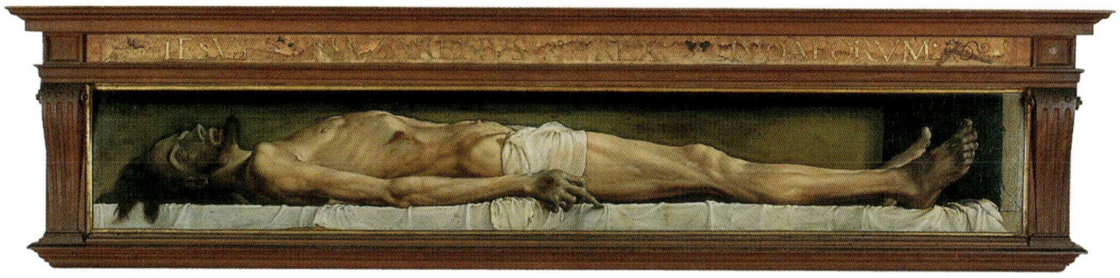

fig. 13
Hans Holbein the Younger,
The body of the dead Christ in the tomb,
1521/22. Panel,
30.6 x 200 cm.
Basel, Kunstmuseum

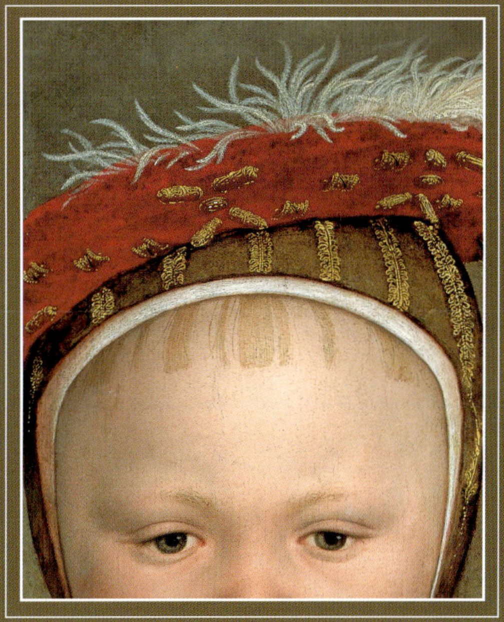

I

Desiderius Erasmus (c. 1466/69–1536), c. 1523

Panel, 42 x 32 cm
Paris, Musée du Louvre
cat.no. 1

Holbein's portraits of Erasmus have permanently shaped our image of the famous humanist scholar. In 1523 Holbein painted no fewer than three portraits of Erasmus: the painting described here from the Musée du Louvre, the variant of it in Basel's Kunstmuseum (fig. 1a; p. 16, colour fig. 11) and the work in a private collection, which is on loan to the National Gallery, London (p. 11, fig. 10).[3] Only the latter actually bears the date 1523. The three portraits are indisputably among the early masterpieces of Holbein's oeuvre. These early commissions by Erasmus — already discussed in the introductory essay by Stephanie Buck— were crucial to the development of Holbein's career in England. For when he journeyed to London in the summer of 1526, he bore letters of introduction from Erasmus, which helped him gain access to numerous potential clients. In England Holbein devoted himself primarily to portrait painting, his sitters including Erasmus's close friend Thomas More (see cat. no. 3). It was a genre into which the prolific artist had ventured only occasionally before then. In Basel he had painted the portrait of the burgomaster Jakob Meyer and his wife Dorothea Kannengießer in 1516 (see p. 17, figs. 12–13),[4] and a year later he had painted the portrait of Benedikt von Hertenstein (New York, The Metropolitan Museum of Art).[5] Benedikt was the son of Jakob von Hertenstein, the wealthy merchant and burgomaster of Lucerne, whose home Holbein decorated with mural paintings in the same period.[6] The well-known portrait of the law scholar Bonifacius Amerbach, who would become an avid collector of Holbein's work, dates from 1519 (p. 18, fig. 14).[7] In 1525–1526 Holbein painted the *Darmstadt Madonna* (cat. no. 2) with portraits of Meyer and his family.

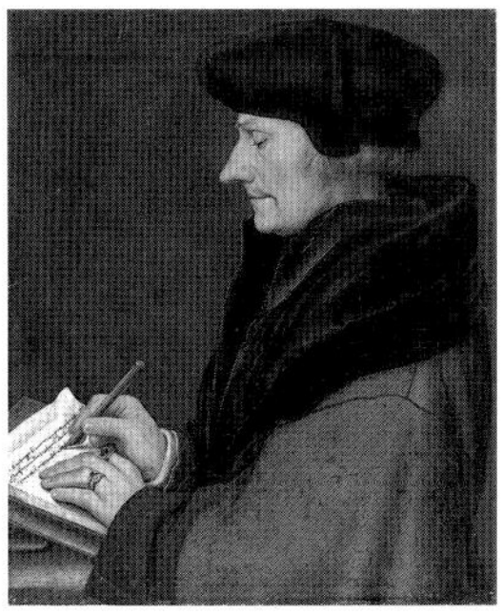

fig. 1a
Hans Holbein the Younger, *Portrait of Desiderius Erasmus*, c. 1523. Paper on panel, 37 x 30.5 cm. Basel, Öffentliche Kunstsammlung, Kunstmuseum

◂ Erasmus, born as the son of a cleric in Gouda, in or around 1469, was one of the most influential advocates of humanism.[8] Having spent his youth in Rotterdam and Deventer, in 1487 he entered the monastery of Steyn, near Gouda, where he studied philosophy, theology and the classics. Erasmus was admitted to the priesthood in 1492. He left the monastery the following year to become secretary to the bishop of Cambrai, whom he accompanied on his travels. On his own study trips to France (1496–1498) and England (1498–1499) Erasmus made the acquaintance of several important humanists. In 1500 he published a collection of Latin and Greek adages that instantly established his reputation. Erasmus returned to England in 1509, Henry VIII's coronation year, and stayed there until 1514. He lectured at Cambridge, and it was there that he wrote his most famous and most popular book, *Praise of folly*. In this satire, he criticised various forms of 'foolish' human behaviour, without sparing the upper classes or the Church. Although Erasmus initially supported Protestantism, he gradually distanced himself from Luther, their differences culminating in a public theological dispute. Erasmus eventually chose the side of the Roman Catholic Church. He lived in Leuven from 1517 to 1521, but when accusations of heresy were made against him he moved to Basel. Holbein too spent much of his early career in this impotant centre of book publishing and humanism. When the Refor-mation came to Basel, Erasmus settled in Freiburg im Breisgau, in order to continue his work undisturbed. Later he returned to Basel, where he spent more than ten years of his life in all, and was laid to rest there in 1536.

◂ Holbein became acquainted with the writings of this celebrated humanist at an early age; he made pen drawings in the margin of a copy of *Praise of folly* in 1515, when only 17 or 18 years of age (p. 15, figs. 5-8). According to Myconius, the book's owner, Erasmus was very taken with these drawings, which are the earliest works by Holbein that have been preserved.[9] One of them probably depicts Erasmus as a scholar, writing in a study (see p. 15, fig. 8).[10]

◂ The painting from Paris discussed here and the closely related portrait in Basel also depict the scholar from the side, writing.[11] In the painting in London —the largest of the three— Erasmus is depicted from a three-quarters angle, with his hands resting on a book.[12] In all three portraits, the scholar wears a cloak that is trimmed with fur (London) or a type of silk (Paris and Basel). In 1517 Pope Leo X had granted him dispensation from wearing a monk's habit.[13] The black cap differed from customary sixteenth-century headgear. An X-

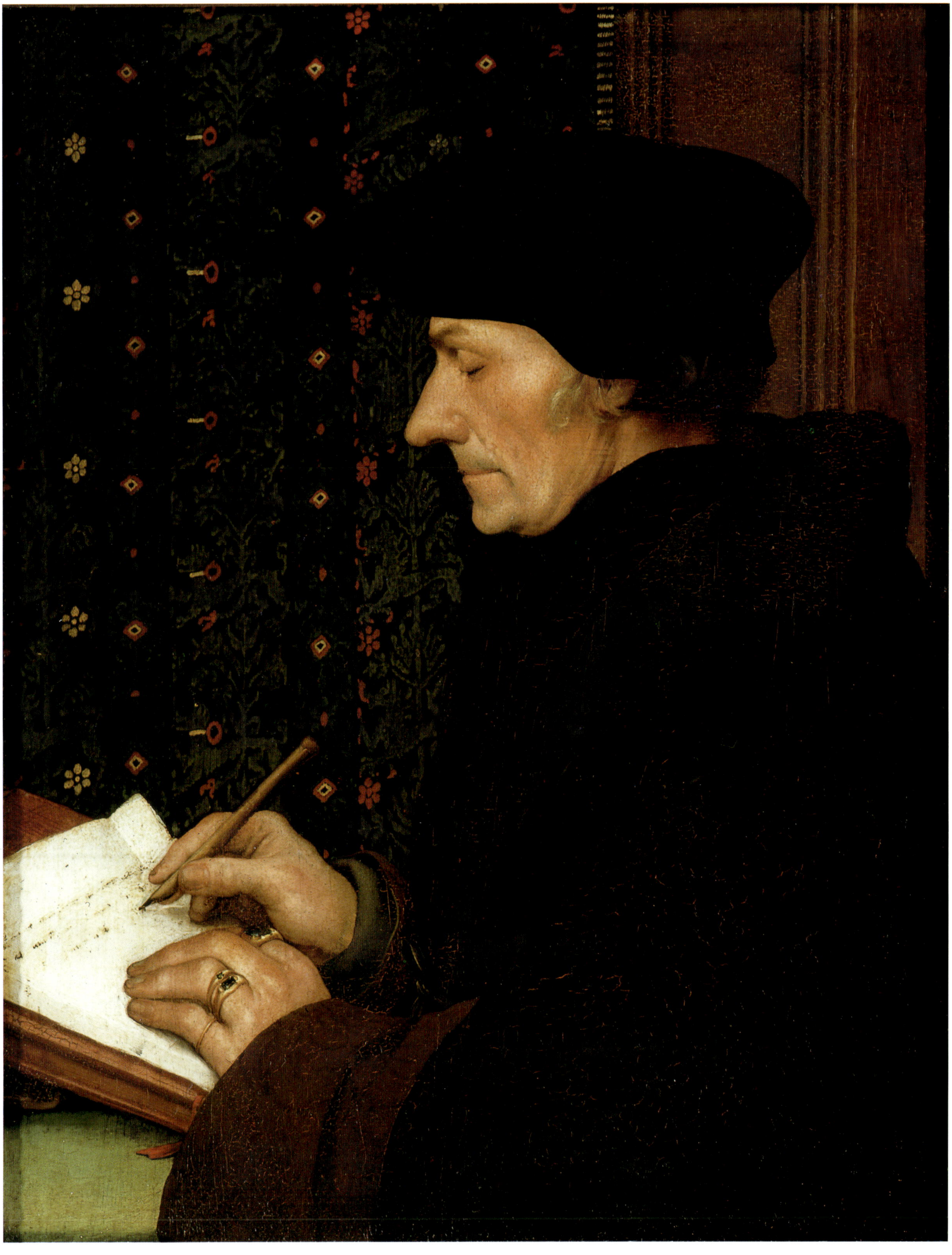

radiograph of the painting discussed here reveals that Holbein enlarged the back of the cap during the painting process.[14]

◂ It is striking that Holbein, who was sometimes rather casual in his rendering of hands (see e.g. cat. no. 7), paid immense attention to the hands in his three portraits of Erasmus. By a stroke of good fortune, a sheet with three studies of Erasmus's hands has been preserved. Like the painting discussed here, it is in the Musée du Louvre (fig. 1b).[15] It is an interesting sheet, because it is the only one that Holbein has filled solely with hands, and it therefore sheds light on his working methods. It shows Erasmus's writing hand, for instance, which is sketched very loosely in black chalk. Holbein depicted this hand, holding a pen, in the portraits in Paris and Basel, though from a slightly different angle. Infrared examination of the painting in Paris has revealed an underdrawing of the hands.[16] This may have been based on a preliminary study, which has since been lost, given that in other portraits Holbein evidently based his rendering of the hands directly on a drawing. In the portrait of Simon George, for instance, the hands were probably traced from a drawing (see cat. nos. 24-25). And Holbein followed the detailed study of the hand with rings on the sheet in Paris when making the portrait in London.

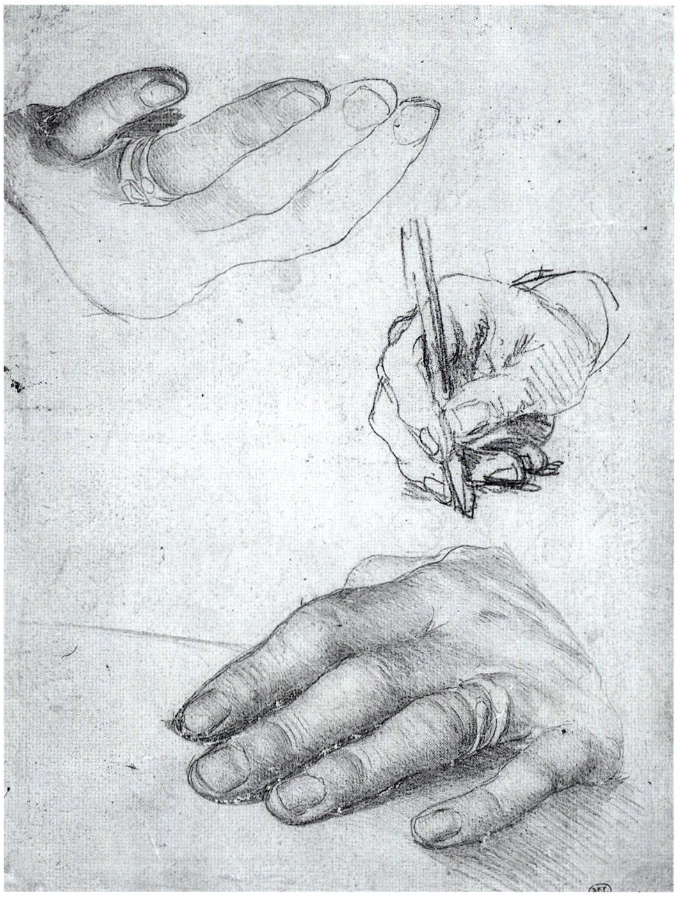

fig. 1b
Hans Holbein the Younger, *Studies of the hands of Desiderius Erasmus*, c. 1523. Silverpoint, red and black chalk, 206 x 153 mm. Paris, Musée du Louvre, Cabinet des Dessins

◂ A second study by Holbein, also preserved in the Musée du Louvre, shows a rough sketch of Erasmus's face, which —like the right hand in this study— served as a preliminary drawing for the portrait in London.[17] No similar sketch of the face has been preserved for the two portraits in profile, nor is there any extant detailed study for them. Perhaps the Basel portrait, which was executed on paper, was simply painted over a more detailed study of Erasmus, or a copy of one; the portrait Holbein painted on parchment of Anne of Cleves (1539) is believed to have been painted directly on top of a copy of the preliminary study (p. 30, fig. 29).[18] It is possible that the Basel portrait was not transferred to a panel for many years. Holbein's wife sold it to the collector Bonifacius Amerbach in 1542, when the artist had been living in London for years. Later that year Amerbach wrote in a letter that he had had the painting pasted to a panel (again?), framed and glazed.[19] Many writers believe that Holbein had taken this portrait with him to France, when he sought unsuccessfully to ingratiate himself with King Francis I.[20]

◂ There has also been some speculation regarding the original destinations of the Erasmus portraits that are now in London and Paris. In a letter of 3 June 1524 to his friend Willibald Pirckheimer, Erasmus wrote that he had recently sent two portraits of himself to England, and that the painter who had made them had taken another portrait of him to France.[21] Erasmus does not mention Holbein by name, but the reference is clear from *Emendationes*, published by the humanist

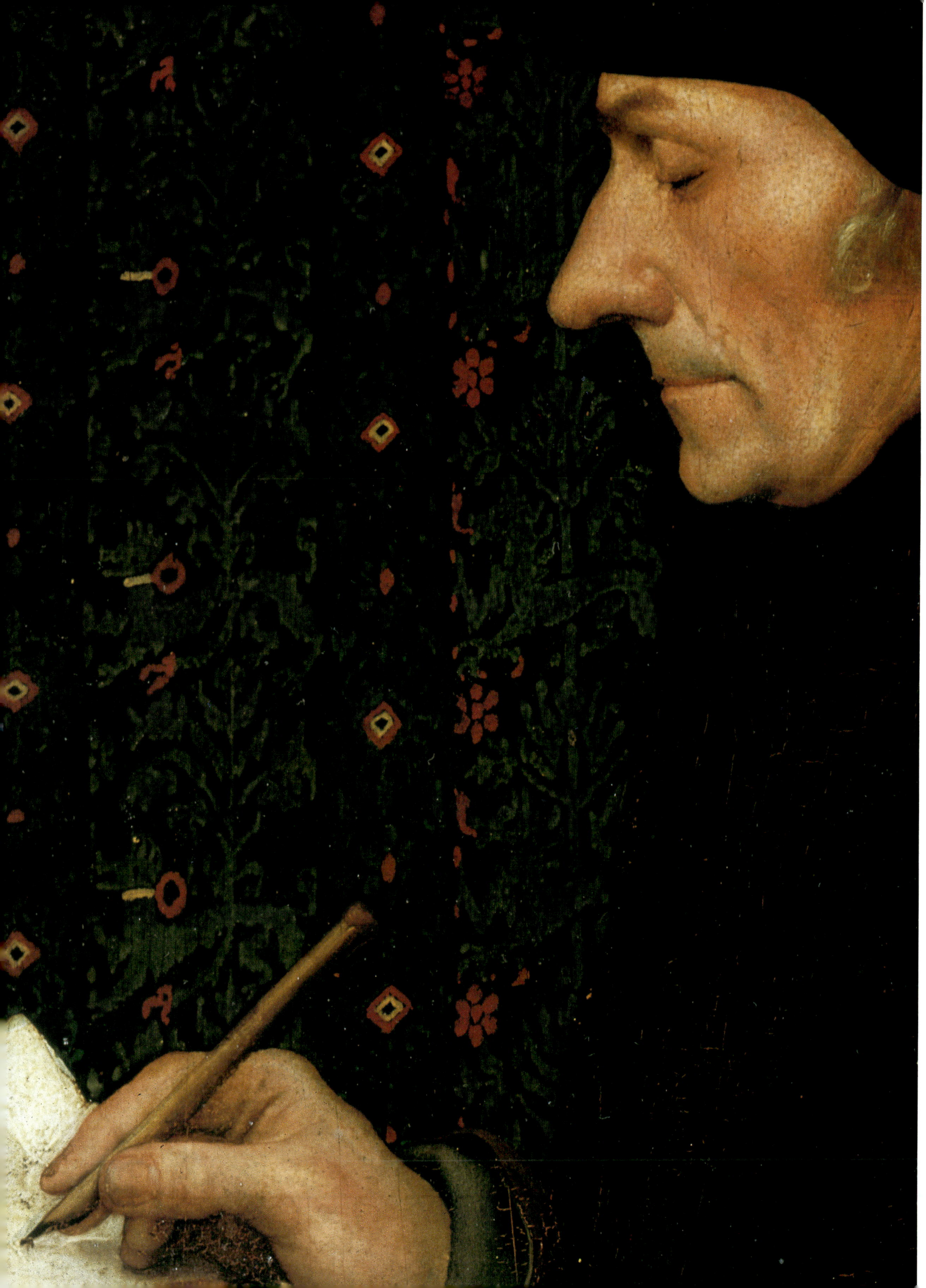

Beatus Rhenanus (1485–1547) with 'corrections' to Pliny's *Natural History*. Rhenanus —whose book was written in 1525 and published in Basel in 1526 by Johannes Froben, an acquaintance of both Holbein, who worked for him in 1516, and Erasmus, who lodged in the publisher's home— refers specifically to two portraits of Erasmus painted by Holbein that had been sent to England.[22] As far as the painting now in London is concerned, it is known to have come from Lambeth Palace,[23] the London residence of the archbishop of Canterbury, then William Warham (p. 23, fig. 22), one of Erasmus's patrons. In another letter from Erasmus, which he wrote to Warham on 4 September 1524, he asked the archbishop whether he had received his portrait yet.[24] Nothing is known about the person for whom the second portrait that Erasmus sent to England was intended. Nor do we know which painting was meant (the Basel or the Paris version), although it may well have been the one described here. The provenance of the Paris panel can be traced back to the collection of Charles I of England, where it was to be found before Louis XIV acquired it in 1671.[25] The intimate ambience of the portrait, in which the viewer looks, as it were, over Erasmus's shoulder, has given rise to the assumption that it was intended for someone in the scholar's immediate circle.[26]

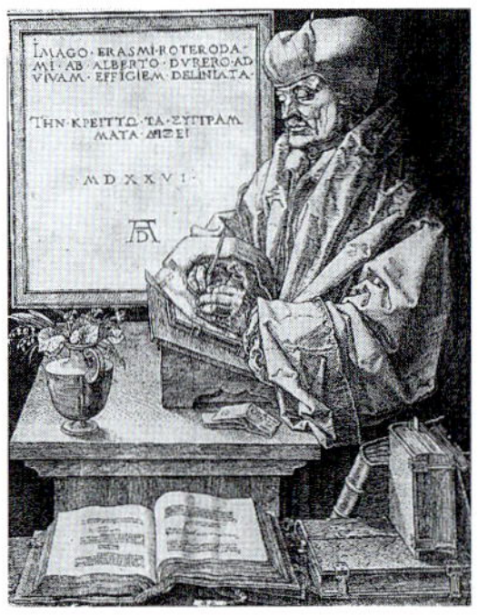

fig. 1c
Albrecht Dürer,
Portrait of Desiderius Erasmus, 1526.
Engraving,
249 x 193 mm.
Basel, Öffentliche Kunstsammlung, Kupferstichkabinett

◂ Notwithstanding the portrait's marked air of intimacy, it presents the 'official' image of himself that Erasmus wished to propagate. It portrays him as an author who actively responds to his vocation, that of making the great works of classical antiquity and Christian literature more readily accessible. The work discussed here shows the humanist absorbed in his writing, his gaze fixed on the paper before him. He also had himself depicted in the process of writing in a portrait engraving by Dürer (discussed below), prints of which became widely available (fig. 1c). Holbein's adoption of a full profile portrait —a rare choice in his oeuvre (cf. cat. nos. 2 and 25)— instils a somewhat official quality into the work. Profile portraits were strictly reserved for the elite, and Amerbach and other contemporaries of Erasmus associated them with emperors' portraits on coins and medallions from classical antiquity. It was believed that a sharp profile expressed the characteristic features of a face to best effect.[27]

◂ Holbein, who here abandoned the tradition of showing scholars in a study filled with books, appears to have depicted Erasmus standing at a table, which was normal practice in this period (see also fig. 1c). His hands attract attention because their flesh colour stands out against both the white paper and the dark sleeves and background. The sheet of paper lies not on a lectern but on two books, a detail that is more clearly visible in the Basel painting. However, the latter variant does not include the red ribbon on the green tablecloth, used to wrap around the book to keep it shut.[28]

◂ The text on the sheet of paper has unfortunately faded so far as to be quite indecipherable, but in all probability it was identical to the text that is legible in the Basel painting. This, in any case, is what close scrutiny of the fragmentary remaining letters appears to suggest. The text in question consists of the opening words in Erasmus's commentary on the Gospel of St Mark, which he had dedicated to King Francis I of France.[29] Partly on the basis of this evidence, the paintings in Basel and Paris can both be dated to 1523, the year in which Erasmus wrote the book in question, which was published in 1524.[30]

◂ In contrast to the portrait in Basel, with its plain-coloured background, the version in Paris suggests an interior: on the left we see fine wall hangings decorated with stylised flowers, plants and mythical creatures, and on the right we see part of a moulded wooden frame, possibly of a door. In the London portrait the imaginary interior is elaborated in more detail, with a handsomely decorated pilaster on the left, a green curtain in the centre background, and a small shelf with three books and a glass carafe on the far right. The book on the left displays the year 1523 in Roman numerals on its cover, while on the side appear two lines of verse in Latin by Erasmus, praising Holbein's work.[31]

◂ Erasmus's admiration for 'Olpeius', as he called Holbein in 1529 in a letter to Thomas More, went beyond mere politeness.

'The painter Holbein depicts people in such a way as to bring them to life', Erasmus enthused.[32] His appreciation is also evident from the fact that he gave the artist other commissions besides the portraits discussed here.[33] This makes it rather curious that the scholar included not Holbein but his fellow countryman Albrecht Dürer among the foremost ranks of artists, even though sources reveal that Erasmus was far from pleased with his likeness in a portrait engraving that Dürer completed in 1526 (fig. 1c).[34] It was presumably Dürer's theoretical writings that Erasmus held in such high regard.[35] Other contemporaries of Erasmus also admired the lifelike quality of Holbein's portraits, including Amerbach, who commented, when purchasing the portrait of Erasmus that is now in Basel, that it was 'vast leblich, gut und doctorn Erasmo gan[t]z enig, als ob er lept' (very lively, good and a superb likeness of Doctor Erasmus, as if he were alive).[36] The same could well be said of the portrait in Paris.

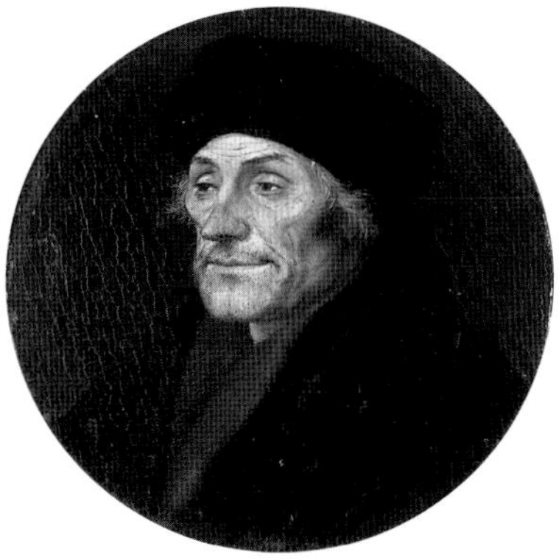

fig. 1d
Hans Holbein the Younger, *Portrait of Desiderius Erasmus*, c. 1530? Panel (circular), 10 cm in diameter. Basel, Öffentliche Kunstsammlung, Kunstmuseum

◂ Aside from the three paintings mentioned here, two other painted portraits of Erasmus are accepted as authentic works by Holbein.[37] One was made as part of a small box (fig. 1d), the lid of which has been lost (cf. cat. no. 20). The intimate little portrait probably came from the collection of Erasmus's friend, Johannes Froben (see above).[38] In addition, numerous variants, copies and prints after Holbein's portraits of Erasmus were marketed in the sixteenth and seventeenth centuries.[39] These images, none of which were by the master himself, were purchased eagerly by admirers of Erasmus and others who endorsed his views. QB

II

THE MEYER FAMILY WITH THE MADONNA, CHRIST AND JOHN THE BAPTIST, KNOWN AS THE

DARMSTADT MADONNA, *c.* 1525/26 *and* 1528/29

Panel (rounded at the top), 146.5 x 102 cm
Courtesy of the Hessische Hausstiftung
cat.no. 2

The *Darmstadt Madonna* is one of Holbein's most impressive scenes. More than that, it is regarded as one of the most important paintings of the German Renaissance. The work was commissioned by Jakob Meyer zum Hasen (1482–1530/31), the presence of whose likeness in this masterpiece has immortalised his name. Meyer had commissioned a portrait of his wife and himself from Holbein before, in 1516 (p. 17, figs. 12-13).[8] Preliminary drawings have survived both of this earlier work and of the one described here (pp. 38-39, figs. 2-4).[9] The event that had prompted the 1516 commission, in which Holbein painted the couple on two separate panels designed as a diptych, was Jakob Meyer's election as burgomaster of Basel on 24 June that year. As the son of a merchant, he must have been delighted to be dignified with an office generally reserved for nobles and patricians. Meyer had accumulated a fortune in a short space of time as a money-changer and an estate agent. He had also been successful commanding Swiss mercenaries in the conquest of Genoa in 1507 and Ferrara in 1510. In 1512 he had served as the Swiss Confederation's envoy to Venice and to Milan, which city was conquered by troops from Basel under his command. In 1521 Meyer was tried for corruption, and following his conviction even served a brief term of imprisonment.[10] Before then, he had used his influence to help Holbein secure some important commissions that helped to shape the artist's career.[11]

‹ In the *Darmstadt Madonna*, Jakob Meyer and his family are depicted at the feet of the Madonna and Child. It was probably in 1512 that Meyer had married Dorothea Kannengießer (*c.* 1490–1549?), the daughter of a tax collector from the Alsace. His first wife, Magdalena Baer, had died the year before. The painting described here includes a posthumous portrait of her, in profile, behind Dorothea Kannengießer. In the right foreground we see Anna, the daughter of Kannengießer and Meyer, who, like the other two women, is depicted kneeling. The boy immediately in front of Meyer is in all probability his patron saint, St James (in German 'Jakobus').[12] In the past some commentators believed this idealised figure to be the posthumous portrait of a son of Meyer who had died in childhood (see the essay by Jochen Sander).[13] The naked child in front of the saint is John the Baptist.[14]

‹ Holbein has depicted the Virgin Mary here as a *Schutzmantelmadonna* or Madonna of Mercy, whose cloak offers protection to those depicted with her. The men are shown on the left of the scene and the women on the right, the customary arrangement at the time.[15] When Holbein's father had painted a similar scene many years earlier, he had followed tradition in portraying the figures sheltering under the cloak much smaller than the Virgin herself.[16] Here, however, Holbein has made no difference between the size of his sitters and the saints, and the Virgin's cloak envelops only his patron. Holbein combined the idea of the Madonna of Mercy with a specifically Italian tradition in which the Virgin Mary and Christ are accompanied by the young John the Baptist.[17] He then incorporated another iconographical tradition, in which Mary stands before her throne, the Christ Child on her arm.[18] All we can see of the throne, which is in front of a wall, is its scalloped upper section and its consoles decorated with stylised acanthus leaves.[19] Mary's imperial crown, unmistakeably based on that of the Holy Roman Empire, identifies her as the queen of heaven.[20] The scene is set in the open air, as is clear from the stylised vines and fig leaves in front of the blue background.[21]

‹ Although Protestantism became the official religion in Basel in 1529, Meyer remained a fervent Catholic. In this context, his commissioning this painting around 1525–1526 was something of a demonstrative gesture.[22] The *Darmstadt Madonna*, the last altarpiece that Holbein was to paint, survived the iconoclastic fury of Basel in February 1529. The panel, which was presumably made for a private chapel,[23] was probably in Holbein's studio at the time. For after his return from England he made several major changes to the work at Meyer's request (for the complicated history of this painting's genesis, see the essay by Sander).

‹ Until 1606, the *Darmstadt Madonna* remained in the possession of Meyer's descendants. Through his daughter Anna, depicted in the painting, it came into the possession of his granddaughter Rosa Irmy, whose second husband, Remigius Faesch I — burgomaster of Basel — sold it in 1606 to the Basel diplomat Johann Lukas Iselin.[24] The latter's widow subsequently sold the painting in 1633, for a considerable sum of money, to the prominent Amsterdam art dealer and engraver Michel Le Blon (1587–1656), a connoisseur of Holbein's work. Either in or before 1638 Le Blon sold the painting, which was by then a renowned work of art, to the Amsterdam banker Jacob Loskaert.[25] For other would-be buyers he had a copy made by Bartholomäus Sarburgh (*c.* 1590–*after* 1637). This copy, perhaps a deliberate forgery, was for many years regarded as the original (p. 41, fig. 6).[26] Later on, the *Darmstadt Madonna* came into the possession of the Cromhouts, a wealthy Amsterdam merchant family.[27] In 1822, after the *Darmstadt Madonna* was unsuccessfully put up for auction, it was purchased by Prince Wilhelm of Prussia as a gift to his wife, in whose family it has continued to be passed down since then.[28] The painting, which has long been exhibited in Darmstadt, is one of the last Holbeins that is still privately owned. QB

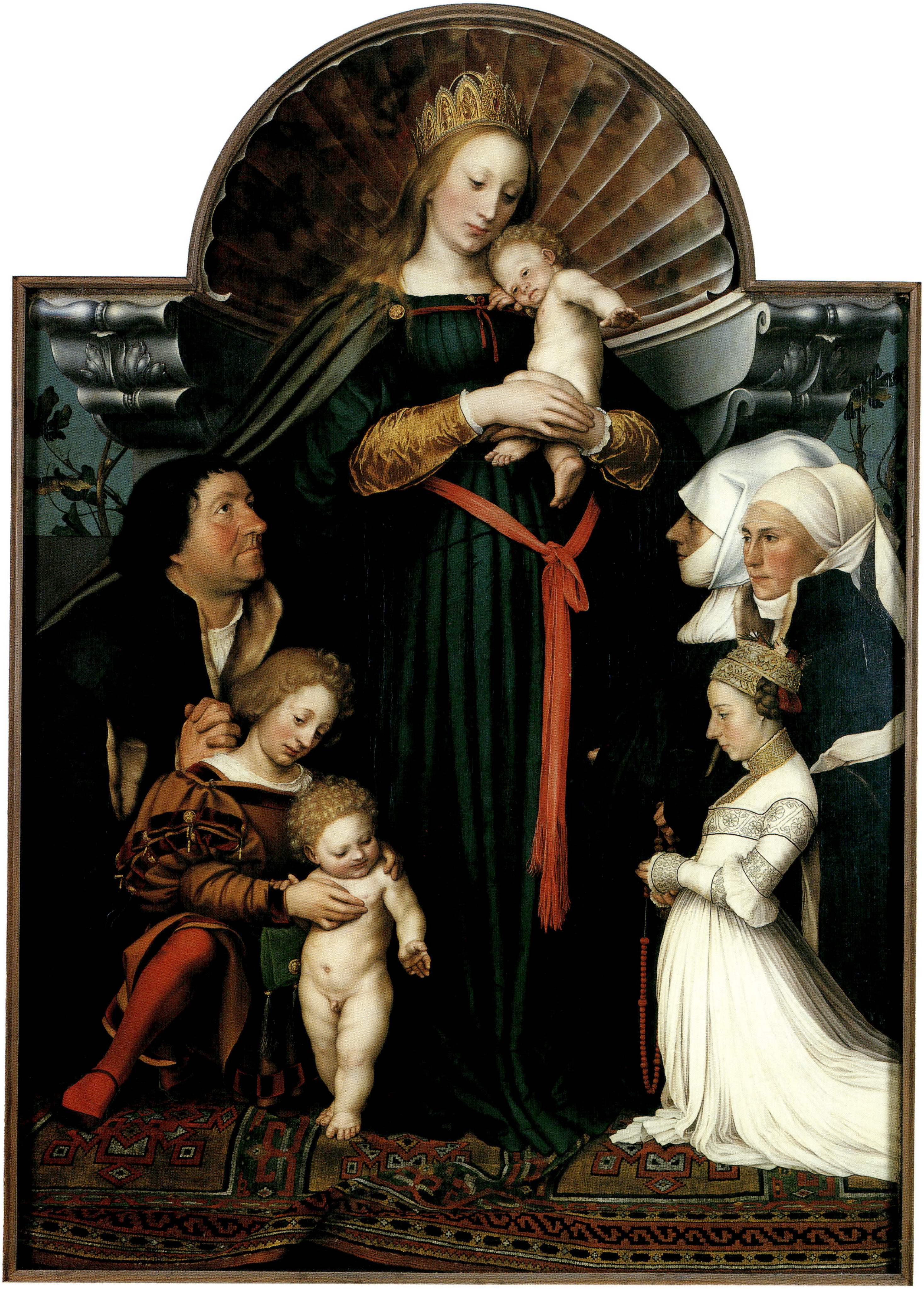

III

Thomas More (1478–1535), c. 1527

Black and coloured chalks on white paper, outlines pricked for transfer, 397 x 299 mm
At upper left, in a later hand: *Tho: Moor Ld Chancelour*
Lent by Her Majesty Queen Elizabeth II
cat.no. 3

Thomas More was one of the great humanists of his day and among the most prominent statesmen in Europe.[1] He achieved fame with his *Utopia* (1516), a witty, erudite description of an ideal society, and he was a pivotal figure in the ecclesiastical and public life of England for decades. Besides his formal education he learnt a great deal while serving as a page in the household of John Morton, Archbishop of Canterbury, and went on to pursue a brilliant career as a lawyer, politician and diplomat. In 1504 he entered the House of Commons, after which he was appointed a judge in 1510 and shortly afterward an undersheriff of London. In 1517 More became a member of Henry VIII's Privy Council, and fulfilled numerous diplomatic missions for the king. In 1523 he became Speaker of the House of Commons, and six years later he succeeded Cardinal Thomas Wolsey as Lord Chancellor, Speaker of the House of Lords — the highest office in the land. More, who had been raised to the peerage in 1521, remained a devout Catholic throughout his life. He therefore opposed the king's intention to seek a divorce from his first wife, Catherine of Aragon. When Henry distanced himself even further from Rome, More resigned as Lord Chancellor, in 1532. Two years later he refused to subscribe to the Act of Supremacy, which recognised Henry as the head of the Church of England. This led to his imprisonment in the Tower of London and his subsequent beheading, on 6 July 1535, following his conviction for high treason. More was beatified in 1886, and canonised in 1935.

Family life was at least as important to Thomas More as his public duties. In 1505 he married Jane Colt, who gave him three daughters and a son. After her death in 1511, he married Alice Middleton, who would survive him. True to the ideals expressed in his *Utopia*, he gave his daughters the same thorough education as his son. The tutors employed in More's household, which Erasmus described as a Christian version of Plato's Academy, included leading scholars such as the astronomer Nicolaus Kratzer (p. 21, fig. 20).[2] Holbein was introduced to Thomas More by More's friend and kindred spirit Erasmus (see cat. no. 1), who had dedicated his *Praise of Folly* to the English scholar in 1509. Thanks to Erasmus's letter of recommendation, Holbein was invited to lodge at the Mores' Chelsea home after his arrival in England in 1526, and he lived there until 1528, when he returned to Basel for a few years.[3]

Holbein's most important commission in this period was a life-sized, monumental group portrait of the More family on canvas,[4] for which this chalk sketch may have been a preliminary study. This first group portrait ever produced in Northern Europe perished by fire in the eighteenth century, but the image it depicted is nonetheless known in part from later variants and in part from a pen-and-ink design by Holbein himself (fig. 3a).[5] It shows Thomas More as a paterfamilias beside his father, the judge John More (c. 1451–1530), surrounded by his young adult children and foster children. Kratzer added the names and ages of the children, all of whom are engrossed in their books.[6] When Holbein returned to Basel in 1528, he probably provided this preliminary drawing as a gift from Thomas More to Erasmus, who responded to it enthusiastically in his letters.[7]

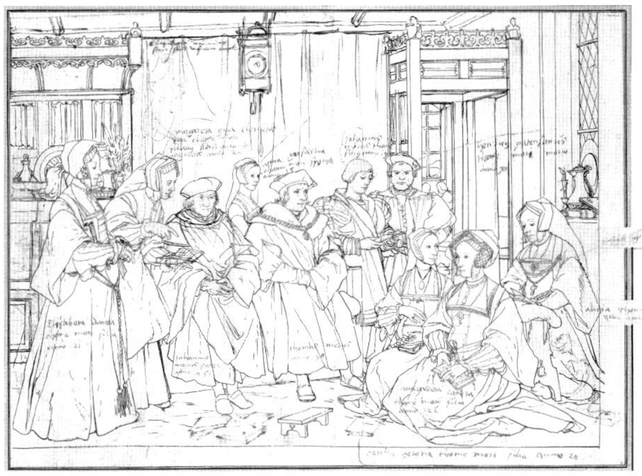

fig. 3a
Hans Holbein the Younger, *Study for a family portrait of Sir Thomas More*, c. 1527. Pen and black ink, finely pointed brush and black wash, inscriptions in brown ink, 389 x 524 mm
Basel, Öffentliche Kunstsammlung, Kupferstichkabinett

Holbein's eight portrait drawings of the More family are preserved in Windsor Castle, all of which were probably made in preparation for the group portrait.[8] They include two portraits of Thomas More, one of which is the sheet discussed here (see also fig. 3b).[9] Both are life-sized, which is exceptional in Holbein's portrait drawings.

The drawing discussed here was executed in black, brown, red and yellow chalks on white paper. This chalk technique is characteristic of the portraits dating from Holbein's first

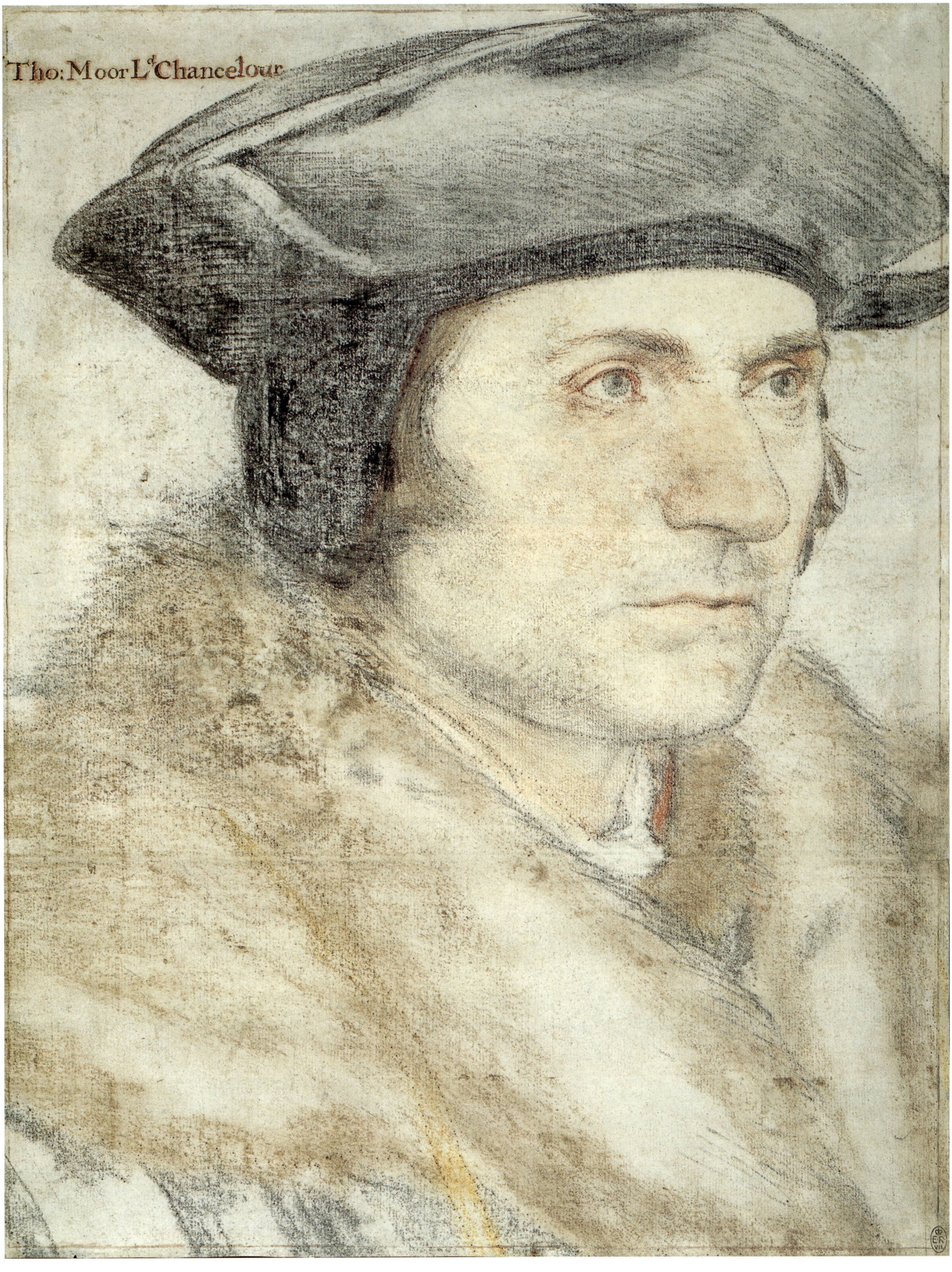
Tho: Moor Ld Chancelour

English period, when he did not cover the paper with a pink ground, as he did after his return to England in 1532.[10] The cap is depicted in black chalk; the hatching on it runs from lower right to upper left, a sure sign of a left-handed artist.[11] More wears this cap over an undercap with earflaps.[12] The soft texture of the fur collar is beautifully conveyed with brown chalk, to which a little black has been added in the shaded parts; some parts of the paper have been left exposed here to suggest the sheen of the fur. More's unshaven face has been subtly rendered in different shades of chalk.

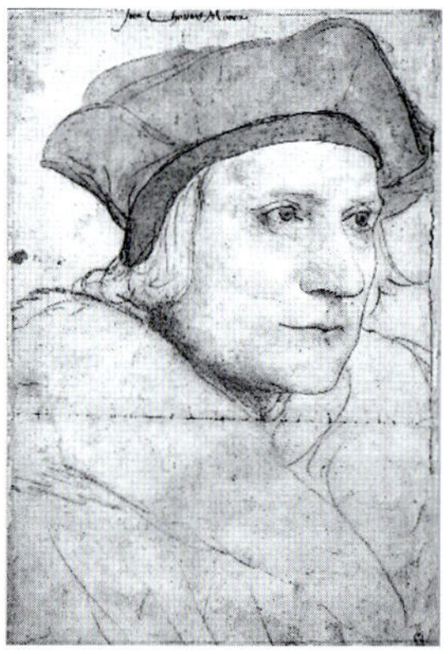

fig. 3b
Hans Holbein the Younger, *Portrait of Thomas More*, c. 1527. Black and coloured chalks, 380 x 258 mm. London, The Royal Collection

◂ This is the only half-length portrait drawing by Holbein whose outlines have been pricked with a needle.[13] The image was transferred by dusting or 'pouncing' charcoal powder over the perforations so that a dotted line representing the outlines of the drawing would appear on the prepared canvas or panel beneath. It has been suggested that the drawing discussed here may have served as a pattern for Holbein's *Portrait of Thomas More* (1527) in the Frick Collection, New York (see p. 20, fig. 18).[14] Infrared reflectography has revealed an underdrawing in this handsome portrait, in which the black dots of a pounced design are discernible.[15] These dots do not correspond precisely to the holes in the drawing, however. The sheet cannot, therefore, have been used to transfer the image to the ground on the panel. Still, there is a close link between the chalk drawing and the half-length portrait painting of More in New York. This is obvious from the rendering of the face, which is almost identical in the two works, except for a minor perspectival distortion near the right eye in the drawing, caused by the outlines of the eye socket and cheekbone being placed too far to the right. Holbein corrected this blemish in the painting. In both drawing and painting More wears the same fur-lined cloak and the same cap, though the latter is a little higher on the forehead in the painting. In his painted likeness More is wearing his chain of S-shaped links and the Tudor rose expressing loyalty to the king.[16] The chain may have been indicated with pricked yellow chalk lines in the sketch, but these have not been followed in the painting.

◂ It is possible that the contours were also pricked into another sheet lying beneath this drawing and then transferred to the painting from this second sheet.[17] This would have removed the need to pounce the black powder through the original preliminary sketch, preserving its condition. This pattern may also have been used for the lost group portrait of the More family, which depicted Sir Thomas from the same angle and wearing identical apparel. Perhaps Holbein disliked the annoying effect of the perforated lines in the drawing discussed here, for he did not use this technique again in his other portrait studies. AvS

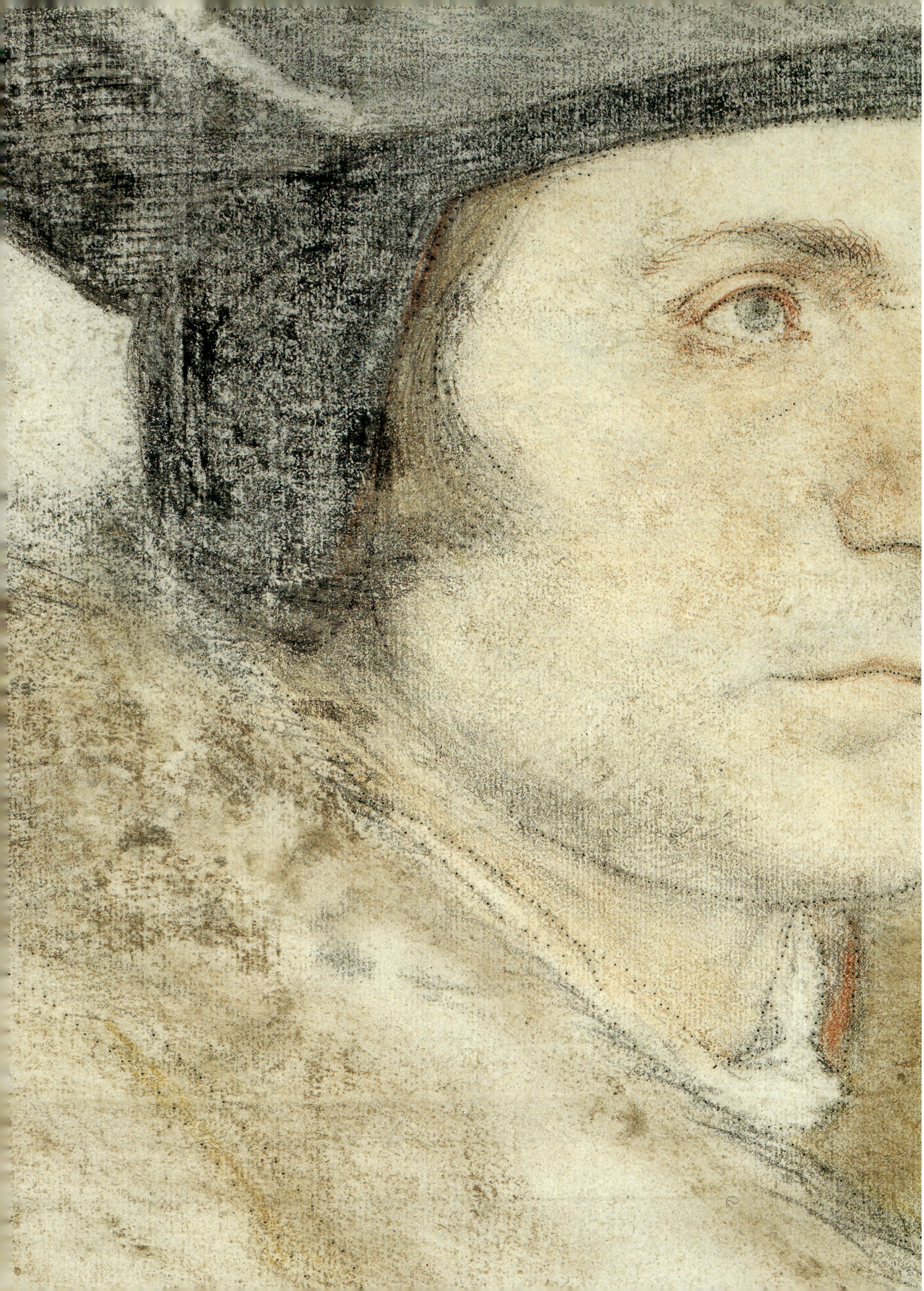

IV

An unknown woman, c. 1526/28

Black and coloured chalks, pen and black ink on white paper, 404 x 290 mm
Annotations by the artist in black chalk (below, from left to right): *dam, ora, atless*
Lent by Her Majesty Queen Elizabeth II
cat.no. 4

The identity of this young woman looking at us sideways is no longer known. Her clothes and headgear do not appear in any other portrait by Holbein and suggest that she is not English but Dutch. Her apparel is quite similar, for instance, to the Dutch garments worn by Albrecht Dürer's wife in a portrait he made of her while travelling through the Low Countries in 1520–1521 (fig. 4a).[1] The drawing is reminiscent of those the artist executed in his first English period (1526–1528) in black and coloured chalks on white paper without prior application of a ground. This has fuelled speculation that Holbein portrayed the woman during his brief stay in Antwerp, *en route* to England for the first time, in the autumn of 1526.[2]

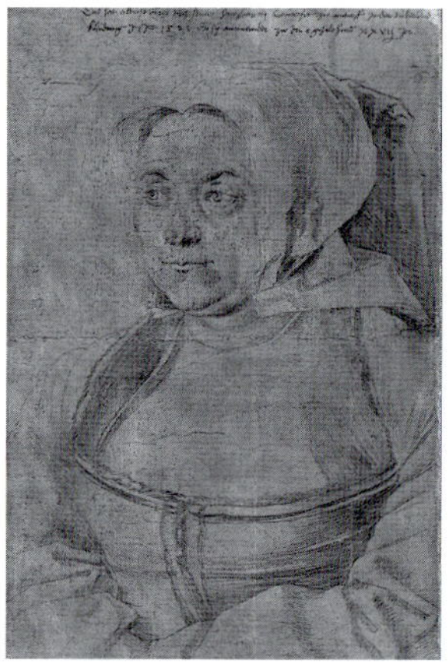

fig. 4a
Albrecht Dürer, *Portrait of Agnes Dürer in Dutch dress*, 1521. Metalpoint on greyish violet prepared paper, 407 x 271 mm. Berlin, Staatliche Museen zu Berlin, Kupferstichkabinett

‹ Although we know of no portrait painting based on this drawing, the notes at the bottom, in the artist's own hand, reveal that the drawing was made as a preliminary study. As an aid for the proposed painting, Holbein noted the words *dam* (damask) and *ora* (gold) next to a zigzag motif above the woman's left arm, and indicated in German on the sleeve at lower right that the material was *atless* (satin).[3] The drawing does not bear any marks indicating that the image was transferred to a panel, like those seen in many sheets from Holbein's second English period: the contours were not traced for that purpose. The chalk drawing therefore conveys the fresh impression of a woman who has just posed for the artist, although the colours have lost some of their vitality.

‹ The woman's face is modelled subtly in different hues of chalk. Whereas drawing with metalpoint on paper is possible only when the paper has been prepared beforehand —a labour-intensive procedure— the use of the new chalk technique made it possible to use unprepared paper. Only by the nostril, the mouth, the chin, and along the lower contour of the cap has Holbein added some accents on the chalk with pen and black ink. The clothes, which are executed in black chalk, have been sketched far more quickly than the face; the parallel hatching in the shaded areas runs diagonally from lower right to upper left, indicative of a left-handed artist.[4] There is a delightful suggestion of translucency in the cap, which is fastened to the hair with a few pins, as well as in the thin piece of white material over the woman's chest. The narrow flesh-coloured strip discernible along the lower edge —probably a fragment of the hands— suggests that the sheet was originally larger.

‹ Holbein's earliest known portrait drawings in black and coloured chalks are the likenesses of Jakob Meyer and his wife and daughter, which he made in 1526 in preparation for the *Darmstadt Madonna* (pp. 38-39, figs. 2-4).[5] In 1524 Holbein used coloured chalks for the first time in his drawings of the polychrome sculptures of Jean, Duc de Berry (1340-1416) and his wife Jeanne de Boulogne, which were then still in the ducal palace in Bourges (p. 19, figs. 15-16).[6] Coloured chalks are ideal for rendering the different tints of a face: the red of the lips, the sheen of blond or brown hair, and the blue or brown of the eyes. In his chalk sketches, Holbein brought the early fifteenth-century sculptures to life by giving a bloom to the cheeks and even adding eyelashes. It is as though he was determined to show that his drawings could be even more lifelike than sculpture.

‹ Given the technical advantages of coloured chalks for representing faces, Holbein understandably reserved them for his portrait drawings, continuing to use ink, watercolours, metalpoint and black chalk for his other drawings. He had occasionally used coloured chalks before, to enhance outlines made with metalpoint or pen and ink or to add red accents in a face.[7] But it was probably not until 1524 that Holbein learnt to draw exclusively in coloured chalks, during his trip to France, where the technique originated.[8] Holbein was probably influenced by the work of the French court portraitist Jean Clouet (c. 1485/90–1540/41), although Clouet's portrait drawings were executed only in black and red chalk. The influence of Leonardo da Vinci (1452–1519) and his followers in France and Italy has also frequently been pointed out. Besides introducing Holbein to the art of drawing in coloured chalks, both Clouet and Leonardo provided innovative portrait compositions that served as compelling examples in his development as a portraitist. AvS

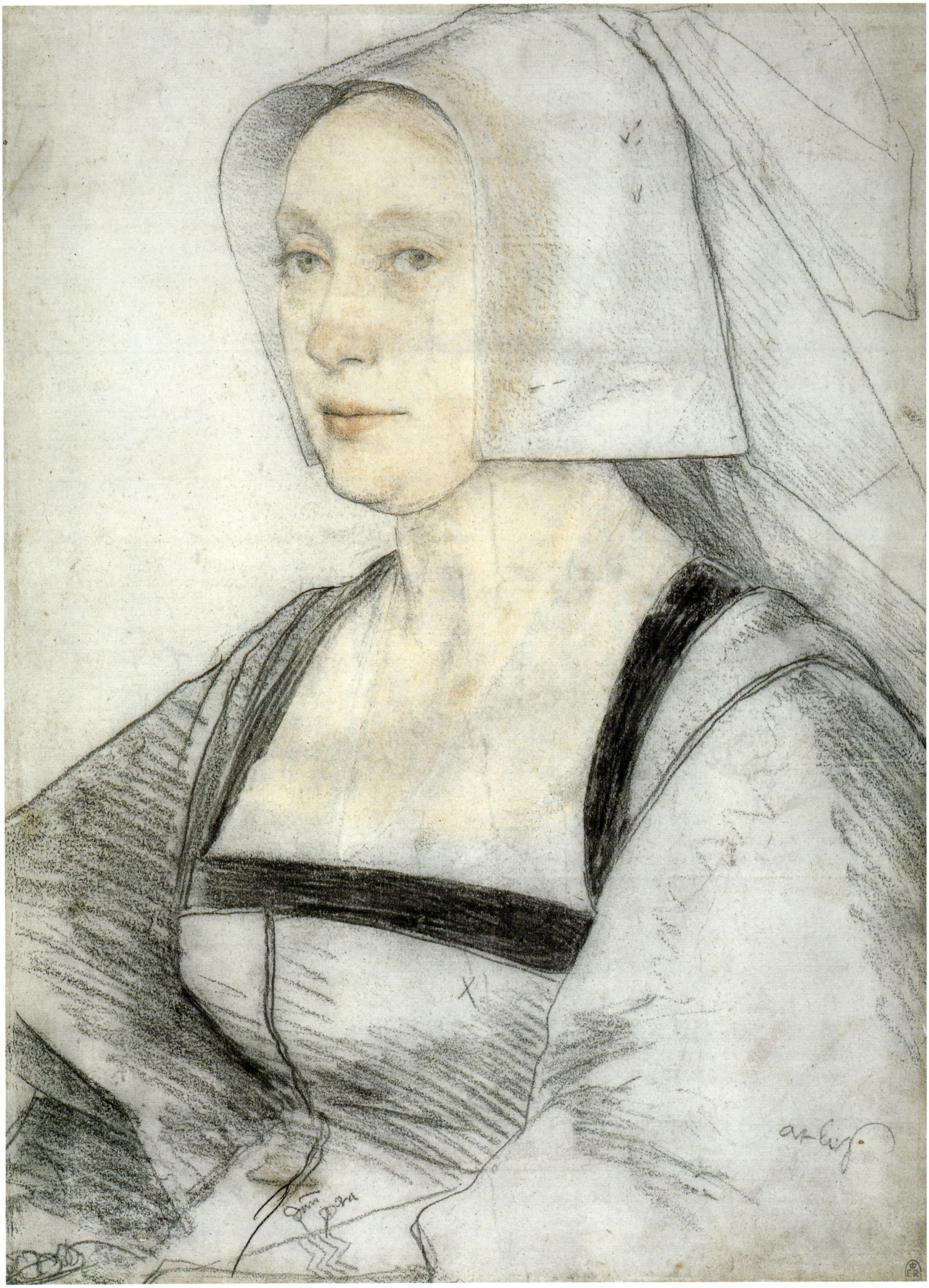

V

An unknown woman, c. 1526/28

Black and coloured chalks, traces of wash, on white paper, 353 x 246 mm
Lent by Her Majesty Queen Elizabeth II
cat.no. 5

This woman's striking white headgear represents an English fashion that Holbein depicted only a handful of times. The wide-brimmed bonnet, possibly made of felt or wool, is worn over a cap stiffened with wire that juts out over the cheeks in two points. The hat was probably attached to the cap with a pin above the forehead, where the hair is just visible. The rendering of these meticulously observed details enhances the effect of intimate authenticity that is so characteristic of Holbein's portrait drawings. For the rest, the woman is wearing a dress with a horizontal neckline characteristic of the age, a shawl and a translucent white cambric over her décolleté similar to that in *Portrait of a lady with squirrel and starling*, made in about 1527–1528 (cat. no. 7).[1]

‹ The drawing (which was not the basis for any existing painting), was executed in black and coloured chalks on unprepared white paper. This technique is characteristic of portrait drawings dating from the artist's first English period (1526–1528). There are traces of wash, but the sheet was not worked with pen or any other instrument, as were many of the portraits from Holbein's second English period (1532–1543). Of the 85 portrait drawings from his estate in Windsor Castle —about 80 of which are attributed to the master himself— only 16 are without inscriptions identifying the sitter; one of them is this portrait of an unknown woman.

‹ The first reference to the 'great booke of Pictures doone by Haunce Holbyn of certyne Lordes, Ladyes, gentlemen and gentlewomen in King Henry the 8' dates from 1590, when the Windsor drawings were in the possession of Lord Lumley.[2] This book included Holbein's portrait drawings, each one identified by 'Sr John Cheke Secretary to King Edward the 6'. Cheke had been Prince Edward's tutor from 1544 onward and later served as his secretary, so he must have known many of the sitters personally (see appendix 1).[3] The inscriptions on the portrait drawings were probably copied from those noted by Cheke in the 'great booke'. We can assume that they were added when the drawings were removed from this collector's album after 1727 to be framed separately.

‹ Twelve of the drawings at Windsor date from Holbein's first stay in England. Only four of these early portraits lack an identifying inscription. Besides the sheet discussed here and the portrait of a woman in Dutch dress (cat. no. 4),[4] these are two of the portraits of Thomas More's daughters, which were made in preparation for the More family portrait (p. 20, fig. 19).[5] The portraits of his other two daughters are named incorrectly.[6] More had long since fallen from grace when Cheke noted his identifications, and it is therefore not surprising that the secretary did not know his daughters or foster-daughters. Cheke was evidently at a loss to identify the woman depicted here too. Given Holbein's close ties with Thomas More's household during his first stay in England, it may be conjectured that she too belonged to this circle.[7] AvS

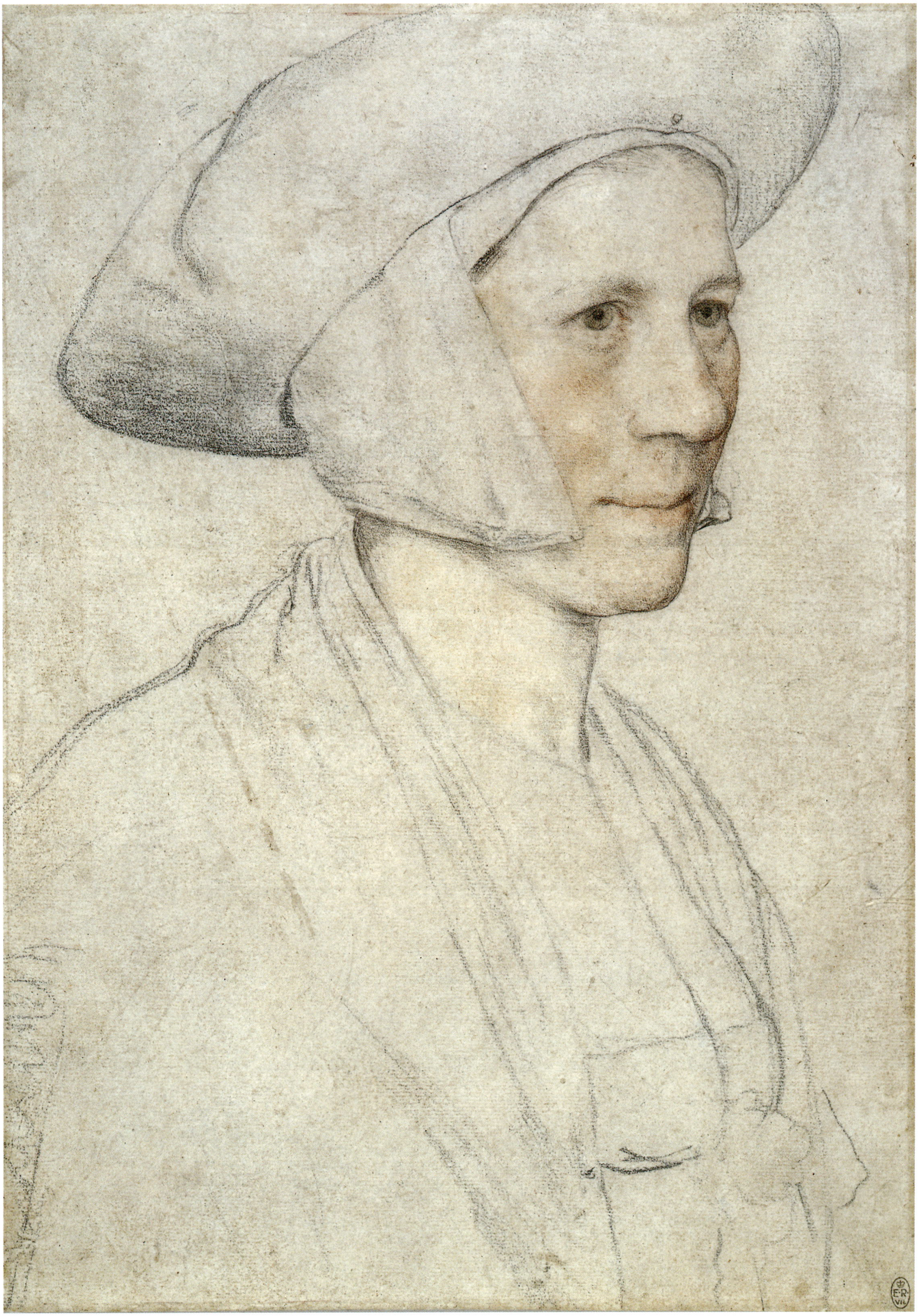

Mary Wotton, Lady Guildford, 1527

Panel, 87 x 70 cm / At upper left, on the architrave: ANNO·MDXXVII·ÆTATIS·SVÆ·XXVII
On the book: ·VITA CHRISTI·
St Louis, Missouri, St Louis Art Museum
cat.no. *6*

The companion portraits of Sir Henry Guildford (fig. 6a) and his second wife Mary Wotton from 1527, now in London and St Louis, respectively, are among the earliest portrait commissions given to Holbein during his first English period. He may have received them in connection with his decorations for a banquet hall and a theatre at Greenwich palace, which the king had built especially for the reception of a French envoy who was coming for the signing of a peace agreement with France. Henry Guildford, as Master of the Revels, was in charge of organising the project, while Holbein —'Master Hans' in the sources— took care of much of the practical implementation. The two collaborated closely in the early months of 1527.[1]

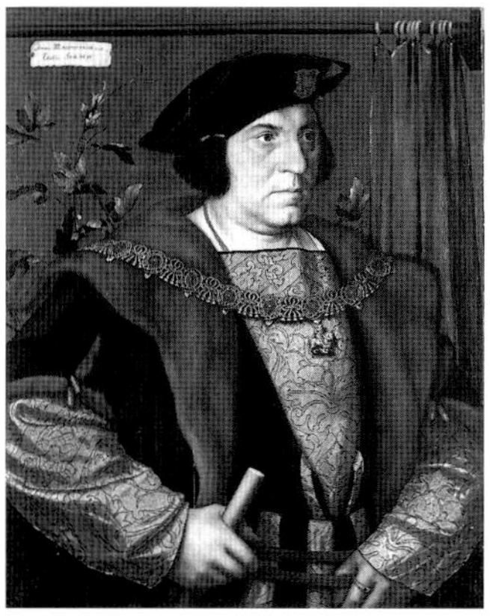

fig. 6a
Hans Holbein the Younger, *Portrait of Sir Henry Guildford*, 1527
Panel, 82.6 x 66.4 cm
London, The Royal Collection

◂ The decorations were evidently finished by 6 May 1527, since Henry received the French envoy on that day. A picture in the banquet hall depicted the Battle of Spurs, which had been fought near the town of Thérouanne, France, in 1513 —a peculiarly inappropriate subject for a room in which a peace treaty was to be signed between the two countries. The French diplomats evidently felt aggrieved when Henry pointedly drew their attention to it.[2] This painting was probably made in a London studio, since a surviving invoice records that it was transported by barge to Greenwich.[3] For the theatre, 'Master Hans' produced a painting on canvas for the ceiling. According to two contemporary sources, it depicted the earth surrounded by the sea. One of the sources also mentions a second painting, containing scenes of the zodiac, the equator, the tropics and poles as well as the seven then known planets, which were probably personified by gods. This latter piece may have been attached beneath the one depicting the earth and the sea. The illusion produced by this arrangement —apparently showing the earth surrounded by celestial bodies— may have been enhanced by special lighting.[4] This ingenious theatrical construction was designed by Holbein's countryman Nicolaus Kratzer, the King's Astronomer, who also advised Holbein on the details of his painting. Painter and astronomer worked on the scene from 8 February until 4 March 1527; a week after its completion, the king came to inspect it. Though the canvas was attached to the ceiling on 10 April, workmen removed it again less than a month later, on 7 May, the day after the ceremony. What happened to it after that is not known.[5]

◂ Shows of ostentation marking special occasions were not uncommon in the early years of Henry's reign, but this particular enterprise seems to have consumed an inordinate amount of time and money. Because of the work's immense size and the limited time available, Holbein was assisted by a team of nineteen painters, at least eight of whom belonged to the London Company of Painter-Stainers, the local painters' guild. Holbein's fee far exceeded that of any of these other artists.[6] The festive event itself was organised by Sir Henry Guildford and Sir Henry Wyatt, a member of the Privy Council. It can scarcely have been a coincidence that Holbein made portraits of both men shortly after completing this work, his first royal commission. In this same period he also painted the portrait of Nicolaus Kratzer, another man directly involved in the project.[7]

◂ Guildford, who was born in 1489 and was hence only two years older than Henry VIII, was the king's favourite and confidant, as both his father and grandfather had been to Henry VII.[8] After Henry VIII ascended the throne in 1509, Guildford consolidated his position at court, culminating in his appointment in 1525 as Comptroller of the Household, in which capacity he supervised the court's finances. In 1531 he fell out with Anne Boleyn, who was to become Henry's second wife in January 1533. Their quarrel arose from Guildford's objections to Henry's plan to forge an alliance with France. The king wanted to shield himself from the wrath of Pope Clemens VII and Emperor Charles V, which his decision to seek a divorce from Catherine of Aragon would undoubtedly unleash. Anne construed Guildford's position in part as a personal rejection and threatened to dismiss him once she became queen. Whether Guildford took this threat seriously

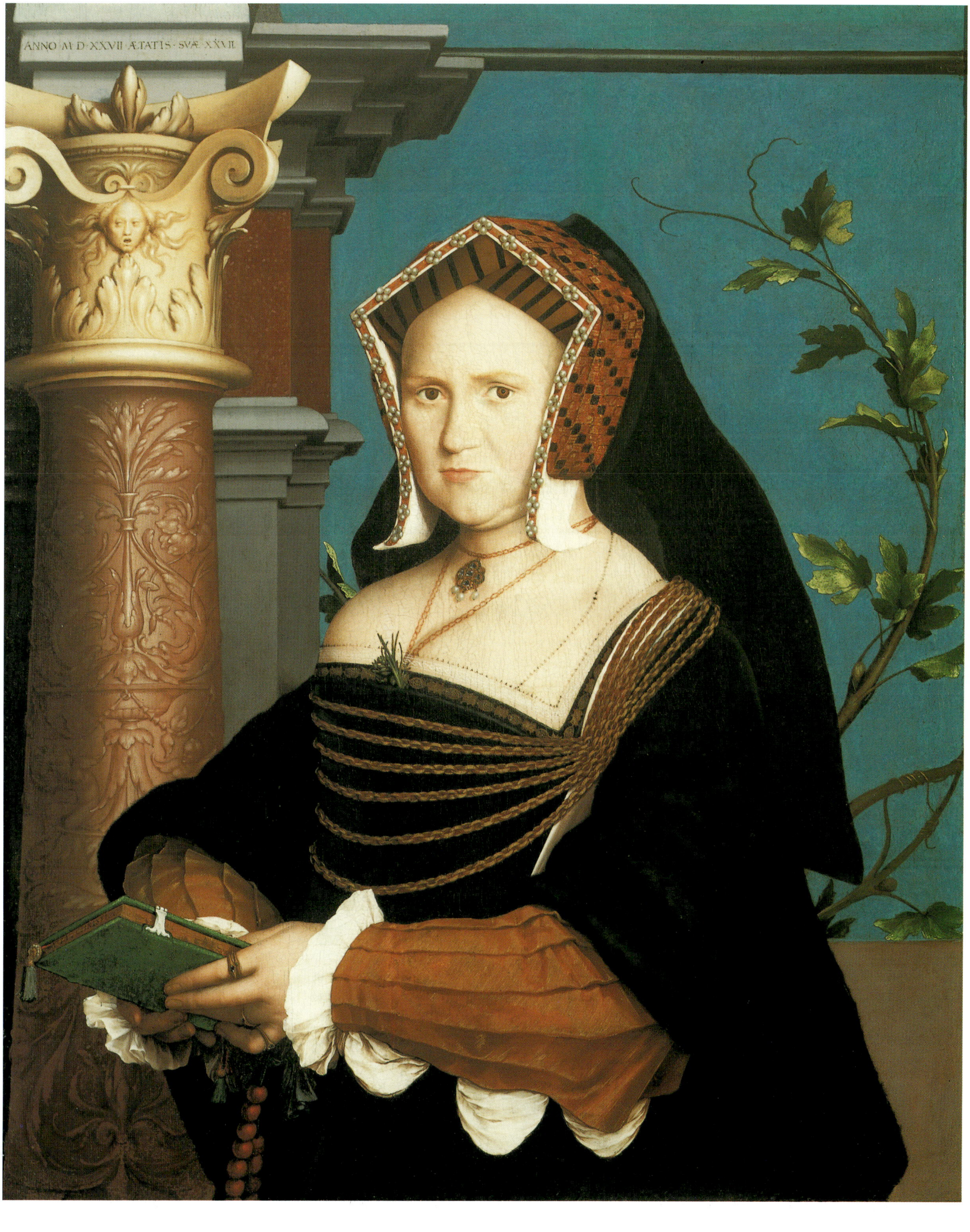
ANNO M·D·XXVII ÆTATIS·SVÆ·XXVII

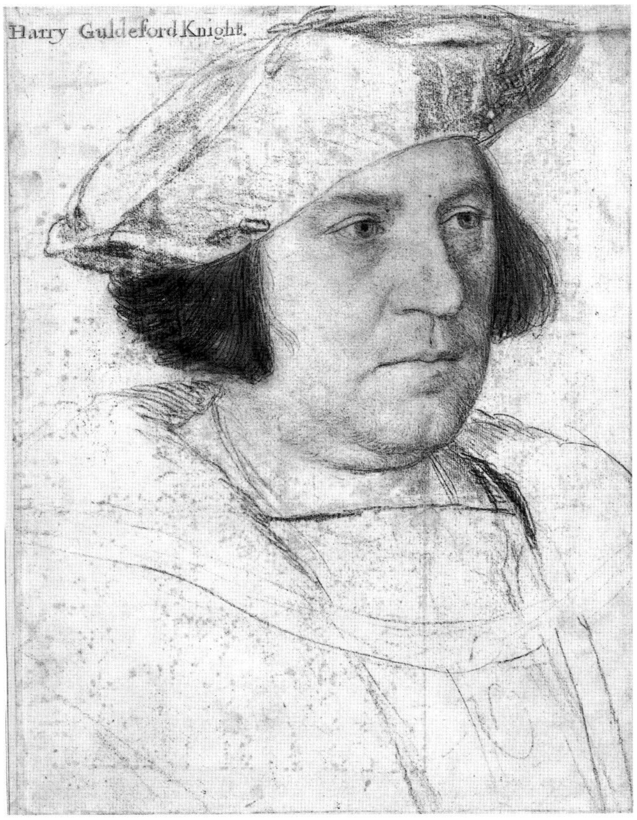

fig. 6b
Hans Holbein the Younger, *Portrait of Sir Henry Guildford*, 1527
Black and coloured chalks, 383 x 294 mm
London, The Royal Collection

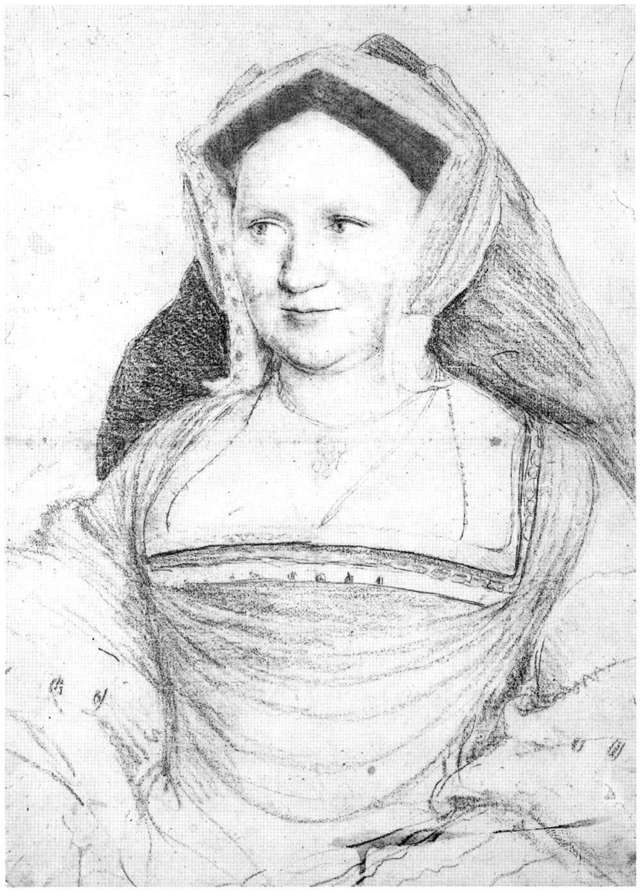

fig. 6c
Hans Holbein the Younger, *Portrait of Mary Wotton, Lady Guildford*, 1527
Black and coloured chalks, 552 x 385 mm
Basel, Öffentliche Kunstsammlung, Kupferstichkabinett

or whether he merely felt aggravated we do not know, but in any case he tendered his resignation as Comptroller of the Household. Although Henry twice tried to persuade him to stay on, telling him that one "should not mind women's talk",[9] Guildford would not relent. He remained in the king's service as counsellor, however, until his death in May 1532.[10]

Holbein has filled the pictorial surface with his sitter's massive frame (fig. 6a). Sir Henry wears a jerkin of precious gold brocade, a material restricted by sumptuary laws to leading nobles and others of high rank. He had been entitled to wear the chain of the Order of the Garter hanging on his chest since 1526, and the white staff in his right hand was the attribute of the Comptroller of the Household.

Lady Guildford, née Mary Wotton, was 27 when she sat for Holbein in 1527, according to the inscription on her portrait in St Louis. She was Henry Guilford's second wife, but it is not known when they were married. In this portrait too, Holbein rendered the clothing with meticulous care, and the splendid black fur of Lady Guildford's cloak and her undersleeves of cloth of gold are particularly striking. Holbein used ample quantities of gold paint to render the cloth of gold, as he did with Sir Henry's gold brocade. Across the bodice of her dress and vertically over her shoulders Lady Guildford wears six gold chains. Her pearl-trimmed gable hood (cf. cat. no. 10) and the gold chains around her neck, the shortest of which bears a pendant decorated with jewels and pearls, complete the image of boundless opulence. Even the bookmark protruding from her book is studded with pearls. The sprig of rosemary tucked into her décolleté strikes a more modest note. Rosemary symbolises remembrance and may refer here to the immortality that the sitter has attained thanks to Holbein's brush — in sharp contrast to physical mortality, something of which Holbein's contemporaries were only too well aware. Lady Guildford's rosary and the small leather-bound volume she is holding express a similar humility. The lettering on the side of the book identify it as *Vita Christi*, a popular narrative of the life of Jesus written by the fourteenth-century writer Ludolf of Saxony (c. 1295-1378).[11]

◂ Holbein conceived the compositions of the two portraits as a single entity. The figures incline toward one another and a curtain-rod in the background of both works provides an optical link. In Sir Henry's portrait this rod serves a clear purpose as a curtain is attached to it, but in the picture of his wife it serves merely to create a visual connection with its companion-piece. The curtain behind Sir Henry has a counterpoise in the column embellished with grotesques in Lady Mary's portrait (cf. also p. 16, fig. 10). Twelve years earlier Holbein had adopted a similar strategy to connect the companion portraits of Jakob Meyer zum Hasen and his wife Dorothea Kannengießer, using the architecture as the cohesive element (p.17, figs. 12-13).

◂ Before embarking on these two portraits, Holbein made preparatory drawings, as was his custom. In this case, however, there are relatively substantial discrepancies between the drawings and the paintings. For instance, Guildford has rather a fleshy face in the study, with eyes, nose and mouth all quite close together (fig. 6b). In the painted portrait, the features have been pulled a little further apart in the vertical plane. These modifications reduce the width of the head, which was no doubt the intention. The changes to Lady Guilford's portrait are of a very different kind. Here, the sitter's proportions as recorded in the preliminary drawing (fig. 6c) and in the painted portrait are the same, but the body in the painting is rotated somewhat to the right relative to the drawing. Furthermore, in the drawing Lady Guildford is smiling amicably in the direction of her husband, while in the painted portrait her face is entirely devoid of expression. Infrared reflectography has revealed the presence of a detailed underdrawing in ink beneath the paint layers of both portraits —especially pronounced in the case of Lady Guildford— executed variously with pen and brush. No corrections are visible in these underdrawings or in the paint layers, however, which suggests that Holbein must have decided on the above changes after completing the studies and before transferring them to the panel, the first stage of the painting process. In the case of Henry Guildford's portrait, he may have moved the drawing a few times when transferring it to elongate the facial features somewhat, but in the companion-piece he only had to alter the position of Lady Guildford's lips and the direction of her gaze.[12]

◂ We do not know Holbein's reasons for altering the likenesses, but it is possible that Henry Guildford considered somewhat more formal portraits to be more appropriate to his position at court.[13] If so, the changes would be indicative of Holbein's flexibility, demonstrating that he permitted his clients to influence the end result. PP

VII

Lady with a squirrel and a starling, *c.* 1527/28

Panel, 56 x 38.8 cm
London, The National Gallery
Exhibited until 1 October 2003
cat.no. 7

Portrait of a lady with a squirrel and a starling is one of a group of paintings that Holbein produced in his first English period (1526-1528). It was then that he produced works such as his impressive portraits of Archbishop William Warham (p. 23, fig. 22) and Sir Thomas More (cat. no. 3). The painting described here bears most similarity to Holbein's portraits of Sir Henry and Lady Guildford, from 1527 (see cat. no. 6 and fig. 6a). The sitters in these pendants are similarly depicted as half-figures against a blue to blue-green background decorated characteristically with stylised vines and fig leaves. Holbein had incorporated this detailed motif before, in a number of history pieces, and he would use it again in 1532 and 1533 in two portraits (cat. nos. 15 and 17), introducing minor variations each time. Fig leaves are traditionally believed to give protection from disease.[1] The leaves depicted here may have borne this significance, although it is not impossible that they were added solely for their decorative value.[2] The vines and the starling are cut off so abruptly as to suggest that the panel was reduced in size, but examination has demonstrated that its original dimensions have not been changed.[3]

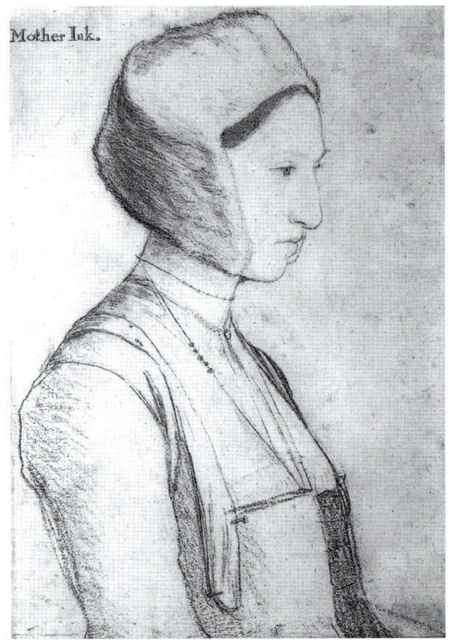

fig. 7a
Hans Holbein the Younger, *Portrait of Margaret Giggs*, c. 1527. Black and coloured chalks, 379 x 269 mm. London, The Royal Collection

‹ In contrast to the Guildford portraits, *Portrait of a lady with a squirrel and a starling* has a restrained, almost intimate ambience. The woman's identity is unknown, and there is no record of any counterpart depicting her husband. On the basis of the characteristic shape of the white ermine headdress, it can be assumed that she lived in England. Margaret Giggs, Thomas More's foster-daughter, wears a similar, though not identical, hat in a portrait drawn by Holbein (fig. 7a).[4] In the past the painting described here was also believed to depict Margaret Giggs — wrongly so, since the facial features, especially the noses, are quite different.[5] The clothing of the woman depicted here is rather sober in comparison to her striking, precious fur hat.[6]

The most striking elements of this painting are the two animals. Nibbling a nut on the woman's lap is a tame squirrel, which she has secured with a little chain around its neck. It was probably her own; squirrels were kept as pets in England from the fourteenth century onward.[7] The starling on a branch is thought to be some reference to her name or family coat of arms.[8] Animals are uncommon motifs in Holbein's oeuvre: there are only two other paintings —both later works— in which they figure so prominently.[9]

‹ Technical examination has shown that the squirrel was not part of the initial composition.[10] This makes it even more unlikely that the woman posed together with it. Holbein probably made a separate study of the creature, as he must also have done with the starling, which is rendered in detail.[11] For the squirrel to be incorporated into the image, the lower section of the painting had to be modified. X-radiography shows that a sash was probably depicted at first in the space now occupied by the squirrel, similar to the sash worn by the Virgin Mary in Holbein's famous painting in Darmstadt (cat. no. 2). It also reveals that the right arm was initially placed lower, and that the hand may also have been altered.[12] It was most probably the client herself who asked Holbein to include her pet in the picture, increasing the painting's appeal.

‹ In this masterful portrait, Holbein's skill as a portrait painter and his phenomenal painting technique appear to full effect. The creased shawl, the transparent upper part of the woman's clothing and her fur hat are almost palpable. The restrained pose and averted gaze give the woman a dignified air. Minor alterations demonstrate that Holbein was not easily pleased: we can see with the naked eye that the hairline was changed during the painting process. On the left, near her temple, the hair initially covered more of her face. Holbein painted some of it away and lowered the hairline near the

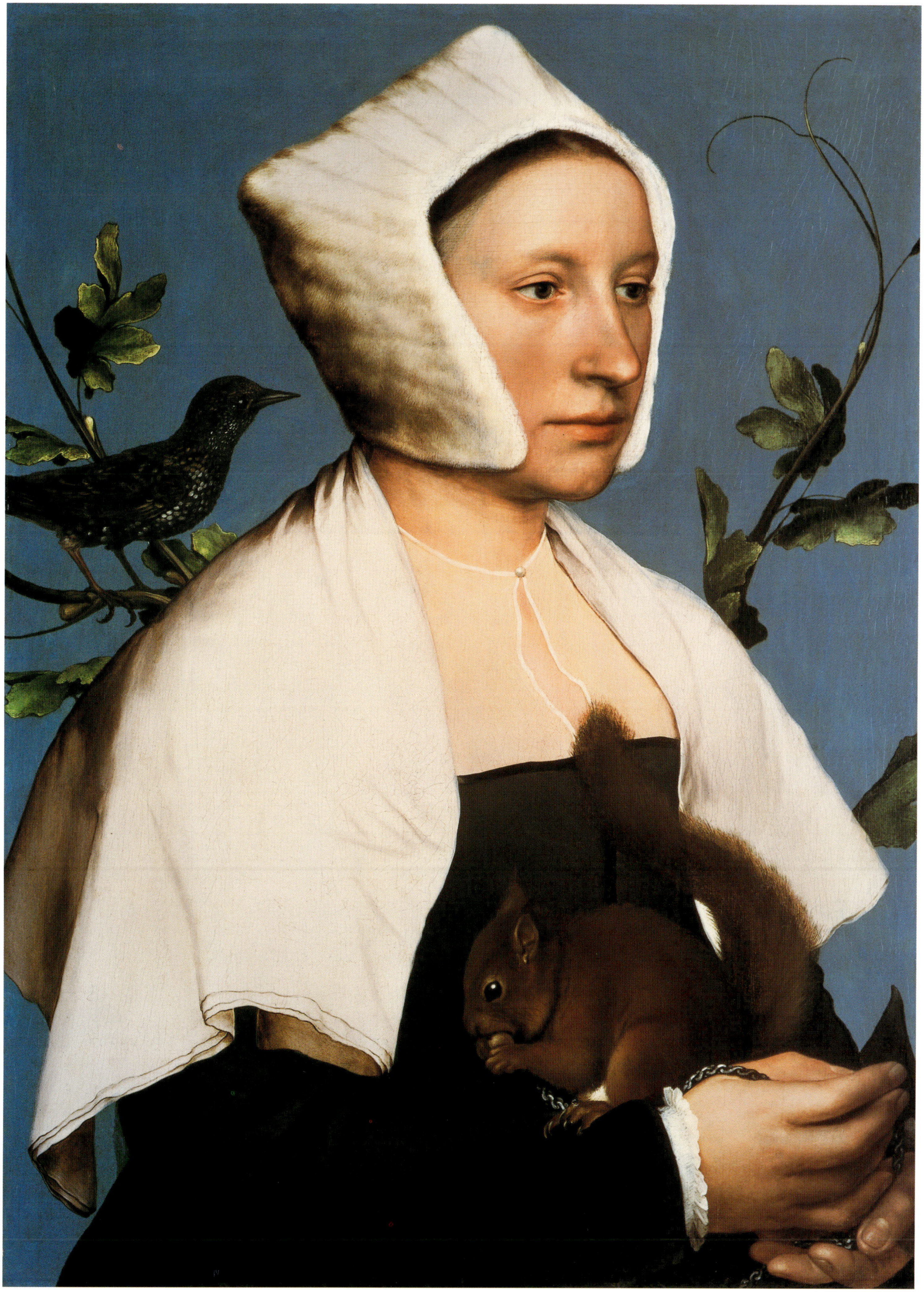

forehead. This *pentimento* became visible with the passage of time; the flesh-coloured paint now glimmers clearly through the hair in this section. The hat was reduced in size to the right of the sitter's face: Holbein partly overpainted it with the blue-green of the background. As the pigment azurite, which contains blue copper, is mixed with a large quantity of white lead, the colour of the background has been remarkably well preserved.[13]

◂ It was not until 1992 that the National Gallery in London acquired the painting from the collection of the Marquess of Cholmondeley. It had previously belonged to the collection of Jan Six (1618–1700), whose portrait had been painted by Rembrandt (1606–1669) in 1654 (Amsterdam, Six Collection).[14] In all probability, the art-loving burgomaster of Amsterdam purchased the work privately in 1658 from the collection of Thomas Howard (1585–1646), Earl of Arundel and Surrey, who had built up the largest existing collection of Holbein's paintings (including cat. nos. 8, 17, 22, 33, 38) as well as acquiring many of his drawings. At the outbreak of the Civil War, Howard had transferred most of his famous collection to the Low Countries.[15] After 1734, when the painting was still in the possession of Six's descendants,[16] it probably belonged to the collection of the Hague tax collector Govert van Slingelandt (1694–1767). This fastidious collector was constantly improving the quality of his small but exquisite collection by exchanging, buying and selling.[17] A year after Van Slingelandt's death, his entire collection was purchased by Stadholder William V (1748–1806), whose paintings in 1816 became the nucleus of the Mauritshuis collection. *Portrait of a lady with a squirrel and a starling* would hang there today, but for the fact that Van Slingelandt sold it at some unknown point in time.
QB

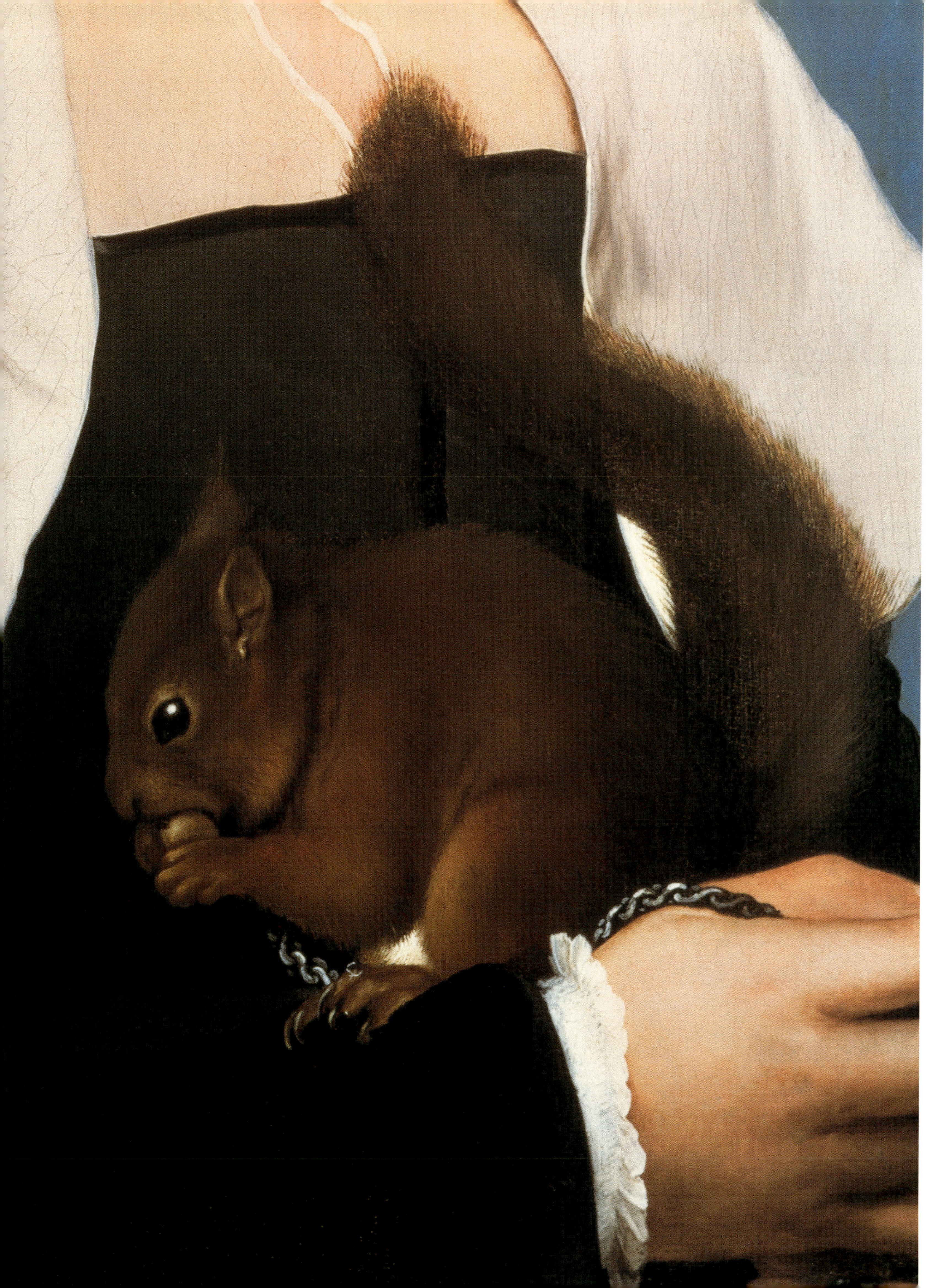

VIII

Thomas Godsalve (c. 1481–1542) and his son John Godsalve (c. 1510–1556), 1528

Panel, 35 x 36 cm / At lower right: *Thomas Godsalve de Norwico Etatis sue Anno quadragesimo septo*
At upper left (not original): *Anno Dmi* M.D. XXVIII
Dresden, Staatliche Kunstsammlungen, Gemäldegalerie Alte Meister
cat.no. 8

In 1528 Holbein portrayed Thomas Godsalve and his son John from Norwich on a small, almost square panel. The inscription on the paper in Thomas's hands, on which he is writing with a quill, gives his name and his age in Latin — 47. The name of his son John, who is about 18, does not appear on the panel, but the similar facial features emphasise their family relationship: the resemblance is further enhanced by their portraits being rendered parallel to each other, in three-quarter view. The boy's identification as John Godsalve is corroborated by the inscription on the drawing of his likeness in Windsor Castle (cat. no. 13). Holbein drew this latter portrait of the son shortly after his return to England in 1532. The double portrait, however, dates from the last year of Holbein's first stay in England. This is striking, since almost all the portraits he made in this period, except those of Thomas More's family, were of prominent courtiers and statesmen.

◂ Thomas Godsalve came from a family of wealthy Norfolk landowners and was Registrar of the Consistory Court of the diocese of Norwich.[1] In 1524 he was listed as one of the fourteen richest men in the city.[2] It was thanks to his good relations with Thomas Cromwell that his son John was also launched into a promising career, starting with his appointment as Clerk of the King's Signet in 1531.[3] In November that year, Thomas Godsalve sent Cromwell 'half a dozen swans of my wife's feeding' in gratitude for all Cromwell's efforts on his son's behalf.[4] By the time Holbein drew John Godsalve's portrait in about 1532 (cat. no. 13), his sitter was a married man holding an important position. In the double portrait, however, he is still depicted as a youth almost hiding behind his father's back. Furthermore, his head, instead of being held erect, inclines very slightly toward his father, another subtle indication of his subordinate position. The fact that John is depicted bare-headed may also be interpreted as a sign of respect to his father. The young John More is also depicted bare-headed beside his father in Holbein's family portrait of the Mores (p. 20, fig. 19), and Jakob Meyer kneels bare-headed before the Madonna and Child (cat. no. 2).

◂ The absence of a hat also provides a good view of the young Godsalve's hairstyle. He has a short fringe and medium-length hair cut straight at the neck, according to the custom of the day; it was a style worn without a beard. The young man is richly dressed, sporting a fur-lined jerkin under his gown, while the collar of his white shirt is decorated with fashionable black embroidery. His father wears a fur-lined gown over his velvet doublet, which is fastened at the neck with a gilt button. On his head he wears a bonnet with turned-up side flaps that are held in place with ribbons tied on top. This is one of the most common men's caps in Holbein's portraits, and John Godsalve also wears one in his individual portrait by the artist.[5]

◂ It was upon his return to Basel in August of that same year, 1528, that Holbein made his portrait of Nicolaus Kratzer (p. 21, fig. 20), a good friend of Thomas More who was appointed astronomer to Henry VIII in 1519.[6] Kratzer too is depicted behind a table, and has his instruments spread out before him. And like the portrait of the Godsalves, his portrait displays a scrap of paper with the sitter's name and the year in which the work was painted. Later on, Holbein would use this motif of a scrap of paper with writing on it, that has a long tradition in Northern European painting,[7] mainly in his portraits of the German Steelyard merchants.[8] But aside from Thomas Godsalve the only person he depicted actually writing was Erasmus, in two portraits made in about 1523 (p. 16, fig. 11 and cat. no. 1).[9] In both these works, Erasmus is intent on what he is writing, whereas Godsalve is looking up from the paper. As his text appears upside down to the viewer, it is rather hard to read. More clearly legible is the year 1528, printed in Roman figures, on the *cartellino* added against the blue background immediately above the son's head. Although this motif is probably not original, we may assume, given the father's age in the inscription, that the year is correct.[10]

◂ Holbein will have found the painting of a double portrait a special challenge, since few examples of such works were available at the time. His father, Hans Holbein the Elder, drew a double portrait of his sons Ambrosius and Hans in 1511 (p. 10, fig. 1), in which he depicted the boys facing each other. Holbein the Younger rejected this rather predictable composition, and concentrated on producing a superb rendition of the faces and on subtly conveying the hierarchy between father and son. AvS

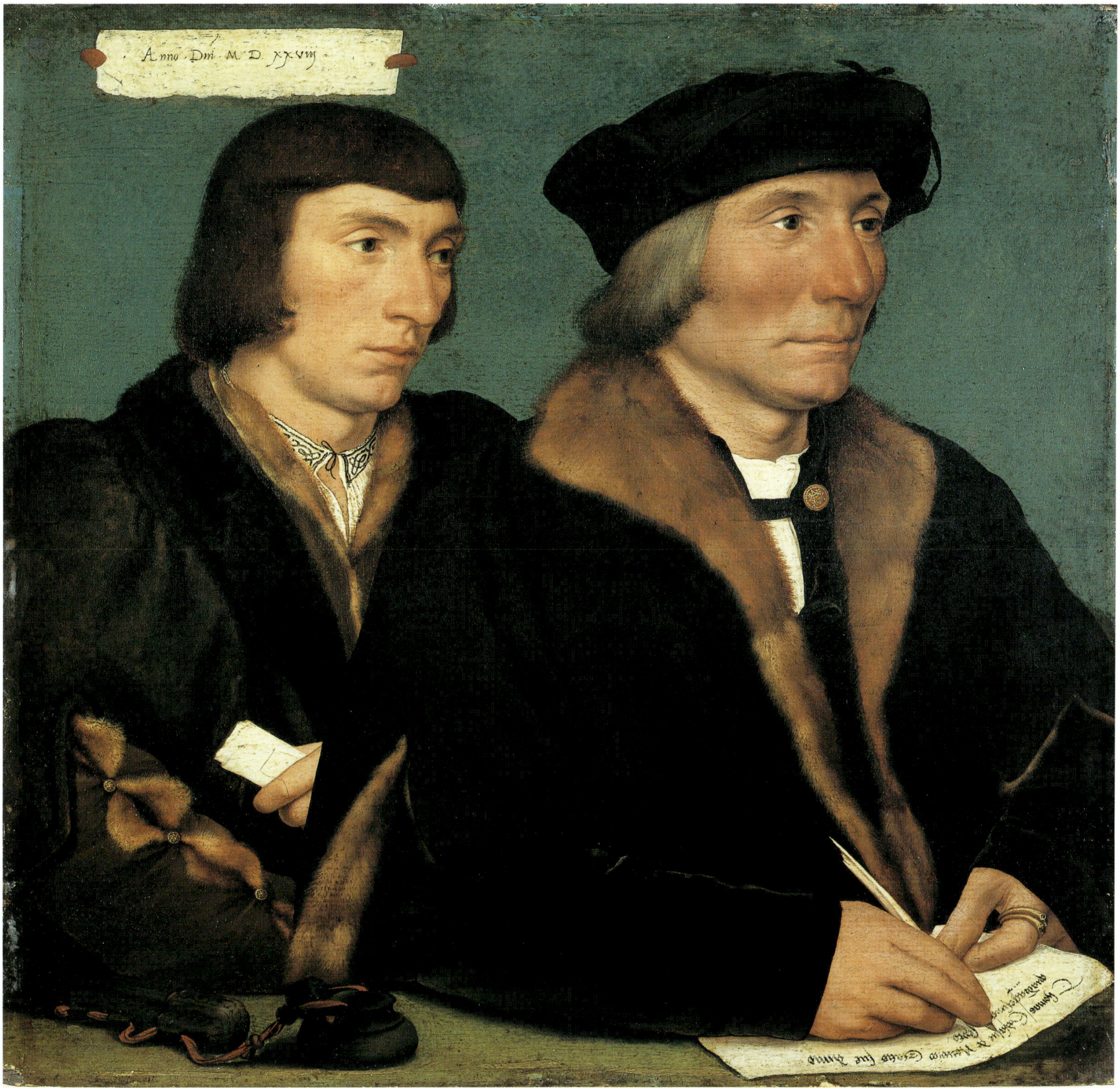
Anno Dni M D xxviij

IX

The Old and the New Law, *c.* 1530/35

(the Old Testament as *Lex* and the New Testament as *Gratia*)

Panel, 49 x 60 cm / Latin inscriptions in gold paint[1]
Edinburgh, National Gallery of Scotland
cat.no. 9

At the foot of a tree that divides the picture in two sits a nude man, gazing upward in grief, hands crossed over his chest in despair. The inscription 'HOMO' above his head on the tree trunk identifies him as the personification of humanity. The stone on which he is seated bears a biblical inscription (in Latin): 'O wretched man that I am! Who shall deliver me from the body of this death?'[2] The two men to the left and right of this allegorical figure may be identified, by the inscriptions beneath their feet, as the prophet Isaiah and John the Baptist. Both are drawing the man's attention to scenes depicted in the background landscape to the right of the tree: Isaiah is pointing to the Virgin Mary, who is depicted at upper right kneeling on Mount Zion at the moment of the Annunciation. Beneath Isaiah's feet is written his prophecy, in gold lettering, 'and the virgin shall [...] bear a son'.[3] John is drawing attention to Christ's role as the Redeemer of mankind. There is a text beneath his feet too: 'Behold, the Lamb of God, which taketh away the sin of the world',[4] and with his left hand he points to Jesus standing with his disciples at the foot of the mountain.

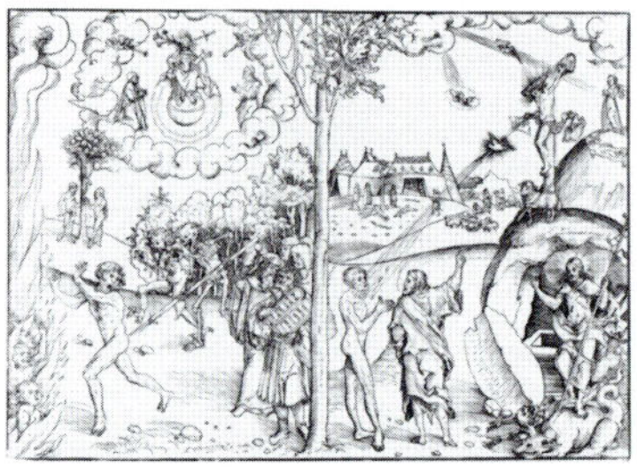

fig. 9a
Lucas Cranach the Elder, *The Fall and Redemption of Man.* Woodcut. London, British Museum

Holbein's allegory links up with a tradition of Protestant woodcuts that expressed Reformed beliefs through a combination of image and text. His many years of residence in Basel had familiarised Holbein with images of this kind. From 1529 onward the studio of Lucas Cranach the Elder (1472-1553) in Wittenberg turned out works that were similar in composition and iconography to Holbein's painting in Edinburgh.[5] A woodcut by Cranach from *c.* 1530 entitled *Fall and Redemption* (fig. 9a), for example, shows a landscape that is divided in two in an identical way by a tree that —as in Holbein's painting— has dead branches on the left while its right side is in full foliage. In both pictures, the left half shows scenes from the Old Testament emphasising sin and penance, while the right has scenes from the New Testament in which the accent is on faith in God and Redemption. Reformers such as Luther and Melanchthon (see cat. no. 20) used this opposition between Old and New Testament as a metaphor for the contrast between beliefs under the old, Catholic faith and those held after the Reformation.[6]

In the upper left corner of Holbein's painting stands Moses on Mount Sinai —the geographical and compositional counterpoint to Mount Zion in the upper right corner, see below— receiving the stone tablets with the Jewish law. Depicted in the distant background is the moment at which he returns to his people, while manna falls from heaven above the camp. A little further toward the foreground is the brass serpent winding around a T-shaped post. Moses conjured up this serpent to save his people from the poisonous serpents that God had sent to punish them for their lack of faith. At the foot of the mountain stand Adam and Eve beside the Tree of Knowledge: they have just eaten the apple, precipitating Man's Fall from grace. At the far left of the painting, in the foreground, we see a skeleton in a coffin, representing Death.

At upper right, on Mount Zion, the kneeling Virgin Mary hears the Annunciation of the birth of her child, the Redeemer. In the far background Holbein has depicted the Annunciation to the shepherds, while further to the foreground Christ is shown on the Cross, as the compositional counterpoint to the brass serpent. In the near foreground on the right we see the Resurrected Christ trampling Death and Sin, represented here as a skeleton and a demon with a globe.

The Old and the New Law are presented emphatically here as opposing values. In the image of the Old Law, the accent is on Law (LEX), the Fall, and Death, while in that of the New Law, which emphasises Grace (GRATIA), the central concepts are redemption and Resurrection.[7] The use of colour and the illumination of the background scenes —sombre and dramatic to the left of the tree, and light and serene to its right— clearly underscores the intended contrast between Good and Evil.

Holbein painted this work around 1535,[8] which means that the painting was probably ordered by an English adherent of the Reformation. The client will undoubtedly have admired the inventive way in which the master used words and images to express the ideas of Reformers such as Martin Luther and Philipp Melanchthon in this painting. PP

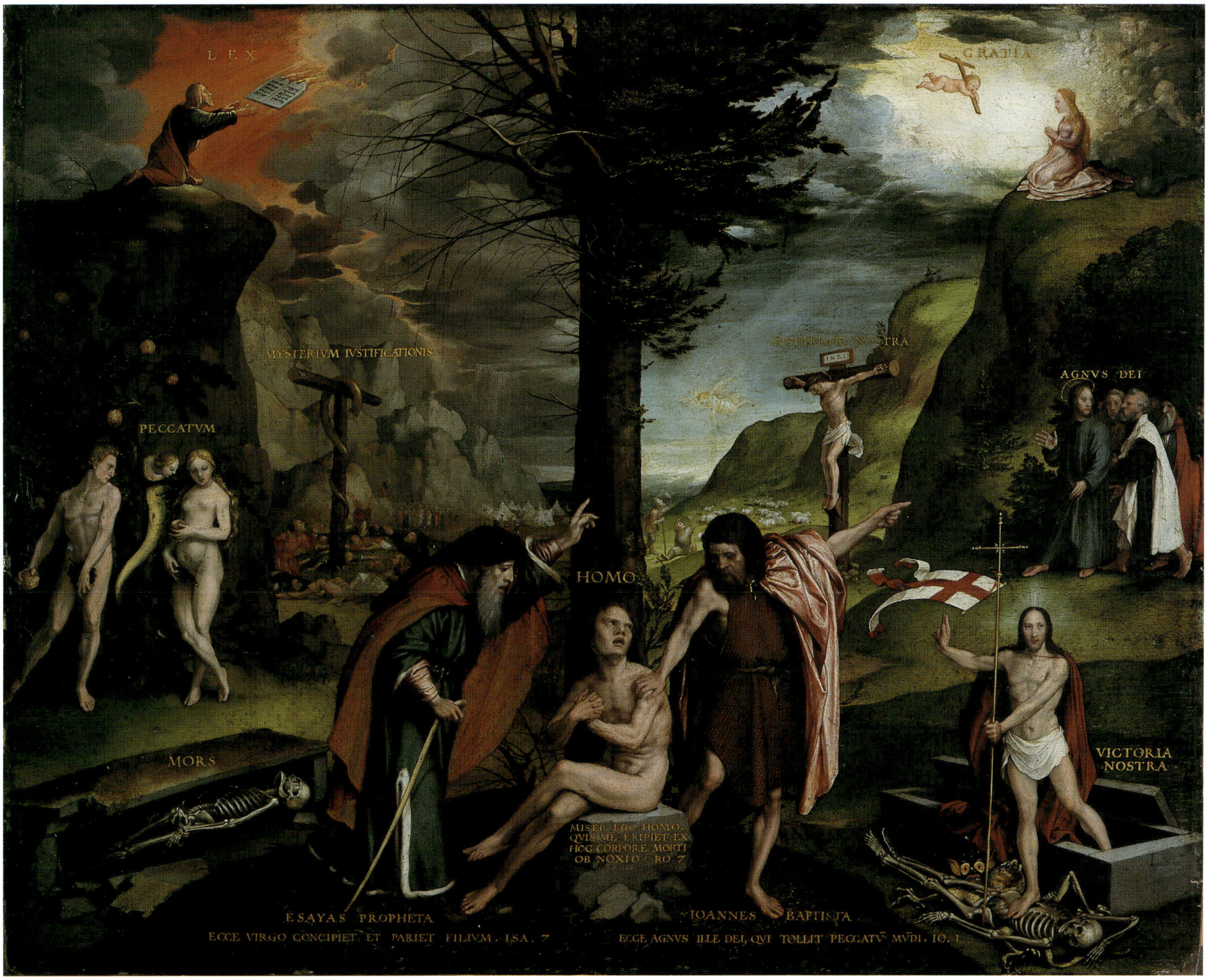
LEX
GRATIA
MYSTERIVM IVSTIFICATIONIS
PECCATVM
AGNVS DEI
HOMO
MORS
VICTORIA NOSTRA
MISER EGO HOMO. QVIS ME ERIPIET EX HOC CORPORE MORTI OB NOXIO. RO. 7
ESAYAS PROPHETA
IOANNES BAPTISTA
ECCE VIRGO CONCIPIET ET PARIET FILIVM. ISA. 7
ECCE AGNVS ILLE DEI, QVI TOLLIT PECCATV MVDI. IO. 1

Lady Margaret Elyot (?–1560), c. 1527/28 or c. 1532/33

Black and coloured chalks, pen and black ink, white body colour on pink prepared paper, 278 x 208 mm
At upper right, in a later hand: *The Lady Eliot.*
Lent by Her Majesty Queen Elizabeth II
cat.no. 10

Lady Margaret and Sir Thomas Elyot, who are immortalised in these beautifully preserved pendant portraits, were among the closest friends of Sir Thomas More (cf. cat. no. 3).[1] Margaret, unusually shown in the heraldic position of precedence (on her husband's right), was a daughter of Sir Maurice à Barrow (or Abarrow), a Wiltshire landowner. According to More's biographer Stapleton, she was tutored in Sir Thomas's humanist household.[2] Some time before 1520, Margaret married Thomas Elyot, who had studied law at Oxford and at the Middle Temple, one of London's Inns of Court. Elyot served as Clerk to the Justices of Assize from about 1510 to 1526 and as Clerk to the Privy Council from about 1523 to 1530. After a spell as Henry VIII's ambassador to Charles V (1531-1532) he held numerous public offices, serving as a member of parliament in 1539 and 1542. In the 1530s he was also involved in the dissolution of the monasteries. Elyot's fame derives chiefly from his *Boke named the Governour*, a humanist treatise that appeared in 1531, on education, ethics, history and politics. Later publications included a Latin-English dictionary (1538) and *The Castle of Helth* (1539), the first handbook on health written in English, which proved his most popular book.[3] Elyot made the ideas of antique authors widely accessible for the first time by his use of the vernacular, and his publications were also of inestimable importance to the English language. In the 1520s Thomas Elyot counted Cardinal Wolsey and Thomas More among his friends, and from about 1530 onward he found favour with the powerful Thomas Cromwell. After More's execution, Elyot wrote a letter to Cromwell repudiating his former friend and kindred spirit.[4]

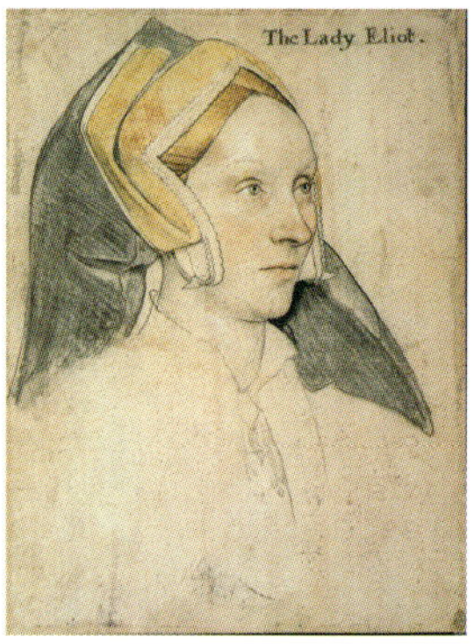

◂ Holbein has rendered the faces of Margaret and Thomas Elyot in chalk with immense subtlety, using white body colour here and there, applied thinly, to add tiny light accents.[5] Thus, Margaret's right eyebrow is suggested by no more than a space in the white highlights, while thin white strokes denote the lower eyelid; the eyelashes are conveyed with just a few dots of black ink. Although her hair is not visible, the resulting impression is that she is fair-haired. The contours of the faces are drawn in ink, the lines varying in thickness and interrupted in places. Holbein also used black ink to render Lady Elyot's head-dress and Sir Thomas's cap, as well as in the latter's brown hair and stubble. While the faces and headgear are elaborated with care, the remaining clothing is indicated only cursorily in chalk. The contours of the drawings do not appear to have been traced to transfer the images to the panel.

◂ Margaret Elyot is wearing a gable hood. This apt term denotes a complex headdress made up of different sections arranged over one another, which fit closely around the face and are drawn together in a point over the head, starched or stiffened with wire. Attached behind are two lappets of black velvet material, which could be worn tied up over the head (cf. cat. nos. 26-28), though Lady Elyot wears them hanging down at the back.[6] The hood always

Sir Thomas Elyot (c. 1490-1546), c. 1527/28 or c. 1532/33

Black and coloured chalks, pen and black ink, white body colour on pink prepared paper, 284 x 205 mm
At upper left, in a later hand: *Th: Eliott Knight.*
Lent by Her Majesty Queen Elizabeth II
cat.no. 11

has a stiffened band or frontlet of striped material on top of the head. A costume study drawn by Holbein, showing the same standing woman from different angles, provides a rear view of the hood (fig. 10a).[7] Both Lady Elyot's hood and Sir Thomas Elyot's hairstyle went out of fashion in the late 1530s. Margaret Elyot's other garments are indicated only with a few chalk lines for the collar and the jewel on her necklace. Her husband's clothes are depicted in slightly more detail, with light hatching in places. The fur trimming at his neck is depicted with brown chalk, while a few yellow lines suggest a cross hanging from a chain.

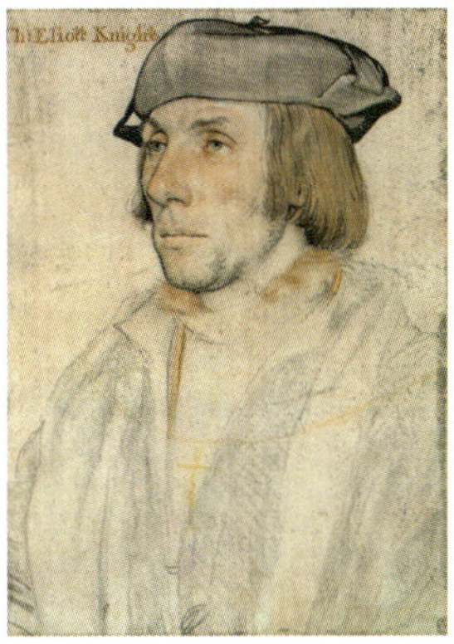

◂ Holbein is generally assumed to have made his portraits of the Elyots —no painted versions of which have been preserved— soon after he settled in England for the second time, in 1532. This is suggested by the pink ground of the paper, which the artist is generally believed not to have used in his earlier portrait drawings.[8] Another feature suggestive of a dating in or after 1532 is the relatively small scale, which is also characteristic of this later period.

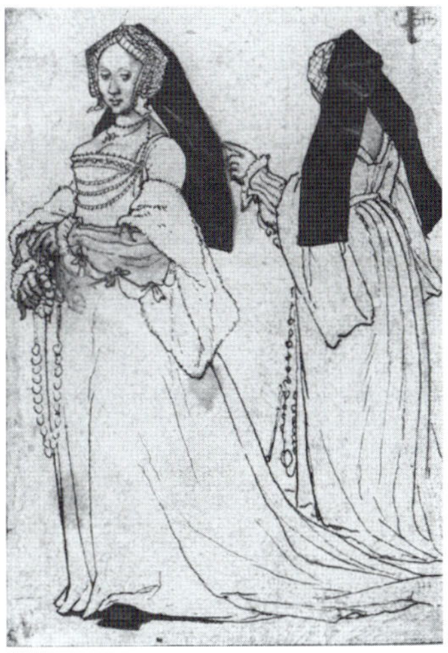

fig. 10a
Hans Holbein the Younger,
Two views of a lady wearing an English hood.
Brush in black, pink and grey wash, 159 x 109 mm.
London, British Museum

◂ Other arguments can be advanced, however, that cast doubt on this traditional dating. In his *Boke named the Governour* (1531), Thomas Elyot complained about the absence of good English artists, as a result of which '[We] be constrayned, if we wyll have any thinge paynted, kerved, or embrawdred, to abandone our owne countraymen and resorte unto straungers'.[9] One wonders if Elyot had already resorted to a foreign artist at this time to obtain portraits of his wife and himself. Furthermore, the youthful appearance of both husband and wife —Thomas Elyot was probably born around 1490, and the couple were married before 1520— makes a dating to Holbein's first English period more plausible. It is not inconceivable that he depicted the couple while he was lodging with Thomas More in the years 1526-1528, when the Elyots belonged to More's intimate circle of friends.[10] AvS

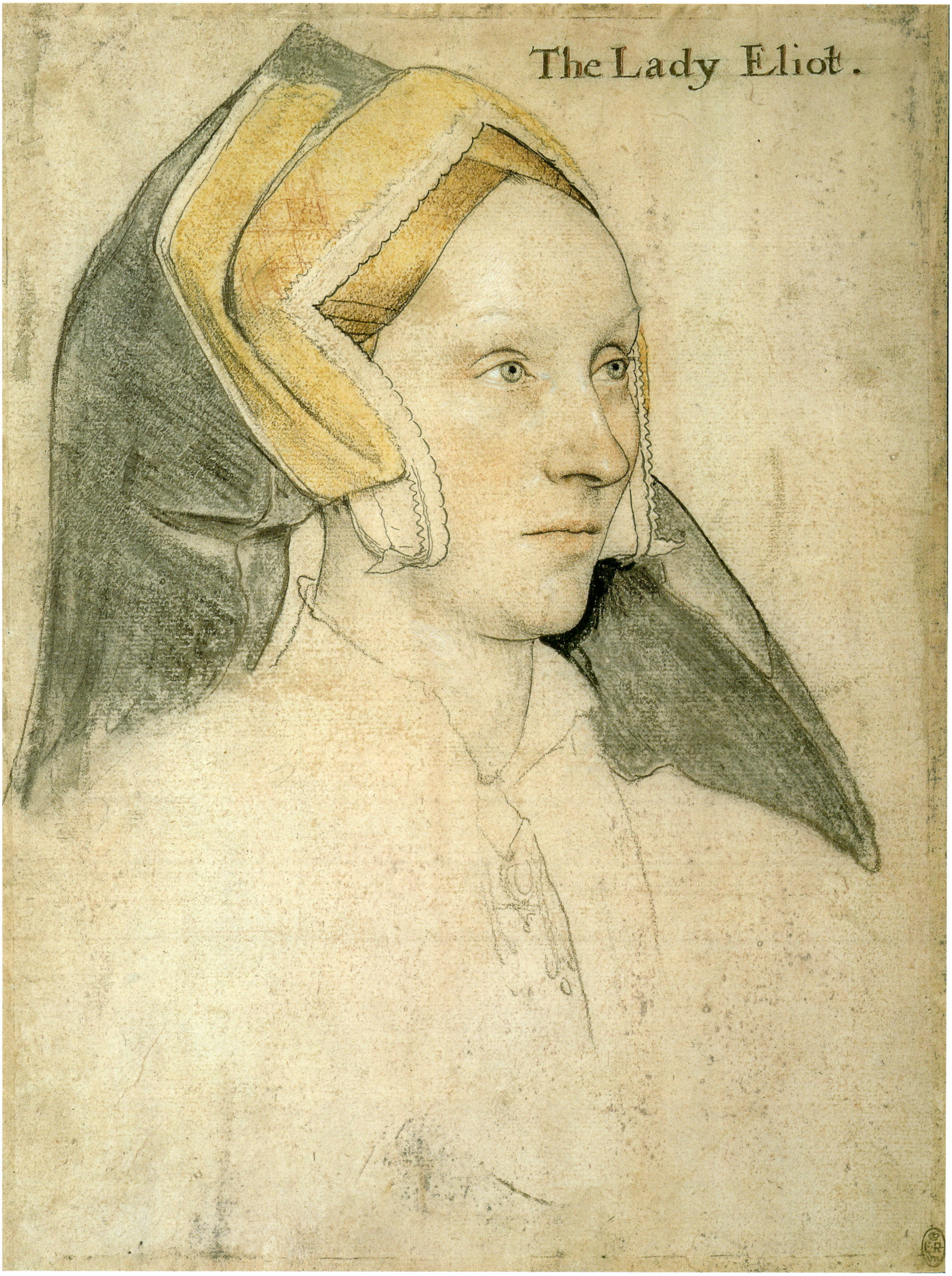
The Lady Eliot.

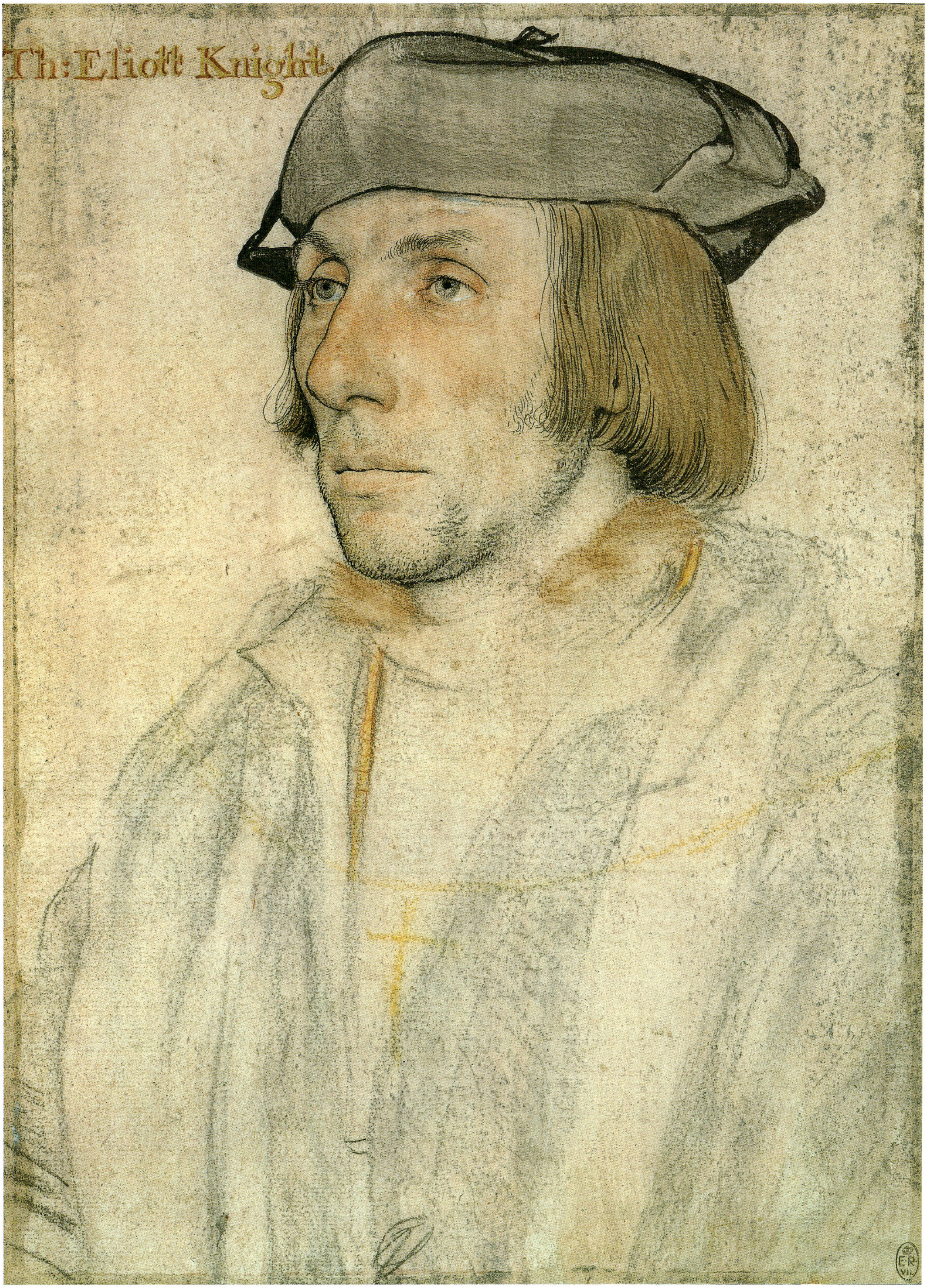
Th: Eliott Knight.

XII

Hermann von Wedigh III (c. 1503–1560), 1532

Panel, 42.2 x 32.4 cm (with a strip 1.3 cm in width added along the lower edge)
To the sitter's left and right: ANNO.1532. / ÆTATIS. SUÆ. *29.*; .; signed with initials on the cover of the book: · H · H ·;
on the side of the book: HER ['W' enclosed in a coat of arms] WID.; on the loose leaf inserted in the book: *Veritas odiu[m] parit:* ˜
New York, The Metropolitan Museum of Art, Bequest of Edward S. Harkness, 1940
cat.no. 12

This portrait dates from 1532, the year in which Holbein returned from Basel to England. His main patrons from his first English period were either deceased, like Archbishop William Warham (p. 23, fig. 22), or had fallen from grace, like Sir Thomas More, one of his most important clients. The latter had been obliged to make do with a meagre income since his dismissal (see cat. no. 3). However, Holbein soon found himself a new clientele among the prosperous members of the Steelyard, who lived at walking distance from his own home. This portrait most probably depicts one of these men. The Steelyard or *Sta[h]lhof* in London was the London branch of the Hanseatic League, a cooperative organisation of mainly German merchants, whose history in England can be traced back to the thirteenth century. In Holbein's day, it was one of the most prominent organisations, capable of exerting considerable political influence because of its good relations with King Henry VIII (p. 28, fig. 27). The merchants were required to observe strict rules, including a pledge to remain unmarried. They lived their lives largely within the confines of a walled area on the banks of the Thames, where they had built their own offices, shops and warehouses, as well as dwellings, an inn and a meeting hall.[1] Around 1533, Holbein was commissioned to produce two monumental, allegorical paintings for this hall, which have unfortunately been lost.[2]

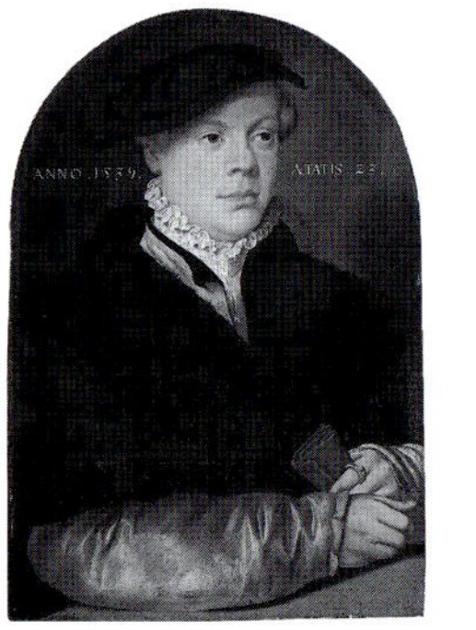

fig. 12a
Bartholomäus Bruyn the Elder, *Portrait of a 23-year-old betrothed man*, 1539. Panel (upper corners rounded), 38 x 26.5 cm. Braunschweig, Herzog Anton Ulrich-Museum

◂ Almost all Holbein's portraits of members of the Steelyard were made in 1532 and 1533 (cat. nos. 17–18).[3] After that he produced only a few incidental examples (cat. no. 35 and fig. 35a).[4] The best-known Steelyard portrait is that of Georg Gisze (1532), now in Berlin (p. 26, fig. 25), which is not only the largest but the most ambitious in conception (see p. 26).[5] The sitter's name is inscribed on it no fewer than seven times. The identity of the 29-year-old man in the painting discussed here, which also dates from 1532, was established on the basis of the inscription on the side of the book: 'HER [...] WID.'. This abbreviation probably refers to Hermann von Wedigh III, who died in 1560. The son of Hermann von Wedigh II and Barbara von der Linden,[6] he was born into a Cologne family of patricians, several members of which were active as merchants in the London Steelyard from 1480 onward.[7] After his stay in England, Von Wedigh married Sophia Hörners (died in 1567) and was appointed as a judge in Niederich and a town councillor in Cologne.[8] Von Wedigh's portrait must have been on show in the latter city before 1539, since the Cologne painter Bartholomäus Bruyn the Elder (1493–1555) made a man's portrait that year that was unmistakeably based on it (fig. 12a). The rendering of the hands and the way in which the sitter grasps his leather gloves are identical,[9] while *pentimenti* to the left and right of the neck show that Bruyn had initially included the shawl collar as well.[10] He also adopted the idea of the Latin inscription, something he had never used in his work before. As Holbein focused on the face in his preliminary studies, paying scant attention to the hands —only two studies of hands by him have been preserved (see p. 50, fig. 1b)— we may assume that Bruyn saw the painting itself and not a preliminary drawing of it.[11]

◂ In 1533 Holbein depicted another member of the Von Wedigh family, in a painting that is now in Berlin (fig. 12b).[12] Like the sitter in this painting, the 39-year-old man wears a signet ring with the Von Wedigh coat of arms.[13] He is believed to be Hermann Hillebrandt von Wedigh,[14] a relative of the Hermann depicted here, probably also a member of the Steelyard community. However, this is not explicitly mentioned in any of the Von Wedigh portraits, in contrast to most of Holbein's other Steelyard portraits.[15]

◂ In the painting described here, there is a second letter 'W' on the side of the book in the abbreviated name 'HER [...] WID.'. The letter is woven into a coat of arms and probably refers to the Windeck, the organisation representing Cologne's merchants.[16] That Holbein and his clients had a fondness for veiled allusions is also clear from the loose leaf inserted into the book, inscribed 'Veritas odiu[m] parit' (Truth breeds hatred). This text comes from the Roman comedy *Andria* (The girl from Andros) by Terence (c. 195–159 BC).[17] It was the motto of the Italian writer Pietro Aretino (1492–1556), but it was also used by Erasmus (see cat. no. 1) and other humanists.[18] How the text should be construed here is not entirely clear, although the fact of its insertion in a volume with gilt clasps —probably a bible[19]— should perhaps be understood in the context of the religious reforms of the sixteenth century. The 'hatred' may refer to the turbulent political and religious climate that resulted from the Reformation, in which there was

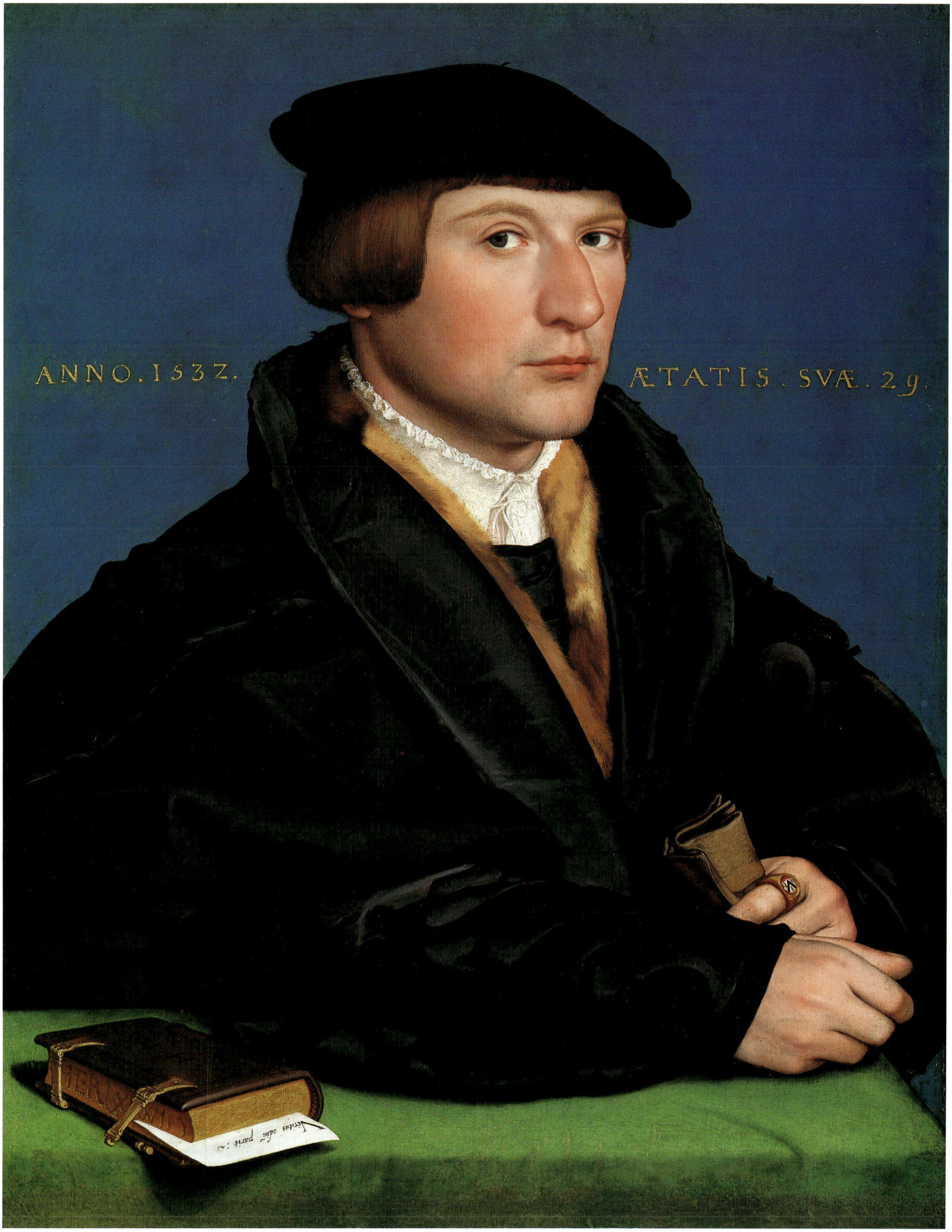
ANNO.1532.
ÆTATIS.SVÆ.29.

a widespread desire to return to the Bible as the source of the 'true' faith. Cicero explained Terence's words as implying that the messenger bringing 'the truth' should not be hated but admired.[20] Von Wedigh, the only person who can clearly read the text depicted and whose name is given, perhaps quite pointedly, on the book itself, therefore appears to be presenting himself here as a supporter of the reforms. He evidently had some considerable say about his portrait. Strikingly, Holbein placed his initials on the cover of the book. Thus interpreted —the letters could be read alternatively as the initials of the sitter, Hermann Hermannsohn— the panel is one of Holbein's few signed portraits.

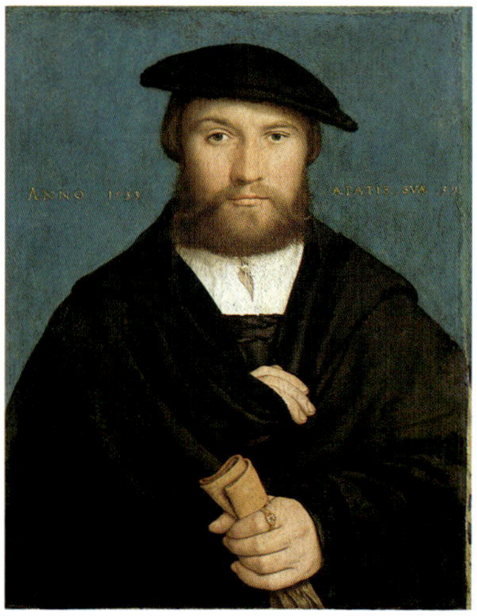

fig. 12b
Hans Holbein the Younger, *Portrait of a 39-year-old man belonging to the Von Wedigh family, traditionally identified as Hermann Hillebrandt von Wedigh*, 1533. Panel, 42 x 32.5 cm. Berlin, Staatliche Museen zu Berlin, Gemäldegalerie

◂ Thanks to the work's superb condition, it gives an excellent impression of the original freshness of Holbein's paintings. The bright blue background has withstood the ravages of time,[21] as have other parts of the representation. The play of light and shade on the folds of the shiny black satin cloak (which is modelled with great subtlety in hues ranging from jet black to grey), is rendered very convincingly.[22] The fine stubble on the man's jaws, rendered with small streaks and dots, also testify to Holbein's keen sense of detail. The artist worked the precious gold leaf into the inscription and book clasps.[23]

◂ The composition relies on a tried and tested formula. The figure is depicted behind a balustrade, in the same way that Holbein had previously placed Nicolaus Kratzer (p. 21, fig. 20) and Thomas Godsalve with his son John (cat. no. 8) behind a table. While in the latter painting Holbein inscribed the year in which it was made on a *cartellino* —as he did on several occasions— here he has recorded the year more ostentatiously, in gold letters against a uniform background. This is apparently the first time that Holbein included the gilt inscriptions giving the year and the sitter's age that would become so characteristic of his portraits. With the introduction of this pictorial motif, Holbein opted for a greatly simplified background: after this, he made only sporadic use of the vines or curtains seen in his older portraits.

◂ A second striking innovation of the Steelyard portraits is that the sitters gaze directly at the viewer (cf. also cat. no. 13).[24] This may be partly because the Steelyard members were required to remain bachelors and their portraits therefore never had counterparts depicting a fiancée or a wife (e.g. fig. 12a). Hermann von Wedigh exemplifies this gaze. In the Steelyard portraits he made the following year, Holbein no longer depicted the face from a three-quarters angle, as here, but more from the front (cat. no. 17), sometimes adopting a full frontal perspective (cat. no. 18 and fig. 12b) that makes the gaze more penetrating still. Eye contact with the viewer is characteristic of this group of portraits.[25] Infrared examination of Holbein's portrait of Hermann von Wedigh has demonstrated the importance that Holbein attached to the rendering of the eyes. It reveals an underdrawing indicating the contours and parts of the face, and showing that Holbein altered the position of the left eye.[26] Interestingly, the lid of the right eye —from the viewer's vantage point— is depicted smaller than that of the other eye, a trait recurring in the portrait of the other member of the Von Wedigh family, in which the frontal perspective makes it more conspicuous still (fig. 12b).[27] In the portrait described here both the sitter's pupils are in the corners of his eyes, making his gaze more penetrating still. QB

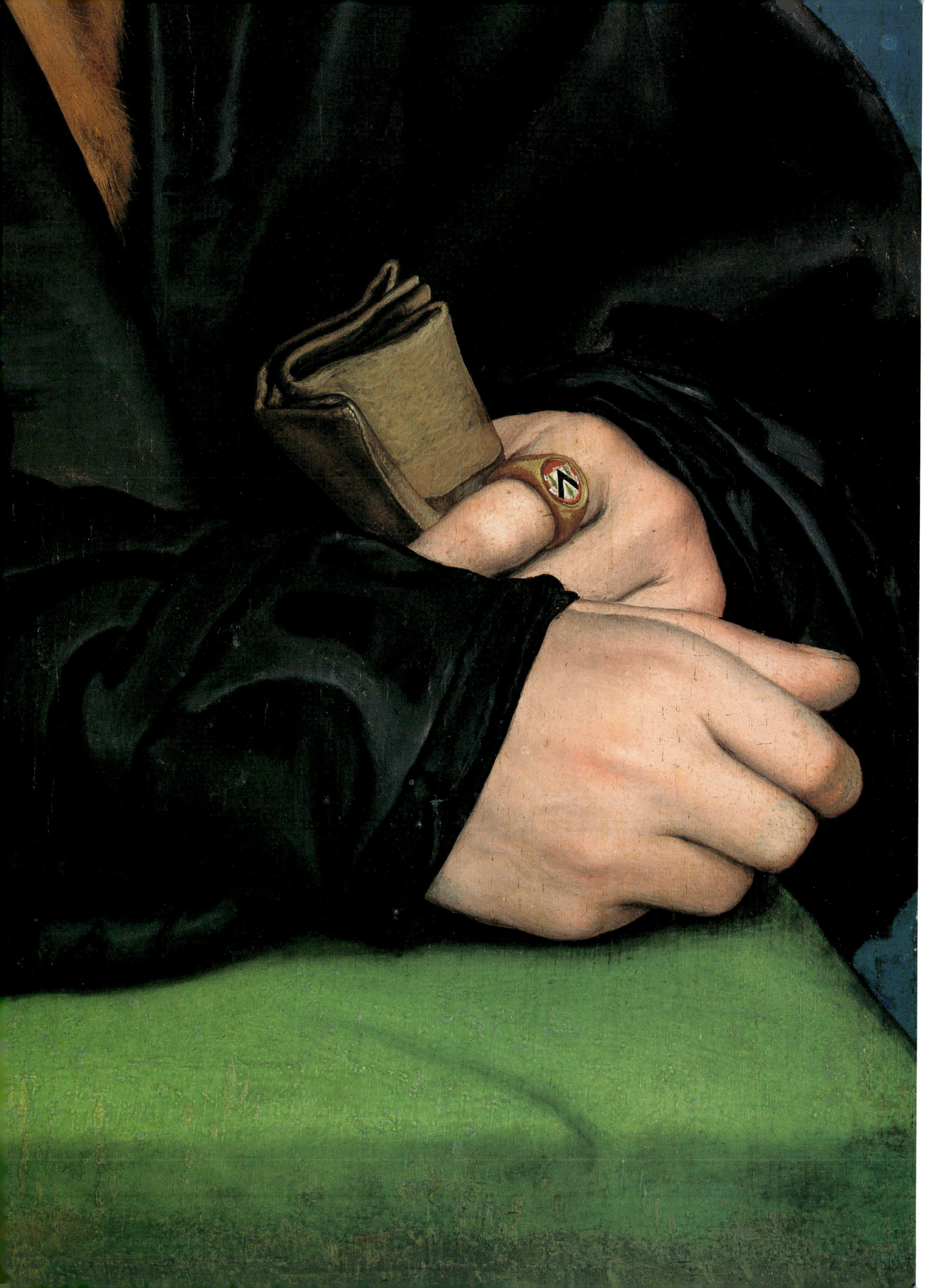

XIII

John Godsalve (c. 1510-1556), c. 1532

Black, white and coloured chalks, pen and brush and black ink, watercolours and white body colour, on pink prepared paper, 362 x 292 mm / At upper left, in a later hand (twice): *Sr Iohn Godsalue*
Lent by Her Majesty Queen Elizabeth II
cat.no. 13

In this drawing John Godsalve has lost some of the youthfulness that he displays in the portrait depicting him together with his father in 1528 (cat. no. 8). His cheekbones are slightly more pronounced, and his side-whiskers and the stubble of his beard are clearly visible. Whereas in the painting he had a subordinate position in relation to his father, here he radiates the self-confidence of a man of the world, holding his head erect and meeting the viewer's gaze.

◂ That the drawing was not a preliminary study for the painting but was made several years later is clear not only from the fact that the sitter appears to be older than the youth in the painting and wears different clothes, but also from the use of a pink ground on the paper. All the portrait drawings from Holbein's second English period (1532-1543) have this flesh-coloured layer, while during his first stay in England he drew his portraits almost exclusively on unprepared white paper.[1] The presence of the pink ground therefore suggests that the drawing should be dated in or shortly after 1532 — the year of Holbein's final return to England.

◂ John Godsalve followed in his father's footsteps, holding public office in a variety of positions in Norwich and London.[2] Like his father, he served, for instance, as Registrar of the Consistory Court of the diocese of Norwich. Godsalve's career got off to a good start thanks to the support of Thomas Cromwell, a friend of his father's. In 1531 he became Clerk of the King's Signet, and the year after he gained a position at the London Office of Common Meter of Precious Tissues.[3] This position brought him into contact with Hanseatic merchants of London's German Steelyard community, who constituted an important clientele for Holbein from 1532 onward (see cat. nos. 12, 17 and 18). In 1544, following his father's death, Godsalve became a Freeman of Norwich.[4] That same year he took part in the English Siege of Boulogne, after which he was knighted in 1547 at the coronation of Edward VI: the letters 'Sr' (Sir) on the drawing, at upper left, indicate that the inscription must date from after 1547.[5] Godsalve was appointed Comptroller of the Royal Mint in the Tower of London in 1548.

◂ The detailed elaboration of Holbein's drawing of John Godsalve makes it one of the most impressive in the Windsor Castle collection. The face, which is drawn in chalks of different hues, has been touched up with great care using pen and brush and black ink, while the clothing, which is generally left unfinished in Holbein's drawings, is elaborated with watercolour and white body colour. Only the medallion on Godsalve's cap is left blank. The sitters' hands are seldom depicted in Holbein's portrait drawings,[6] but here they play an important role, and even the shading on them is suggested with fine hatching. The right hand, in which Godsalve holds a sheet of paper, seems to be resting on a plinth or frame at the bottom of the portrait: a trompe l'oeil motif that was frequently used by artists such as Hans Memling (c. 1440-1494). This hand at the outer edge of the image also suggests that the sheet is still more or less its original size, which is unusual. This appears to be confirmed by the faint dark line framing the drawing on all four sides. Another feature seldom encountered in Holbein's portrait drawings is the blue background, which has been applied over the pink ground. The ground shows through the blue throughout, but along the lower left side of the sheet a wash has been applied over it, producing a more even blue there. Perhaps the background is unfinished, and was meant to be an even blue surface, as we often see in Holbein's painted portraits.

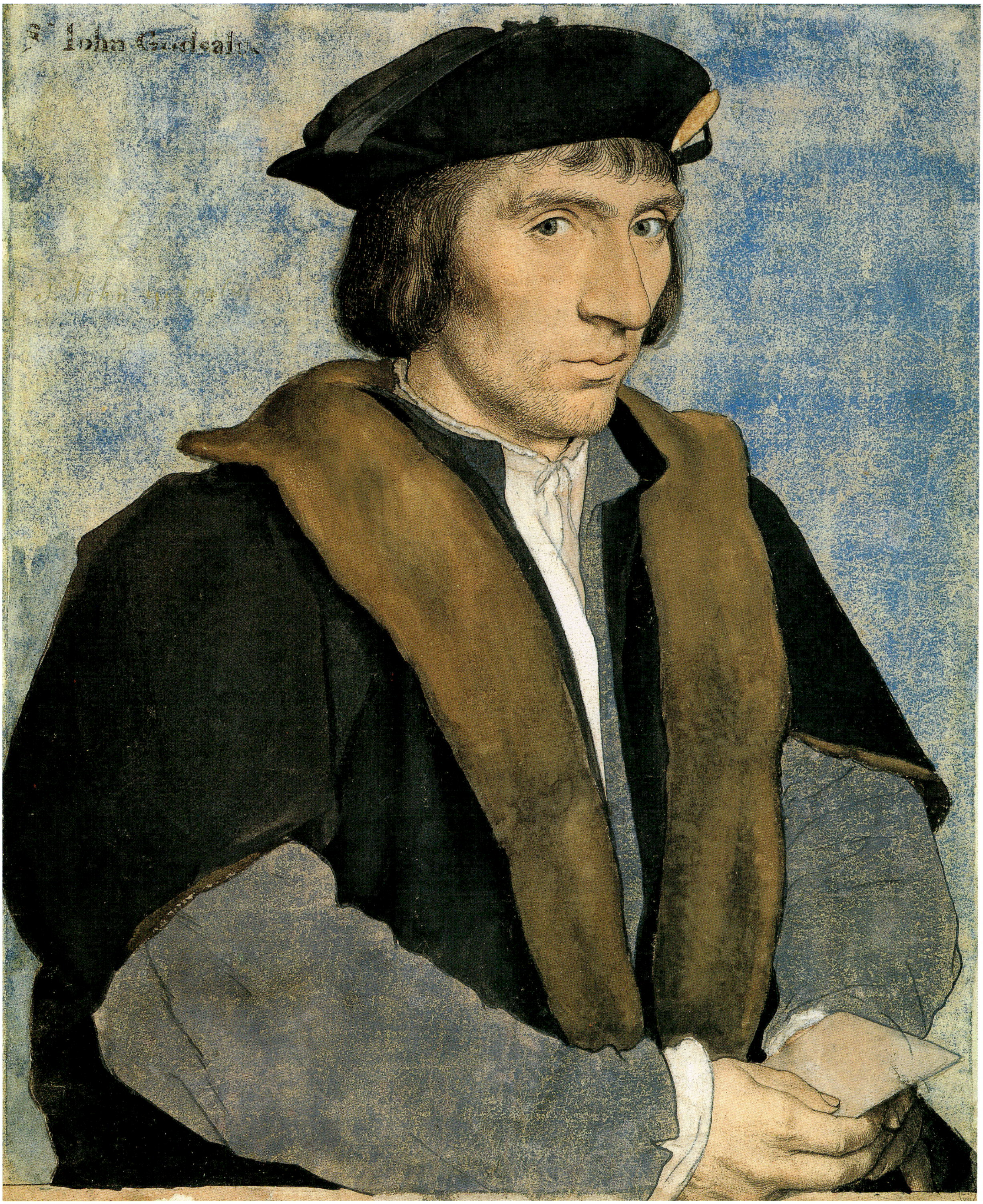

The only other portrait drawing by Holbein that displays a degree of finishing similar to *The Portrait of John Godsalve* is the one in Basel depicting a small boy with a lemur, which also has a blue background (fig. 13a).[7] Holbein generally elaborated only the faces in his portrait drawings, most of which served as preliminary studies for paintings.[8]

The drawing discussed here is executed in such detail as to suggest that it was intended not as a preliminary study, but as an independent work of art.[9] Nevertheless, it evidently did not come into the sitter's possession, since it is one of the group of drawings at Windsor Castle, all of which are thought to have come from Holbein's studio estate. AvS

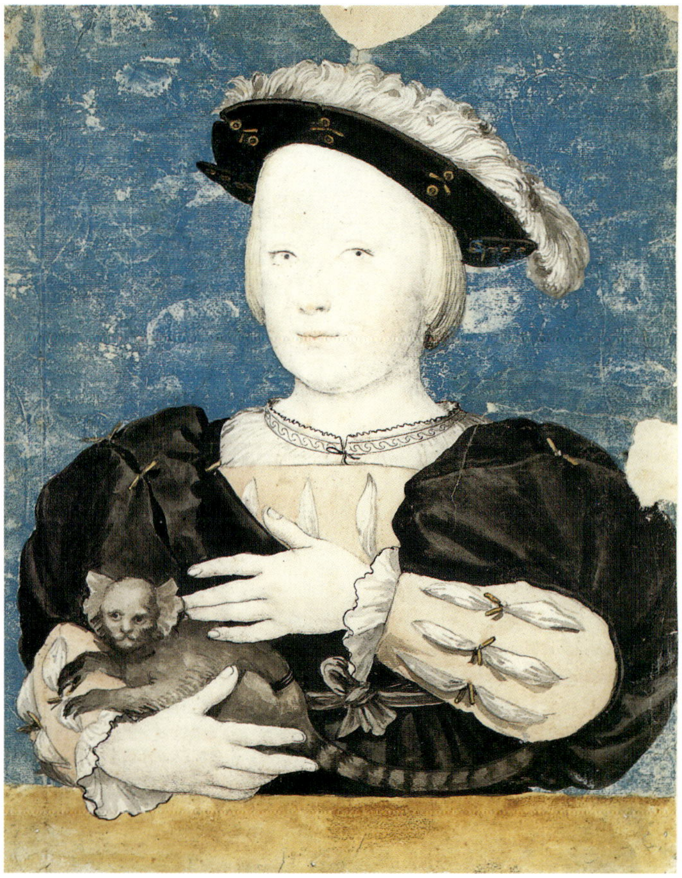

fig. 13a Hans Holbein the Younger, *Portrait of a boy with a lemur.* Black and coloured chalks, wash, 400 x 307 mm. Basel, Öffentlichen Kunstsammlung, Kupferstichkabinett

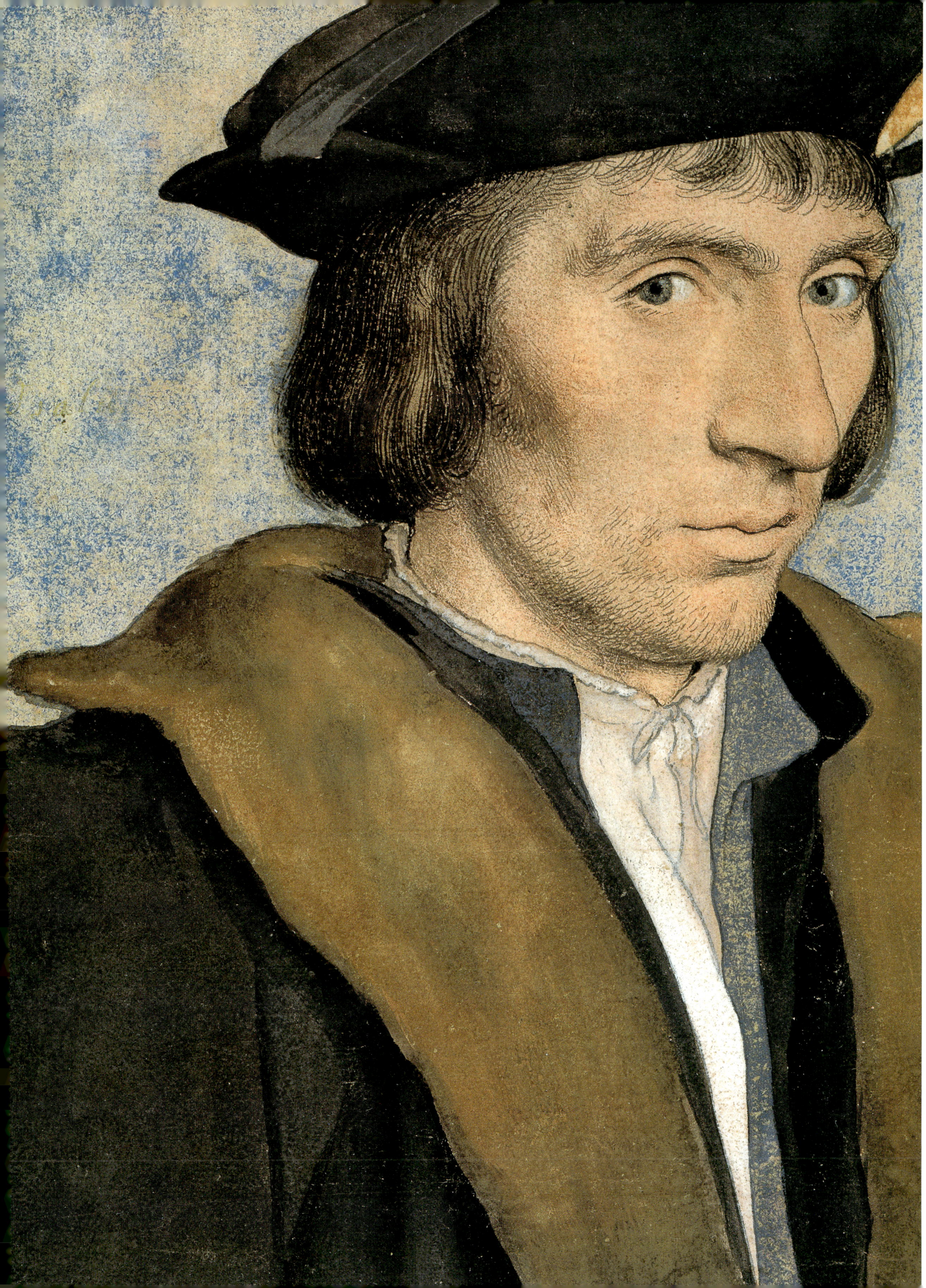

William Reskimer (?-1552), c. 1532/33

Black, white and coloured chalks, metalpoint on pink prepared paper, 290 x 210 mm
At upper left and right, in a later hand: *Reskemeer a Cornish Gent:*
Lent by Her Majesty Queen Elizabeth II
cat.no. 14

At the top of Holbein's portrait drawing in Windsor Castle of a man with a striking pointed red beard, wearing a cap, is an inscription in bold lettering, reading 'Reskemeer a Cornish Gent'. This identifies the sitter as William Reskimer, the youngest son of John Reskimer of Merthen, Cornwall. After his appointment as Page of the Chamber in 1526 he served for years at the court of Henry VIII in London, where Holbein probably depicted him not long after his return to England in 1532. The drawing served as a sketch for a painted portrait showing the sitter almost in profile against a deep blue background enlivened with decorative vines. The painting also shows Reskimer's hands, which are not depicted in the drawing: with his right hand, that is twisted around towards his body, he is holding the two-pointed end of his beard. The hanging cords of his white shirt provide a conspicuous accent in the painting that was not foreseen in the drawing.

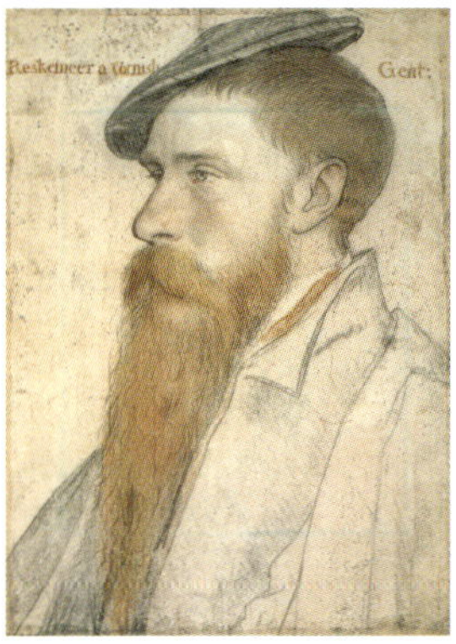

‹ About twenty of Holbein's extant drawings — including that of Reskimer — can be linked to painted portraits, some of which were executed by studio assistants.[2] Many other works have not survived: in numerous cases there are paintings for which the preliminary drawings have been lost, and the reverse situation is also found. Even so, using cases in which both sketch and painting have survived, we can make a fair reconstruction of Holbein's working methods. Infrared reflectography of the under-drawings beneath the layers of paint plays an important part here.[3] This reveals that the artist devised a standardised production method using drawings as working material for painted portraits,[4] a method he applied with particular frequency in his second English period (from 1532 onward).

‹ While his sitter was posing Holbein made a chalk sketch, on which he often made notes about the clothing, jewellery and colours. He modelled the face in chalk with the utmost care, meticulously observing nuances of colouring in skin and hair, as we see here. He also observed in minute detail the colour of the eyes, the reflected light on the pupils, and the red accents on the translucent skin of the eyelids. In contrast, his rendering of clothes in his portrait drawings was sketchy. Holbein would then make his painting on the basis of the sketch; his sitter probably did not pose for him again at the painting stage. He generally kept the drawing: the Windsor Castle collection of eighty portrait drawings by Holbein, fifteen of which are on show at the present exhibition, were most probably from his studio estate.[5]

‹ Before painting the portrait, Holbein would studiously transfer the most important outlines of the drawing — in particular, the contours of the face, nose, mouth, eyes, and ears — to the panel, to which in the case of Reskimer's portrait a flesh-coloured layer (the *imprimatura*) had been applied (see also cat. nos. 28 and 33).[6] The result was a painting with exactly the same dimensions and proportions as the original sketch, as we see here.[7] To transfer the drawing to the panel Holbein probably used a sheet of paper blackened with charcoal or chalk, which he placed between the drawing and the prepared panel.[8] The contours of the drawing were then traced, with the application of light pressure, using a metalpoint for instance, leaving an imprint of the lines in charcoal or chalk on the panel. This was a well-known technique described by Vasari, and used for instance by the French court portraitist Jean Clouet (c. 1485/90–1540/41),[9] whose work served as a major source of inspiration for Holbein. Some drawings still display the light indentations caused by tracing, but in most cases the passage of time has rendered them invisible. The metalpoint lines are visible in many of the drawings, as in the portrait described here, but the tracing may sometimes have been done using a stylus that did not leave any marks. The delicate charcoal or chalk lines on the panel were subsequently enhanced with pen or brush in ink, after which the rest

William Reskimer (?-1552), c. 1532/33

Panel, 46.4 x 33.7 cm
Lent by Her Majesty Queen Elizabeth II
cat.no. 15

of the image could be sketched in slightly freer lines before the paint was applied: the part precise, part loosely sketched underdrawing that resulted from this process has been revealed in some of Holbein's portraits by infrared reflectography.[10] After the contours were transferred to the panel, the preliminary drawing continued to serve as Holbein's model during the painting process. He built up the composition of his portraits, whether paintings or drawings, from the contours; thus, in the painted portrait of William Reskimer, these lines do not blend completely with the adjoining flesh tints. The artist rendered the skin of his sitters with a subtle and varied palette, which closely follows the diverse nuances of the chalk in the drawings.

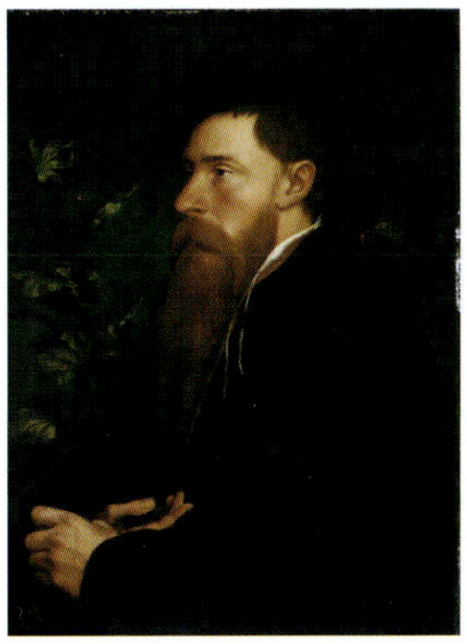

◂ Holbein occasionally enlivened the background of his early religious paintings and early portraits with stylised vines, some of which look more like figleaves (cat. nos. 2, 6 and 7). At the beginning of his second English period he used this motif only in the portraits of Derich Born (cat. no. 17) and William Reskimer.[11] Perhaps the medicinal, protective qualities traditionally attributed to these plants played a role in his addition of this motif.[12] The leaves in Reskimer's portrait are not cut by the edge of the pictorial plane; furthermore, the unpainted edges of the panel prove that the work was never reduced in size.

◂ The man with the red pointed beard was once thought to be William's elder brother John Reskimer (c. 1499–1566).[13] In 1521 John was in the service of Cardinal Thomas Wolsey, whom he accompanied to France in 1527, but he later appears to have moved back to the family's property in Cornwall. William Reskimer, on the other hand, was active at the court as Henry VIII's page. In 1543 he was appointed Keeper of the Posts of the Duchy of Cornwall, and three years later he became Gentleman Usher, another ceremonial position at court.[14] The identification of the sitter as William rather than John Reskimer derives support from the provenance of this painting, which Sir Robert Killigrew presented to Charles I at the beginning of the seventeenth century. One of Killigrew's daughters was married to a grandson of William Reskimer, whereas John Reskimer died childless.[15] AvS

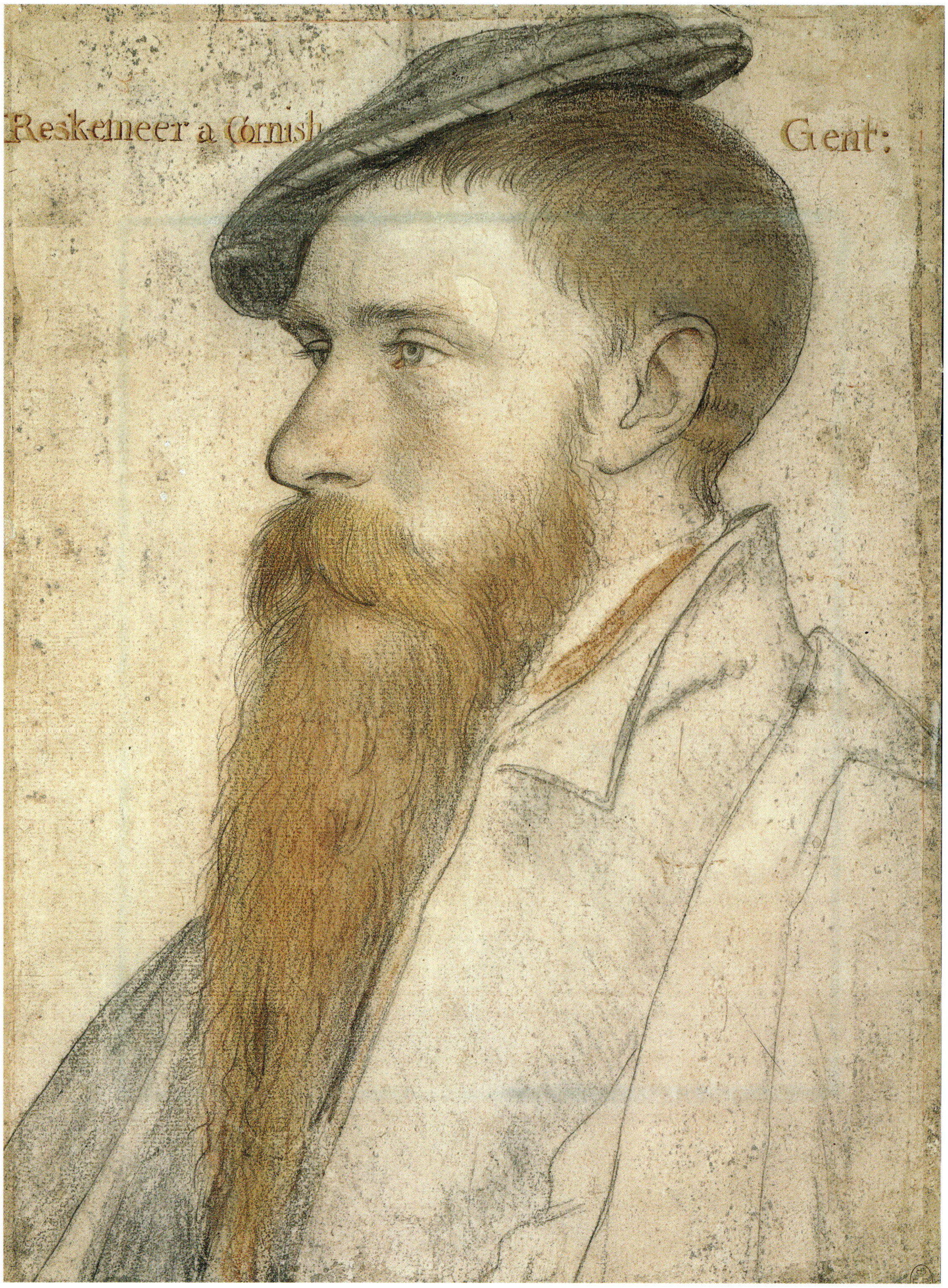
Reskemeer a Cornish
Gent:

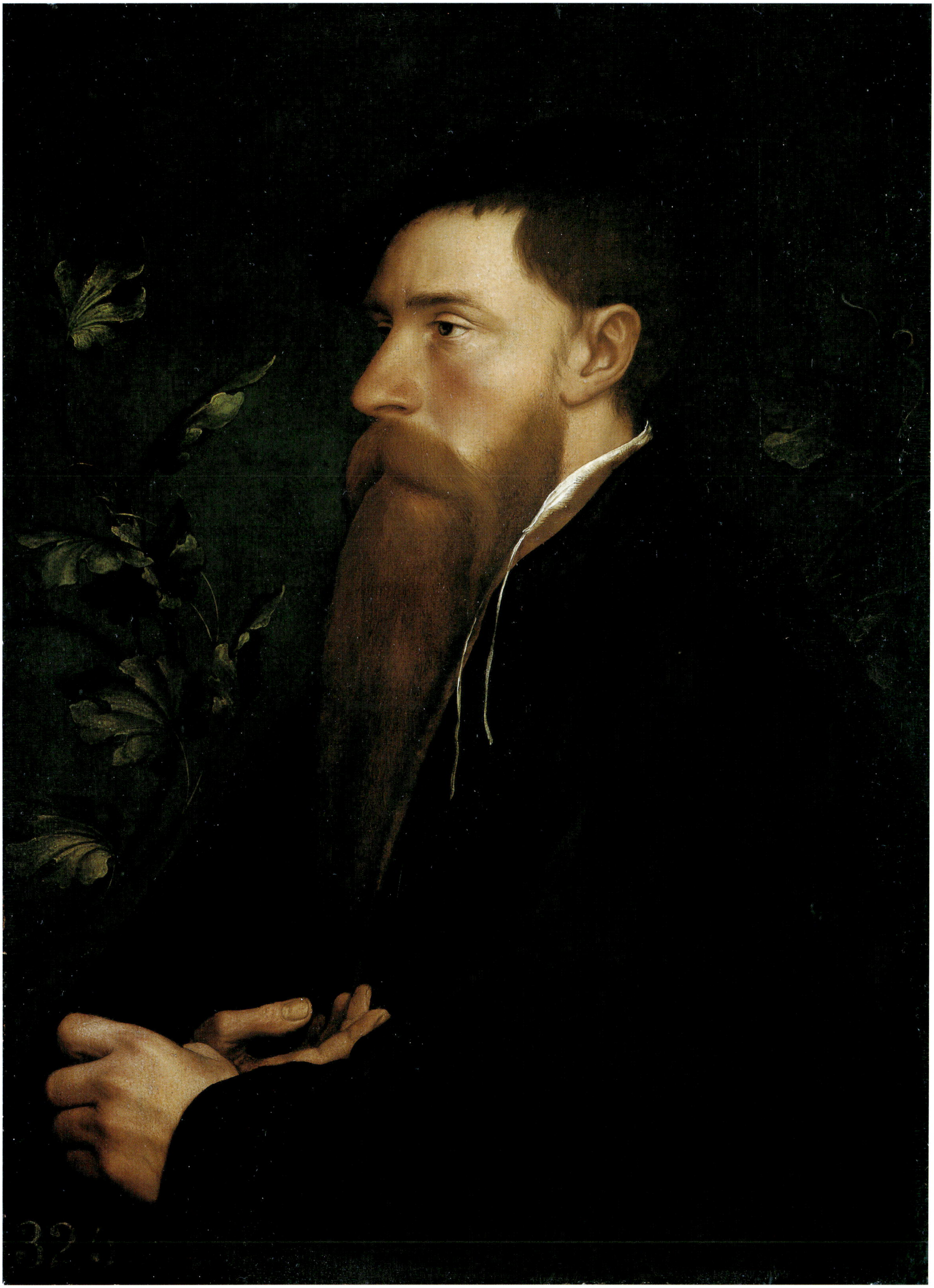

XVI

An unknown man, c. 1532/34

Black, white and coloured chalks, pen and brush and black ink, on pink prepared paper, 272 x 210 mm
Annotations by the artist in pen and black ink, from left to right: *S*, *at* [twice] and *atlass*
Lent by Her Majesty Queen Elizabeth II
cat.no. 16

The drawing discussed here shows Holbein's superb mastery of the combined use of chalk, pen and brush. Having first laid in the man's face in chalk, he then added subtle pen and ink accents, such as the outlines of the upper eyelids and the line between the lips. The eyebrows are indicated with thin lines executed with the pen, while the hair and cap have been laid in with quite broad brushstrokes. Holbein used the pen to add a few springy hairs, while in the dark wash of the beard he added wavy pen lines to suggest curly hair. He rendered the clothing with bold lines in black ink, using the tip of his brush.

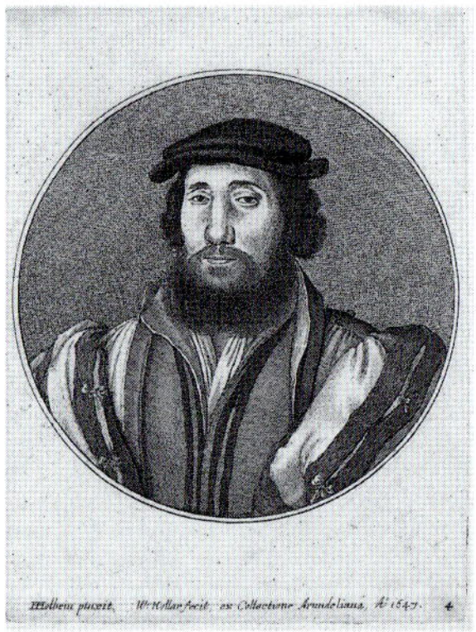

fig. 16a
Wenceslaus Hollar after Hans Holbein the Younger, *Portrait of an unknown man*, 1647. Etching, 128 x 108 mm. Amsterdam, Rijksmuseum, Rijksprentenkabinet

The pen inscriptions on the apparel of this man with a broken nose and curly beard confirm that the drawing was made, like many others, as a preliminary study for a painting. On the band to which the sleeve is fastened on the left appears the letter 'S', standing for 'Samt' (velvet) or 'schwarz' (black). Aside from this, on the collar and chest section Holbein twice added the word 'at' and once 'atlass', the German word for satin. Despite these indications, no painted portrait of this dark-haired man has been preserved.[1] What has survived, however, is an etching in reverse image after the portrait, made by the Bohemian artist Wenceslaus Hollar (1607–1677), in which the clothing is further elaborated (fig. 16a).[2] A striking detail is the inscription 'HHolbein pinxit', which appears to suggest that the etcher worked from a painting rather than the drawing: perhaps its circular shape reflects that of the panel.[3]

From about 1627 onward, Holbein's portrait drawings from Windsor Castle—including the one described here—were in the possession of Thomas Howard, Earl of Arundel (1585-1646), and his wife Aletheia née Talbot (c. 1590–1654),[4] who had taken their celebrated art collection with them when they went into exile in the Netherlands in 1642.[5] That Arundel (of whose ancestors Holbein made several portraits; see cat. nos. 31, 32 and 34) was a passionate collector of Holbein's work is clear, among other things, from an inventory drawn up in Amsterdam in 1655, after the death of Arundel's wife: it lists an astonishing 44 paintings by Holbein,[6] added to which the earl had also managed to acquire the 'great booke' of portrait drawings. Hollar produced many reproductive etchings of works in the Arundel collection besides the print mentioned above,[6] and they are often inscribed 'ex Collectione Arundeliana'. Seventeen of them depict portraits by Holbein. AvS

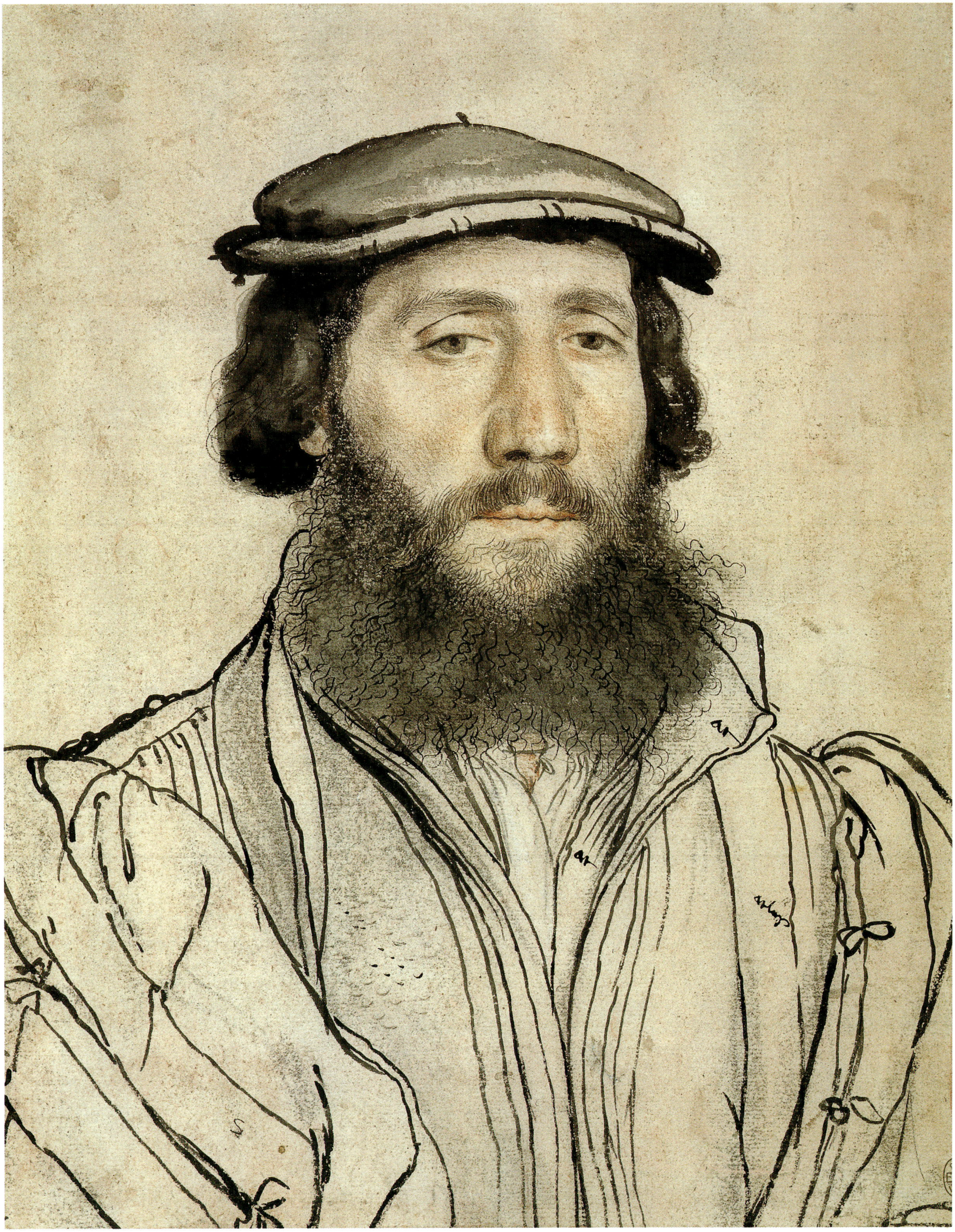

XVII

Derich Born (1509/10–*after* 1549), 1533

Panel, 60.3 x 45.1 cm / On the balustrade: DERICHVS SI VOCEM ADDAS IPSISSIMUS HIC SIT / HVNC DVBITES PICTOR FECERIT AN GENITOR / DER BORN ETATIS SVAE 23. ANNO 1533
Lent by Her Majesty Queen Elizabeth II
cat.no. 17

When Holbein returned to England from Basel in the summer of 1532, all his former English patrons had either lost their lives or fallen from political favour. But he soon discovered a new circle of clients among the German merchants of the Steelyard, the London establishment of the Hanseatic League: almost all Holbein's portraits of these prosperous men date from the period 1532–1533 (cf. cat. nos. 12 and 18).[2] It is striking that each one displays the sitter's name and age, as well as the year in which it was made. Thus the inscription on the balustrade in this painting identifies the sitter as the 23-year-old Derich Born from Cologne, the youngest of the Steelyard merchants portrayed. Holbein produced a second portrait of the young man, probably also in 1533, on a small circular panel.[3]

◂ Born is portrayed against a dark blue background with stylised vines (cf. cat. nos. 6, 7 and 15). Of the few details that have been preserved concerning his life and his presence in London, most relate to commercial disputes.[4] Derich Born and his elder brother Johannes were expelled from the Steelyard in 1541 after a dispute with the duke of Suffolk —another of Holbein's patrons[5]— concerning the payment for a consignment of lead; the two men were accused of jeopardising the privileges of the German business community in London. In 1542 their presence was documented in Antwerp, and the last reference to Derich Born dates from 1549, when he submitted a formal complaint about his expulsion, while in Cologne. Since Holbein's portrait of Born was already in the English royal collection in the early seventeenth century, it seems fair to assume that it stayed behind in England after its subject had left.

It has sometimes been speculated that Holbein's portraits of the German merchants in London were made for the decorations for the guildhall of their *Stahlhof* or Steelyard,[6] for which Holbein in any case made monumental allegories.[7] It seems more likely, however, that they were intended to serve as souvenirs to take home:[8] many of them bear inscriptions alluding to London and to the sitter's membership of the Hanseatic League there (cf. cat. no. 18).[9] In contrast to Holbein's portraits of the British nobility, the Steelyard portraits were not duplicated, as far as is known, nor are any preliminary drawings for them known.[10] Examination of the *Portrait of Derich Born* using infrared reflectography has revealed an underdrawing (fig. 17a).[11] It shows that the painter had difficulty capturing the outline of the face on the right, drawing it three times. The IRR assembly also reveals that the contours of the shoulders were initially placed higher up.

◂ A telling detail is the Latin inscription ostensibly carved into the stone balustrade, which refers to the painter's skill in dissolving the dividing-line between illusion and reality: 'Once you add the voice, you see Derich himself here, such that you wonder whether it was the painter or the Creator who made him.'[12] The use of the past tense emphasises the work's perfection; barring the voice, nothing could possibly be added to it. The same figure of speech for verisimilitude was used by others, including Erasmus in his praise of the 'new Apelles' Albrecht Dürer (1471–1528), with whom Holbein appears to be competing here. Thus, the pose of the sitter, who meets our gaze self-confidently over his shoulder while resting his right arm on a balustrade, resembles Dürer's in a

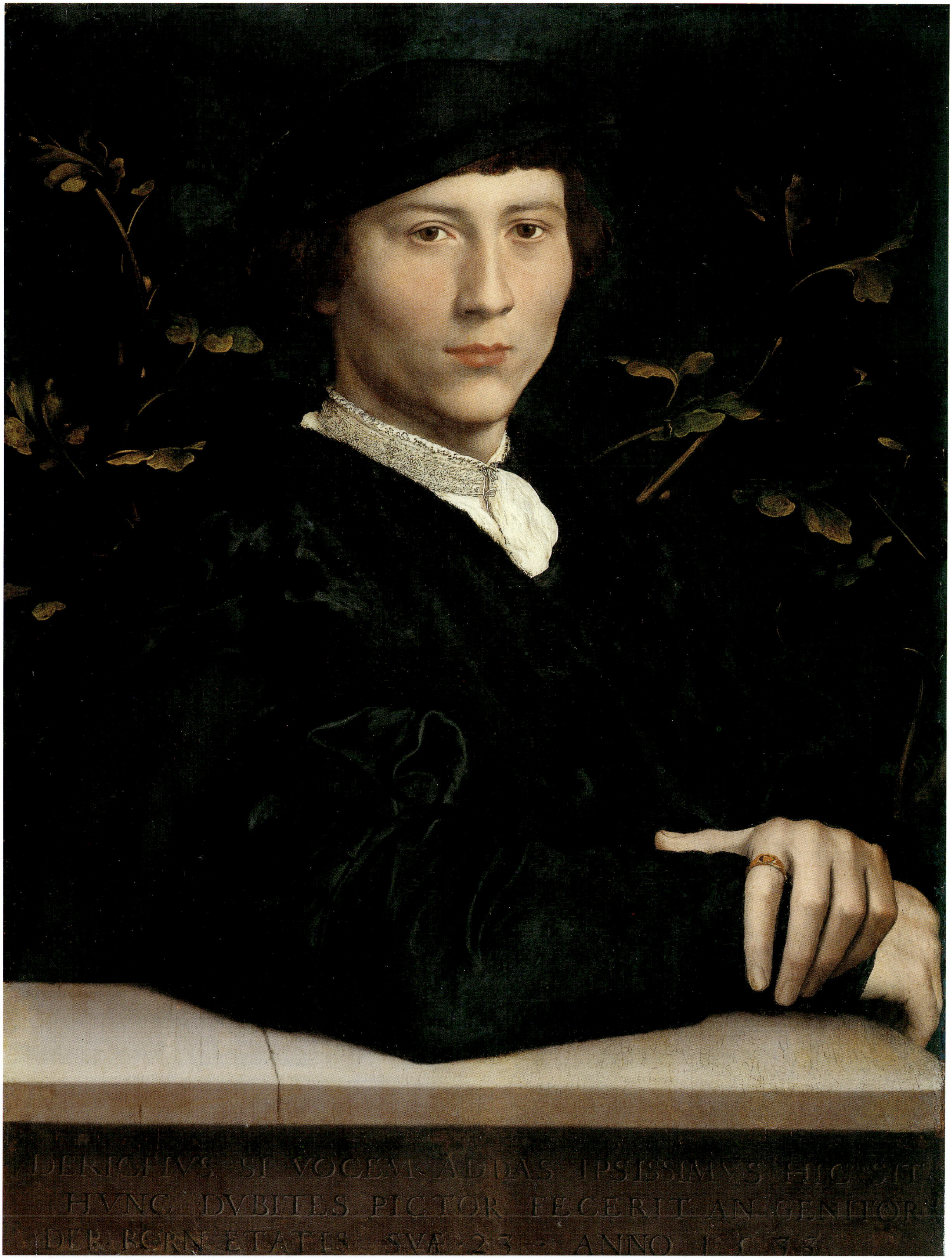
DERICHVS SI VOCEM ADDAS IPSISSIMVS HIC SIT
HVNC DVBITES PICTOR FECERIT AN GENITOR
DER BORN ETATIS SVÆ 23 ANNO 1533

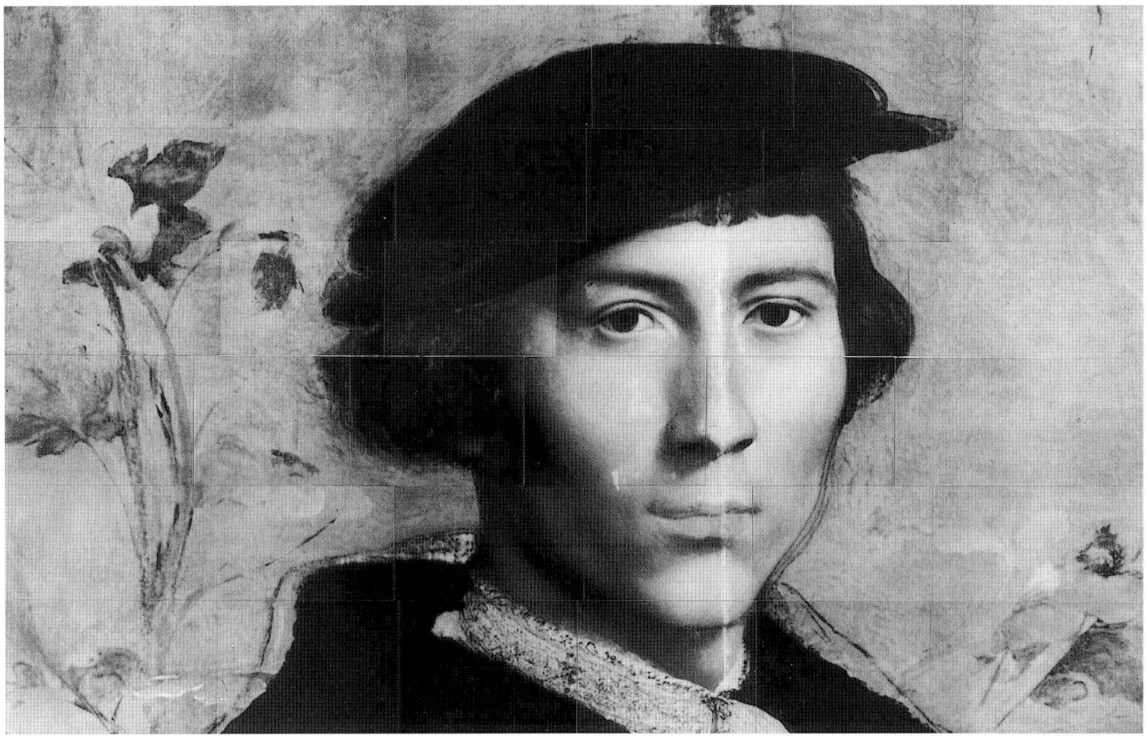

fig. 17a
Derich Born (detail)
Infrared reflectogram assembly, Rachel Billinge, The National Gallery, London

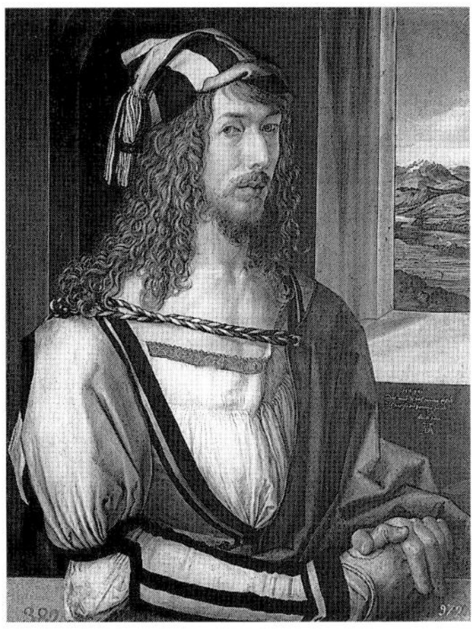

fig. 17b
Albrecht Dürer, *Self-portrait*, 1498. Panel, 52 x 41 cm. Madrid, Museo del Prado

self-portrait from 1498 (fig. 17b). This pose became popular in early sixteenth-century Italian portraiture, for instance in the work of Titian (1477–1576) (fig. 17c), who may also have served as a source of inspiration here.[13] With the pose and the addition of the eloquent inscription, Holbein's portrait of his young fellow countryman gave notice of his artistic ambitions. AvS

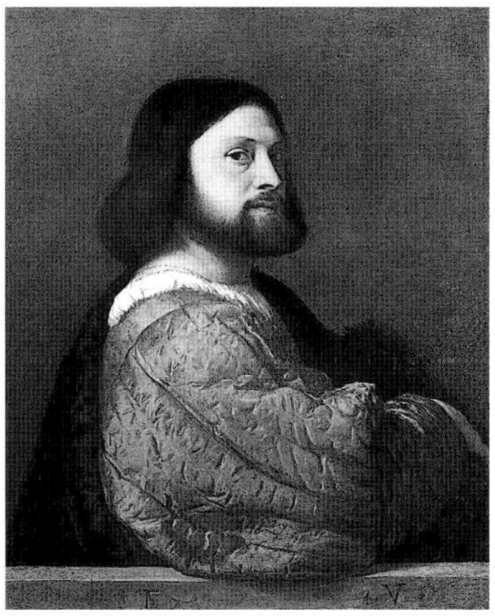

fig. 17c
Titian, *Portrait of an unknown man*, c. 1512. Canvas, 81.2 x 66.3 cm. London, The National Gallery

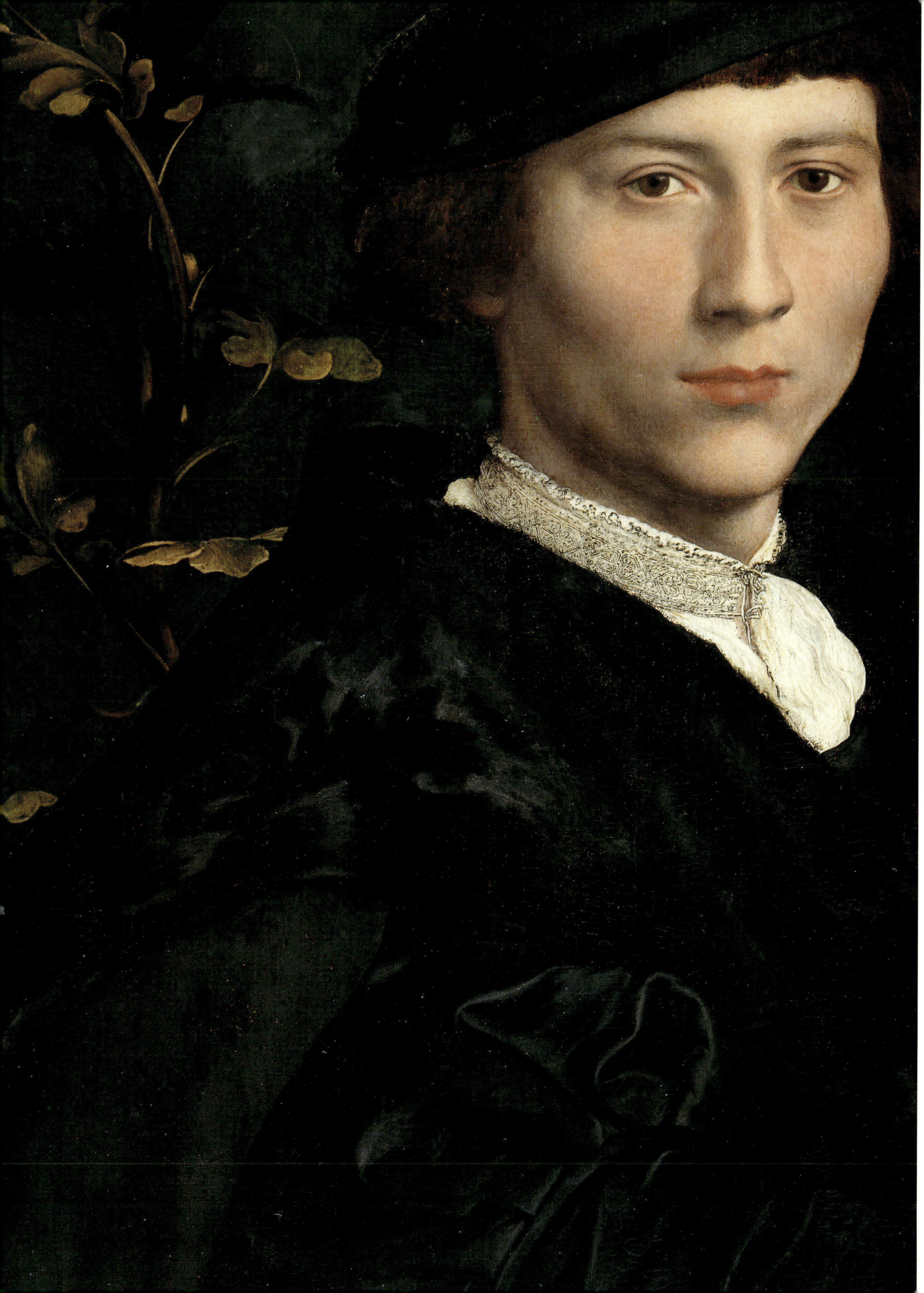

XVIII

Cyriacus Kale (c. 1501-?), 1533

Panel, 60 x 44 cm. / Inscription in left and right background: IN ALS GEDOLTIG / SIS ALTERS ·32 / ANNO ·1533·
Text on the two notes: *Dem ersamen syriacuss Kalen to Lu[n]den up stalhoff sy disser Briff* and
Dem ersamen + [esten] syriacus Kallenn in Lunde ... stalhoff sy dies[er] ..
Braunschweig, Herzog Anton Ulrich-Museum, Kunstmuseum des Landes Niedersachsen
cat.no. 18

A recurrent feature of the small group of Steelyard portraits to which this painting belongs is that the sitter appears to be seeking direct contact with the viewer by meeting his gaze (see cat. nos. 12 and 17). Nowhere is this more striking than in the portrait of Cyriacus Kale in Braunschweig. This effect is produced partly by the frontal vantage point; furthermore, Kale's massive figure almost fills the pictorial surface, while his arms are cut off by the edge of the picture. The directness is further enhanced by the fact that Kale is not positioned behind a table or a balustrade, as in most of the Steelyard portraits. This means that there is no visual barrier between the sitter and the viewer. All this lends the portrait an air of monumentality that transcends its modest dimensions. Moreover, Holbein has completely excluded staffage from the Braunschweig painting. Aside from the two notes and the gloves in Kale's hands, at the lower edge of the painting, there is nothing to distract the viewer's gaze from the sitter's fleshy face and piercing brown eyes.

◂ Holbein painted this portrait with an extremely muted palette. The black fur of the cloak, the greenish-brown satin sleeves, the gloves and the background are all depicted in similar colours. Aside from Kale's face, the white of his shirt and the notes in his hands are the only small highlights in the otherwise almost monochrome picture.

Both notes bear the sitter's name: Cyriacus Kale. The address, in German — 'stallhof' — indicates that he was a member of the London Steelyard (see cat. no. 12). The uppermost note also displays a mark consisting of a long arrow with an X beneath it and a cross in the middle — Kale's merchant's mark, which served as an additional address on the letter.[1] We know almost nothing else about Kale.[2] Because the portrait was in Braunschweig at an early stage — it was probably purchased by Duke Anton Ulrich (1633–1714) — it has always been assumed that Cyriacus belonged to the Kale family of merchants whose presence is documented in Braunschweig city archives from 1281 onwards. He may have been the son of Gerloff Kale (1446–1523), who was burgomaster of Braunschweig in 1521. The inscription in the background, 'IN ALS GEDOLTIG / SIS ALTERS · 32 / ANNO · 1533 ·', indicates that Cyriacus was born in or around 1501. It is not known exactly how long he stayed in London and whether he took the portrait with him if and when he returned to Braunschweig, or whether he had it sent from London to a relative in Braunschweig before then. In the latter case, the first part of the inscription, 'in als gedoltig' [patient in all things], besides being his own personal motto, could also have been intended as a message to his relatives admonishing them to wait patiently for him to return home.[3] PP

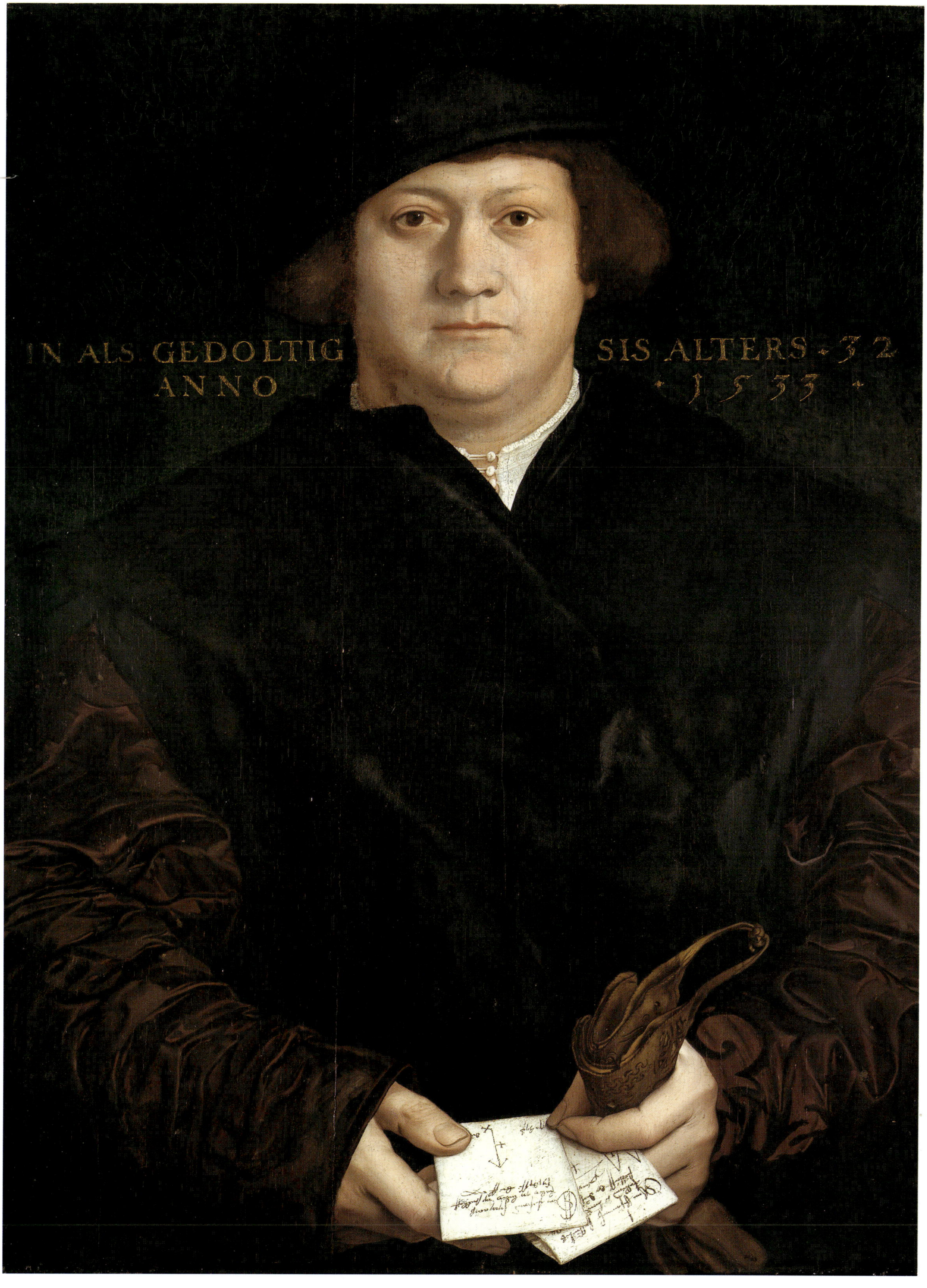
IN ALS GEDOLTIG
SIS ALTERS · 32
ANNO
· 1533 ·

XIX

Robert Cheseman (1485–1547), 1533

Panel, 58.8 x 62.8 cm / To the sitter's left and right: ROBERTVS CHESEMAN . / ETATIS . SVAE . XLVIII . / ANNO . DM̄ . / M . D . XXXIII .
The Hague, Royal Cabinet of Paintings Mauritshuis
cat.no. 19

The Latin inscription informs us that this painting from 1533 is a portrait of Robert Cheseman (1485–1547) at the age of 48.[1] Cheseman, a nobleman who was held in high regard at the court of Henry VIII, is dressed in a tabard with slits at elbow level to put the arms through. Under this he wears a red jerkin and a black garment glimpsed near the collar of the tabard. The different materials of Cheseman's clothes are rendered very convincingly. Holbein has also devoted a great deal of attention to the play of light on the creased satin sleeves. The meticulous rendering of the white shirt's smockwork trimming further exemplifies his sense of detail.

◂ The most beautiful part of this picture is the gyrfalcon with its different-coloured feathers rendered down to the smallest detail.[2] The gyrfalcon is not only the largest of the hunting falcons but also the best equipped for the task, with its powerful claws and rapid flight. Holbein has depicted the bird in profile, fitted with hunting gear. Its hood is attached with laces, and the jess with a bell on its left leg is an aid in retrieving the creature after it has killed its prey (see also cat. no. 36). The cord of the leash with which Cheseman secured the bird is wound around the middle and ring fingers of his left hand, which is protected by a chamois glove.[3] On his other hand Cheseman wears two gold rings: a finely worked ring on his index finger, and a smaller one on his little finger.

◂ Until 1792 falconry was the prerogative of the nobility in England. Cheseman is nonetheless depicted here with a rare and precious falcon, because he held the privileged position of king's falconer.[4] Cheseman must have accompanied Henry VIII regularly on his hunting trips. A scion of a prominent aristocratic family, he held several offices in the king's service.[5] In 1531 he was made 'a Justice of the Peace' in Middlesex, his home county, and he sat on several councils appointed by the king. He often represented Middlesex at important occasions, such as the reception of Anne of Cleves (p. 30, fig. 29) as Henry VIII's fourth bride on 31 December 1539. Two years later, Cheseman was involved in the trial of Catherine Howard (1521–1542), Henry's fifth wife. That Cheseman was wealthy as well as powerful is clear from the fact that he raised troops in 1536 to be deployed against rebels in the north of England.

◂ Cheseman was the son of Joan Lawrence and Edward Cheseman, cofferer to Henry VII (1457-1509).[6] The family home was Dormans Well at Southall Manor in Norwood, Middlesex. In 1543 Robert became lord of Southall and Norwood by purchasing the manors of those names from Henry VIII.[7] Cheseman died four years later. He was buried in the local church of Norwood, where visitors can still see his tomb today. His first marriage to Eleanor, a sister of the court dignitary John Tawe, was childless. After her death, Cheseman married Alice Dacres —also related to a courtier— with whom he had a daughter, Anne.

◂ The recently completed restoration has transformed this portrait of Cheseman.[8] The image was once obscured, especially in the background and the inscription, by a yellowed layer of varnish and overpainting. In its new state the nuances of colour and the modelling of Cheseman's face have become clearly visible again, and the figure with its dark cloak and cap stands out more sharply against the now lighter background. The original uniformly blue background, the azurite pigment of which had acquired a greenish quality over the years with the ageing of the medium and remains of varnish, wholly accorded with other paintings by Holbein such as one dated 1533, in Berlin (p. 82, fig. 12b).[9] In addition, the rendering of the folds of the orange-red sleeves is very similar to that in other portraits by Holbein from the early 1530s, such as the *Portrait of Georg Gisze* (p. 26, fig. 25) from 1532 and *'The ambassadors'* from 1533 (p. 27, fig. 26).[10] The near-square format of the painting discussed here, on the other hand, is exceptional.[11] Perhaps Holbein chose this shape here to create more space for the figure in the pictorial field. The intense concentration with which Holbein has his sitter in this painting peer beyond the representation —maybe Cheseman was looking for suitable prey— gives this portrait a particularly expressive quality. The man's head is turned to the left, which is counterbalanced by the slightly raised right arm and the almost tender gesture of the right hand, with which Cheseman appears to be stroking the falcon.[12]

◂ Holbein modified parts of the composition during the painting process, as we can see chiefly along the outlines. Since the paint layers have become more transparent in the course of time, it is now possible to see with the naked eye that the thumb was reduced in size. For the rest, research has shown that the black cap was also made smaller on the left, where it overlaps the background for half a centimetre. The contours of the satin sleeves were also retouched along the lower side.[13] QB

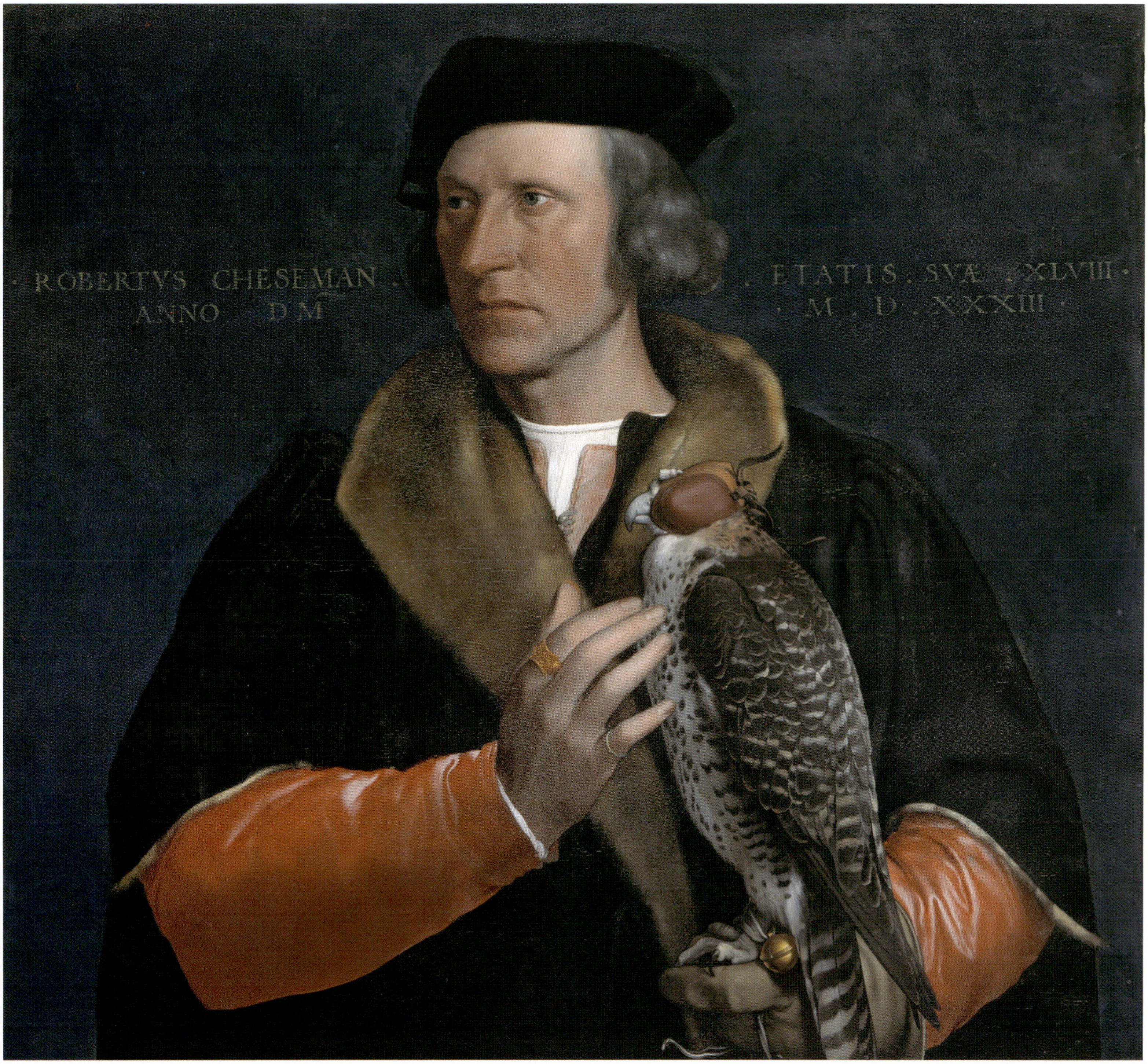

Photographed during restauration

XX

Philipp Melanchthon (1497–1560) and Decorated lid, c. 1535

panel, 9 cm diameter / Inscription inside lid: QVI CERNIS TANTVM NON, VIVA MELANTHONIS ORA, HOLBINVS RARA DEXTERITATE DEDIT / Hannover, Niedersächsische Landesgalerie
cat.no. 20

Holbein painted his portrait of Philipp Melanchthon inside the base of a small circular box. He also painted the inside of the lid, with decorative motifs surrounding a Latin inscription. Holbein often made medallion portraits of this kind,[1] but this is the only example of which both box and lid have been preserved.

◂ Medallion portraits were generally intended for personal use: they were presented as gifts to relatives, sweethearts or admirers — or, conversely, ordered by someone who wanted to possess a likeness of a loved one. Since these portraits were small and could be covered for protection, they could be carried on one's person or kept in a small cabinet together with other valuables.[2]

◂ Philipp Melanchthon played a leading role in the German Reformation. Born in 1497 as Philipp Schwarzerdt, he was given the humanist name Melanchthon —Greek for 'Schwarzerdt' (black earth)— on account of his gift for this language by his teacher at the Latin school in Pforzheim, the humanist Johannes Reuchlin (1455–1522). Melanchthon went to the university of Heidelberg at only 12 years of age, followed by that of Tübingen. In 1518, at 21 years of age, he was offered the new chair in Greek at the University of Wittenberg. This appointment would determine the course of his life, since it was in Wittenberg that he met Martin Luther. He attended Luther's theology lectures and was deeply affected by his Reformist views. He in turn encouraged Luther to study Greek. Luther's translation of the Bible into German, a milestone in the history of German culture, may have been inspired by Melanchthon, who gave a structured exposition of the principles and ideas of the Reformation in numerous influential publications, starting with *Loci communes rerum theologicarum* (1521). Through these writings, and thanks to his gift for rhetoric, Melanchthon became one of the primary spokesmen of the Reformation.[3]

◂ It used to be assumed that Holbein and Melanchthon once met, and that Holbein produced the portrait described here on that occasion, in 1529. In fact they almost certainly never met, and the portrait was most probably made later, around 1535, during Holbein's second stay in England.[4] After the founding of the Church of England in 1531, the English became interested in the Reformation in continental Europe. This interest was heightened in 1535, when Henry VIII was forced to acknowledge that the break with Rome threatened to precipitate England into political isolation: Catholic Europe was turning against him. He therefore made overtures to German rulers who were well-disposed to the Reformation and tried to forge diplomatic and religious ties with them. The duke of Saxony gave him permission to engage in religious consultations, and Henry therefore wrote to Melanchthon. In the same period, two prominent English clerics travelled to Wittenberg on Henry's instructions to discuss religious matters with Melanchthon.[5] As a direct result of these exchanges, Melanchthon sent Henry a copy of the revised edition of his *Loci communes*, an English translation of which appeared the following year, with a title page designed by Holbein. Strikingly, some of the decorative elements on the title page —the music-making fauns and the curved lines of the foliate motifs— recur inside the lid of the medallion portrait in Hannover. Given the widespread interest in Melanchthon's ideas and Holbein's collaboration in the illumination of his book, it is quite plausible that an English admirer of Melanchthon ordered the portrait from Holbein around this time.[6]

◂ It was unusual for Holbein to work without the subject posing for him, but the result shows that this was clearly not an insuperable obstacle. Several artists had already produced portraits of the popular Melanchthon by 1535. Holbein probably took as his models a copperplate engraving by Albrecht Dürer from 1526, which depicts Melanchthon virtually in profile,[7] and a painted portrait by Lucas Cranach the Elder —or one of the many copies made of it— which adopts a more frontal perspective.[8] Even though he had no direct contact with his subject, Holbein succeeded in producing a lifelike rendering of Melanchthon's refined features. He may have slightly exaggerated his subject's paleness to identify him as a scholar. The clear gaze and astute expression emphasise Melanchthon's intrepid nature and formidable intellect. The Latin inscription inside the lid —possibly written by Henry's court librarian John Leland— is an ode to the painter's virtuosity: 'Behold Melanchthon's features, almost as if alive: Holbein has captured them, with a skill defying belief'.[9] PP

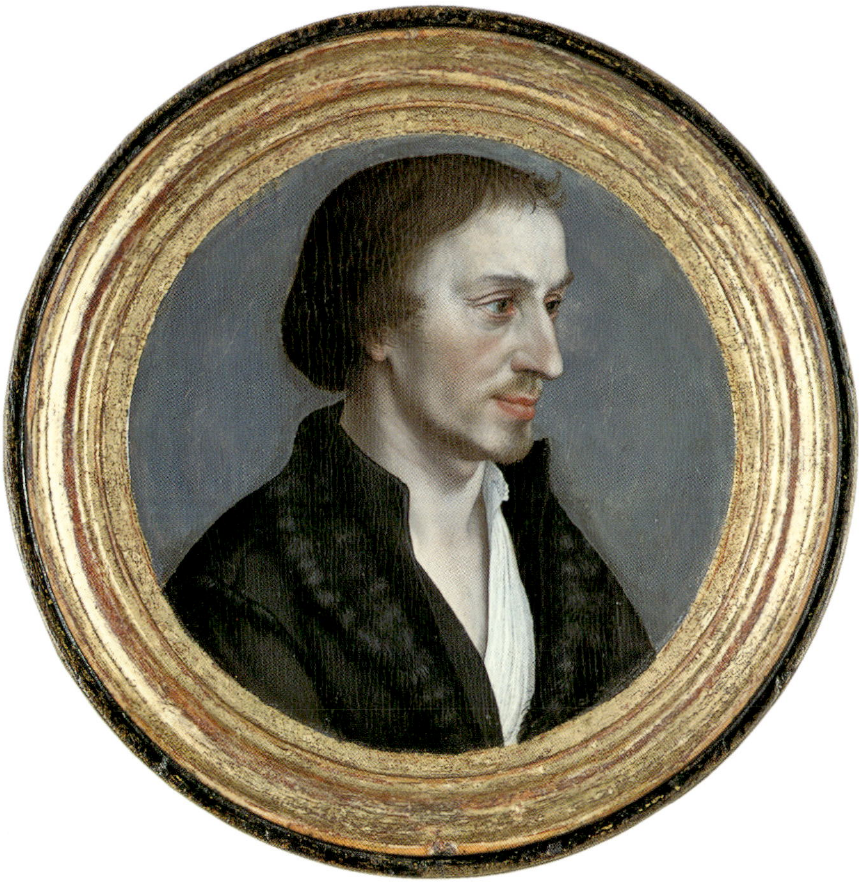

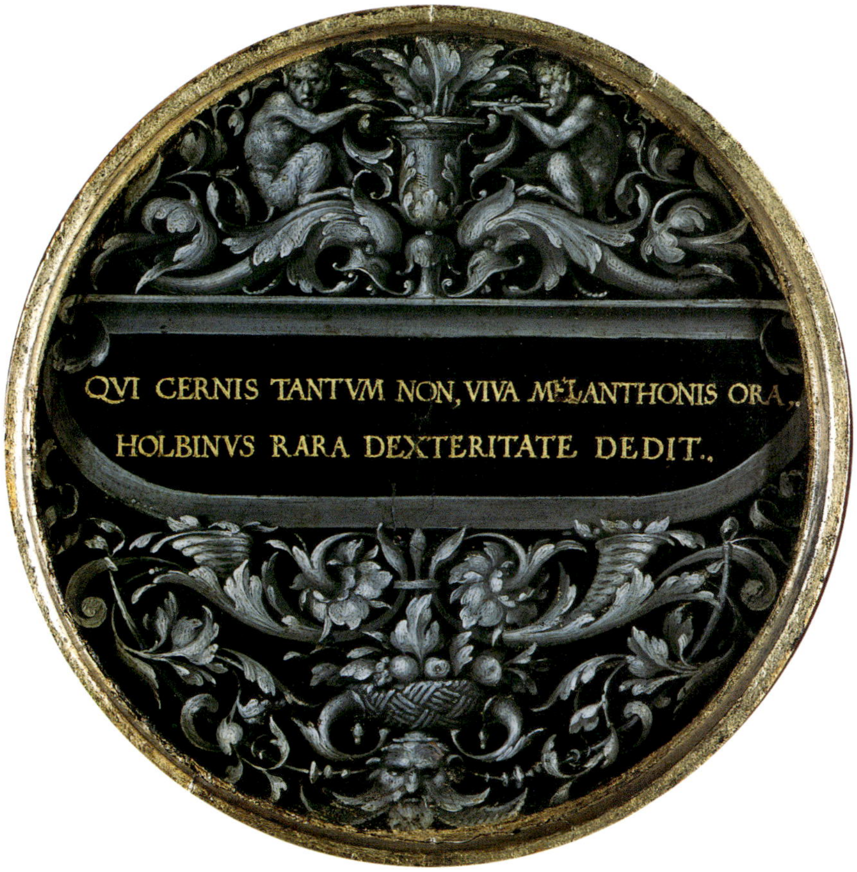
QVI CERNIS TANTVM NON, VIVA MELANTHONIS ORA,
HOLBINVS RARA DEXTERITATE DEDIT.

Richard Southwell (1503/4–1564), c. 1536

Black and coloured chalks, pen and brush and black ink, metalpoint, on pink prepared paper, 366 x 277 mm
At centre left: [A]NNO and, in a later hand, RI / At centre right: ETTATIS SVA[E] / .33 / and: *die augen ein wenig gelbart*
At upper left, in a later hand: Rich: *Southwell Knight.*
Lent by Her Majesty Queen Elizabeth II
cat.no. 21

Richard Southwell, a son of the wealthy country gentleman Francis Southwell of Norfolk, was one of the most ambitious, loyal and ruthless of the men who worked for Thomas Cromwell.[1] In 1531 he was involved in a murder, but after paying a fine of 1,000 pounds he was allowed to go free. In spite of this stain on his character, he was appointed sheriff of Norfolk and Suffolk in 1534. From that time onward, he was involved in the dissolution of the monasteries, which proved a very lucrative occupation. Thus, in 1536 he became Receiver of the Court of Augmentations, a new government body that was responsible for transferring the property owned by the monasteries in England to the Crown.[2]

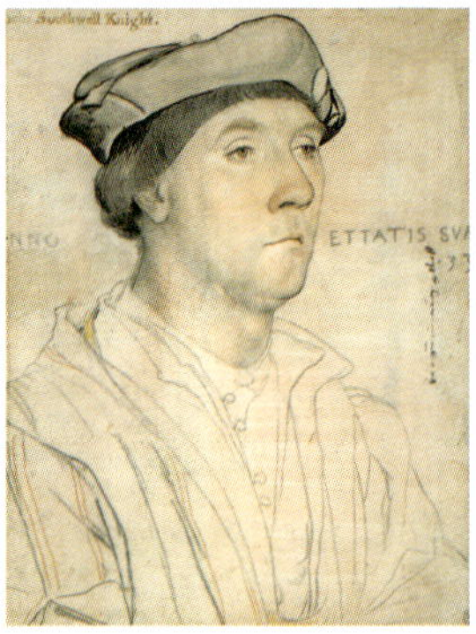

◂ Southwell became a member of parliament for Norfolk in 1539, and three years later he was raised to the peerage. During the reigns of Edward VI and Queen Mary he was a member of the Privy Council. That even a loyal servant like Southwell could not always be certain of his life is clear from the fact that he was imprisoned for a time in 1549 following a charge of sedition. Southwell played an unsavoury role in the conviction of Thomas More in 1535: he was present in the Tower when More was interrogated by the Solicitor General, Richard Rich,[3] but later denied that he had heard More's replies, after which More was sentenced to death on the basis of Rich's perjury.[4] Southwell was also one of the accusers in the trial of his boyhood friend Henry Howard,[5] the son of the Duke of Norfolk, Thomas Howard (cat. no. 34), who was executed for high treason in 1547.[6]

◂ Most exceptional in Holbein's portrait of Richard Southwell in the Uffizi is its gold inscription with a very precise date, namely 10 July of the 28th year of Henry VIII's reign — in other words 1536, since the king had been crowned in June 1509.[7] The sitter was undoubtedly seeking here to express his loyalty to the sovereign, but whether anything particular happened on 10 July 1536 that could have prompted him to commission a portrait is unknown. The date on the panel also helps to date the preliminary portrait drawing of Southwell in Windsor Castle, which was probably made the same year. In the case of most of Holbein's drawings from his second English period, the date is a matter of guesswork.[8] The drawing of Southwell is also the only one with an inscription in the background, in capitals, written by Holbein himself. The inscription, giving Southwell's age, is similar to those on his painted portraits, but differs slightly from the one on the panel. The sheet has been cut along the sides —virtually all of Holbein's portrait drawings in Windsor Castle were reduced in size— removing some of the letters. Very different in nature is the vertical inscription that the artist added in pen at centre right: 'die augen ein wenig gelbart' (the eyes a little yellowish). This note was undoubtedly intended to jog the artist's memory when painting, since Southwell was not present and Holbein had to base himself on his study.

◂ The modern viewer may see Southwell's half-closed 'yellowish' eyes and thin lips as reflecting the deviousness bespoken by the events of his life, but neither the artist nor the client will have had anything of the sort in mind. Holbein has drawn the face in chalk, with immense feeling for detail, subsequently enhancing the lines in the face subtly with the pen. In the hair and the cap he chose to enhance the lines with brush and black ink. The right contour of the face has been marked with metalpoint or hard chalk.[9] The chalk lines denoting the clothing have been traced with the same material, all of which was undoubtedly done for the purpose of transferring the composition to the panel.[10] With care Holbein rendered the small scars on his sitter's neck and forehead, which have sometimes been misconstrued as blemishes on the paper, and followed them faithfully in the painting.[11] The drawn contours of the clothing, such as those of the four black buttons that stand out against Southwell's white shirt, were also followed meticulously. In the painting the artist followed the line of the neck drawn in ink in the drawing, not the original chalk line to its left.[12] The heavy gold chain is indicated in the drawing with yellow chalk, and only the outline is given of the medallion on the cap. Holbein has elaborated this jewel in detail: it is a red coral woman's head in relief—possibly

Richard Southwell (1503/4–1564), 1536

Panel, 47.5 x 38 cm / At centre left: .X°.IVLII. ANNO. / .H.VIII. XXVIII°.
At centre right: ETATIS SVÆ / ANNO XXXIII.
Florence, Galleria degli Uffizi
cat.no. 22

Lucretia— mounted in gold.[13] Southwell's smoothly shaven cheeks and his hairstyle were going out of fashion in 1536, when gentlemen were starting to cut their hair short and grow beards.

◂ The absence of arms and hands in the drawing suggests that the sheet was also cut along the lower edge. In the painting, by contrast, Southwell's right arm and his hands, one folded over the other, seemingly resting on the frame, are an important element of the composition. The shadow that the figure casts on the even bluish-green background, combined with an inscription, is exceptional. It creates the impression that the sitter is enclosed within a very small space between the background and frame, enhancing the figure's plasticity. The rendering of the different black materials of the clothing, ranging from shiny satin to matt velvet, and the play of light on them, exemplifies Holbein's consummate skill.

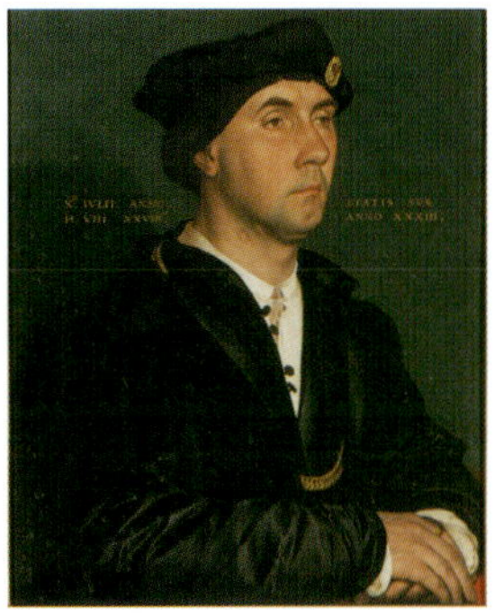

On 12 September 1620, Grand Duke Cosimo II de' Medici of Tuscany wrote to Thomas Howard, Earl of Arundel, a famous collector of Holbein's art, telling him of his desire to own a painting by the German master.[14] Arundel responded by giving the Grand Duke Southwell's portrait, in February 1621. In the accompanying letter he described the work as 'una pittura delle migliore et meglio conservate' (one of the best and one of the best preserved paintings). For the occasion he even had a new ebony frame made for the painting, with four silver medallions, enclosing names among which were those of Holbein and Richard Southwell, 'private counsellor to Henry VIII'.[15] One wonders whether Arundel was aware, in 1621, of the disgraceful role that Southwell had played in the execution of his great-grandfather Henry Howard, almost three-quarters of a century before. Perhaps this was precisely why he decided he could do without this portrait, which has remained in Florence ever since.[16] AvS

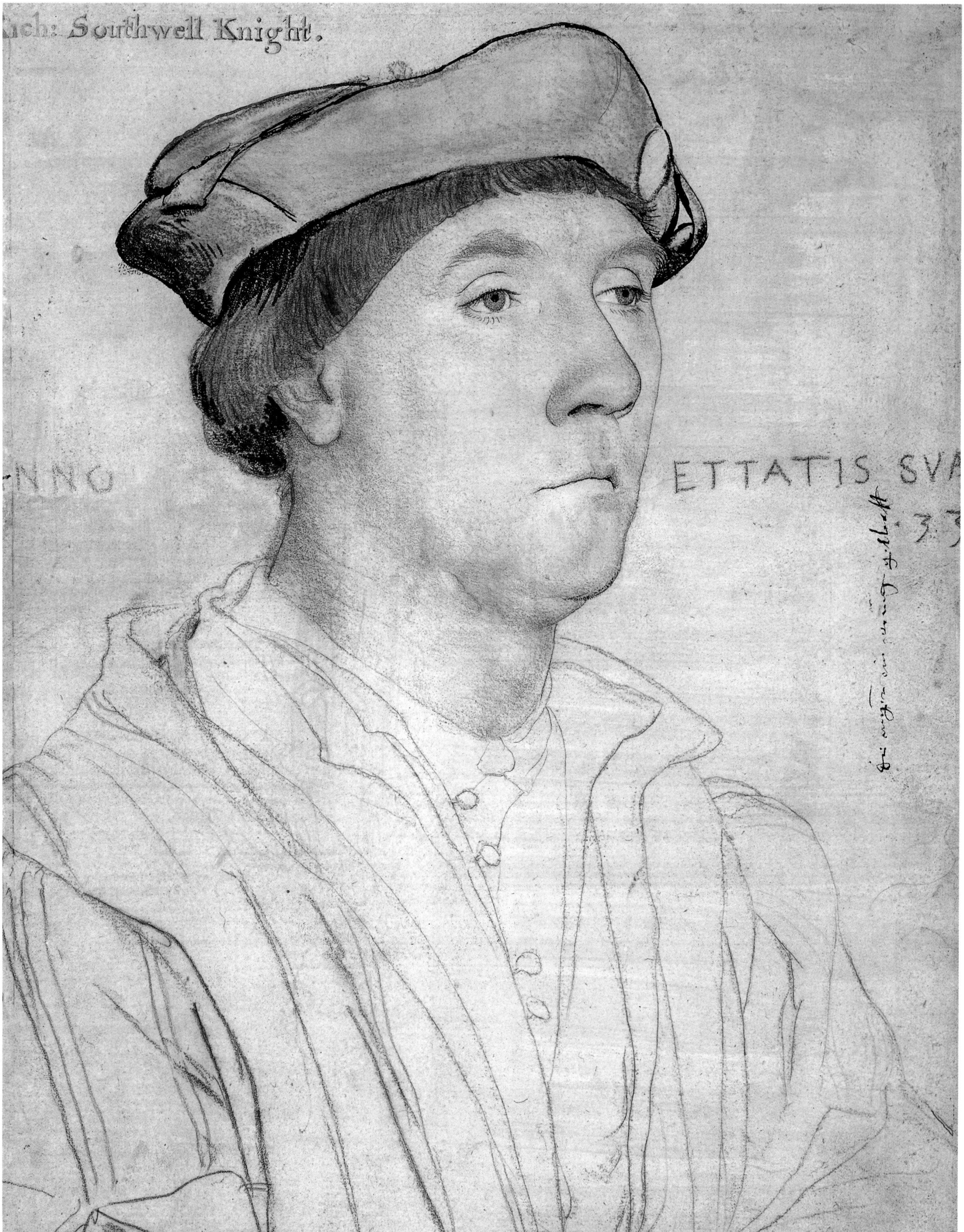
ich: Southwell Knight.
NNO
ETTATIS SVA

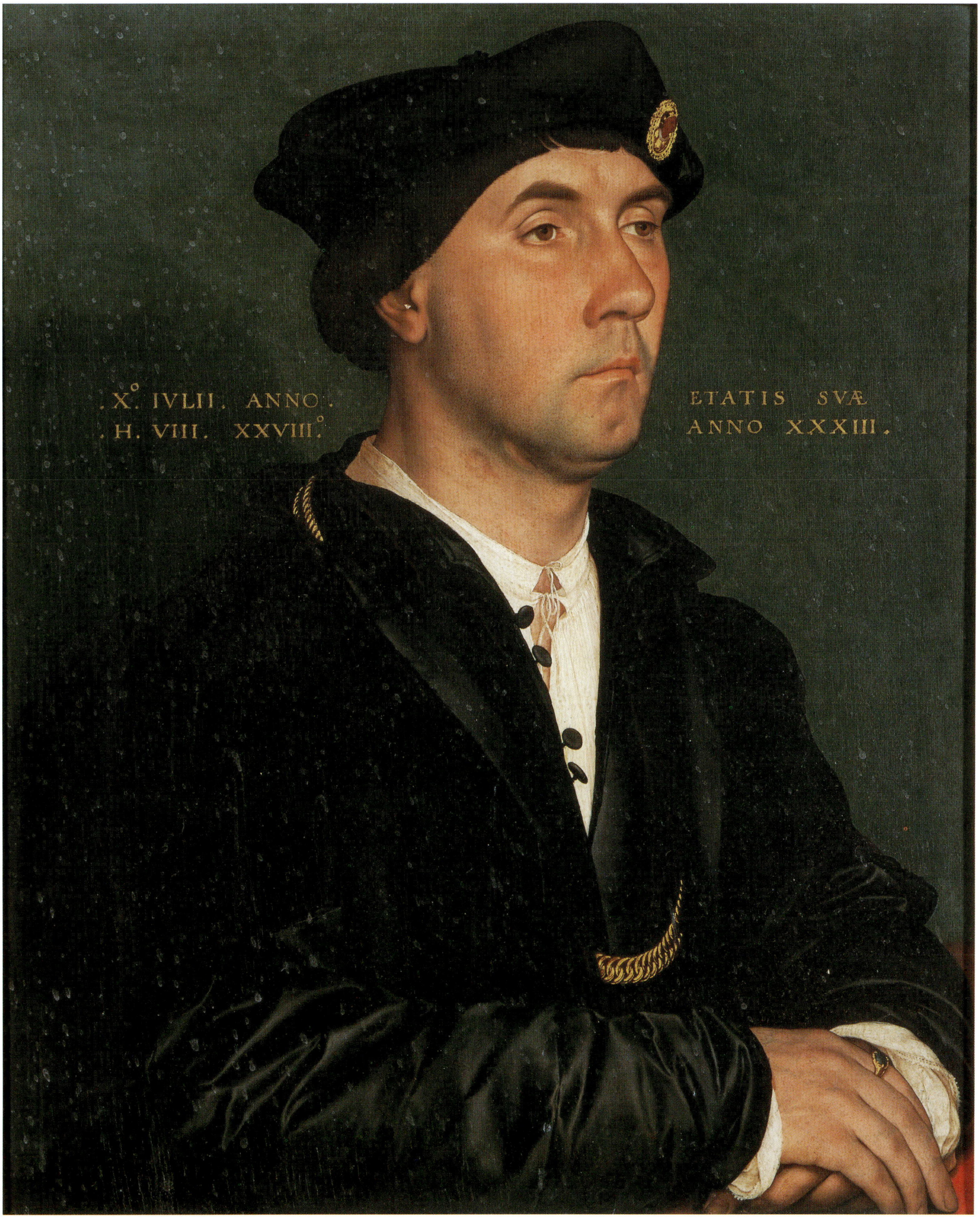
.X.º IVLII. ANNO.
.H. VIII. XXVIII.º
ETATIS SVÆ
ANNO XXXIII.

Thomas le Strange (1493–1545), c. 1536

Black and coloured chalks, brush, metalpoint, on pink prepared paper, 243 x 210 mm
At upper left, in a later hand: *Tho: Strange Knight.*
Lent by Her Majesty Queen Elizabeth II
cat.no. 23

Thomas le Strange came from Hunstanton in Norfolk.[1] In 1501, at only 7 or 8 years of age, his parents arranged for him an advantageous marriage to Anne Vaux, who would bring sixteen children into the world.[2] Le Strange became Esquire of the Body of Henry VIII in 1520, and accompanied the king to the Field of the Cloth of Gold near Calais, where Henry conducted peace negotiations with King Francis I of France in a gold tent, a regal meeting of unprecedented grandeur, which however failed to produce the desired peace. Thomas le Strange was knighted in 1529, and the following year he became sheriff of Norfolk and Suffolk. As the representative of the Crown, he was actively involved in the dissolution of the monasteries in England. He was responsible, for instance, for an investigation into the revenue of Walsingham Abbey in Norfolk, which led in 1538 to the destruction of England's most famous mediaeval place of pilgrimage.

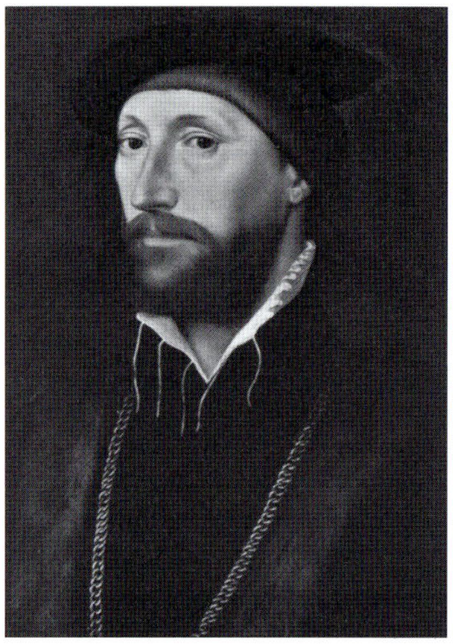

afb. 23a
Hans Holbein the Younger, *Portrait of Thomas le Strange*, 1536.
Panel, 41 x 28.5 cm.
Fort Worth, Kimbell Art Museum

◂ Holbein's portrait drawing of Thomas le Strange was most probably a preliminary study for a painting, which has not however been preserved. On a flesh-coloured preparatory layer he sketched his sitter using chalks of different colours, after which he added washes with the brush in the cap and the hair. After that the most important lines in the face, along the hair, and the upright collar were traced using a metalpoint or a hard type of chalk: we can still see the slight depressions in these lines.[3] In this way the most important parts of the portrait were transferred, using an intermediate sheet of blackened paper, to the ground of the panel, which was then painted according to the example in the drawing (cf. cat.nos. 14-15). The loosely drawn chalk lines used to give a rough indication of the clothing in the drawing were not traced.

◂ A painted portrait of Thomas le Strange by Holbein —which at the beginning of the twentieth century was still in the possession of the Le Strange family in Hunstanton and was then shipped to America (fig. 23a)— was only indirectly based on the drawing.[4] It includes some identical details such as the little cords dangling from the white collar, but the face in the painting is rather larger and turned more towards the pictorial plane. Furthermore, the sitter meets the viewer's gaze and his eyes are dark instead of blue, as in the drawing.[5] At some time in the past the panel was sawn to make it smaller, after which the inscription 'ANNO DE 1536 ... AETATIS SVAE 43' was added. This later inscription, which was removed again during restoration work before 1950, may have been based on an original inscription.[6] Holbein never dated his portrait drawings, but the year inscribed on the painting in Fort Worth is an aid to help us date the drawing discussed here to the same year or just before it. AvS

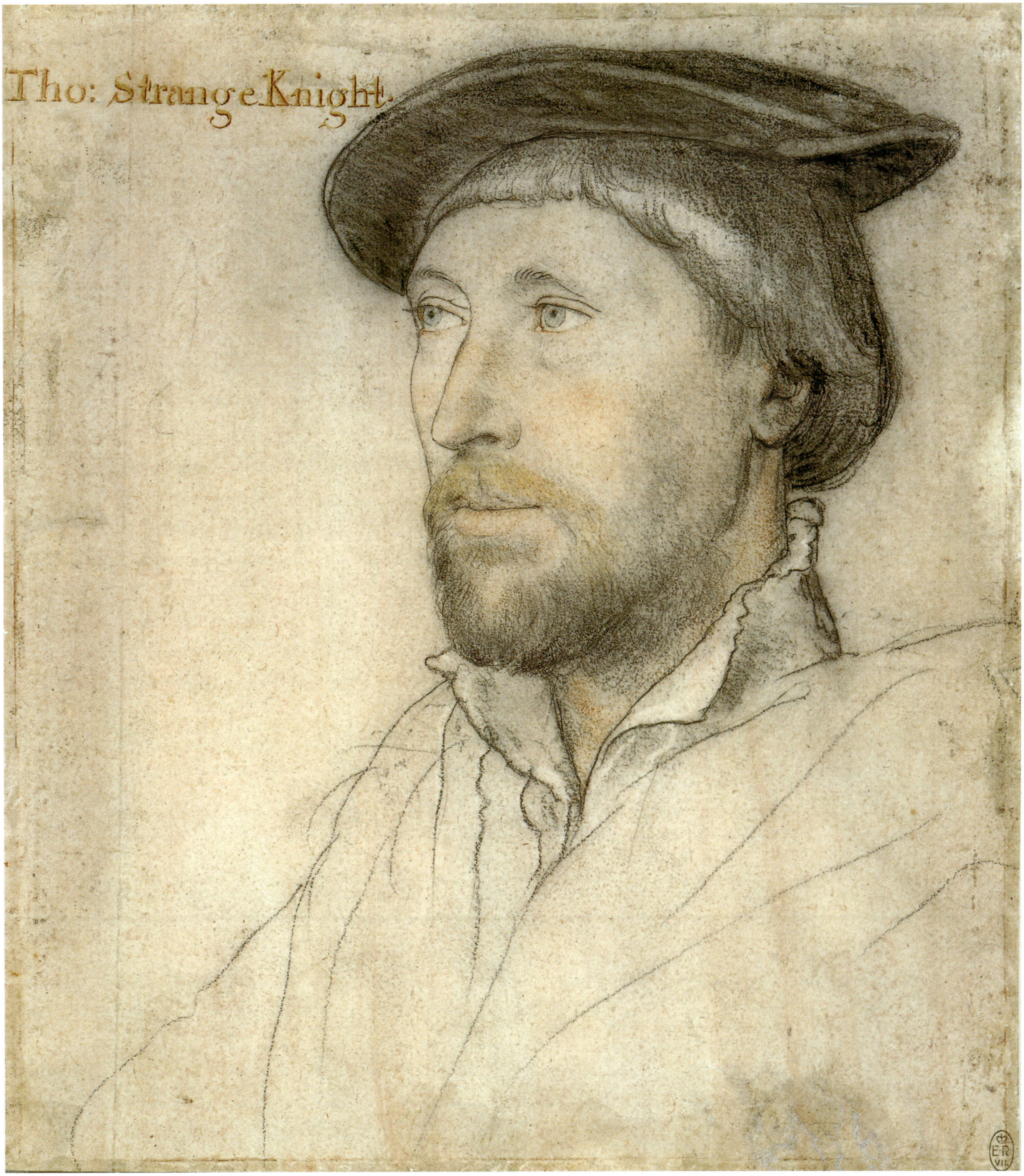
Tho: Strange Knight.

SIMON GEORGE, c. 1536/37

Black and coloured chalks, pen and brush and black ink, metalpoint on pink prepared paper, 279 x 191 mm
At lower right, in a later hand: *S. George of Cornwall*
Lent by Her Majesty Queen Elizabeth II
cat.no. 24

One striking difference between Holbein's preliminary drawing for the portrait of Simon George and the painting based on it is that in contrast to the stubble seen in the sketch, the painting depicts the sitter with a full beard. In addition, the clothing is depicted only cursorily in the drawing, while in the painting it is elaborated in detail, most notably in the fashionable black embroidery on the collar of the undershirt and on the cuffs, but also in the decorative stitching on the red shirt and the elegant pattern in the shiny black material of the cloak. Simon George's cap is decorated with an ostrich feather, gold aiguillettes, a medallion with an image of Leda and the swan, and enamelled violets. His rich apparel suggests that the sitter was a prominent citizen, but almost nothing is known about his life; we know only that his family originated from Dorset and that he married Thomasine Lanyon, a daughter of Richard Lanyon, in Cornwall.[1] We know nothing at all about the circumstances in which Holbein made his portrait or whatever ties George may have had with the court.[2] The red carnation in his right hand suggests, however, that he had his portrait made to commemorate his engagement or marriage, since this flower frequently bears such connotations.[3] In that case, a pendant portrait must have existed, showing his fiancée or bride in profile and gazing to the right, but there is no trace of any such work. Interestingly, this putative woman's portrait would hence have assumed the heraldic position of precedence, that is, to the right of the man. Generally it is the man's prerogative to be on the right, although there are other cases in which the traditional positions are reversed, as in the pendant portraits of Thomas and Margaret Elyot (cat. nos. 10 and 11).[4]

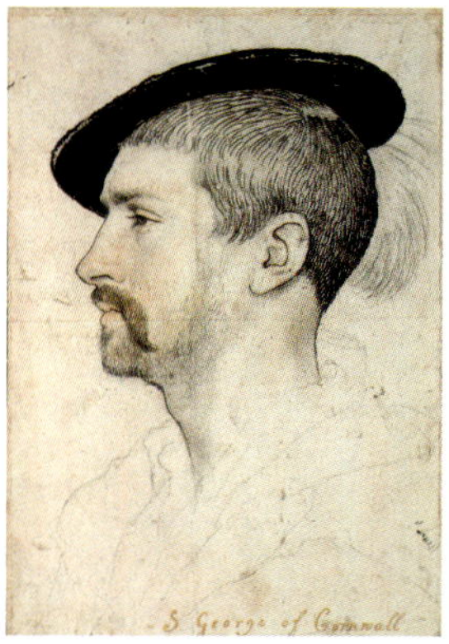

◂ Holbein drew the profile of Simon George in chalk and black ink on paper that had first been prepared with a pink ground — a practice that the artist adopted in his second English period. In the drawing under discussion he enhanced the contours of the face with pen lines of variable thickness. The short hair, drooping moustache, stubble, eyelashes and eyebrows are likewise accentuated with pen and black ink, while the cap has been coloured in using the brush. The thin chalk lines used to roughly indicate the clothing have been traced with metalpoint, probably to transfer the design to the panel. The face was probably also traced with metalpoint, but this has been obliterated by the ink that was added afterwards with pen: only by the ear lobe are traces of metalpoint still discernible.

◂ Infrared reflectography has revealed an underdrawing beneath the layers of paint on the panel.[5] The contours of the face were underdrawn very precisely using pen and brush, corresponding exactly to the preliminary study. The underdrawing also included the clothing: however, these lines differ from the eventual painted surface, although they do correspond, strikingly enough, to the sketch on paper.[6] Holbein evidently altered the costume during the painting process. He may have made a separate preliminary study of Simon

Simon George, c. 1536/37

Panel, diam. 31 cm
At centre right, in a later hand: NOBA / IOHAN[N]
Frankfurt am Main, Städelsches Kunstinstitut
cat.no. 25

George's hand, which he subsequently used as a pattern for his underdrawing on the panel. This is suggested by the rather stiff, broken lines of the underdrawing of the hand, to which a few strokes have been added freely.[7] Only two studies of hands drawn by Holbein have been preserved — sketched from life in preparation for his portraits of Erasmus (p. 50, fig. 1b),[8] but he evidently made such sketches as part of his preparatory work on other occasions.

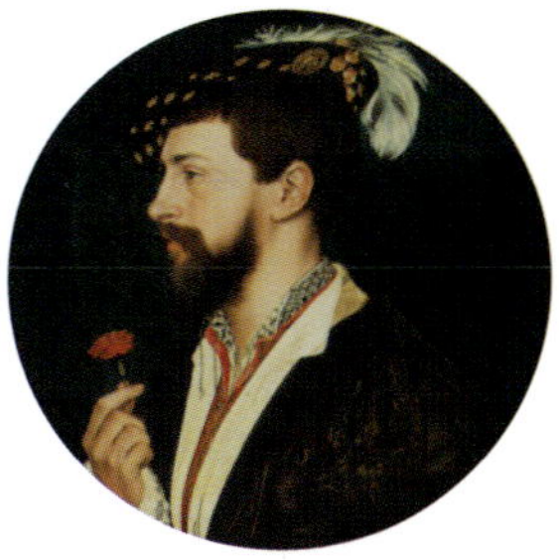

◂ X-radiography of the panel reveals that here too Holbein initially portrayed his sitter with stubble.[9] He added the beard, which he depicted overlapping the black embroidered collar, at a later stage, with the moustache protruding slightly beyond the contours of the face.[10] This latter detail has the effect of lessening the degree to which the sitter's head appears in profile, relative to the drawing. It has been suggested that George grew a beard in compliance with a decree issued by Henry VIII on 8 May 1535, ordering gentlemen at court to cut their hair short and to grow beards. In all probability, however, this decree was never actually promulgated,[11] so that the beard cannot corroborate the —perfectly plausible— dating of both drawing and painting to about 1535.[12]

◂ At some point the panel was sawn and corners were added to make it rectangular, but in about 1930 it was reconstituted in its original circular format.[13] Holbein often painted circular portrait miniatures on vellum, and other portraits on small round panels with a circumference of 10 to 12 cm,[14] but a circular portrait of this size is exceptional in his oeuvre.[15] AvS

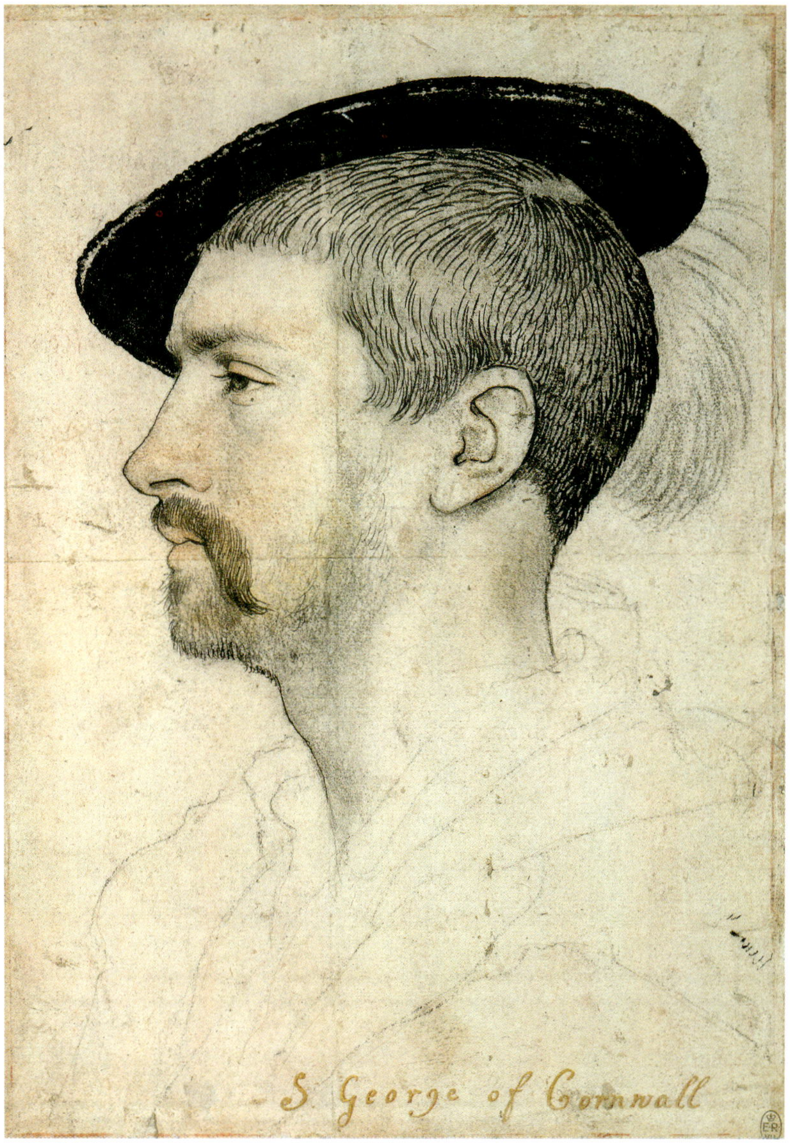
S George of Cornwall

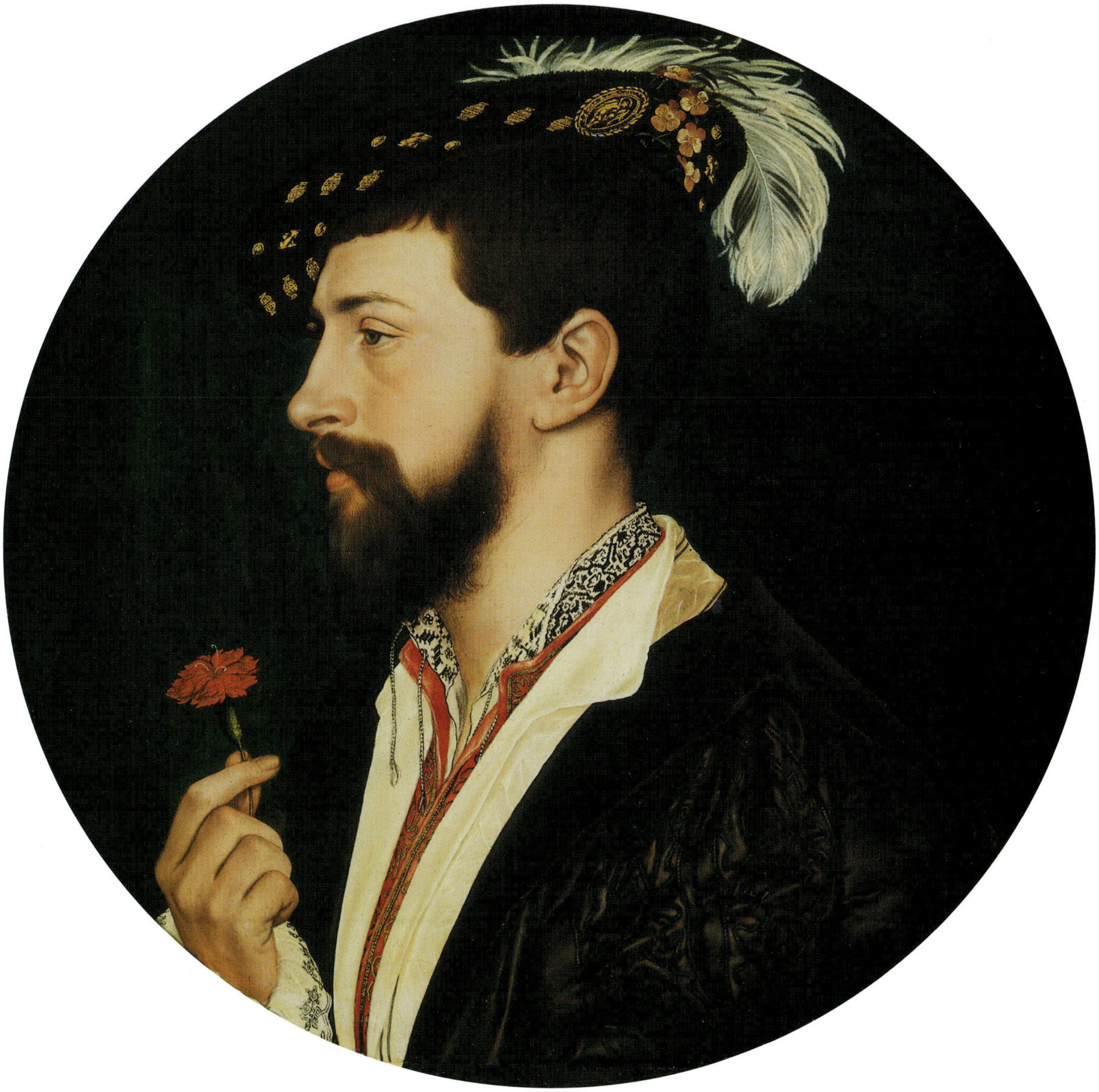

XXVI · XXVII · XXVIII

Jane Seymour (1508/9–1537), c. 1536/37

Black and coloured chalks, pen and black ink, metalpoint, on pink prepared paper,
500 x 285 mm (lower 65 mm enhanced) / At upper left, in a later hand: *Iane Seymour Queen.*
Lent by Her Majesty Queen Elizabeth II
cat.no. 26

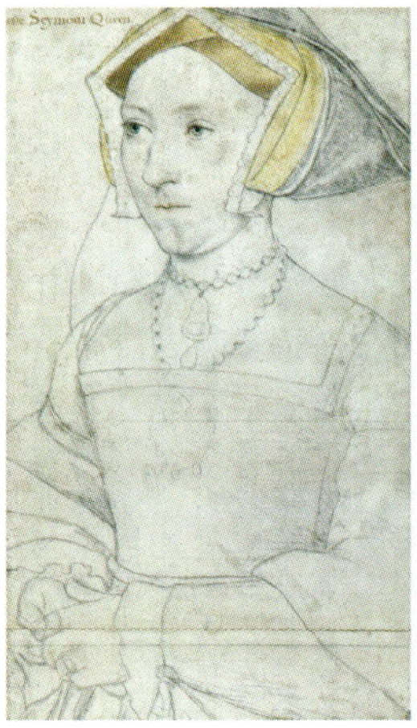

Jane Seymour (1508/9-1537), the daughter of John Seymour of Wolf Hall in Wiltshire and Margaret Wentworth, was a direct descendant, on her mother's side, of King Edward III.[3] She served as lady-in-waiting to both Catherine of Aragon and Anne Boleyn, Henry VIII's first and second wives respectively. The king became formally betrothed to Jane the day after Anne's execution, and ten days later, on 30 May 1536, she became his third wife, after which he had her proclaimed queen on 4 June. But before she could be crowned she died, on 24 October 1537, twelve days after giving birth to the long-awaited heir to the throne, Prince Edward (cat. no. 33). The mother of Henry's only legitimate son, Jane Seymour was the only one of his six wives to be given a state funeral in St George's Chapel, Windsor. In 1547, Henry was buried beside her. The king is said to have sincerely mourned the passing of his third wife, which did not however stop him casting around for someone to replace her soon afterwards. The Imperial ambassador to the English court, Eustace Chapuys, described Jane Seymour in 1536 as 'of middle stature, and no great beauty, so fair that one would call her rather pale than otherwise'.[4]

◂ The court painter Hans Holbein made several portraits of Jane Seymour in the barely seventeen months that she was queen. The most important work in which he depicted her likeness was the large mural painting of the Tudor dynasty in the Royal Palace of Whitehall in London, made in 1537, including a full-length, life-sized portrait of her, together with her husband and his parents. Though the work perished by fire, we know its composition from a small painted copy dating from 1667 (p. 32, fig. 31).[5] A cartoon drawn to scale with the portraits of Henry VIII and his father Henry VII has been preserved (p. 124, fig. 30a).[6] Holbein will undoubtedly have prepared the portraits of Jane Seymour and of Henry's mother, Elizabeth of York, with similar life-sized drawings. He will also have produced smaller-scale studies before embarking on the mural, and the portrait drawing from Windsor Castle discussed here may be one such study. Judging by the seventeenth-century copy of the mural, its depiction of Jane Seymour closely resembled the portraits described here. The copy shows her resting her left hand on the upturned palm of her right hand in an identical fashion. There are minor differences in her clothing, however. Thus, in the Whitehall mural a lappet of her headdress hung down over her left shoulder, while in the portraits described here it is pinned up. Moreover, there are no strings of pearls gracing her breast in the latter works.

Of the painted portraits of Jane Seymour once attributed to Holbein, only the one in Vienna is now believed to have been made by the master, while the smaller version in the Mauritshuis is generally described as a good copy produced in his studio.[7] The Vienna painting depicts the queen on exactly the same scale as the portrait drawing in Windsor Castle: the latter's contours were probably transferred to the unpainted panel by tracing. It is striking that the drawing's rendering of the jewellery differs from the painting in Vienna, but corresponds to the Mauritshuis version. Exactly the same may be said of the folds in the sleeves.

◂ In both paintings Jane Seymour is royally attired in garments of precious material and adorned with costly jewels.[8] However, the Vienna painting displays a good deal more pearls, gold and precious stones —in the jewellery as well as in the decoration on the clothing— and the precious stones are blue instead of red. While the undersleeves in the Hague painting are made of a white material, the Viennese version displays silver brocade that recurs in the underskirt, a garment not depicted in the former work. In both portraits Jane Seymour wears a white shift with blackwork embroidery at the cuffs; the embroidery is rather more opulent in the work in Vienna. Over this she wears separate sleeves with open undersides revealing her shift; the sleeves are held together with jewels. Her red velvet dress displays the square neckline that was customary at this time, set off with pearls and precious stones. The sleeves of this over-garment are turned well back over her arms, revealing the lining with a lattice of gold thread. Jane Seymour is always depicted wearing a gable hood (cf. cat. no. 10), unlike her predecessor Anne Boleyn, who preferred the more modern rounded French hood.[9] Jane's hood is trimmed with a strip of gold brocade, while the border of her under-cap is decorated with pearls and precious stones. Jane Seymour insisted that her ladies-in-waiting emulate her in wearing an English gable hood instead of the more fashionable French type.[10]

◂ The shorter of the queen's two strings of pearls bears a pendant with two large stones, from which hangs a pear-shaped pearl. Next to it, in the middle of her chest, is pinned a large jewel bearing the monogram of the name of Christ, IHS, an item from Henry VIII's immensely rich jewellery collection.[11] Holbein probably rendered the queen's jewellery and clothing accurately from life. Thus, one of the inventories of Jane's property lists sleeves lined with gold thread: 'item oone peir of sleevis of crymsen satten embraudred with venice gold'.[12] We can assume that Holbein

Jane Seymour (1508/9–1537), c. 1536/37

Panel, 65 x 40.5 cm
Vienna, Kunsthistorisches Museum, Gemäldegalerie
cat.no. 27

drew more detailed studies of the precious pendant hanging from the necklace and the IHS jewel, which are indicated in the Windsor Castle drawing with a few rough chalk lines, but no such drawings have survived. It is not impossible that these jewels were based on his own designs, since Holbein was very active as a designer of jewellery and other precious items — for which Henry VIII was undoubtedly his most important patron; many of his designs for delightful pendants and other jewels have been preserved (none of which, it should be said, corresponds exactly to any jewel that appears in his paintings), but the jewels themselves have not survived the ravages of time.[13] Henry VIII had a passion for jewels, and his contemporaries described him with some disdain as draped with gold and precious stones.[14] He ensured that all his wives were richly endowed with precious jewels. For Jane Seymour he commissioned from Holbein a design for a gold standing cup, two sketches for which have been preserved (fig. 26a).[15] The priceless cup, which is listed in the royal inventories until 1626, bore Jane's personal motto 'Bound to obey and [serve]' and its decorations included the initials of the royal couple, 'HJ', linked with love knots.

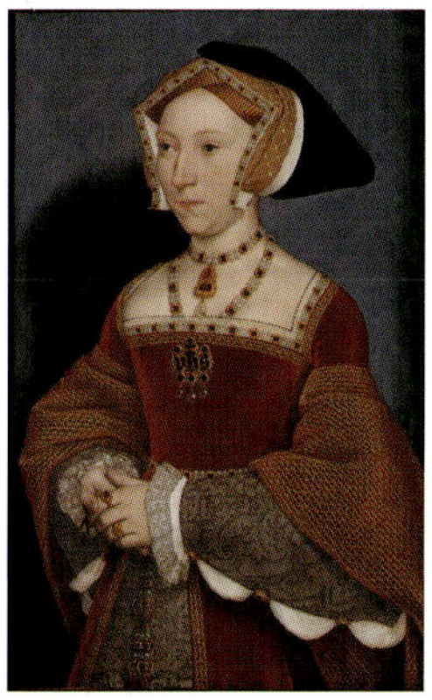

‹ While the portrait drawings from Holbein's second English period generally depict only the head and shoulders, the drawing in Windsor Castle is a three-quarter-length portrait of Jane Seymour. The sheet may have been even larger at the beginning, for it has been cut on all sides. Along the lower edge, however, the drawing has been expanded with a strip of paper 65 mm wide, on which the sleeve and part of the hands have been drawn again. Some have questioned the drawing's authenticity,[16] but the delicate rendering of the head points to Holbein's hand. The thin ink lines used to indicate the eyes, eyelashes and nose and to enhance the line between the lips are also extremely subtle and cannot prompt any doubts. The irises of the queen, who was clearly blond, have been coloured in with blue chalk.[17] Her headdress has been elaborated in various hues of chalk, beautifully suggesting the effect of light on the various different materials. In contrast, the rendering in metalpoint of the clothing and necklaces in the drawing is so stiff as to cast doubt on its authenticity. One of Holbein's assistants probably re-drew the lines in this section when they became too faint. Perhaps it was on this occasion that the strip of paper was added along the lower edge, on which the same hand continued the drawing. Two folds in the paper —at 210 mm and 55 mm from the lower edge— also reveal just how intensively this drawing was used: numerous copies were painted of such royal portraits, and it is quite possible that the drawing was consulted as an example each time afresh.

‹ The painted portrait of Jane Seymour from the Kunsthistorisches Museum in Vienna may be the 'portrait depicting one or other queen of England' by Holbein that Karel van Mander saw in Amsterdam's Warmoesstraat. In his *Schilder-boeck* (1604) Van Mander refers, in his biography of Hans Holbein, to 'a costume of silver cloth which looks like real silver [...] it almost looks as if there is some tin or silver foil underneath':[18] Holbein worked silver leaf into the brocade of the sleeve and skirt in the Vienna painting.[19] Several copies were made after this painting, all of them depicting the queen in three-quarter length and sharing the same details of clothing.[20]

‹ The artist based his composition for the Vienna panel on the drawing in Windsor Castle, the contours of which were traced and transferred to the ground of the panel through an intermediate sheet covered with black chalk (cf. cat. nos. 14–15, 21-22 and 24-25).[21] The metalpoint and pen lines in the face and headdress correspond to the underdrawing on the panel that has been revealed using infrared reflectography (IRR).[22] The underdrawing displays the highly controlled style that is characteristic of this method. The rendering of the clothing has been modified a little in comparison to the drawing, some parts of which cannot be seen with IRR because of the thick layers of paint.

‹ The pearls in the jewellery and decoration on the clothing in the Vienna portrait appear in clusters of four, alternating with precious stones. The necklaces in the drawing, on the other hand, are threaded

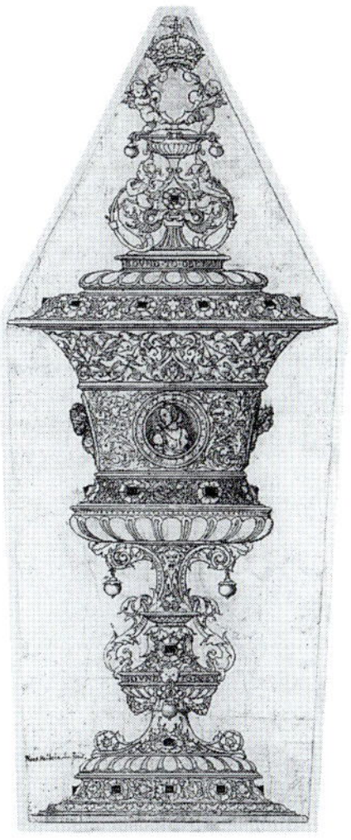

fig. 26a Hans Holbein the Younger, *Sketch for a standing cup for Jane Seymour*, 1536/37.
Pen and black ink, wash, gold paint, 375 x 155 mm.
Oxford, Bodleian Library

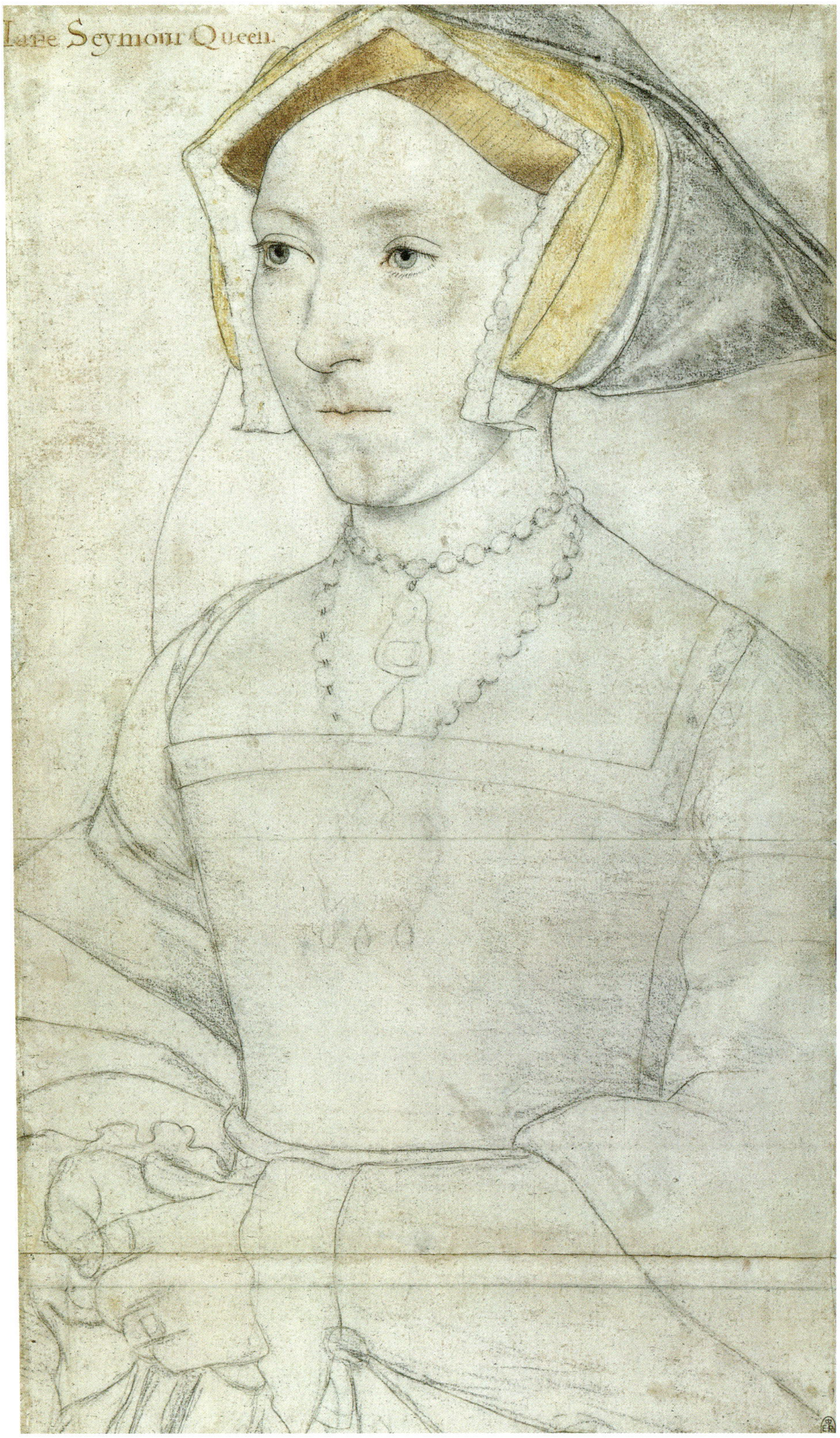
Iane Seymour Queen

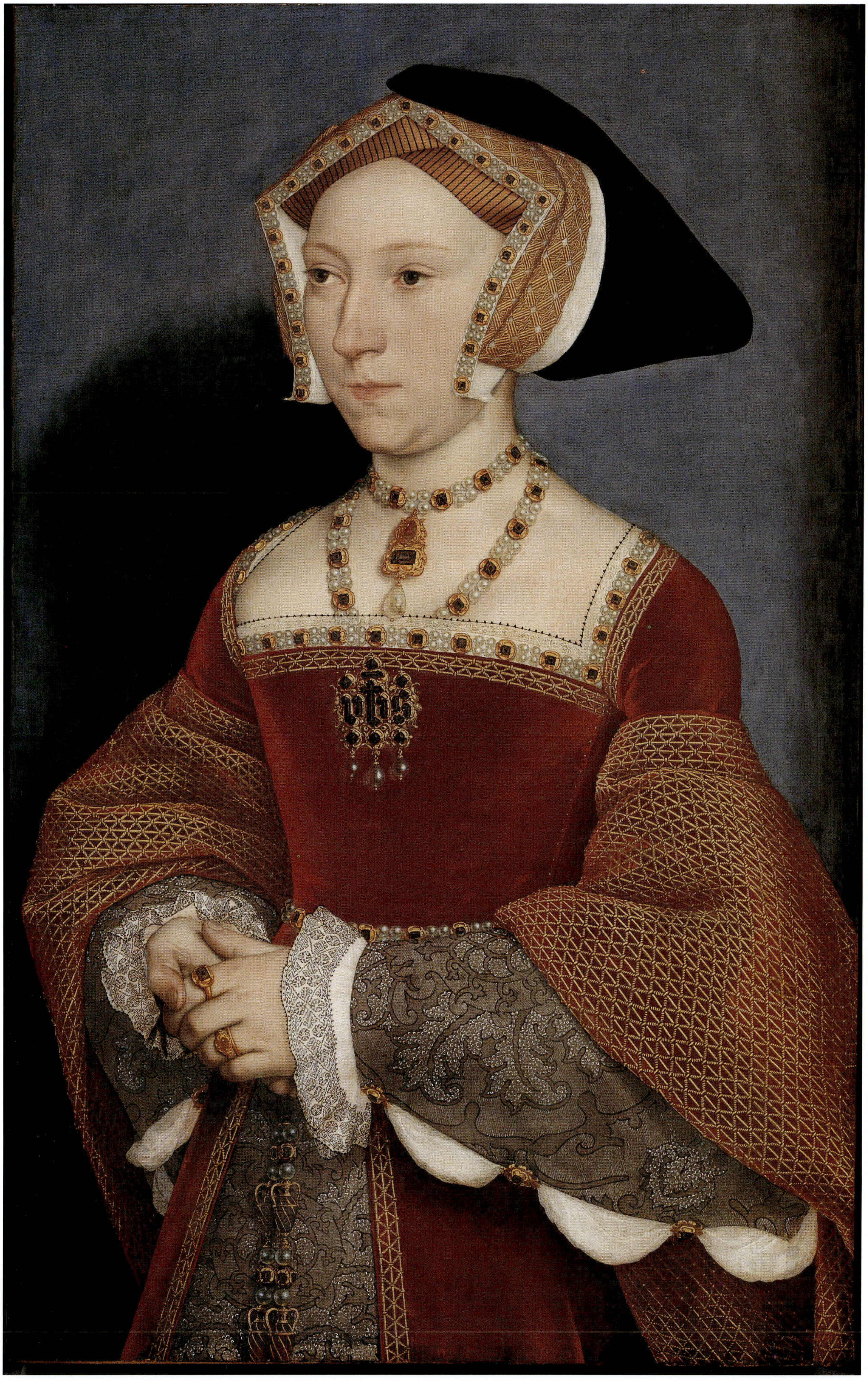

Jane Seymour (1508/9–1537), c. 1540

Studio of Hans Holbein the Younger
Panel, 26.4 x 18.7 cm
The Hague, Royal Cabinet of Paintings Mauritshuis
cat.no. 28

with single strings of pearls, depicted in an unnaturally large size. In the Viennese painting too, the decorations on the headdress consist of a pattern of four-pearl clusters alternating with precious stones, while the drawing in this section —which is by the master himself— has clusters of three pearls; Holbein appears to have deliberately deviated from his preliminary drawing here. The blue background of the painting in Vienna, which has become discoloured partly through wear, was laid in on a pink imprimatura (the first layer applied over the ground),[23] as has since been demonstrated in a number of other portraits by Holbein (cf. cat. nos. 15 and 33). The background of the Hague portrait too – now dark green but originally blue or bluish green – was built up on a pink imprimatura, but this work does not show a cast shadow to the figure's left.[24]

◂ The portrait of Jane Seymour in the Mauritshuis is of such high quality that it might well have been attributed to Holbein himself if the larger version in Vienna had not been preserved as well. The face is painted with great precision: details such as the eyelashes and eyebrows and a little vein at the sitter's temple have been rendered with the utmost care. In addition, a striking amount of gold leaf has been used in the clothing and jewellery, although part of it has worn away. In some respects Jane Seymour's clothing and jewellery are executed more simply than in the Vienna painting, although it is clear that the Hague work too must be based on the preliminary drawing in Windsor Castle that was touched up in these sections, as already noted, by a later hand. Thus, the single strings of pearls in the Mauritshuis painting correspond to those in the drawing, as do, for instance, the folds in her right sleeve; these fall differently in the painting in Vienna. One striking detail is the pendant on the string of pearls, which hangs unrealistically from a pearl in both the drawing and the Hague painting: in reality, a pearl would break under such a weight. This testifies to a lack of technical understanding of such jewels, which would have been inconceivable in the case of Holbein himself; in the Vienna painting, the pendant hangs more plausibly in between the pearls, and is attached to the string.[25] Where painterly technique was concerned, however, the maker of the Mauritshuis portrait was clearly very close to the master; he also had Holbein's preliminary drawing at his disposal.[26] Perhaps the portrait was even made by the same artist who touched up the lower section of the drawing.

◂ Dendrochronological analysis of the growth rings in the oak wood has revealed that the Hague panel was painted at some time after 1527,[27] which tallies with the hypothesis that it was made shortly after the original version of 1536–1537. In 1542 Jane Seymour's powerful brother Edward paid ten shillings to 'Hance that made quene Janes picture'. Perhaps this was for a portrait of his royal sister from Holbein's studio, given that many documents refer to the artist only by his first name.[28] It has also been suggested that the Hague panel, which King William III acquired in London at the end of the seventeenth century, was originally part of a diptych with a portrait of Henry VIII, since a royal inventory of 1547 refers to a diptych with portraits of the royal couple: 'a table like a booke, with here pictures of Kyng Henry theight and Quene Jane'.[29] However, the back of the panel in the Mauritshuis was probably never painted, as one would expect in the case of such a diptych.[30] That Holbein's portrait of Henry VIII in the Museo Thyssen-Bornemisza in Madrid served as a pendant to this (p. 28, fig. 27) is unlikely, if only because this work is entirely by the master. Furthermore, the back of this panel too has been left unpainted, and it has a different —ultramarine— background.[31] The current exhibition provides the first opportunity to compare the two painted portraits of Jane Seymour and the preliminary drawing, so that the differences and similarities between them, in terms of quality and in other respects, can be examined and perhaps re-assessed. AvS

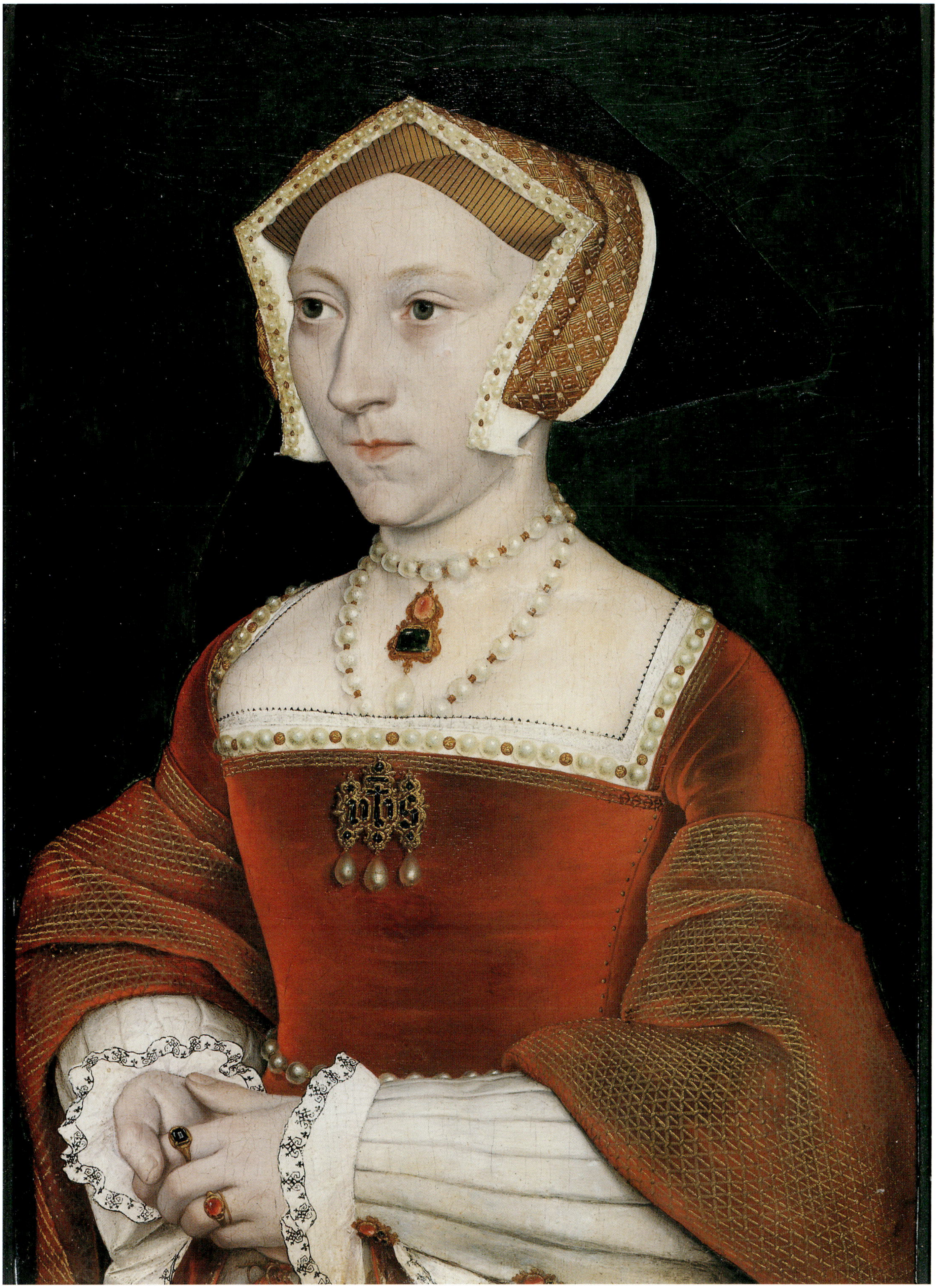

XXIX

William Fitzwilliam, first Earl of Southampton (c. 1490-1542), c. 1536/40

Black and coloured chalks, metalpoint on pink prepared paper, 383 x 270 mm
At upper left, in a later hand: *Fitz Williams Earl of Southampton.*
Lent by Her Majesty Queen Elizabeth II
cat.no. 29

William Fitzwilliam grew up at court as a companion for Prince Henry, who was the same age and shared his passion for sport. After Henry's coronation, in 1509, Fitzwilliam stayed on in the royal household, fulfilling many senior positions. However, his primary commitment was always to his military career, in which he excelled, notably in expeditions against the French. He also took part in several diplomatic missions to France. In 1513 the young Fitzwilliam was wounded while commanding the English fleet at Brest, after which he was knighted for services rendered to his country. Not long afterward he was promoted to vice-admiral of the English fleet. In 1518 William Fitzwilliam entered the service of the powerful Lord Chancellor, Cardinal Wolsey, who sent him as an envoy on a mission to Francis I in 1521. From 1524 to 1526 Fitzwilliam was encamped in France, where he helped to negotiate an Anglo-French truce. Returning home in 1526, he gained the important position of Comptroller of the King's household and was admitted to the Order of the Garter, the highest chivalric order in England. In 1529, Fitzwilliam actively helped to procure the fall of his former patron Wolsey, and that same year he succeeded Sir Thomas More as Chancellor of the Duchy of Lancaster. Henry Norris, when tried for adultery with Anne Boleyn in 1536, declared that his confession had been wrung out of him through the treacherous machinations of Fitzwilliam, who was a member of the trial bench. In August that same year Fitzwilliam's military career reached its acme with his appointment as Lord High Admiral, a position he held until July 1540. In 1537 he was made first Earl of Southampton. In December 1539 Fitzwilliam escorted Henry's fourth bride, Anne of Cleves (see p. 30, fig. 29), from Calais to her new country. Later on he would be accused of arousing false expectations in the king by praising the bride's beauty in his letters. In October 1542 Fitzwilliam died while travelling to join the war against the Scottish insurgents. Leaving no male heir, he bequeathed to the king not only his ship but also 'his collar of the Garter, with his best George beset with diamonds'.[1]

◂ Fitzwilliam is depicted wearing this precious chain in the portrait dated 1542 in the Fitzwilliam Museum, Cambridge (fig. 29a). It is a copy after a painting by Holbein that has been lost, for which the sheet described here served as a preliminary drawing.[2] The drawing has been traced with metalpoint to transfer the most important elements to the panel. The position of the chain of the Order of the Garter and the contours of the admiral's staff of office are indicated only with a few rough lines. Fitzwilliam's angular face, on the other hand, seen slightly from below, is carefully modelled with chalk, paying great attention to the effects of light on the skin. Furthermore, Holbein has taken pains to make the stubble and the characteristic hair implant of the eyebrows as realistic as possible. It is with individual details of this kind that Holbein breathed life into his sitters. Fitzwilliam's cap, on which the outline of a medallion has been sketched, exhibits the left-handed hatching in black chalk that is characteristic of Holbein: from lower right to upper left. The ribbons of the cap are tied in a bow under the fleshy chin. The structure of the fur collar is indicated only cursorily in chalk, while the rest of the clothing is indicated with a few sketchy lines traced with metalpoint.

◂ The copy in Cambridge, which was bequeathed in 1816 by the founder of the museum, Richard, 7th Viscount Fitzwilliam, is a full-length portrait of the earl, resting his admiral's staff on the ground. The background, a coastal landscape with ships, is a scene so unlike Holbein's usual settings that it must have been the copyist's invention. The full-length portrait may well have been based on Holbein's original painting, which probably perished by fire at Fitzwilliam's residence, Cowdray, in 1793:[3] the drawing already

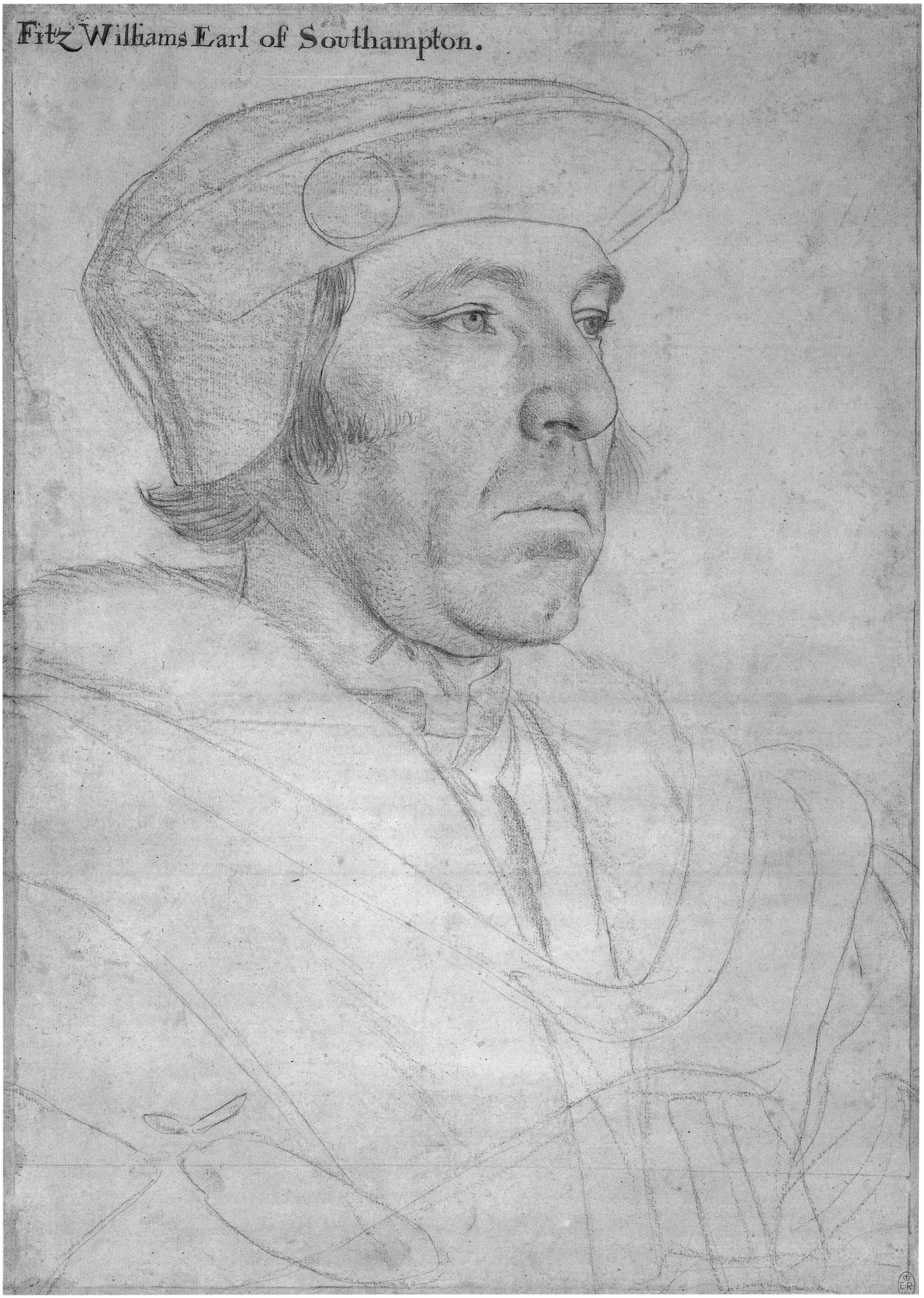
Fitz Williams Earl of Southampton.

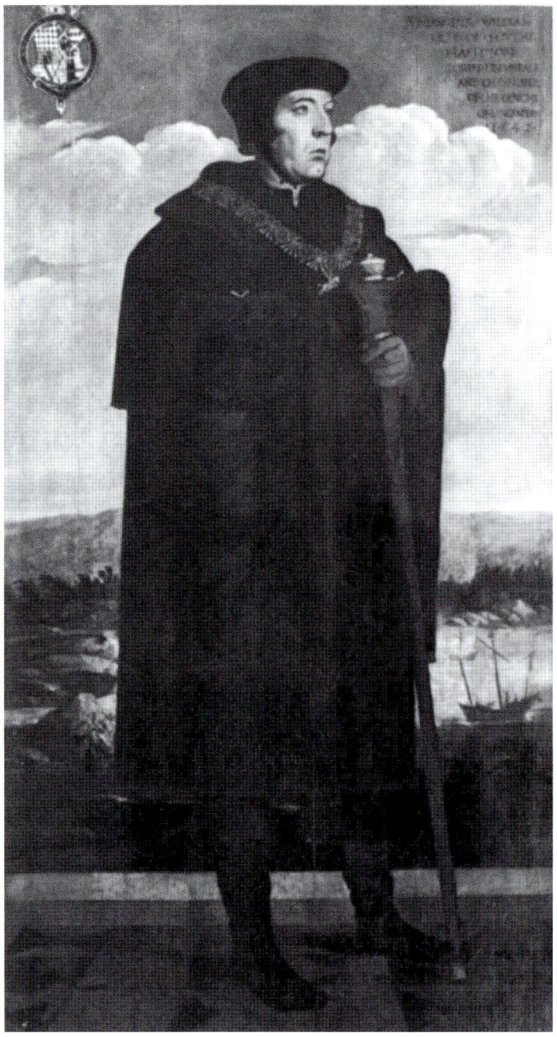

fig. 29a
Anonymous, after Hans Holbein the Younger, *Portrait of William Fitzwilliam, first Earl of Southampton.* Panel, 187.1 x 100 cm. Cambridge, Fitzwilliam Museum

displays the contours of the knob of the admiral's staff, its length almost equal to a man's height, while the viewer's low vantage point gives Fitzwilliam a martial air that comes out well in a monumental, life-sized portrait.

◂ The presence of this staff dates the drawing to between August 1536 and July 1540, when Fitzwilliam was Lord High Admiral. He had previously commissioned a portrait in 1521, while residing as an ambassador at the French court, but was dissatisfied with the result: he complained that the —unknown— artist 'did not do my portrait well ... he made [it] in haste'.[4] In the late 1530s, when Fitzwilliam's military and social power was at its height, he had no mind to take any more risks, and chose the best portraitist in England, Hans Holbein. That he probably ordered a full-length portrait —a type with a regal air, which Holbein tended to reserve, after *The ambassadors* in 1533 (cf. p. 27, fig. 26), for court commissions (cf. p. 29, fig. 28 and p. 124, fig. 30a)— speaks volumes about Fitzwilliam's pretensions. The monumental portrait was intended to be hung in Cowdray, the house in West Sussex he had purchased in 1529, where, after a series of ambitious renovation projects, he regularly entertained King Henry VIII. AvS

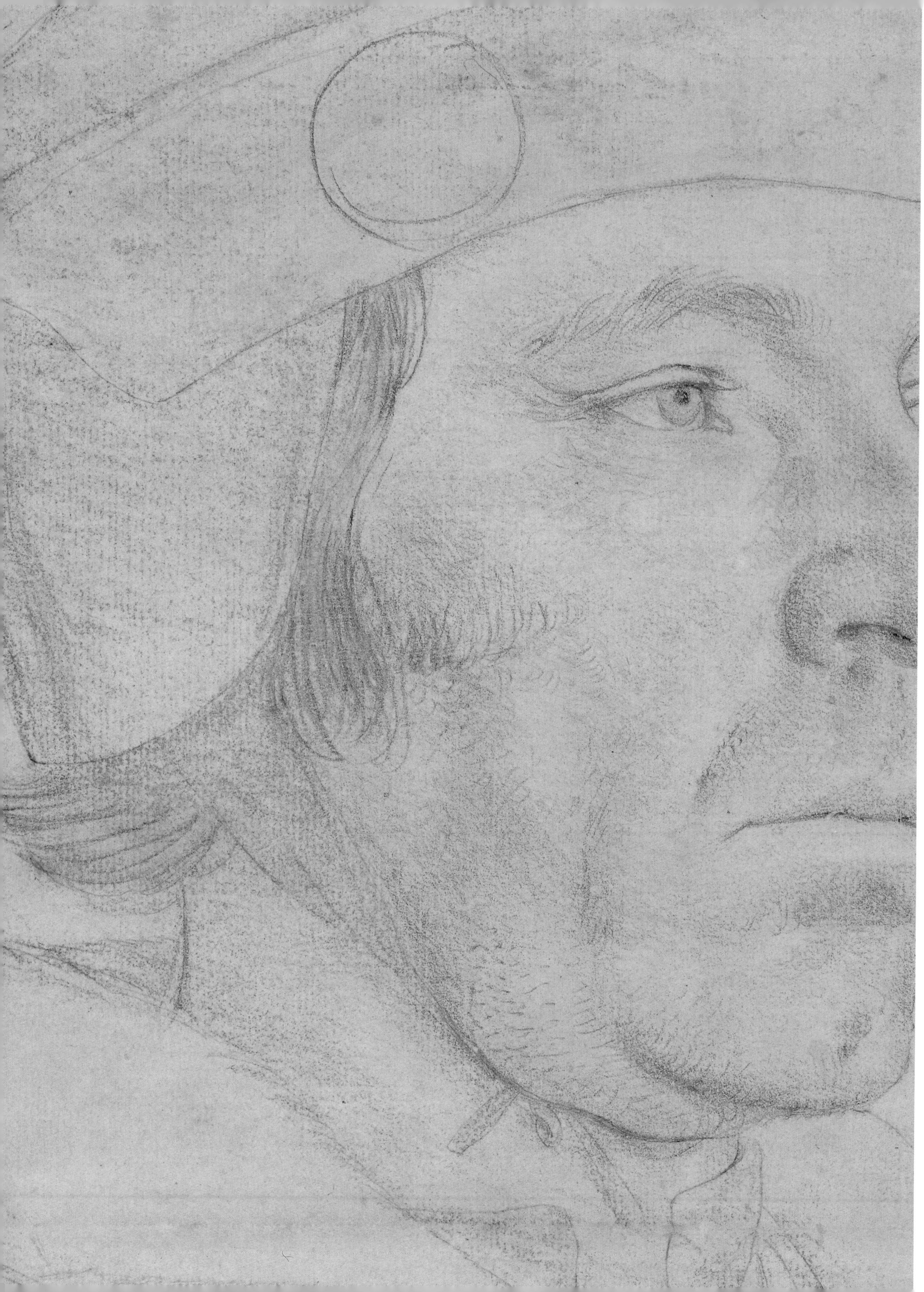

XXX

James Butler, 9th Earl of Ormond (c. 1504–1546), c. 1537

Black, white and coloured chalks, watercolour and body colour, pen and brush and black ink, on pink prepared paper, 401 x 292 mm / At upper centre, in a later hand: *Ormond*
Lent by Her Majesty Queen Elizabeth II
cat.no. 30

The inscription 'Ormond' on this sheet created some confusion about the subject's identity, since there were two rivals for the title of Earl of Ormond in the reign of Henry VIII: Thomas Boleyn (1477–1539), the father of Henry's second wife Anne Boleyn, and Piers Butler (1467–1539). After the latter's death, his son and heir James Butler (c. 1504–1546) also laid claim to the title.[1]

◂ Piers Butler was a loyal servant of Henry VIII in Ireland, who was rewarded in 1524 by being appointed Lord Treasurer of Ireland.[2] At Henry's request he had surrendered the earldom of Ormond in 1529 in favour of his cousin Thomas Boleyn, who was to be the king's father-in-law. Anne Boleyn's execution in 1536 brought about a very different situation, and two years later Piers Butler's title was restored to him: this meant that until Thomas Boleyn's death in 1539 there were two earls of Ormond. Boleyn died without leaving a male heir, so that when Piers Butler died —also in 1539— his son James was the sole Earl of Ormond. The old identification of the man on this portrait as Thomas Boleyn is untenable, since he was already well into his fifties in the 1530s, while the man depicted has a far younger appearance. James Butler, 9th Earl of Ormond, is the only candidate of the right age.[3]

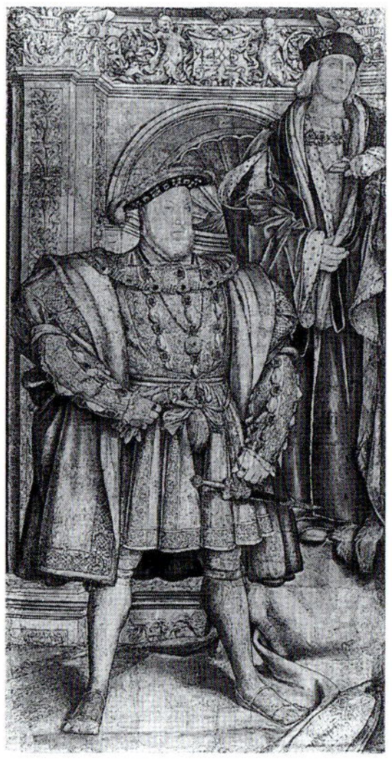

fig. 30a
Hans Holbein the Younger, *Henry VIII and Henry VII*, cartoon for the Whitehall mural, 1537. Pen in black, with gray, brown, black and red wash, on paper mounted on canvas, 257.8 x 137.1 cm
London, National Portrait Gallery

◂ James Butler, nicknamed 'James the Lame', grew up at the English court, but spent most of the 1530s in Kilkenny in southeast Ireland, which his parents had transformed into a centre of Anglo-European art and culture. In 1535 Butler became admiral of Ireland and was elevated to Viscount Thurles. Holbein may have made his portrait in the autumn of 1537 while he was staying at the English court to attend Prince Edward's christening, after a visit to the Netherlands.[4] In this period, James Butler successfully applied for the restitution of the estates and title of Ormond to his family. A dating of the portrait to 1537 would also appear consistent with Butler's apparel, since Henry VIII wears clothes cut in the same fashion, though richer in execution, in the life-sized cartoon depicting him with his father Henry VII that Holbein made for the mural of 1537 (which perished by fire) in Whitehall Palace (fig. 30a). The upper sections of both men's jerkins are tied such as to form a deep V-shape, which is covered by a chest-piece with a straight neckline and slits — in Butler's case exposing his white shirt. Over the jerkin, of which part of the skirt is also visible, Butler, like the king, wears a gown with big puffed sleeves. Both men have black ribbons around their necks, each probably attached to a relic or amulet worn under the clothing.[5] James Butler, who died of poisoning while visiting London in 1546, was not in fact Earl of Ormond yet in 1537, as the inscription on the drawing suggests: the explanation is probably that John Cheke did not identify the portrait until years after it was made.[6]

◂ In the portrait described here, Holbein again displays his wonderful control of his drawing materials, which included the paintbrush as well as chalks and pen. He used the tip of his brush for his bold delineation of Butler's clothes and of his hand, which rests on the edge of an imaginary frame. The artist had previously used this *trompe l'oeil* motif in his portrait drawing of John Godsalve (cat. no. 13). These two portraits are also similar in execution, although James Butler's portrait is sketchier than that of Godsalve, especially in the rendering of the sitter's right sleeve and hand. The fact that washes have only been added to the red beret and the chest-piece gives the impression that the sheet is unfinished. Perhaps it was not originally intended to serve as a preliminary study for a painting, but as a portrait on paper in its own right. AvS

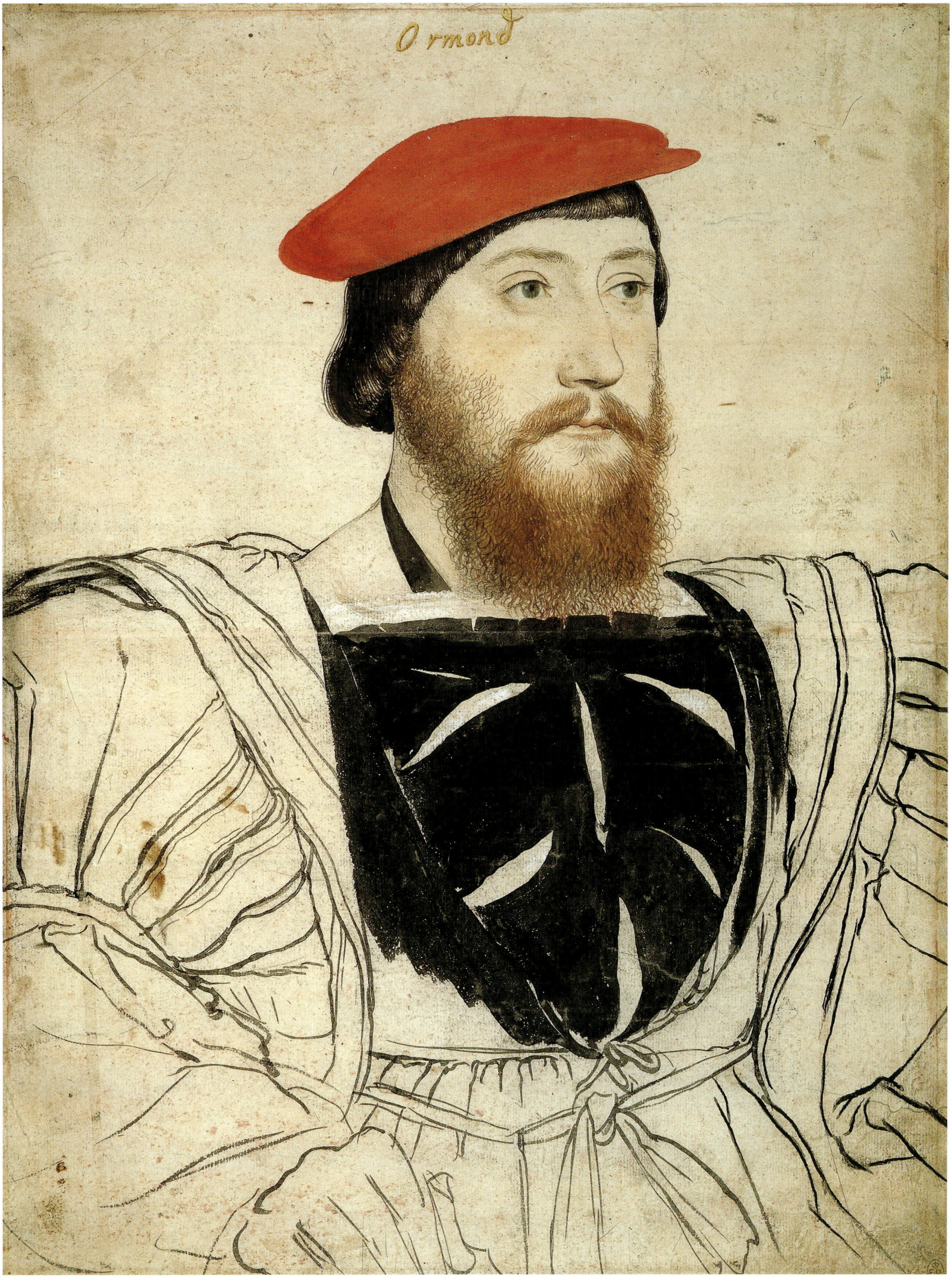
Ormond

XXXI · XXXII

Lady Elizabeth Audley (?-1564), c. 1538

Black and coloured chalks, pen and black ink, metalpoint on pink prepared paper, 292 x 207 mm
Annotations by the artist in metalpoint: *samet, rot damast, rot, w, go* [?], small heart-shaped leaf [denoting the colour green]
At left and at upper centre, in a later hand: *The Lady Audley*
Lent by Her Majesty Queen Elizabeth II
cat.no. 31

So versatile was Holbein, and so extraordinarily gifted as a painter, that he could make portraits of any size, from murals covering entire walls (see p. 32, fig. 31) to miniatures measuring no more than a few square centimetres (cat. no. 35) In 1528, Holbein added decorated initials to a manuscript by Nicolaus Kratzer, the astronomer at the court of Henry VIII, which shows that he was already familiar with the technique of painting miniatures on vellum at this time.[2] His earliest independent miniature —dating from about 1534— depicts the Queen of Sheba presenting gifts to King Solomon (whose features some have compared to those of Henry VIII) (fig. 31a).[3] This image, painted in shades of grey, reminds us that the art of limning (painting miniatures) developed from book illumination. However, this work is an exception within the oeuvre of Holbein, to whom a small group of thirteen to fifteen portrait miniatures can be attributed.[4]

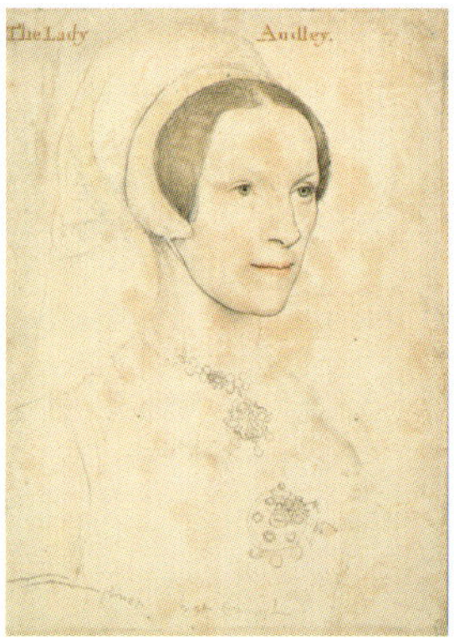

◂ Karel van Mander's *Schilder-boeck* (1604) relates that Holbein learnt the art of painting miniatures from an artist working for the king, one master Lucas, whom he soon surpassed 'as the light of the sun outshines that of the moon'.[5] The master in question was undoubtedly Lucas Horenbout (c.1490/5–1544), who came from a Ghent family of book illuminators. Horenbout worked at Henry VIII's court from about 1525 onward, making portrait miniatures of the king, his relatives, and court dignitaries.[6] It was thus a Flemish artist who launched what would become a popular English tradition, in which the portrait miniatures that Holbein started to paint about ten years later are the supreme achievement.

◂ Like Horenbout, Holbein used vellum, a fine type of parchment made from the skin of unborn calves, as the support for his miniatures. To prevent the vellum from cockling under the influence of the watercolour, it was pasted to card using starch. The white back of a playing card was often used for this purpose, as in the case of this miniature portrait of Lady Audley. After the vellum had been prepared and smoothed, a flesh-coloured layer of ground was applied. This could then be painted with both transparent watercolour and body colour, generally mixed with gum arabic, producing a glossy effect.[7] Also like Horenbout, Holbein depicted his sitters against a blue background in a circular format. He added a narrow gilt rim around the image, in the tradition of book illumination. The precious little works of art were mounted in costly frames or placed in boxes; sometimes they were actually worn as jewellery. None of the original frames or boxes of Holbein's miniatures has been preserved, however.[8] A valuable miniature portrait made an ideal gift. While Horenbout worked only for a small circle of clients at court, Holbein also produced miniatures for other clients.[9]

◂ Around the same time as Horenbout, the Brussels artist Jean Clouet (c. 1485/90–1540/41) was working at the court of King Francis I of France on his first independent portrait miniatures, which may also have inspired Holbein.[10] In 1526, Madame d'Alençon, Francis's sister, sent some tiny portraits of her brother and his two sons that had been painted by Clouet to Henry VIII, who responded in kind by sending her miniature portraits of himself and his small daughter Princess Mary, presumably made by Horenbout.[11]

◂ Probably unlike Horenbout, by whom no preliminary studies are known, Holbein seems to have prepared his miniatures with the aid of preliminary sketches. Although there are no known studies by him in miniature format, larger ones have been preserved that served as examples for his miniature portraits.[12] Thus, the portrait drawing of Lady Elizabeth Audley served as the basis for the miniature with her likeness. The face on the drawing, the contours of which were enhanced with

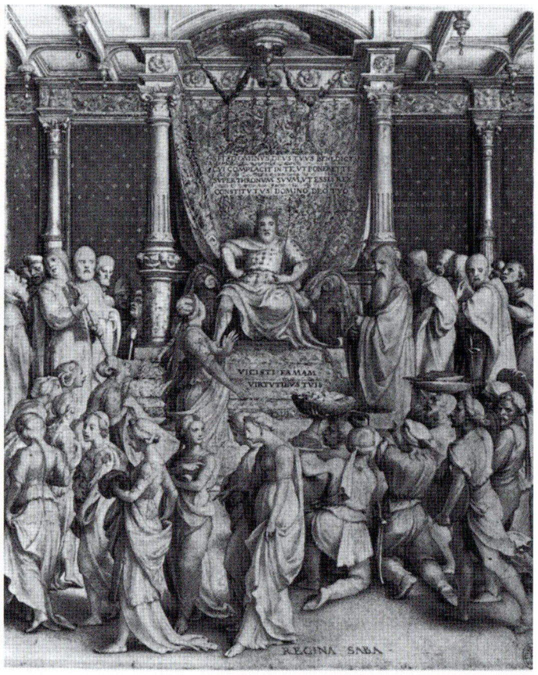

fig. 31a Hans Holbein the Younger, *Solomon and the Queen of Sheba*. Watercolour and body colour on vellum pasted to card, 228 x 181 mm. London, The Royal Collection

Lady Elizabeth Audley (?-1564), c. 1538

Watercolour and body colour on vellum on a piece of a playing card (circular), diam. 56 mm
Lent by Her Majesty Queen Elizabeth II
cat.no. 32

fine ink lines, clearly served directly as the model for the subtle portrait in miniature form to which Holbein subsequently added hands. He added notes to the sheet in metalpoint: 'samet' (velvet) and 'rot damast' (red damask) for the material of the clothing, and 'rot' (red), 'w' (white) and 'go[?]' (gold) to the pendant on Lady Audley's breast. A small clover-leaf to the pendant's right signifies the colour green. The indications for the use of colour were not in fact heeded,[13] besides which the piece of jewellery was altered in the miniature: the three pendant pearls are absent, and the details are different. What is more, Lady Audley's French hood —which supplanted the angular gable hood (cf. cat. nos. 10 and 26-28) in the 1530s— is executed far more sumptuously in the miniature than in the drawing. While in the study she wears a simple white cap over her blond hair, in the miniature her cap is trimmed with a striped band of gold material and a richly worked border, while the hood is decorated with a band of precious stones and pearls. Finally, Lady Audley wears two necklaces in the miniature, instead of one as in the sketch. In view of all these differences, perhaps the drawing served not just as an example for the miniature, with the sheet being followed only in the rendering of the face, but also for a painting on the same scale, which has been lost. This theory derives some support, perhaps, from a detail at upper right in the drawing: a small sketch of a female torso in thin chalk lines. This little figure may indicate a decorated architectural element in the background of the intended painting, such as those to be found in a number of other portraits by Holbein (cf. p. 16, fig. 10 and cat. no. 6).

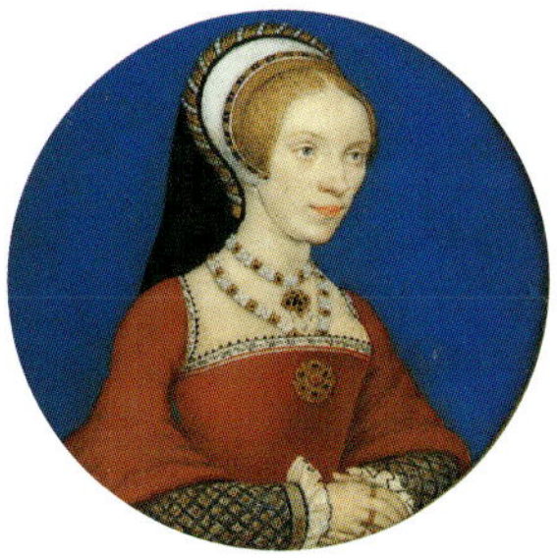

‹ Unlike Horenbout, Holbein generally included his sitters' arms and hands in his portrait miniatures, as a result of which these works were almost as monumental in nature as his panel portraits. With very fine modelling, Holbein created a convincing effect of depth in his figures against the even blue background. In this respect too he surpassed the flat portrait miniatures of his predecessor Horenbout. One of those to comment on Holbein's innovations in portrait miniatures, over fifty years later, was the English miniaturist Nicholas Hilliard (1547-1619) —court painter to Queen Elizabeth I— who wrote in his treatise *The Arte of Limning* (c. 1598–1603), 'Holbean's manner of limning I have ever imitated and howld it for the best'.[14]

‹ The inscription 'The Lady Audley' on the drawing, which is not by Holbein, generated some confusion about the identity of the sitter, since two ladies bore this title around this time. One was Elizabeth Tuke, the daughter of Brian Tuke[15] — an influential man at the court of Henry VIII whose official posts included that of Treasurer of the Chamber, and who was also depicted by Holbein.[16] Elizabeth Tuke was the wife of George Touchet, the ninth Lord Audley, who however did not acquire this title until 1557, some twenty years after Holbein made this portrait. It is therefore likelier that the woman in this miniature is Elizabeth Grey, a daughter of Margaret Wotton (also immortalised by Holbein)[17] and Thomas Grey, the second Marquis of Dorset, who was Master of the Household to Princess Mary.[18] In April 1538 Elizabeth became the second wife of Thomas Audley (1488-1544), who on 29 November that year was made the first Baron Audley of Walden, a former Benedictine monastery in Essex that he had converted into a country house.[19] Audley was a powerful man, who had succeeded Thomas More in 1532 as Lord Chancellor. He played a role in the conviction and execution not only of More himself but also of John Fisher, Anne Boleyn and Thomas Cromwell. After Audley's death, Elizabeth married Sir George Norton. She died in 1564. Holbein may have made his portrait of her on the occasion of her marriage in 1538,[20] as this dating would tally with the style of the drawing and miniature discussed here. AvS

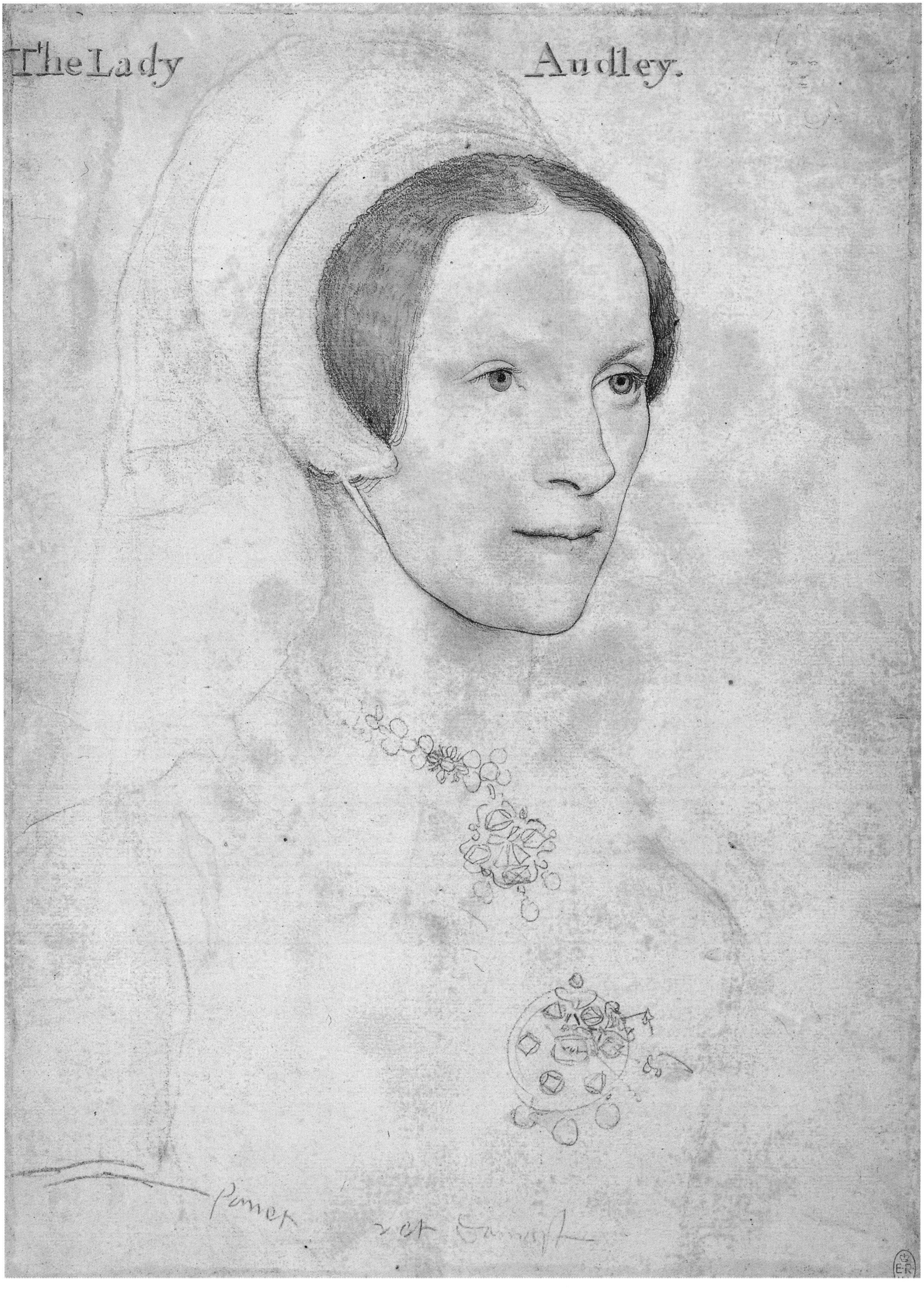
The Lady Audley.

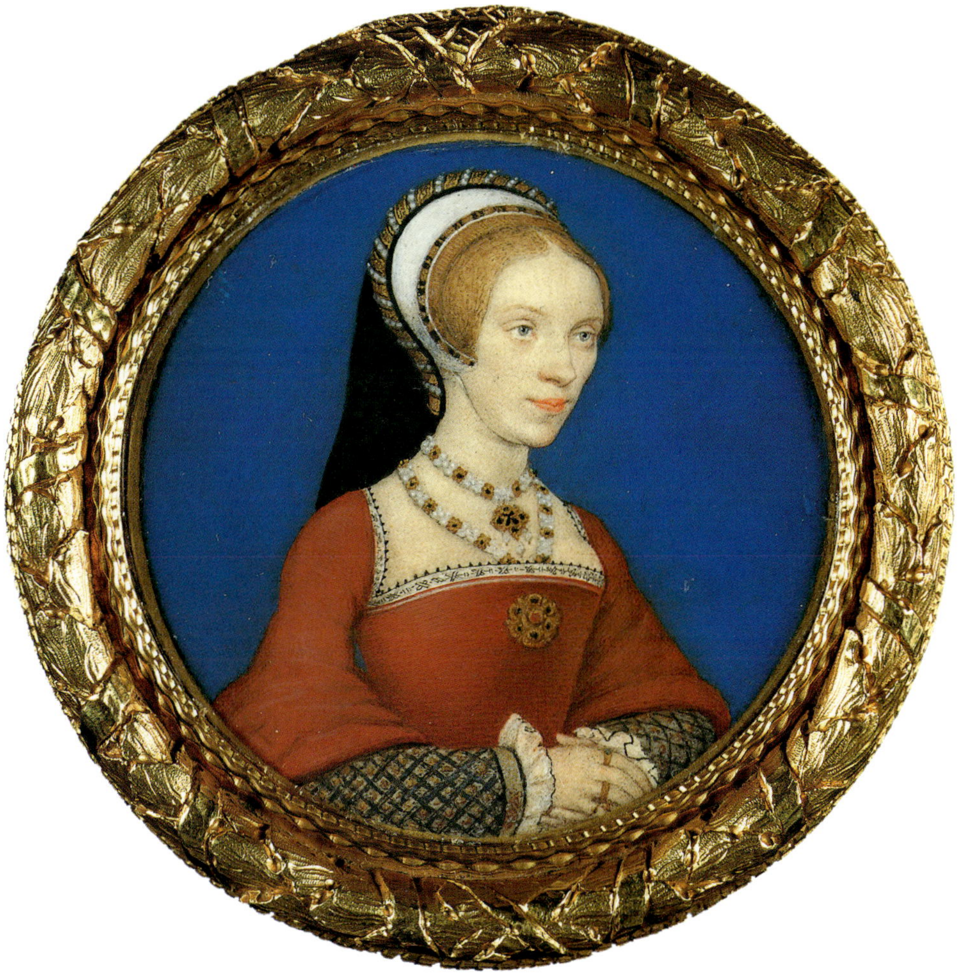

XXXIII

Edward (1537–1553), Prince of Wales, *c.* 1538

Panel, 56.8 x 44 cm / Inscription: PARVVLE PATRISSA, PATRIÆ VIRTVTIS ET HÆRES / ESTO, NIHIL MAIVS MAXIMVS ORBIS HABET.
GNATVM VIX POSSVNT COELVM ET NATVRA DEDISSE, / HVIVS QVEM PATRIS, VICTVS HONORET HONOS.
ÆQVATO TANTVM, TANTI TV FACTA PARENTIS, / VOTA HOMINVM, VIX QVO PROGREDIANTVR, HABENT / VINCITO, VICISTI,
QVOT REGES PRISCVS ADORAT ORBIS, NEC TE QVI VINCERE POSSIT, ERIT. *Ricard: Morysini. Car:*
Washington, National Gallery of Art, Andrew W. Mellon Collection
cat.no. 33

As court painter to Henry VIII of England, Holbein painted many of his prospective brides from 1538 onward, but he rarely depicted the king's family. This portrait of Henry's son Edward (1537–1553), Prince of Wales, is the earliest known likeness of the crown prince and the only painting of him by Holbein that has been preserved.[1] Edward was born at Hampton Court on 12 October 1537 as Henry's only legitimate son. Holbein also produced a portrait of his mother, Jane Seymour (cat. nos. 26-27), who died twelve days after giving birth to her son.

◂ The prince is depicted regally attired, with a tightly fitting cap known as a biggin on his head. The feathered cap worn over it is a miniature version of a man's headgear such as that worn by Henry VIII in his portrait by Holbein (p. 28, fig. 27). What little of the prince's hair we can see is combed tightly over his forehead. Like the feathered cap and biggin, the boy's clothes are handsomely embroidered: particularly striking is his red tunic decorated with gold thread, worn over a white shirt that is also trimmed with gold thread at the neck. The gold brocade sleeves are decorated with stylised acanthus leaves, a motif that recurs on the gold bands of the tunic. Edward holds a gold rattle in his left hand that evokes associations with a royal sceptre. His right hand is raised, as if blessing the viewer.

◂ At first sight the child depicted here appears —certainly to a modern viewer— far older than twelve or fourteen months, Edward's age when this portrait was made. But Holbein set out not to depict Edward as a child, as he did with his own two-year-old daughter Katharina in the well-known family portrait in Basel (p. 24, fig. 23),[2] but as the heir to the throne. That the painting should be construed as an official portrait explicitly presenting the prince as the future king is clear both from the pose and costume of the prince, who looks down at us from behind a balustrade, and from the Latin inscription below. This text was written by Richard Morison (died 1556), a protégé of Thomas Cromwell (*c.* 1485–1540), secretary to Henry VIII.[3] Freely translated, it reads as follows:

> Little one, emulate thy father and be the heir of his virtue; the world contains nothing greater. Heaven and earth could scarcely produce a son whose glory would surpass that of such a father. Do thou but equal the deeds of thy parent and men can ask no more. Shouldst thou surpass him, thou hast outstript all kings the world has revered in ages past.

In short, the text emphasises the heavy burden of responsibility resting on Edward's shoulders as heir to the throne. Holbein often placed a text in a prominent position in his works of art. At the very centre of his mural painting in Whitehall, which included the portraits of Henry VIII and Jane Seymour (p. 32, fig. 31), was a Latin inscription.[4] It proclaimed that the glory of Henry VII had been surpassed by that of his son and successor, Henry VIII (see p. 32). Similarly, the lines inscribed on the portrait of Edward that was completed about a year later express the hope that he in turn will surpass his father. In the past the lines of verse on the painting described here have been interpreted in the context of Thomas Cromwell's campaign to place Henry VIII's secular and religious power on a secure footing.[5] For Henry's defiance of the pope in securing the annulment of his marriage to Catharine of Aragon had led to a breach with Rome, throwing the country into turmoil.

◂ The reign of Edward VI was destined to be brief. The prince had been sickly since infancy, although there is little trace of this in his portrait. His eyesight was poor and he had bouts of deafness. Even so, he was not spared the rigours of a stern tutor.[6] He distinguished himself on the lute at an early age, and he took a lively interest in astronomy. Following his father's death he was crowned king of England and Ireland in Westminster Abbey on 25 February 1547, at nine years of age. But a mere six years later the young king died at Greenwich on 6 July 1553, three months before his

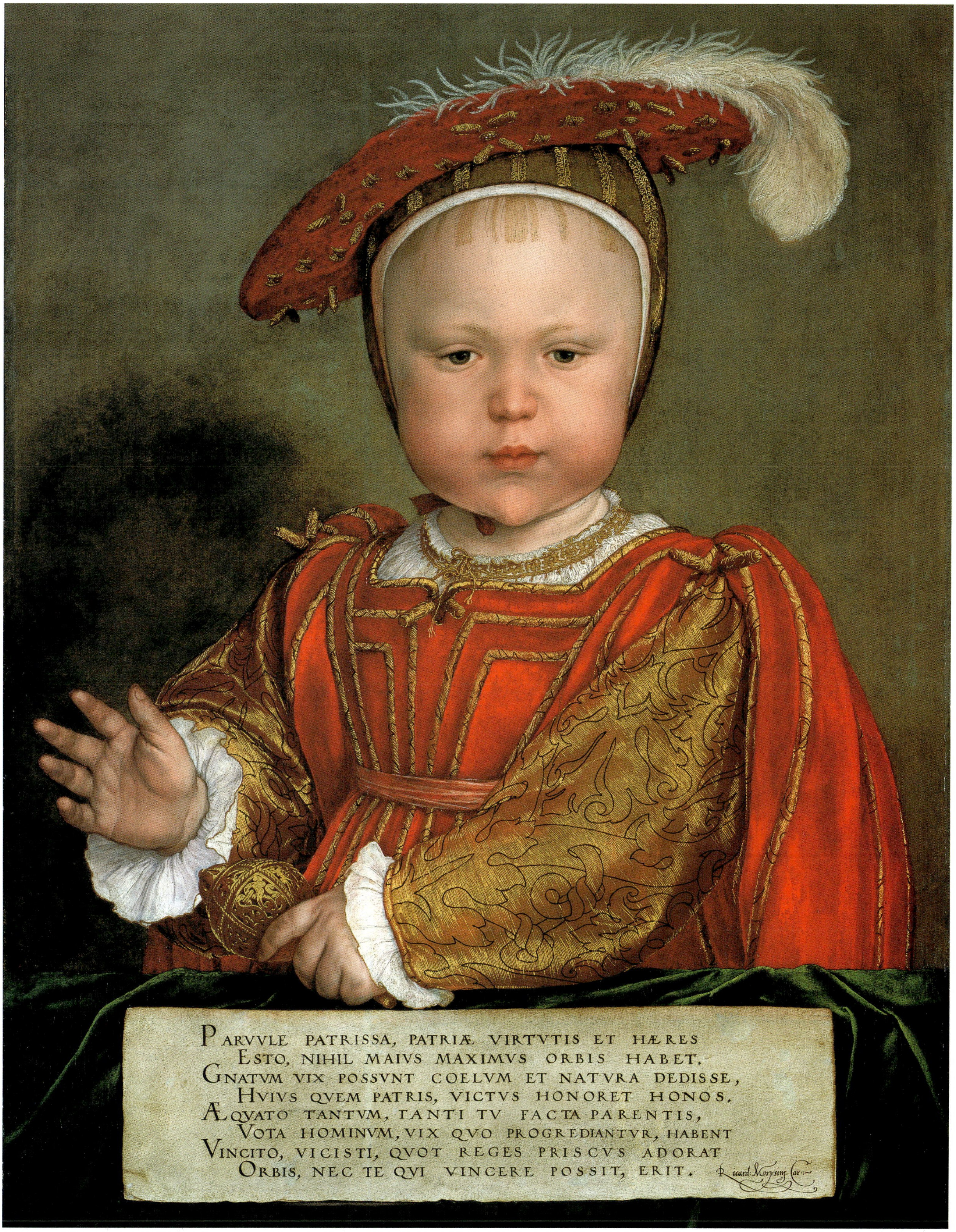
PARVVLE PATRISSA, PATRIÆ VIRTVTIS ET HÆRES
ESTO, NIHIL MAIVS MAXIMVS ORBIS HABET.
GNATVM VIX POSSVNT COELVM ET NATVRA DEDISSE,
HVIVS QVEM PATRIS, VICTVS HONORET HONOS.
ÆQVATO TANTVM, TANTI TV FACTA PARENTIS,
VOTA HOMINVM, VIX QVO PROGREDIANTVR, HABENT
VINCITO, VICISTI, QVOT REGES PRISCVS ADORAT
ORBIS, NEC TE QVI VINCERE POSSIT, ERIT.
Ricard: Morysini. Car:

sixteenth birthday, probably of tuberculosis. Edward's brief reign was marked by a full adherence to the doctrines of Protestantism, something that was welcomed enthusiastically by supporters of the Reformation in other parts of Europe.

◂ In all probability the painting described here is the portrait of Edward that Holbein presented as a gift to Henry VIII on 1 January 1539 —'By hanse holbyne a table of the pictour of the p[ri]nce grace'— prompting the king to give him a gilded goblet in token of his gratitude.[7] This seems likely, since it is the only portrait of Edward painted by Holbein that has been preserved.[8] If the painting was indeed presented to the king on New Year's Day 1539, it must have been finished by the end of 1538. This means that it was made in a relatively short period of time. For it was in October 1538 at the earliest that Holbein returned to London from his travels in France, where he had made portraits of several potential brides for the king.[9] The portrait of Edward must therefore have been painted in November or December 1538. Perhaps the artist intended this gift (his only documented gift) to demonstrate his loyalty to Henry, after Basel city council had expressed its desire to take Holbein into its service once again.[10]

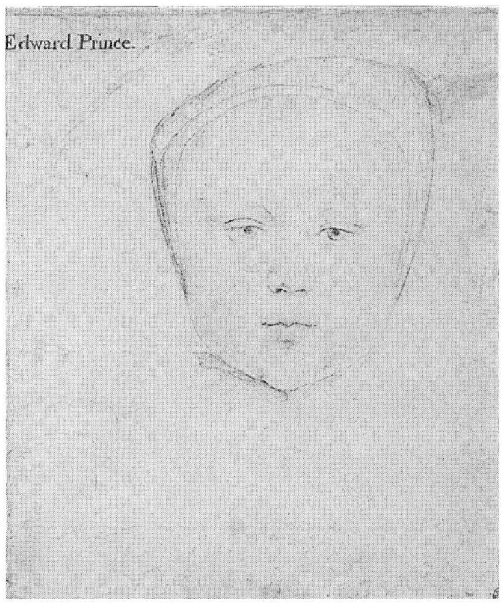

fig. 33a Hans Holbein the Younger, *Portrait of Edward, Prince of Wales*, c. 1538. Black and coloured chalks, on pink prepared paper, 262 x 223 mm. London, The Royal Collection

◂ It must have been a difficult task for Holbein to make a good likeness of such a young and probably lively child. There is a preliminary study of Edward's face in the Royal Collection in England (fig. 33a).[11] This portrait, which was drawn in very thin lines and later gone over by another hand, already displays an initial design for the prince's handsome headgear. In the painting itself, Holbein applied a very light underdrawing over the salmon-coloured ground.[12] This can be seen with the naked eye, but emerges much more clearly with the aid of infrared reflectography. This technique also reveals a few minor alterations to the eyelids (in the underdrawing they were placed somewhat higher) and to the fingers of the hand with the rattle.[13] In contrast to Holbein's practice in other paintings, here he appears not to have traced the contours from the preliminary drawing onto the panel, since the head in the preliminary study is slightly smaller than in the painting.[14] It has recently been suggested, however, that Holbein did indeed transfer the drawing to the panel, but enlarged the face later.[15]

◂ The portrait from Washington is a superb example of Holbein's astonishing technique. Even while applying the lowest layers of paint he took account of how the finished painting would appear. Thus, it can be demonstrated that the gold aiguillettes on the cap were painted over a light ochre-coloured layer of paint — applied not just as a solid ground but as a warm underlying tone. For the biggin, Holbein mixed gold powder and even silver leaf into the paint.[16] The portrait has been preserved in a reasonably good state, although the background has become badly discoloured — it was originally an even blue colour,[17] in common with that in several of Holbein's other portraits from the 1530s. The dark green drapery hanging over the balustrade must once have formed a sharp contrast with the bright blue background, contributing to the effect of depth. Today, the painting derives depth largely from the fact that the prince is positioned behind a balustrade and from his shadow in the background. QB

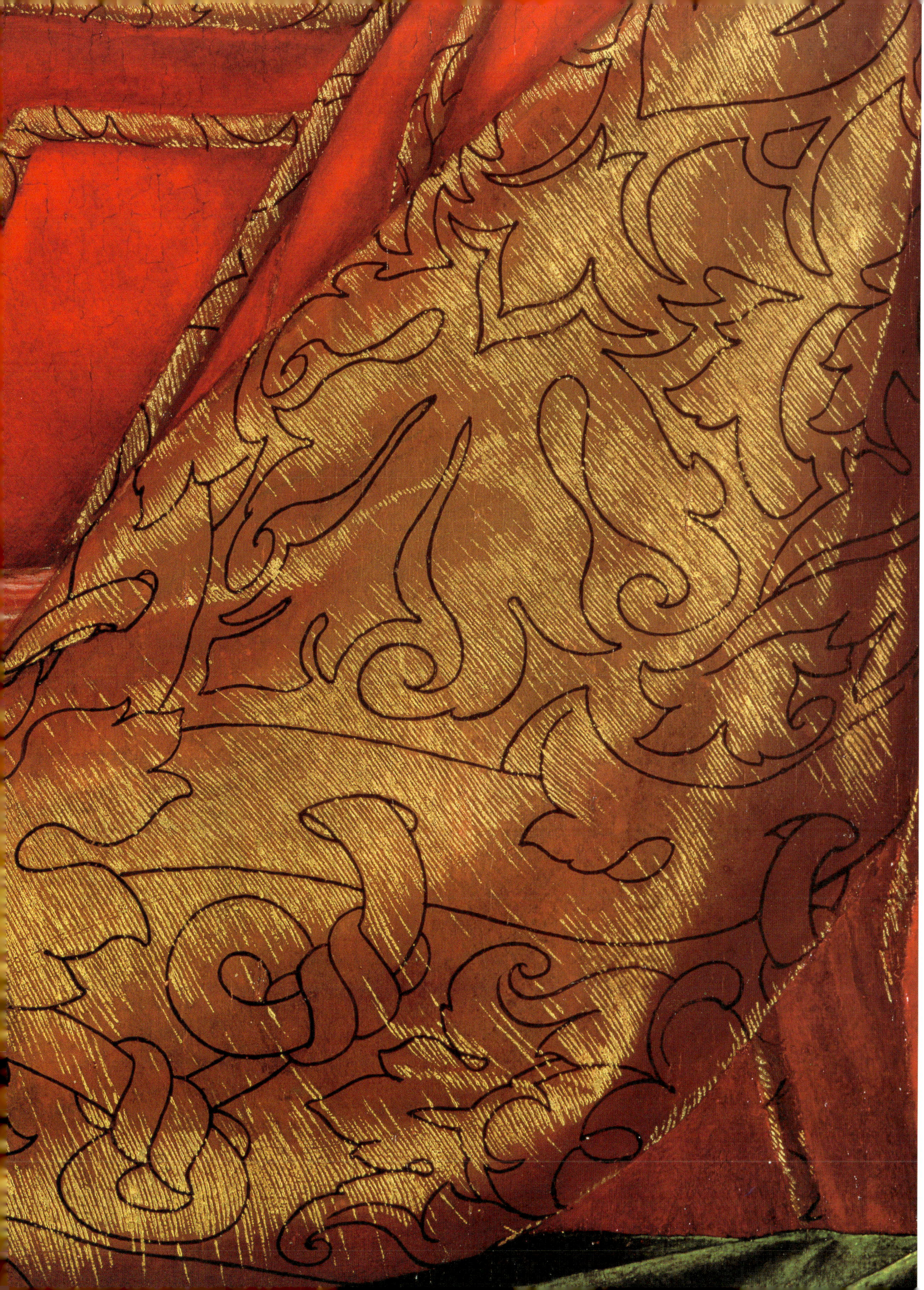

XXXIV

Thomas Howard, third Duke of Norfolk (1473-1554), c. 1539/40

Panel, 80.6 x 60.9 cm / At upper left and right: THOMAS. DUKE OFF NORFOLK. MARSH[ALL / AND] TRESVRER OF INGLOND[E] / THE [.L]X[VI] YERE [O]F HIS AGE
Lent by Her Majesty Queen Elizabeth II
cat.no. 34

Thomas Howard, third Duke of Norfolk, was one of the most powerful nobles in England. He was a loyal servant of King Henry VIII, whose uncle he was able to call himself three times over.[1] Thus in 1495 he married the sister of Henry's mother Elizabeth of York, Princess Anne Plantagenet (1475–1512/13). Later on, Henry twice chose one of Howard's nieces as his bride: Anne Boleyn in 1533 and Catherine Howard in 1540 (his second and fifth wives, respectively). Both ended their lives on the scaffold. Thomas Howard actually presided over the bench that sentenced Anne Boleyn to death, after serving for years as her principal adviser. On top of all this, Howard was godfather to Prince Edward, and married his daughter Mary to Henry's illegitimate son Henry Fitzroy, Duke of Richmond.

When Holbein made Thomas Howard's portrait in 1539–1540, the nobleman was 66 years of age, and could look back on an impressive military career. He had initially served under his father in Scotland. In 1512, as lieutenant-general, he had fought the French, and a year later he was appointed Lord High Admiral of the English fleet, in which capacity he succeeded his deceased brother Edward. Instead of leading the fleet against France, he joined the army under his father's command and fought the Scots, helping to procure the overwhelming English victory at the Battle of Flodden in 1513. Thomas was rewarded by being made Earl of Surrey in 1514, while his father —who had held the supreme command in this battle— became Duke of Norfolk. In the years that followed, the Howards turned against Cardinal Wolsey and his policies, which were aimed at stripping the old aristocracy of its power. Thomas Howard strengthened his ties with the country's leading nobles in 1513, after the death of his first wife, by marrying Elizabeth Stafford, a daughter of the Duke of Buckingham. The marriage was not a success, and the couple separated in 1533.

In 1520 Howard left on a mission to enforce English rule in Ireland, after which he fought against France with the English fleet in 1521–1522. In the summer of 1522 Howard burned the town of Morlaix in Brittany to the ground and pursued a scorched earth campaign in the vicinity of Boulogne. Following his return to England he succeeded his father as Lord High Treasurer in 1522. The following year he led another punitive expedition against Scotland, laying waste the entire border territory.

After his father's death in 1524 he became Duke of Norfolk. The following year he conducted peace negotiations with France. After the peace was concluded, Henry's divorce from Catherine of Aragon was the issue dominating English politics. In this matter too, Howard unswervingly supported his king, although he would always remain loyal to the Roman Catholic Church. The events surrounding the royal divorce led in 1529 to the fall of Cardinal Wolsey as the most powerful minister in the kingdom, a fall that Howard had happily helped to precipitate. However, it was not Howard who was called upon to fill the ensuing power vacuum, but the far more astute Thomas Cromwell — a man that Howard viewed as an upstart. Like many other nobles, Thomas Howard profited enormously from the dissolution of the monasteries in the 1530s, following Henry's revolt against the pope. In 1533 he was appointed Earl Marshall, which put him in charge of all ceremonial occasions at court. As a military commander, he played a key role in the suppression of the Pilgrimage of Grace in 1536–1537, the largest and most dangerous revolt against Henry's religious and fiscal policies. He crushed the rebellion ruthlessly. The next few years were dominated by the power struggle between Howard and his arch-rival Cromwell, whom he eventually arrested in person on 10 June 1540. Howard's triumph was complete when Henry VIII married his niece on the day on which Cromwell was beheaded, but this marriage too ended in disaster. Now advanced in years, Howard again fought in successive battles against the Scots and the French. His influence at court was nonetheless waning, and in 1546 he and his son Henry were arrested on charges of high treason. Henry was beheaded, but Thomas narrowly escaped the same fate because the king died the night before he was due to be executed. Under Henry's successor, Edward VI, Howard was imprisoned for a further six years, until he was released and rehabilitated by Queen Mary ('Bloody Mary') in 1553. He died a year later.

Holbein's portrait shows Thomas Howard at the height of his fame, accompanied by the main attributes of his

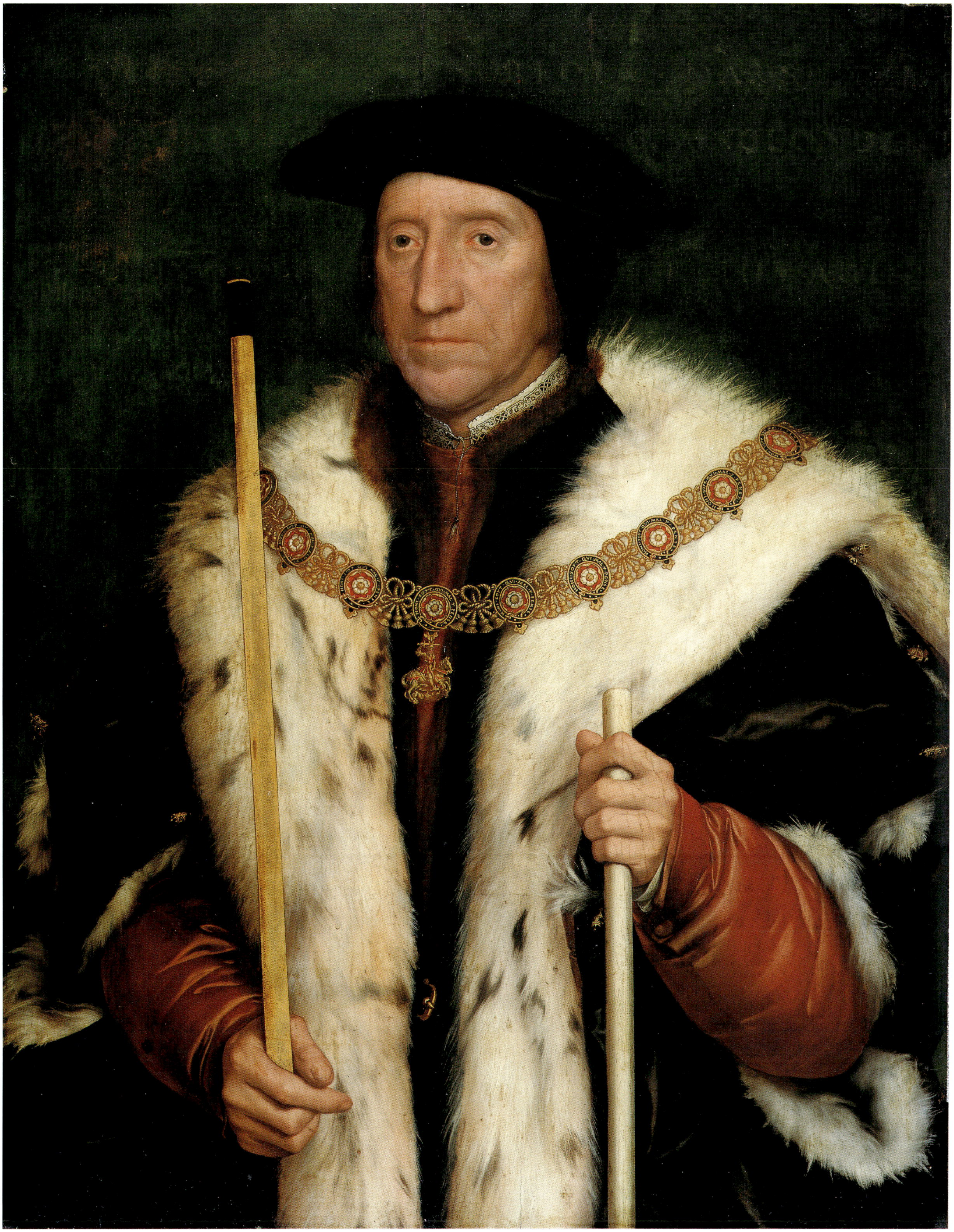

power and status. In his right hand is the gold truncheon that went with the office of Earl Marshall, and in his left he holds the Lord High Treasurer's white staff of office. Both positions are mentioned in the now near-illegible inscription, which can be deciphered with the help of several copies of the portrait.[2] Over the precious lynx fur of his cloak the duke wears the chain of the Order of the Garter, to which he was admitted in 1510. Edward III, on establishing this highest chivalric order in England, had restricted its ranks to only twenty-six 'persons of the highest honour'. This number is reflected in the twenty-six Tudor roses in the chain, each of which is enclosed by a blue garter bearing the motto 'Honi soit qui mal y pense' (Shame be to him who thinks evil of it). From the chain hangs an image of St George, the Order's patron saint, who kills the dragon from his mount.[3]

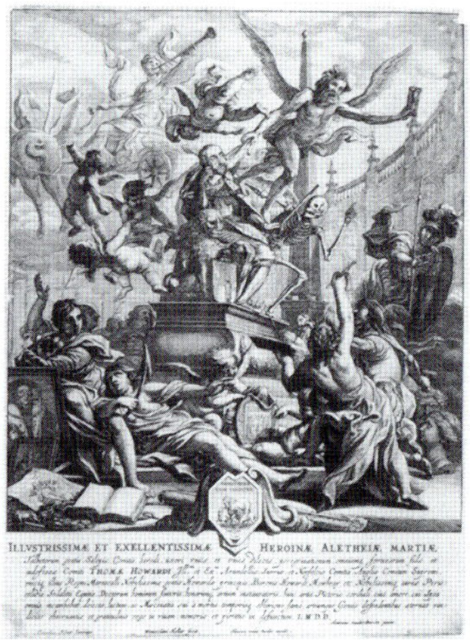

fig. 34a
Wenceslaus Hollar after Cornelius Schut, *Apotheosis of the Earl of Arundel*, c. 1650. Etching, 378 x 313 mm. Amsterdam, Rijksmuseum, Rijksprentenkabinet

Howard was expelled from the Order after his arrest in December 1546, and his insignia were presented to Edward Seymour[4] — after Cromwell's death Howard's main rival at court. The staffs of office that went with his positions as Lord High Treasurer and Earl Marshall —also rendered by Holbein— were also taken from him and given to Jane Seymour's brother Edward, who succeeded Howard in both of these important positions.[5] After the death of Henry VIII in the early morning of 28 January 1547, Edward Seymour, who had since been made the first Duke of Somerset, enjoyed supremacy for a few years as Protector of the Realm and regent for his young nephew, Edward VI. But although Seymour had won a battle in his power struggle with Thomas Howard, he lost the war, as it were: himself a victim of intrigues, he went to the scaffold in 1552. Howard was released from prison in 1553; he was soon given back his title of Duke of Norfolk and readmitted to the Order of the Garter.

At the time of his arrest in 1546, Thomas Howard owned twenty-eight portraits of famous people, testimony to his fascination for the genre.[6] Besides his own likeness he also commissioned portraits of his children from Holbein. Perhaps the works served together as a family portrait gallery. The artist depicted Howard's son Henry three times, first as a boy of fifteen in 1532, when he married Frances de Vere, whose portrait Holbein also made at this time.[7] He also produced a portrait drawing of Howard's daughter —probably another preliminary study— and a sheet bearing the inscription 'Lady Ratcliffe' may depict Howard's half-sister.[8] A portrait painting by Holbein shows Henry at the age of twenty-five (Museo de Arte, Sao Paolo). Both this work and the portrait discussed here are depicted in the background of a watercolour drawing from 1643 by Philip Fruytiers, a family portrait of Thomas Howard, Earl of Arundel (1585–1646), which was probably a copy of a painting by Anthonie van Dyck, since lost.[9] Arundel was the greatest ever collector of Holbein's work (cf. cat. nos. 7, 8, 17 and 22) and the portrait of his great-great-grand-father that is discussed here was among his collection. His pride in his illustrious ancestor is beautifully expressed in an etching by Wenceslaus Hollar, *Apotheosis of the Earl of Arundel* (fig. 34a).[10] This memorial print celebrates the deceased earl —seated high up on a sarcophagus— among other things as a patron of the arts: at lower left, it includes the portrait of Thomas Howard by Holbein that is discussed here. AvS

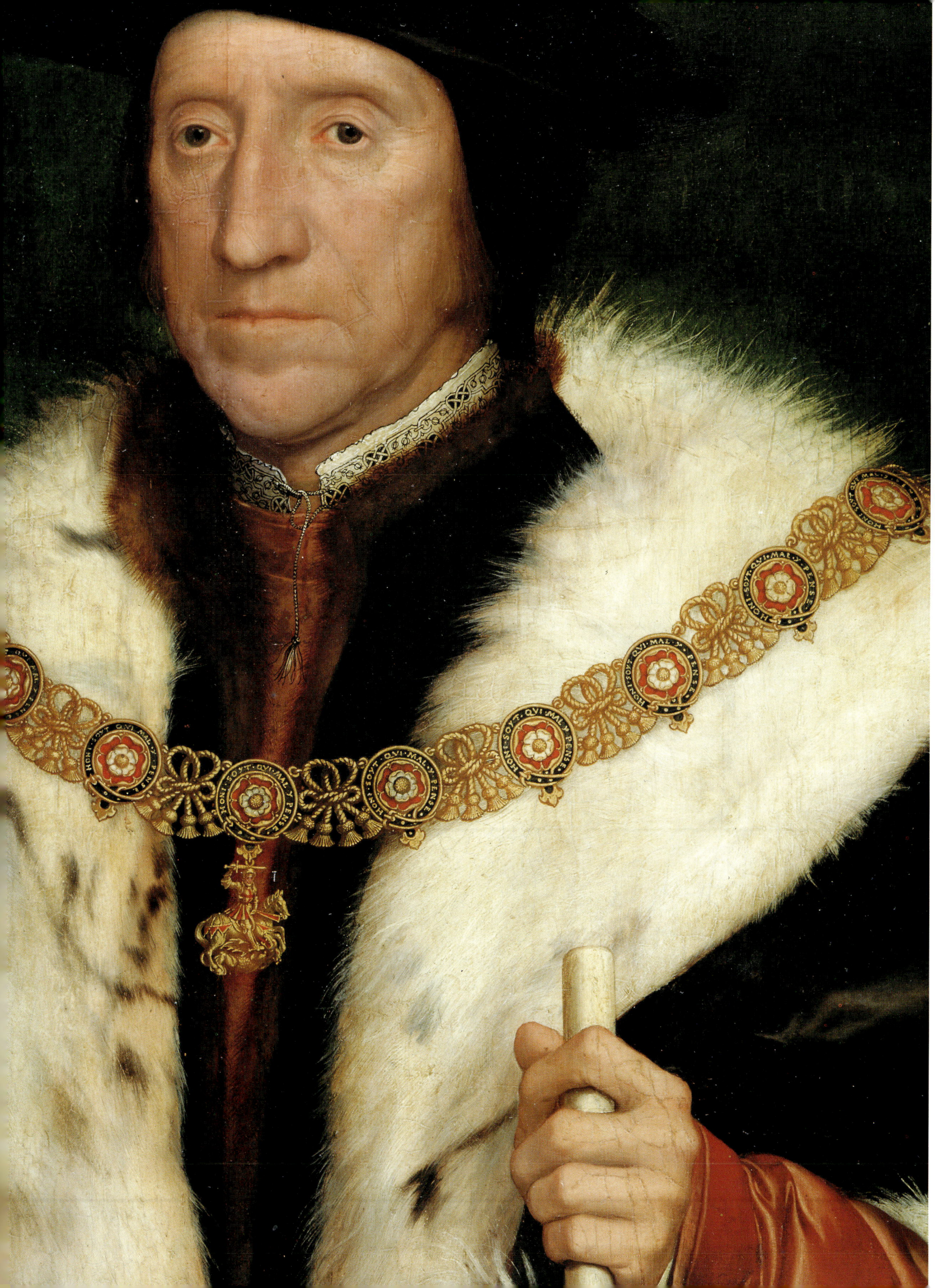
HONI SOYT QVI MAL Y PENSE

XXXV

An unknown young man, c. 1540/43

Watercolour on vellum (circular), pasted to a piece of a playing card, diameter 3.8 cm
The Hague, The House of Orange-Nassau Historic Collections Trust
cat.no. 35

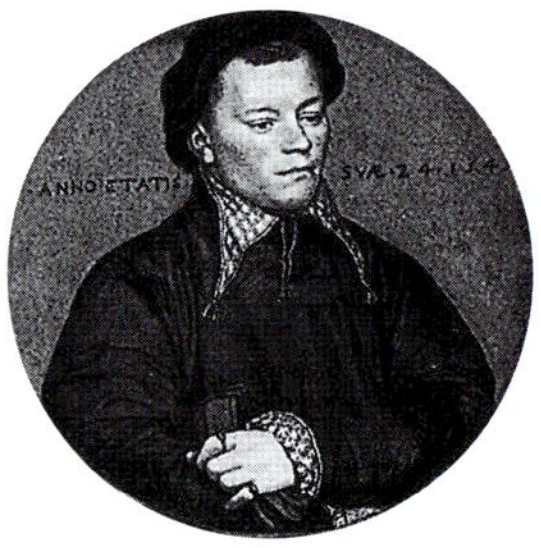

fig. 35a
Hans Holbein the Younger, *Portrait of a 24-year-old youth, probably a member of the Von Schwarzwaldt family*, 1543. Watercolour on vellum (circular), diameter 5.3 cm. Taken from the Stadtmuseum, Gdansk (photograph: RKD, The Hague)

This delightful little portrait of a young man is part of the small oeuvre of miniatures attributed to Holbein (see also cat. no. 32).[1] The image is painted with watercolour on vellum, fine parchment that was made from the skin of unborn calves.[2] This was very popular as a support for portrait miniatures in the fifteenth and sixteenth centuries. Holbein also used it for other miniatures, the earliest of which were made around 1535 during his second period in England. His portrait miniatures are often framed with a painted gilt rim, which is also present in this case but is concealed by the frame. To stop the vellum from wrinkling in reaction to the moisture of the paint, it was often pasted to a playing card, as here.[3] The tiny circular portrait —the original frame of which has been lost— is only 3.8 cm in diameter,[4] making it Holbein's smallest extant miniature. In spite of the work's modest dimensions and the use of watercolour, we see the same meticulous detail here as in Holbein's oil paintings. The pattern of the material of the dark jerkin with puff sleeves is rendered highly convincingly, as is the young man's cropped hair. In 1604 Karel van Mander (1548–1606) wrote admiringly, in his *Schilder-boeck*, of the subtle way in which Holbein contrived to depict 'beard or hair' in his portraits.[5] The little cords attached to the collar of the white shirt add almost imperceptibly to the effect of depth in this portrait miniature: since the young man is depicted turning slightly to one side, one of the four small white cords overlaps the uniformly blue background, enhancing the three-dimensionality of the image.

‹ The sitter's contemplative, almost melancholy gaze, is relatively rare, though not unique, in Holbein's oeuvre. The same expression, with the lips pressed tightly together and the eyes directed downward, can be seen in a portrait miniature of a 24-year-old member of the London Steelyard community from Gdansk (fig. 35a).[6] This miniature, long attributed to Holbein, the whereabouts of which have been unknown since the Second World War, has a uniformly blue background, like the work described here. This little portrait, dated 1543, is so similar in conception to the one described here that the latter must have been made in the same period, roughly 1540–1543.[7] The informality of the open collar in the miniature discussed here, in which the sitter's hands are not shown, enhances the portrait's intimacy.

‹ The young man's identity has long been a mystery. Portrait miniatures as such were not the exclusive preserve of members of the Royal Family or Household, as is clear, for instance, from Holbein's portrait of Jane Small (London, Victoria and Albert Museum), who was the wife of a prosperous London merchant.[8] Only one of Holbein's known portrait miniatures has the sitter's name inscribed on it, although several give the person's age.[9] In this case even the age is omitted. Nor do we have any information about the earliest provenance of the little portrait, which was probably acquired in the nineteenth century by Queen Sophie (1818–1877), the first wife of King William III (1817–1890).[10] On the basis of the youth's clothes, it has been assumed that he was English.[11] However, it is just as plausible that he was a member of the London Steelyard community,[12] like the sitter in the miniature dated 1543, which would mean he was from Germany rather than England. On the basis of the similarity of facial features and in particular the characteristic angle of the cropped hair, it could even be conjectured that the two portraits depict the same person. If so, the present portrait would depict him when somewhat younger. QB

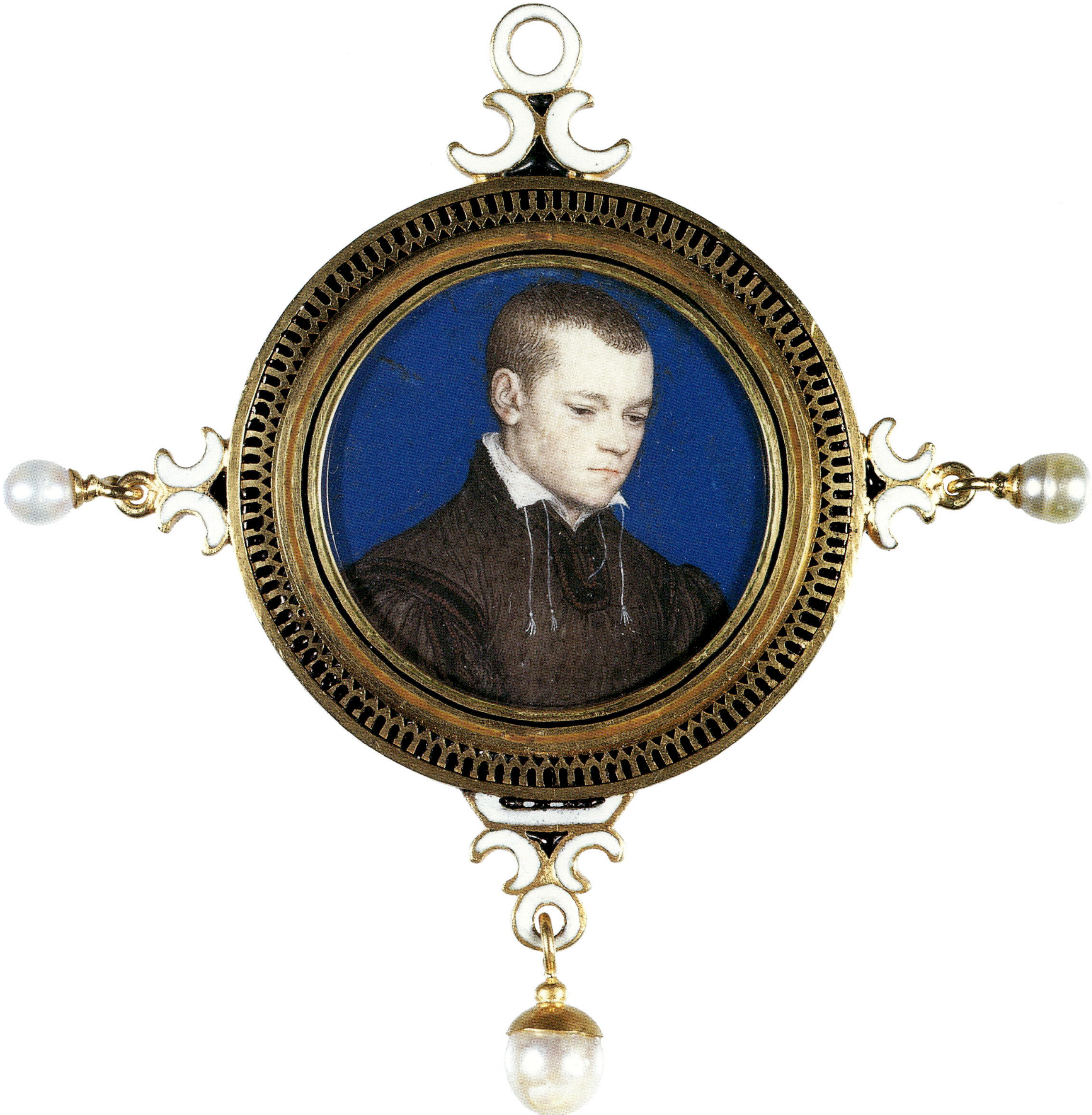

XXXVI

Nobleman with a hawk, 1542

Panel, 24.6 x 18.8 cm / At upper left and upper right: 15 / 42 / .*ANNO . ETATIS . / . SVÆ . XXVIII*
At lower left: N 28 ('N' in spiegelbeeld)[1]
The Hague, Royal Cabinet of Paintings Mauritshuis
cat.no. 36

This small painting, dating from 1542, is a half-length portrait of a man with a hawk on his left hand. It is one of a group of paintings that Holbein produced in the last years of his life. The figure almost fills the pictorial field, and his body is slightly twisted around, adding to the liveliness of the image. The close-up, near-frontal rendering of the face gives the portrait a special air of directness and intimacy. Furthermore, the frontal pose enabled the artist to achieve the best possible rendering of the sitter's individual facial features. The layers of paint have lost their intensity in patches, and the painting must initially have had a far stronger effect of depth, as the background probably had a more even, bluer colour that contrasted sharply with the dark figure. Chemical processes have caused a discoloration in the relatively light background (which contains smalt) over the centuries, so that it now appears bluish-grey.[2] The well-preserved gilt inscription with the year 1542 and the sitter's age in the background dispel the illusion that the man is outdoors. Holbein appears to have deliberately chosen an indeterminate background in order to give the portrait a timeless quality (cf. p. 29).

◂ In spite of the ageing and discoloration of the paint layers —especially in the background— this portrait demonstrates that Holbein continued to produce works of high quality until his premature death in 1543. The convincing rendering of the flesh tints of the face and the shadow falling on it has been achieved by building up the paint layers in a differentiated process. The flesh tints were enhanced by the prior application of a layer of pink, with a greyish-pink layer being applied beneath the shaded areas. The darkest shadows have been accentuated using an initial layer of dark brown. The image derives added appeal from gold-coloured details such as the gilt letters in the background, the highlights on the man's two gold rings, and the little bell attached to the bird's leg (see cat. no. 19). These are all executed in gold leaf applied over a cream-coloured mordant.[3]

◂ The man wears a black jerkin, the front and sleeves of which are trimmed with a woven *passementerie* with geometrical patterns. The right sleeve has a vent near the seam fastened with two little cords, revealing the red material of the lining. On the man's left hand, which is protected by a thick brown leather glove, sits a hawk.[4] The landed nobility and affluent middle classes hunted with hawks in sixteenth-century England. In his right hand the sitter holds the bird's hood, used to keep it calm when not hunting.

◂ All we know about the man in this portrait is what the inscription tells us, namely that he was aged 28 in 1542, when Holbein immortalised him. As the oak panel has been planed down, making it considerably thinner —this was probably done at the end of the seventeenth century— old inscriptions clarifying the man's identity or his portrait's provenance may have been lost. The sitter's name had already sunk into oblivion by the seventeenth century, as is clear from old inventories of the British royal collections, into which the painting had already been incorporated before 1649.[5] Some critics have suggested that this painting, though made in England, depicts a Frenchman.[6] In all probability, however, it depicts an English nobleman,[7] whose high status can be inferred from his rich apparel and gold rings. It is generally assumed that the man was not a professional falconer but an occasional huntsman, since he is depicted not with a falcon, like Robert Cheseman, the king's falconer (cat. no. 19), but with a hawk.[8] Here we see one of the bird's eyes, while the falcon in Cheseman's portrait, which is also preserved in the Mauritshuis, is shown hooded.

◂ Technical examination reveals that Holbein made major alterations to the composition while he was painting.[9] These changes cannot be seen with the naked eye, but can be demonstrated with the aid of infrared reflectography (IRR; fig. 36a). In the first design the sitter wore a wide-brimmed hat largely covering his forehead, similar to a hat in a man's portrait that Holbein painted a year earlier (fig. 36b).[10] This hat was painted out, producing one of the artist's few paintings to depict the sitter bare-headed. Also visible in the IRR image, close to the man's shoulder and neck, are the contours of what was once a fur-trimmed cloak, a garment that occurs in several of Holbein's paintings (cf. fig. 36b). The most striking discovery

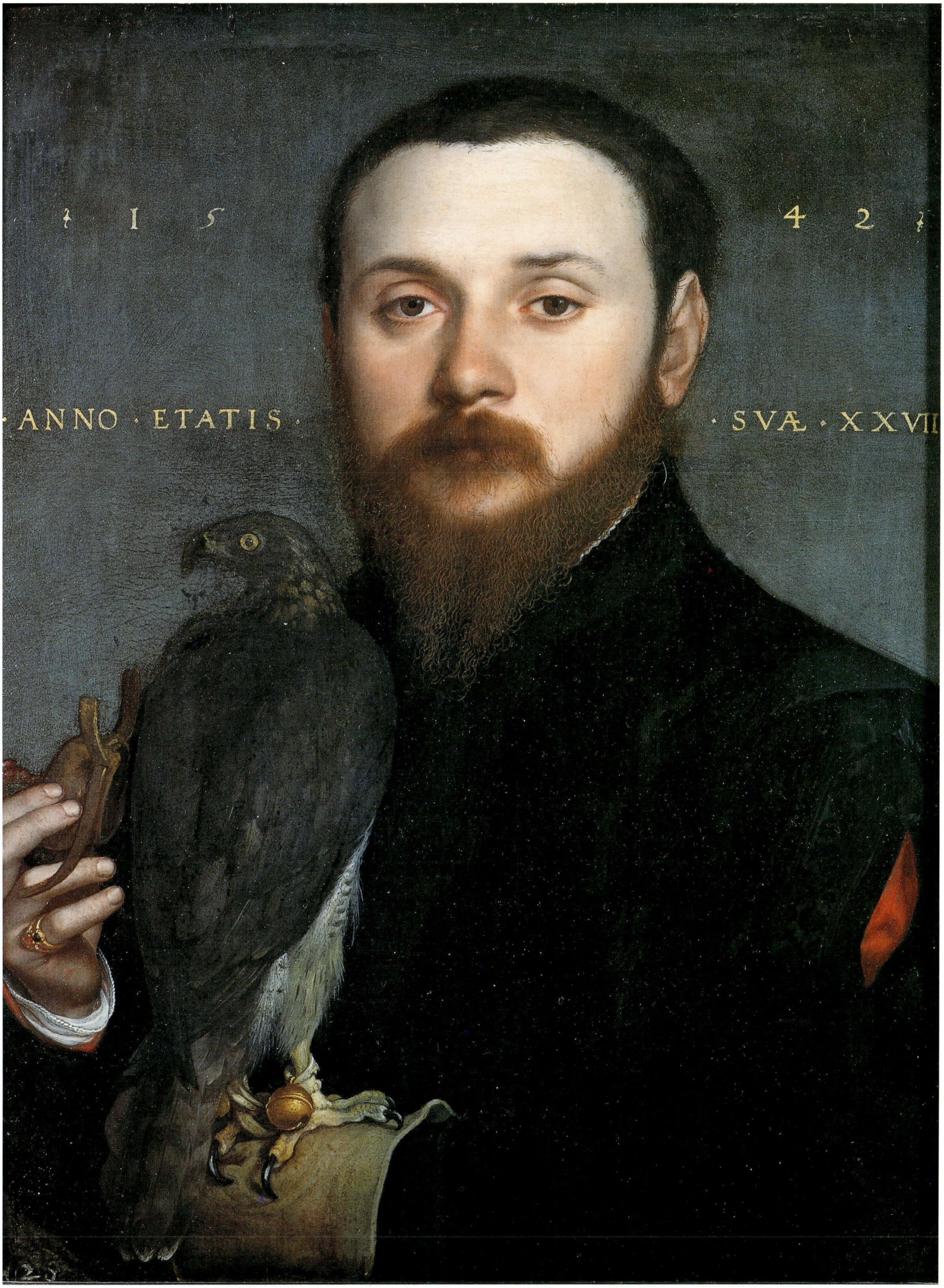
1 5 42
ANNO · ETATIS · SVÆ · XXVII

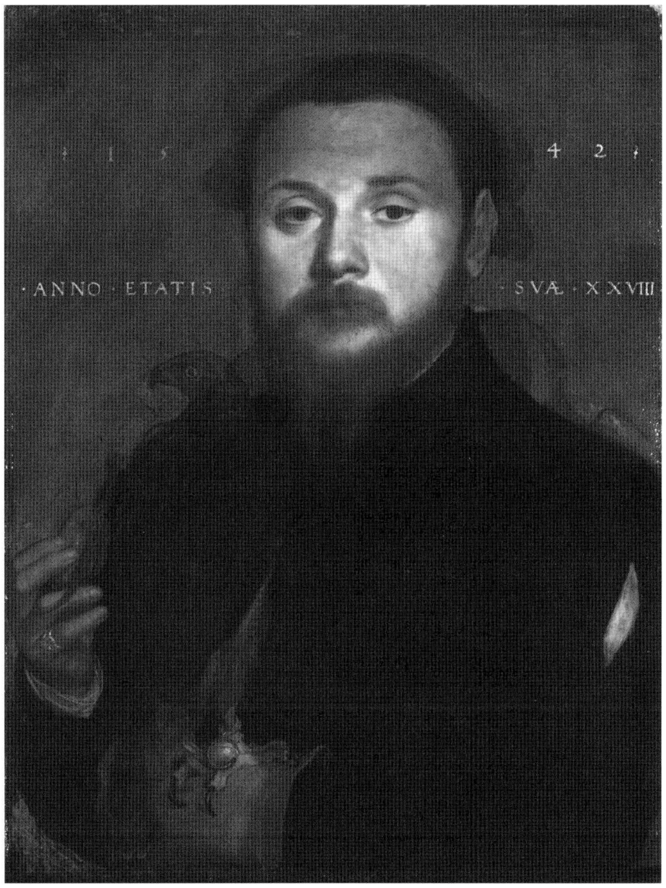

fig. 36a
Infrared
reflectogram of
cat. no. 36

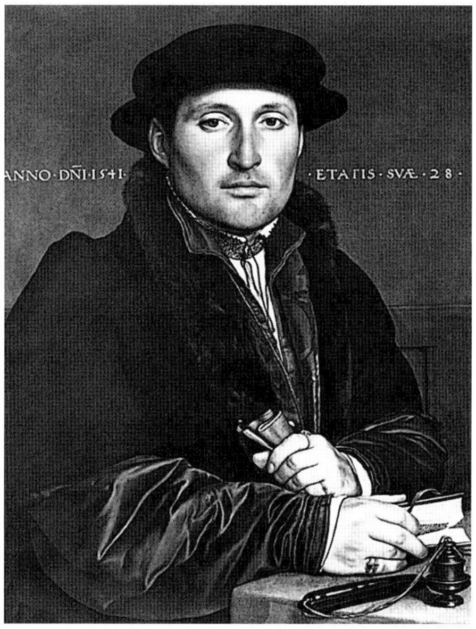

fig. 36b
Hans Holbein
the Younger,
Portrait of a 28-year-old man at his desk, 1541.
Panel, 46.4 x 34.8 cm.
Vienna,
Kunsthistorisches
Museum,
Gemäldegalerie

arising from the IRR examination, however, is that the hawk was added relatively late in the painting process. The glove was painted over an initially uncovered hand and part of the red sleeve of the jerkin, while the bird itself was depicted over the dark apparel and the background.[11] Had the hawk been planned from the outset, Holbein would have reserved space for it, as was his usual practice. Interestingly, in the *Portrait of a lady with a squirrel and a starling*, one of the few other paintings in which Holbein depicted animals, the prominently placed squirrel was also painted in at a relatively late stage (see cat. no. 7), most probably at the client's request. Perhaps the unknown man in the Mauritshuis portrait sought to enhance his status by adding a hawk to his portrait. QB

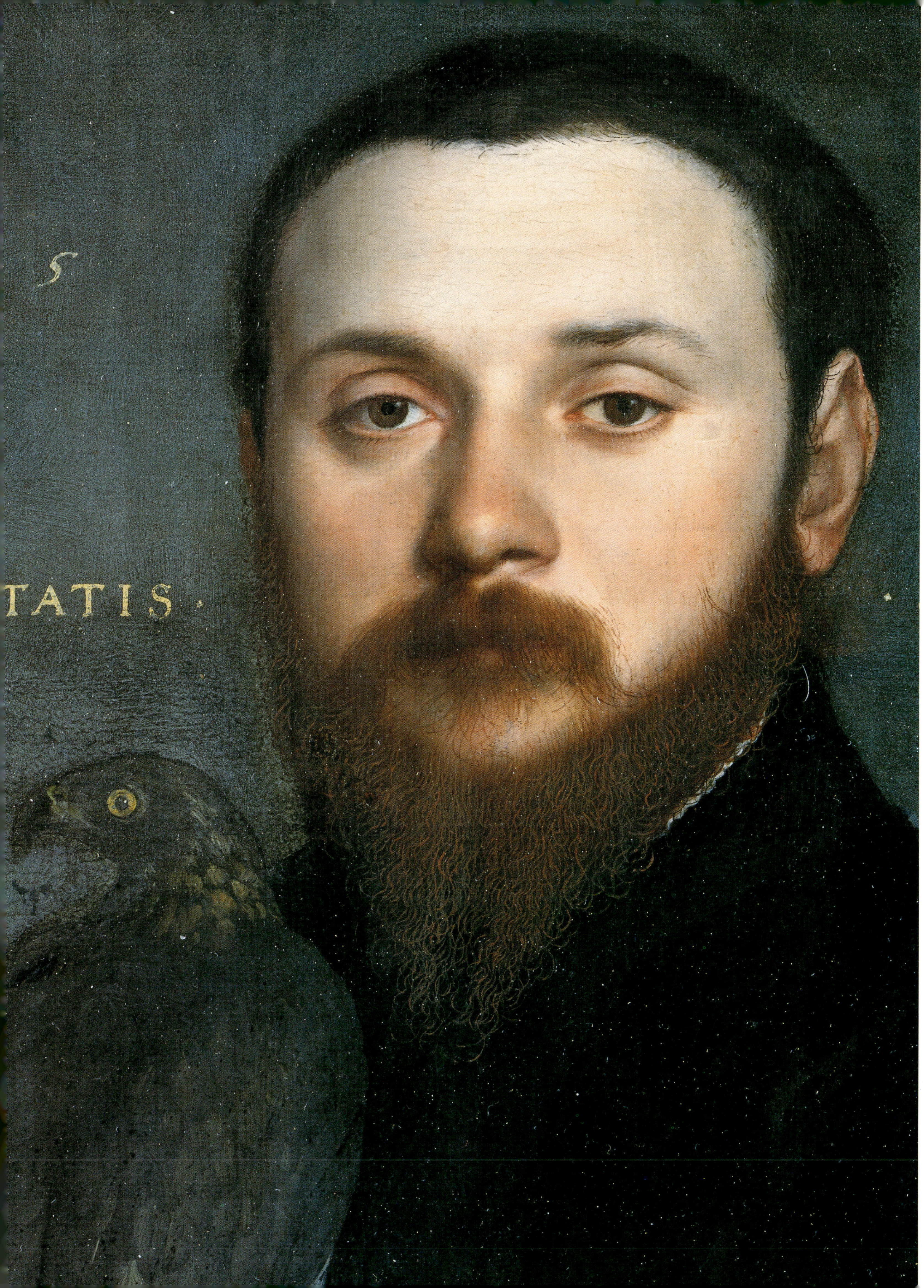
TATIS

Anton the Good, Duke of Lorraine (1489–1544) ?, c. 1543

Panel, 51 x 37 cm. / Inscription in left and right background: ÆTATIS · SVÆ · 54 ·
Berlin, Staatliche Museen zu Berlin, Gemäldegalerie
cat.no. 37

The man in this portrait cannot be identified with complete certainty as Anton the Good, Duke of Lorraine. The German art historian Oskar Fischel, who published the identification in 1926, based himself primarily on the similarity between this portrait and a seventeenth century copy after an older portrait that is in the portrait gallery of the Uffizi, Florence (fig. 37a). The Florentine portrait contains an inscription identifying the sitter as Anton, Duke of Lorraine. The great difference in quality between the two portraits impedes an objective comparison of the facial features, but there is undeniably a resemblance between them.[2]

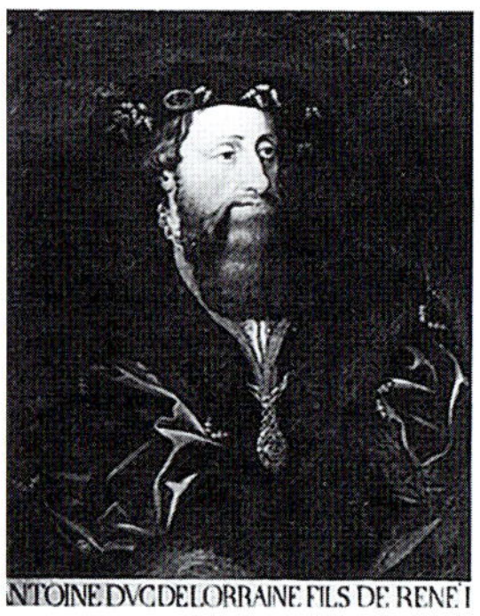

fig. 37a
Anonymous (French, seventeenth century?)
Portrait of Anton the Good, Duke of Lorraine
Canvas, 70 x 56 cm.
Inscription: ANTOINE DVC LORRAINE FILS DE RENE II
Florence, Galleria degli Uffizi

◂ Although the sitter's identity is not unassailable, it is supported by circumstantial evidence. Thus, the generally accepted dating of Holbein's portrait —to about 1543[3]— accords with Anton the Good's date of birth and the age of 54 given on the panel. More importantly perhaps, the duke is a 'plausible' candidate to have had his portrait made by Holbein, because he moved in the same circles as the artist's other sitters and because he could have met the painter, which is more or less a condition for the making of a portrait such as this one. If the two men did in fact meet, it must have been in the summer of 1538, the year in which Holbein made several trips to continental Europe in the service of Henry VIII to make portraits of potential brides for him. In March he went to Brussels to visit Christine, Princess of Denmark and Duchess of Milan (see p. 31, fig. 28), whom Henry had visions of marrying. In June he depicted Marie de Vendôme. Finally, in August he journeyed to Joinville and Nancy to make the portraits of two daughters of the de Guise family and of Anne of Lorraine, a daughter of Duke Anton the Good.[4] Holbein may well have met the duke in the course of this latter visit, and perhaps it was then that he made a preliminary drawing of him, which he used five years later as a basis for the painting discussed here.[5] In the event, none of these women married Henry. After three marriages, two of which the king had deliberately ended himself, many marriageable ladies of the nobility no longer saw him as an ideal match. Christine of Denmark married François, Duc de Bar, Anton the Good's eldest son, in 1541, and hence became Anton's daughter-in-law. In 1540 Anton's daughter Anne married René of Chalon, whose title of Prince of Orange would pass, upon his death on the battlefield in 1544, to William of Nassau-Dillenburg, the later William of Orange.

◂ From 1508 until his death in 1544 Anton the Good was Duke of Upper Lorraine, which encompassed roughly the current northeast region of France, part of Luxembourg, and the border area with Germany. Much of his career was taken up with France's military campaigns in Italy. He used his diplomatic abilities to build up a firm friendship with Louis XII and later on, in order to protect his duchy, he adopted a neutral position in the skirmishes between Louis's successor François I and Emperor Charles V. Holbein has depicted him in three-quarter profile. He is wearing a jerkin with red sleeves and a jet-black cloak, against which his greyish-black beard stands out in fine contrast. The gold or gilded decorations on the thread in his cap harmonise with the gilded inscription in the background. The painter's primary aim in this portrait was to create an effect of motionlessness and introspection. The most tangible evidence for this is the way in which the sitter's head is positioned —sunk forwards slightly— and his half-shut eyes; the concealment of the hands and the simplification of the body's contours add to this effect. X-radiography has revealed that these latter interventions were entirely deliberate. Holbein initially painted the collar slightly away from the head; it was only in the final stages that he altered it to end higher up, against the back of the sitter's head, greatly enhancing the portrait's monumentality and expressiveness.[6] PP

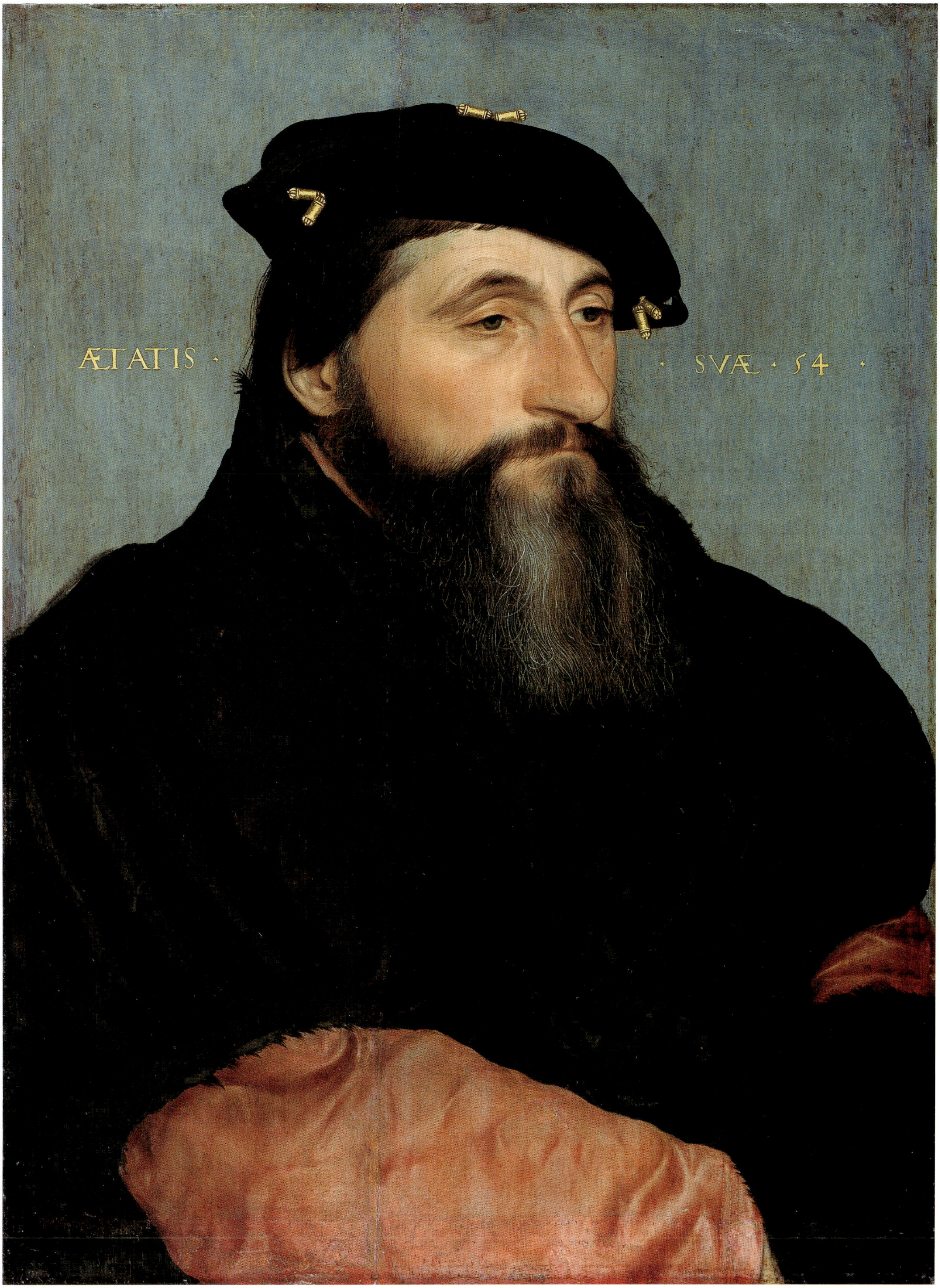
ÆTATIS ·
· SVÆ · 54 ·

XXXVIII

John Chambers (1470?-1549), c. 1543

Panel, 51 x 44 cm
Inscription in left and right background: AETATIS · SVE · 88
Vienna, Kunsthistorisches Museum, Gemäldegalerie
cat.no. 38

On 24 July 1540 the English parliament endorsed the merger of two London guilds, those of the barbers and the surgeons. The ensuing Barber-Surgeons' Company commissioned a large group portrait painting from Holbein to mark this momentous occasion (fig. 38a). It shows Henry VIII enthroned, handing the royal charter for the merger to Thomas Vicary, Master of the new guild. Behind Vicary we see a large group of guild members, identifiable as such by their red sashes. The text in the cartouche above their heads extols the king. Henry is depicted as the personification of the highest authority, with his attributes of crown, ermine royal robe, and sword. Holbein's formal and somewhat static rendering of the scene recalls similar images in the form of miniatures that often decorated the charters themselves; it may also be explained by the fact that no such meeting ever took place.[1]

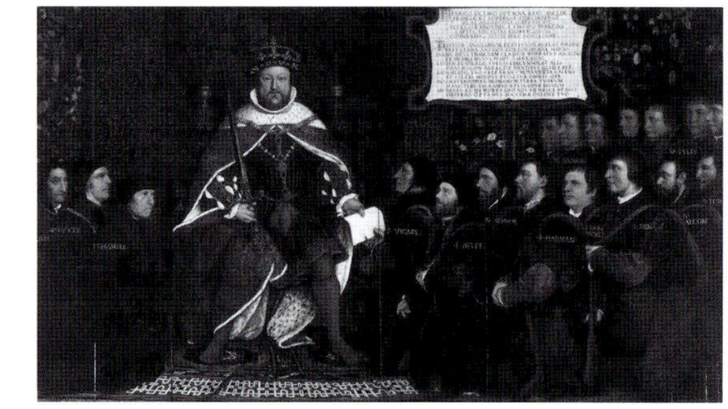

fig. 38a Hans Holbein the Younger, *Henry VIII and the Barber Surgeons*, c. 1540/43. Panel, 180.3 x 312.4 cm. London, Royal College of Surgeons of England

Almost all the sitters can be identified by names painted over their robes. The men standing at the king's right hand, from the edge of the pictorial plane inward, are the court apothecary Thomas Alsop and the court physicians Sir William Butts and —closest to the king— John Chambers. None of these men belonged to the guild. Their inclusion in this group portrait —in the place of honour at the king's right hand— was undoubtedly attributable to their close relationship with him. John Chambers was a cleric as well as Henry's personal physician. He taught medicine at Merton College, Oxford, and later became dean of St Stephen's, Westminster. He was also among the founding members of the Royal College of Physicians in 1518.[2]

The group portrait for the Barber Surgeons' Company led to two new commissions for Holbein, namely individual portraits of William Butts and John Chambers.[3] The portrait of Chambers, which is in Vienna, is virtually identical to his likeness in the group portrait in London. The underdrawing in the Vienna painting reveals that the painter based it either on a preliminary drawing (now lost) for Chambers' likeness in the group portrait or on the cartoon for that painting.[4] For in the group portrait, Chambers —depicted kneeling— directs his eyes upward, towards his king, a detail that was copied exactly in the underdrawing of the Vienna portrait, but subsequently changed, at the painting stage, into a more horizontal gaze.[5] The most significant difference between the two likenesses is the depiction of the hands: in the group portrait Chambers holds them almost reverently under his robe, whereas in the individual portrait they have taken on an important compositional and psychological role. The determined manner in which Chambers grasps his gloves serves rather to emphasise his indomitable facial expression.

The complete absence of any staffage and the marked focus on the sitter's facial features in the panel in Vienna are characteristic of Holbein's late work. Its immediate relationship with the group portrait in London does not enable us to date it with any precision, since the latter's genesis was rather complicated and not entirely clear.[6] Nor is the inscription with Chambers's age particularly helpful, since it does not tally with his date of birth: if Chambers was indeed born in 1470, he would have been aged only 70 or a little older in the period in which Holbein made his portrait —between 1540 and 1543— and not 88, as the inscription records. This great age together with the letters 'SVE' instead of Holbein's customary 'SVÆ' and the rather clumsy appearance of the number suggests that the inscription was altered by a later hand or was perhaps altogether a later addition.[7] Technical examination has not yet confirmed this, however.[8] The background of the portrait must originally have been lighter, but it is now covered with dark overpainting. In spite of this far from delicate intervention, the work remains today one of Holbein's most impressive portraits. Besides compelling admiration for sheer craftsmanship, the rendering of Chambers's lined, slightly hollow-cheeked face and his introverted expression has produced a thoroughly moving portrait. PP

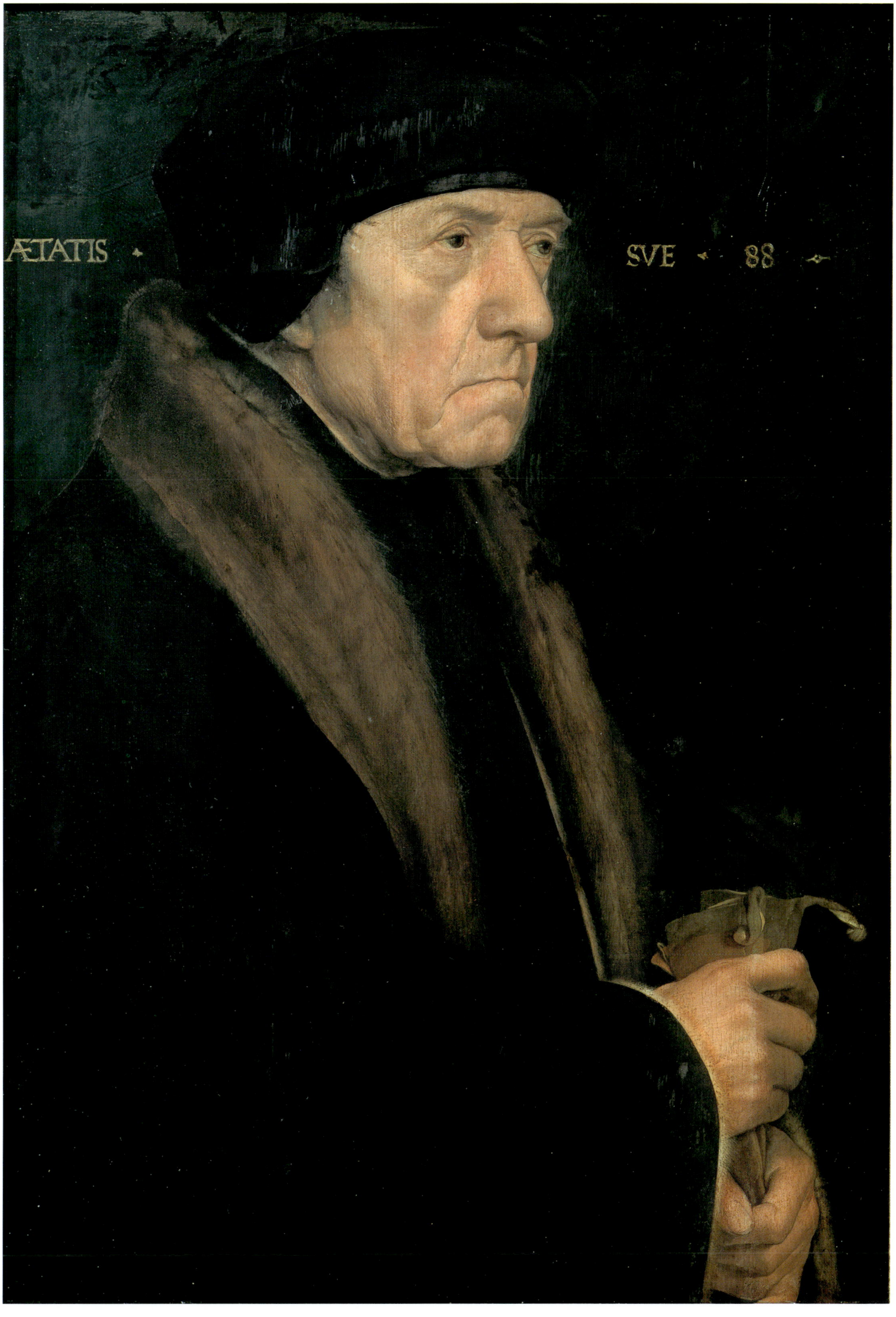
ÆTATIS · SVE · 88 ·

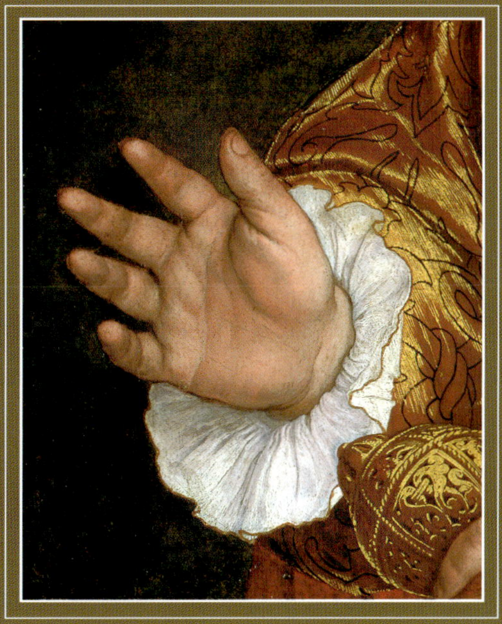

Appendices

The history of Holbein's portrait drawings in Windsor Castle

The British Royal Collections contain an astonishing eighty portrait drawings by Hans Holbein, produced during the artist's first and second periods in England, in 1526–1528 and 1532–1543. Most are studies for painted portraits, as is clear from surviving paintings and from notes that the master added to some of the sheets. Where the painted portraits have been lost, the drawings preserve their memory. Furthermore, as preparatory studies they shed light on Holbein's working methods as a portraitist, and the identifications on the sheets tell us about his English clientele. Last but not least, the drawings are beautifully executed portraits, long appreciated as independent works of art.

The large group of portrait drawings probably derives from Holbein's studio estate. It seems likely that they came into the possession of King Henry VIII after the master's death in 1543. 'A booke of paternes for phisioneamyes' is mentioned in a royal inventory from 1547, made when Edward VI ascended the throne. After Edward's death in 1553 the drawings were acquired by Henry FitzAlan, 12th Earl of Arundel (1512–1580), who had served as Lord Chamberlain in Edward's reign. When FitzAlan died, his collection passed to his son-in-law Lord John Lumley (c. 1533-1609), who possessed an important portrait collection. The first unequivocal reference to an album with Holbein's drawings is in an inventory of Lumley's property, drawn up in 1590: 'a great Booke of Pictures doone by Haunce Holbyn of certyne Lordes, Ladyes, gentlemen and gentlewomen in King Henry the 8: his tyme, their names subscribed by Sr John Cheke Secretary to King Edward the 6 wch booke was King Edward the 6'. Significantly, this tells us that John Cheke (1514–1557) was the man who had noted the sitters' names. Cheke was Prince Edward's tutor from 1544 onwards and later served as his secretary, so that he probably knew many of these men personally. Cheke may have written his notes directly on the sheets - many of which have been substantially cropped — or added them to the drawings pasted into the book. The present inscriptions in gold paint were copied from his inscriptions, possibly at the moment when the sheets were removed from the 'great booke' in the eighteenth century.

The next phase in the complex history of Holbein's portrait drawings came after the death of Lord Lumley in 1609. The latter's celebrated collection of drawings and books — the 'Lumley Library' — came into the possession of Henry, Prince of Wales (1594–1612), who died three years later. The next owner of Holbein's drawings was Henry's younger brother and heir, the later King Charles I (1600–1649). Around 1627, however, the king exchanged his precious album for a painting by Raphael, *St George and the dragon* (now in the National Gallery of Art, Washington). The new owner of the drawings, Philip, 4th Earl of Pembroke (1584–1649/50), who served as Lord Chamberlain from 1626 to 1640, made a gift of his acquisition, almost immediately after the exchange, to his brother-in-law Thomas Howard, Earl of Arundel (1585–1646). Arundel confessed to having a 'foolish curiosity' about Holbein: he owned the largest collection of the master's paintings and drawings that has ever been amassed. There is no record of the portrait drawings' eventual return to the Royal Collections, but it must have occurred before 1675, in the reign of Charles II (1630–1685). In 1727, shortly after George II (1683–1760) came to the throne, his wife, Lady Caroline, found the album in a desk at Kensington Palace. She had the drawings cut out of the album and framed separately, after which the portraits hung on the walls of the royal palaces for several decades. Before 1774 they were placed in bindings again, ending up in the Royal Library in Windsor Castle in the 1830s. There, the drawings were again removed from the books and stored separately. A full fifteen of these precious portrait drawings by Hans Holbein are on loan from the Royal Collection to the Mauritshuis for this exhibition. AvS

Chronology

Events in Holbein's life		*Other events*
Born in Augsburg	1497/98	
	c. 1505	Painting of the *Mona Lisa* by Leonardo da Vinci
Initial training in the studio of his father Hans Holbein the Elder, together with his elder brother Ambrosius	c. 1508	
	1509	Henry VIII crowned king of England followed by his marriage to Catherine of Aragon Erasmus's *In praise of folly*
Trains in Basel together with Ambrosius, under the artist Hans Herbst	1515	Francis I crowned king of France
First official commission: the portraits of Jakob Meyer zum Hasen and Dorothea Kannengiesser	1516	
Departure for Lucerne to make wall paintings for the Hertensteinhuis; from there possibly journeys to northern Italy	1517	Luther disseminates his 95 theses: the beginning of the Reformation
Master painter in Basel; marries Elsbeth Binzenstock (†1549)	1519	Charles V crowned Holy Roman Emperor
	1521	Erasmus settles in Basel for the second time
Makes a portrait of Erasmus	1523	
Travels to France, probably to secure commissions from Francis I	1524	
Travels via Antwerp to England	1526	
Lives with Thomas More in Chelsea and makes portraits of More's family	1527	
Returns to Basel and purchases a house in the St Johann quarter on the banks of the Rhine	1528	
Completes the *Darmstadt Madonna*, but secures few commissions	1529	Iconoclasm in Basel Erasmus departs for Freiburg Thomas More becomes Lord Chancellor
	1530	Thomas Cromwell greatly consolidates his power
Leaves for London for the second time, and rents a house in Mayden Lane, London	1532	Thomas More resigns as Lord Chancellor and falls into disfavour
Acquires numerous clients among the Steelyard members and courtiers	1533	Henry VIII has his marriage to Catherine of Aragon annulled and marries Anne Boleyn
	1534	Act of Succession, Act of Supremacy and the founding of the Church of England
	1535	Thomas More executed
Appointed as court painter, with an annual salary of 30 pounds	1536	Execution of Anne Boleyn Henry VIII marries Jane Seymour
Mural painting of the royal family in Whitehall Palace	1537	Crushing of the Pilgrimage of Grace Birth of Edward, heir to the throne Death of Jane Seymour
Makes portraits of possible brides for Henry VIII, first in Brussels and then in Nancy, visiting Basel as part of this trip	1538	
Undertakes another journey, this time to Düren in Germany, to make a portrait of Anne of Cleves	1539	
	1540	Henry VIII marries Anne of Cleves; the marriage is annulled a few months later and Henry marries Catherine Howard Cromwell disgraced and beheaded
Holbein receives no more royal commissions after Cromwell's death		
Holbein draws up his will in his home in Aldgate, London on 7 October. A little while later he dies, at about 45 years of age	1543	

In Basel he leaves behind a wife and two daughters, Katharina and Küngold.
His sons are serving apprentices as goldsmiths: Philip the eldest in Paris, Jakob in London
There are also two illegitimate children in London.

Biographies

Petrus Aegidius see **Pieter Gillis**

Bonifacius Amerbach (1495–1562)
Amerbach studied at the universities of Basel and Freiburg, and was a pupil of the writer, judge and music theorist Andreas Alciatus in Avignon. Holbein made his portrait of the learned humanist in 1519 (see p. 18, fig. 14). In 1521 Amerbach was offered a chair in Roman law at the University of Basel. Amerbach was a very close friend of **Erasmus**, who named him as his sole heir. Bonifacius's son Basilius collected works by Holbein. In 1661 Basel city council purchased his Holbein collection, which became the basis of one of the first public museums in the world.

Catherine of Aragon (1485–1536)
The Spanish princess Catherine of Aragon married Arthur, heir to the English throne, in 1501. The marriage did not last long, as Arthur died only six months later. His brother Henry VIII then married Catherine, when he became king in 1509. At length they had a daughter, Mary, but their union did not produce a male heir. When Henry fell in love with the beautiful Anne Boleyn, he sought the annulment of his marriage, which the pope however refused to grant. The emperor Charles V, Catherine's nephew, also opposed the annulment, generating a political dispute. The controversy eventually led to the establishment of the Church of England. The king married Anne Boleyn (1533) and Catherine was expelled from the court.

Anne Boleyn (c. 1501–1536)
While still married to **Catherine of Aragon**, **Henry VIII** became interested in Anne Boleyn. Letters from the king have been preserved that reveal his passion for her. He promised Anne that he would secure an annulment of his marriage to Catherine so that he could marry her, and this is in fact what happened. After an enormous political and ecclesiastical conflict, Henry married Anne in January 1533. She gave him a daughter, the later Elizabeth I. Still, when no male heir was forthcoming, the king wanted to be rid of her. Anne was arrested and made to answer charges of adultery, witchcraft and incest. On 19 May 1536 she was beheaded. Shortly after her execution, Henry married one of Anne's ladies-in-waiting, **Jane Seymour**.

Hans Burgkmair (1473–1531)
Hans Burgkmair was one of the most important German artists of his day. When he returned home after a stay in Italy he brought the new Renaissance style of painting to Augsburg. Together with **Hans Holbein the Elder**, Burgkmair painted the seven great churches of Rome on panels in St Catherine's monastery in Augsburg (1501–1504). Burgkmair was probably Holbein the Elder's brother-in-law. Besides being a painter, Burgkmair was also a designer of woodcuts; like **Dürer** he worked on the *Triumph of Maximilian*, a series of large prints depicting the procession of the emperor and his retinue. Hans Holbein the Younger drew inspiration from his work.

Charles V (1500–1558)
Upon the death in 1506 of his father, Philip the Fair, Charles became king of a large number of Netherlandish territories. At 16 years of age he also became king of Spain (1516–1556) and three years later he succeeded his grandfather **Maximilian I** as Holy Roman Emperor (1519–1558). He became embroiled in a protracted conflict with **Francis I**, the king of France. Charles displayed little interest in humanism and the arts. He nonetheless had a number of artists at his court, his favourite being Titian.

Anne of Cleves (1515–1557)
After **Jane Seymour**, the third wife of **Henry VIII**, died in childbirth, **Thomas Cromwell** was instructed to find a suitable replacement. Cromwell's main concern was to ensure that Henry's next marriage consolidated ties with Protestant Germany. Holbein was dispatched to make portraits of the various candidates so that the king could form an opinion of their appearance. Anne of Cleves, the sister of the duke of Cleves, was among them. Henry VIII was delighted with the woman in Holbein's portrait (see p.30, fig. 29), but when he saw his fiancée for the first time he was greatly disappointed and is said to have called her a 'Flemish mare'. They were married nonetheless, on 6 January 1540. Soon afterwards Henry became enamoured of **Catherine Howard** and therefore sought to divest himself of Anne. Cromwell was told to arrange it. Since it emerged that Anne had officially never severed her engagement with the duke of Lorraine, her marriage to Henry could be annulled. Anne resigned herself to her fate. In recompense for her cooperation she was richly rewarded, and given the honorary title of 'the King's Sister'.

Thomas Cranmer (1489–1556)
Thomas Cranmer, fiercely loyal to the king, was appointed Archbishop of Canterbury in 1533. It therefore fell to him to pronounce the annulment of the marriage between **Henry VIII** and **Catherine of Aragon**. When Henry wanted a divorce from his second wife, **Anne Boleyn**, in 1536, Cranmer obliged once again. Cranmer's writings include the *Book of Common Prayer* (1549), containing the liturgy of the **Church of England**. When Henry died in 1547, Cranmer was at his deathbed. After the brief reign of **Edward VI**, Mary—the daughter of Henry and Catherine— became queen of England. This Catholic queen turned against Cranmer. The archbishop was taken prisoner and convicted of treason and heresy. He tried to exculpate himself with recantations, but to no avail. Cranmer was burned at the stake on 21 March 1556.

Thomas Cromwell (c. 1485–1540)
Thomas Cromwell was a highly influential statesman. He began his career as secretary to **Thomas Wolsey**. After Wolsey's fall from grace, Cromwell took his place as **Henry VIII**'s primary advisor. He helped Henry achieve the split from Rome and establish the **Church of England**. After the death of **Jane Seymour**, Cromwell toured Europe to find a new wife for the king. At length he fixed upon **Anne of Cleves** — the sister of the Duke of Cleves, to forge ties between England and the Protestant movement. The marriage was solemnized but soon annulled. By this time Henry was surrounded by people who hated Cromwell and were plotting against him. **Thomas Howard**, Duke of Norfolk, convinced the king that Cromwell was guilty of heresy, a charge serious enough to warrant a death sentence. Cromwell was beheaded at the Tower of London on 28 July 1540. A few months after the execution, Henry was stricken by remorse. In a fit of fury, he accused his counsellors of lying to him and of deliberately precipitating the fall of his 'most loyal servant'. Cromwell is regarded as one of the most important political figures in English history. Holbein painted his portrait in 1534 (p. 25, fig. 24).

Albrecht Dürer (1471–1528)
Albrecht Dürer was one of the greatest German artists of the Renaissance. To complete his training as a painter (under Michael Wolgemut), Dürer spent several years (1490–1494) travelling around the German territories. He then visited Venice, where he was particularly influenced by the art of Giovanni Bellini and Andrea Mantegna. Back in Nuremberg, Dürer set up his own studio, where besides painting he produced prints for the open market. From 1515 onward he received from Emperor **Maximilian I** an annuity for his work on the series of monumental woodcuts entitled *The triumph of Maximilian* (published in 1526). On his way to the Netherlands (1520–1521) he attended the coronation of Emperor **Charles V** on 23 October 1520. Dürer had a lifelong friendship with the humanist **Pirckheimer**, and **Erasmus** admired him for his intellect as well as his art. Dürer wrote three treatises on art theory.

Edward VI (1547–1553)
Edward was the son of **Henry VIII** and **Jane Seymour**. Holbein painted his portrait in 1539 (cat. no. 33). Edward became king of England upon the death of his father in 1547. Since he was still a minor, his uncle **Edward Seymour** ruled as Protector of England, enjoying all the powers of a sovereign. Edward VI was known for his intelligence and piety. His health was poor, however, and he died at 16 years of age.

Desiderius Erasmus (1466/69–1536)
Erasmus, one of the most influential humanists in history, played an important role in launching Holbein's career as a painter. He commissioned several portraits of himself from the artist (see cat. no. 1 and the essay by Stephanie Buck) and gave the artist letters of recommendation, giving him access to men who would become some of his main clients in England.

John Fisher (1459/69–1535)
John Fisher was bishop of Rochester and professor of theology at the University of Cambridge. He hired Erasmus's services as a lecturer and was probably the author of the royal treatise of Henry VIII against Luther (1521). Henry's plan to seek an annulment of his marriage with Catherine of Aragon precipitated Fisher's demise. The cleric took Catherine's side, advising and assisting her throughout the controversy. When the annulment was almost a fact, in May 1533, Fisher was imprisoned to prevent him from causing trouble. He was released a few days after Henry's new wife Anne Boleyn was crowned queen, on 1 June 1533. But when Fisher refused to take the oath required by the Act of Succession, he was imprisoned again on 26 April 1534 and sentenced to death the following year. He was canonised in 1935.

Francis I (1494–1547)
At 20 years of age Francis succeeded his uncle Louis XII as king of France. His reign was not distinguished by military or political success. After the death of Emperor Maximilian I he made a vain attempt to secure the succession. In Italy a succession of wars broke out between Francis's troops and those of Charles V — his rival, who had bribed his way to the position of Holy Roman Emperor. None of these wars ended well for France. Francis is looked on as France's first Renaissance king. He was a great patron of art; celebrated artists such as Leonardo da Vinci, Andrea del Sarto and Benvenuto Cellini worked at his court.

Johannes Froben (c. 1460–1527)
The celebrated German publisher Johannes Froben settled in Basel. A friend of Erasmus, he published a range of humanist writings, including a reprint of Erasmus's *Praise of folly*, with commentary by the scholar Gerhard Lister of Utrecht (1515). He also printed the Latin version of the New Testament (1516), which Erasmus had edited and translated from the Greek. Holbein painted portraits of him in 1522/23 and in 1531/32.

Oswald Geisshüsler (1488–1552)
Oswald Geisshüsler, better known as Myconius, studied the classics at the University of Basel. In 1514 he became a schoolmaster there. The brothers Hans and Ambrosius Holbein painted his signboard. When Erasmus came to live in Basel, he made Geisshüsler's acquaintance, and it was probably he who named him 'Myconius'. The Holbein brothers scribbled little drawings in the margins of Myconius's copy of Erasmus's *Praise of folly*. In 1516 Myconius went to work in Zürich, where he joined a Reformed group. Thanks to his efforts, Ulrich Zwingli —the leader of the Swiss Reformation— came to Zürich, and the Reformation took hold there. In 1531 he returned to Basel, where he acquired the office of town preacher. Myconius wrote a number of treatises and a life of Zwingli (1532), as well as a statement of Protestant doctrine that was adopted in 1534 and that is known as the First Confession of Basel.

Pieter Gillis (c. 1486–1533)
Pieter Gillis, also known by his Latinised name of Petrus Aegidius, was the town clerk of Antwerp. Erasmus often stayed with him in that city. He was also a good friend of Thomas More, who gave him a role in his book *Utopia*. At the end of 1526, Holbein was able to stay with Pieter Gillis on his way to England, thanks to a letter of introduction from Erasmus.

Henry Guildford (1489–1532)
Sir Henry Guildford was one of Henry VIII's favourite courtiers. One of the gentlemen of the Privy Chamber, he held a variety of honorary positions such as *Comptroller of the Royal Household*. In 1526 he received the Order of the Garter, the highest distinction that an English monarch can award. The following year, Holbein painted the portraits of Guildford and his wife, Mary Wotton (cat. no. 6).

Henry VIII (1491–1547)
Henry Tudor was born on 28 June 1491 as the second son of Henry VII and Elizabeth of York. When his elder brother Arthur died in 1502, Henry became heir to the throne. After his father's death in 1509, the athletic, good-looking young man was crowned king of England. That same year he married Catherine of Aragon, his brother's widow. During his reign he succeeded, with the assistance of Thomas Wolsey, in building England into a powerful nation. In 1521 his open opposition to Martin Luther prompted Pope Leo X to grant the title of *Fidei Defensor* (Defender of the Faith). However, his annulment of his marriage to Catherine in 1533 culminated in a break with Rome. Henry became the head of the new Church of England.

◂ Henry would marry six times in total. His wives were Catherine of Aragon (marriage annulled, 1533), Anne Boleyn (executed 1536), Jane Seymour (died 1537), Anne of Cleves (divorced 1540), Catherine Howard (executed 1542) and Catherine Parr (died 1548). Three children were born of these marriages: Mary (the daughter of Catherine of Aragon), Elizabeth (the daughter of Anne Boleyn) and Edward (the son of Jane Seymour). As he grew older, Henry became obese and suffered from a variety of other ailments. He died in 1547. His three children all reigned after him, so that the Tudors held power until 1603. Holbein painted several portraits of Henry VIII (see p. 28, fig. 27 and p. 32, fig. 31). These portraits determine to a large extent the image that we now have of this king: large and indomitable.

Hans Holbein the Elder (1460/65–1524)
Hans Holbein the Elder was the paterfamilias of a family of painters, including his two sons, Ambrosius and Hans Holbein the Younger, and his brother Sigmund. Born in Ulm, Hans Holbein the Elder settled in Augsburg around 1493, where his work was soon in great demand. He is known primarily for his Late Gothic altarpieces, but he also designed stained- glass windows. In addition, numerous silverpoint drawings display his talent and insight as a portraitist. Renaissance influence is visible particularly in his later paintings, into which he incorporated decorative elements of classical architecture.

Catherine Howard (1521–1542)
Catherine Howard was an impoverished niece of Thomas Howard, duke of Norfolk. Her late cousin Anne Boleyn was Henry VIII's second wife, and she was executed in 1536. At the end of 1539, Catherine was appointed as lady-in-waiting to the king's fourth wife, Anne of Cleves. The king became interested in her, had his marriage to Anne of Cleves annulled and took Catherine as his new bride. Catherine proved to be a flirtatious young woman, who had a number of extra-marital affairs. Before long, this conduct led to her arrest, after which she suffered the same fate as her cousin Anne Boleyn: Catherine was beheaded at the Tower on 13 February 1542. Holbein painted her portrait in 1540/41.

Thomas Howard (1473–1554)
Thomas Howard, third duke of Norfolk, was one of the most powerful nobles in England and a loyal servant of Henry VIII. Two of his nieces married the king: Anne Boleyn and Catherine Howard, who were Henry's second and fifth wives, respectively. Howard had an impressing military career, besides which he held important positions at court. In 1546 he was imprisoned, together with his son Henry Howard, the duke of Surrey. Henry was executed for high treason in January 1547, but Thomas Howard just escaped this fate, as the king died the night before he was due to be executed. After six years in prison, Howard was released during the reign of Queen Mary; like the queen, he was a Catholic. Holbein painted his portrait in or around 1539 (cat. no. 34).

Nicolaus Kratzer (1486–1550)
Nicolaus Kratzer studied mathematics and astronomy at the universities of Cologne and Wittenberg and worked as an instrument maker. In 1517 he went to England, where Cardinal Thomas Wolsey secured for him a chair in mathematics at the University of Oxford. As a humanist he built up a friendship with Thomas More. In 1519 he was appointed as court astronomer to Henry VIII.

Holbein painted Kratzer's portrait in 1528 (see p. 21, fig. 20).

Martin Luther (1483–1546)
The Augustinian monk Martin Luther was ordained priest in 1507. The following year he embarked on a study of theology at the University of Wittenberg. He became acquainted with the ideas of humanism, and embraced the notion of a return to Scripture. After taking his doctorate in 1512, Luther accepted a chair in biblical theology. The ideas he propagated led to the **Reformation**. Thus he denounced the abuses of the Catholic Church, such as the trade in indulgences. In 1517 he drew up his 95 Theses, provoking responses ranging from enthusiastic agreement to fierce criticism. At length Luther was excommunicated by Pope Leo X, and **Charles V** placed him under an imperial ban as an outlaw. With the help of the elector Frederick the Wise he went into hiding at Warburg. Here he wrote the first German translation of the New Testament, which made the Bible accessible to far more readers. In 1522 Luther returned to Wittenberg to bring the chaos that the Reformation had unleashed there under control. He lost a good deal of his popularity when he sided with the authorities in the revolutionary Peasants' War (1524–1525). **Erasmus** too turned against Luther in this period. Urged on by Luther, many monks abandoned their monasteries. Luther too discarded his monk's habit, and married Katharina von Bora, a former nun. He wrote a German mass (1526) and produced the first evangelical church music. In 1529 he compiled the Small and Large Catechisms. In 1534 Luther completed his German translation of the Bible, which was published that same year.

Maximilian I (1459–1519)
Maximilian was the son of Emperor Fredrick III, of the House of Habsburg. In 1477 he married Mary of Burgundy, so as to gain control of the Burgundian as well as the Habsburg territories. In 1493 Maximilian succeeded his father as Holy Roman Emperor. He became involved in the Italian wars, with the aim of expanding the Habsburg kingdom and curbing the power of France. The flowering of the realm under his grandson **Charles V** was to a large extent attributable to Maximilian's shrewd policy of marital alliances.

Jakob Meyer zum Hasen (1482–1531)
The merchant's son Jakob Meyer zum Hasen made a fortune as a money changer. In 1516 he was elected burgomaster of Basel. That same year he gave Hans Holbein his earliest known independent commission: a double portrait of Meyer and his wife Dorothea Kannengießer. In 1521, Meyer became embroiled in an extortion scandal that tarnished his reputation beyond repair. After this he served only as the spokesman of the Catholic party in Basel, which was losing ground as the **Reformation** gathered steam. When he was in these dire straits, Meyer commissioned Holbein, in 1526, to paint an altarpiece with the Madonna and Child, flanked by himself and other members of his family. The resulting work became known as the *Darmstadt Madonna* (cat. no. 2).

Thomas More (c. 1478–1535)
After studying widely, including courses in the classics and law at the universities of Oxford and London, Thomas More was admitted to the bar in 1501. An encounter with Erasmus during the latter's first visit to England led to a lifelong friendship. Erasmus dedicated his *Praise of folly* to More. More was strongly drawn to the religious life, and spent several years in a Carthusian monastery in London. But he was also attracted to political life, and in 1504 More became a member of the House of Commons. He spent some time in Flanders in 1515 as **Henry VIII**'s envoy. The following year his book *Utopia* was published, in which More criticised the economic and political fabric of England and outlined his own ideal world. In 1517 he became a member of the **Privy Council** and in 1521 he was knighted. In 1526–1528 Hans Holbein stayed in More's house, and made portraits of his host (cat.no.3). More made no bones about his disapproval of the king's plans to seek an annulment of his marriage to **Catherine of Aragon**, but was nonetheless made Lord Chancellor in 1529. He finally resigned in 1532. When he subsequently refused, in 1534, to assent under oath to the **Act of Succession** and the **Act of Supremacy**, More was sentenced to death for high treason and beheaded on 6 July 1535. He was canonised by Pope Pius XI in 1935.

Myconius see **Oswald Geisshüsler**

Catherine Parr (1512–1548)
Catherine Parr was the sixth and last wife of **Henry VIII**. Twice widowed when she married the king, she was actually in love with Thomas Seymour, the brother of the late **Jane Seymour**, Henry's third wife. She accepted Henry's proposal all the same, and the royal marriage took place on 12 July 1543. Catherine was a good stepmother to Henry's children and made sure that Elizabeth received a good education. She was interested in Protestantism and took part in the religious debates of the day. Henry construed this as undermining his authority, and it was only by expressing the most profound contrition that Catherine was able to escape being arrested. When the king died, on 28 January 1547, there was no longer any impediment to her marrying Thomas Seymour. They were married that same year. One year later, Catherine died as a result of childbirth.

Willibald Pirckheimer (1479–1530)
This famous German humanist served as counsellor to emperors **Maximilian I** and **Charles V**. He described Maximilian's struggle against Switzerland, translated Greek treatises into German, and published humanist books. Together with Fabius Zonarius, Pirckheimer edited the famous satire on the Catholic theologian Johannes Eck, entitled *De Eckius dedolatus*. He corresponded with famous contemporaries such as **Dürer** and **Erasmus**.

Edward Seymour (c. 1500–1552)
Edward Seymour was a prominent soldier and diplomat. He was the brother of **Jane Seymour**, who married King **Henry VIII** in 1536. When the king died in 1547, the heir to the throne, **Edward VI**, was too young to rule the country. Seymour was appointed Protector, with all the powers of a sovereign, and he was also made Duke of Somerset. With the help of **Thomas Cranmer**, Archbishop of Canterbury, he accomplished major Protestant reforms in the **Church of England**. He led the English troops against the Scots, culminating in a great victory at Pinkie (1547). That same year his brother Thomas Seymour married **Catherine Parr**, Henry's widow. After Catherine's death in 1548, Thomas made an unsuccessful bid to obtain the hand in marriage of Princess Elizabeth (the later queen of England). In consequence, Edward had his brother arrested, and Thomas was sentenced to death for high treason. In 1549 Seymour's enemies engineered his downfall. He was imprisoned, and though released in 1550 he was arrested again the following year, this time followed by his execution.

Jane Seymour (c. 1509–1537)
The day after **Anne Boleyn**'s execution, **Henry VIII** became engaged to Jane Seymour, one of Anne's ladies-in-waiting. They were married on 30 May 1536, and Jane became Henry's third wife. She gave him his only legitimate son, **Edward**, but she died twelve days after the delivery from complications arising from the Caesarean section. She is believed to have been Henry's favourite wife. She was mild-mannered, and achieved a reconciliation between Henry and Mary, his daughter by **Catherine of Aragon**. Holbein painted her portrait in 1536/37 (cat.nos. 26-28).

William Warham (c. 1450–1532)
As Archbishop of Canterbury (1504-1532) and Lord Chancellor (1504–1515), William Warham was immensely influential in all affairs of state. During **Erasmus's** second stay in England (1509–1514), Warham was one of his patrons. In 1524, Erasmus sent Warham a portrait of himself that had been painted by Holbein. In 1515 Warham resigned as Lord Chancellor because he disapproved of the anti-French policy pursued by **Henry VIII**. Cardinal **Thomas Wolsey** succeeded him. Holbein painted Warham's portrait in 1527 (p. 23, fig. 22). In 1530, Warham was compelled to sign the petition asking the pope to annul the marriage between Henry VIII and **Catherine of Aragon**. During the founding of the **Church of England**, Warham remained loyal to the pope and was therefore no longer certain of his life. Nonetheless, he died a natural death in 1532.

Thomas Wolsey (1471/74–1530)
The cleric Thomas Wolsey held a variety of diplomatic and senior official positions at the English court from 1507 onwards. In 1514 he became Archbishop of York. He succeeded **William Warham** as Lord Chancellor. Such was his power at this stage that he

was called *Ipse Rex* (the king himself). In 1521 and 1523 Wolsey put his name forward unsuccessfully as a candidate for the papacy. The question of the annulment of **Henry VIII**'s marriage to **Catherine of Aragon** precipitated Wolsey's fall. Wolsey fell from grace when he failed to persuade the pope to grant the annulment. He was compelled to resign as Lord Chancellor, in which office he was succeeded by **Thomas More**. In 1530 charges of treason were brought against him. Before he could be tried, however, Wolsey died in Leicester Abbey. BvdM

—

Explanations of Historical Terms

Act of Succession
After the annulment of the marriage between Henry VIII and Catherine of Aragon, the Act of Succession of 1534 determined that their daughter Mary (born in 1516) was illegitimate, and therefore could not succeed to the throne. Instead, the future queen was Elizabeth, then just a few months old, who was the daughter of Henry and his second wife, Anne Boleyn. The birth of Henry's legitimate son, Edward, in 1537, produced a new heir to the throne. In February 1544 Parliament eventually adopted a new Act of Succession, determining that Edward was first in line, followed by Mary (who had by then been rehabilitated), while Elizabeth was now third in line to the throne. The three Tudor monarchs later ascended the throne in this order.

Act of Supremacy
On 3 November 1534, Parliament adopted the Act of Supremacy recognising Henry VIII as the 'Supreme Head in earth, immediately under God, of the Church of England', thus formalising the break with Rome. All government officials had been placed under an obligation to take an oath declaring their allegiance to the Act. Those who refused, such as Thomas More and John Fisher, were executed for high treason.

Church of England
The Church of England was founded in 1534, largely in consequence of an escalating conflict between Henry VIII and the pope in Rome. The king wanted his marriage with Catherine of Aragon annulled, so that he could marry his new love, Anne Boleyn. When the pope refused permission, Henry and Thomas Cromwell side-stepped the pope's authority by founding an independent Church of England. This Reformation made the sovereign the head of the new Protestant Church. Directly below him were the Archbishop of Canterbury (see Thomas Cranmer) and the Archbishop of York.

Greenwich Palace
Greenwich Palace — sixteenth-century Greenwich was a village about 7 kilometres to the east of London — was a complex beautifully situated on the banks of the Thames. Henry VIII spent a fortune on building and decorating his palaces. By the end of his life he had fifty, including Windsor, Richmond and Hampton Court. Greenwich Palace, where he was born, was initially his favourite residence. During his marriages to Catherine of Aragon and Anne Boleyn the court spent most of its time here. Holbein painted decorations for a temporary banquet hall in this palace in 1527 to commemorate the signing of a peace treaty with France. In the seventeenth century the palace was largely demolished to make room for the Royal Naval Hospital, for destitute sailors.

Humanism
Humanism was the intellectual movement that determined the course of the Renaissance. Its name derived from its emphasis on human rather than theological development. It derived its inspiration primarily from philosophical and contemplative texts from classical and early Christian times, which were once again studied with great enthusiasm and published. The invention of printing around 1450 was key to this development, as it enabled accurate copies of texts to be distributed rapidly. Humanism developed first in Italy, and gradually spread to all parts of Europe, through an international network of thinkers and scholars, as a philosophical and religious movement. Erasmus was a pivotal figure in this network.

Iconoclasm
During the rise of Protestantism, religious works of art in churches and monasteries in many parts of Northern and Central Europe were destroyed. This Iconoclasm was driven by the Reformists' revulsion of the worship of images and the wealth of the Church. The destruction of images began in Wittenberg, in 1522, followed by Zürich in 1523, Copenhagen in 1530, Münster in 1534, Geneva in 1535, and Augsburg in 1537. Many years later, in 1566, the Iconoclasm reached the Netherlands. Holbein witnessed it at first hand in Basel on 8 February 1529. Erasmus described this event as follows: 'Nothing was left of the sculptures, either in the churches or in the cloisters, in the portals or in the monasteries. Whatever painted pictures remained were daubed over with whitewash, whatever was inflammable was thrown upon the pile, whatever was not was broken to pieces.'

London
In Holbein's day, London was a walled city with a population of about 85,000. Although more and more buildings sprang up outside the walls, the centre of government in Westminster was not yet engulfed by the city. In 1532 Holbein moved into the house he rented in Mayden Lane, near St Paul's Cathedral. He later lived in Aldgate, in a neighbourhood that was popular among foreigners.

1. Westminster, the centre of government
2. Whitehall Palace, the residence of Henry VIII
3. Mayden Lane, the location of Holbein's first home in London
4. Steelyard, the site occupied by the German merchants
5. Aldgate, the location of Holbein's second London home
6. Tower of London, where prominent figures who had been disgraced were executed

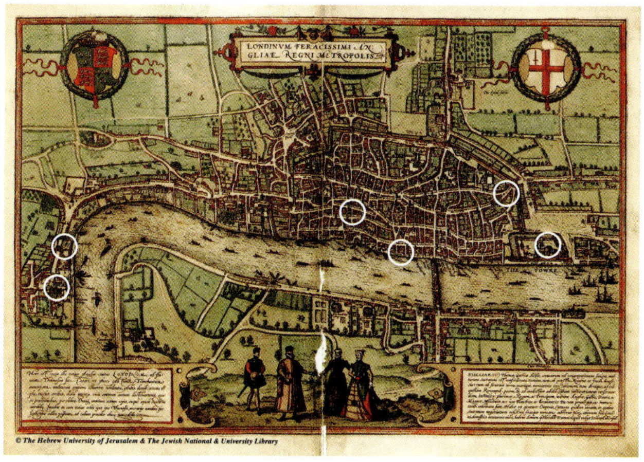

Map of London around 1560, taken from G. Braun and F. Hogenberg, *Civitates orbis terrarum*, Cologne 1572 (© The Hebrew University of Jerusalem & The Jewish National & University Library)

Monasteries, dissolution of the
The English Reformation led to the dissolution of all the country's monasteries. Through its chief representative Thomas Cromwell, the Crown confiscated all the monasteries' property and sold the estates, a vast operation in which Thomas le Strange (cat. no. 23), Thomas Elyot (cat. no. 11) and Richard Southwell (cat. nos. 21-22) were among those who cooperated. The small monasteries were dissolved in 1536, followed by the larger ones in 1538-1540. Virtually all the nobles profited from this and thus came into the possession of enormous estates. But merchants,

lawyers, doctors, and other members of the middle ranks of society also acquired land and the status that went with it. The dissolution of the monasteries greatly increased the income of the Crown.

Order of the Garter

The Order of the Garter is the oldest and highest chivalric order in Britain, founded by Edward III in 1348. The members —always twenty-six in number, including the king— were personally chosen by the king. Much about this order is hard to explain, such as its emblem of a blue garter, and its motto, 'honi soit qui mal y pense' (commonly rendered, 'Evil to him who evil thinks'). The order's patron saint is St George, the patron saint of England.

‹ In his efforts to boost the pomp and circumstance at court, Henry VIII reinvigorated the Order of the Garter, which he awarded to his most important advisors and connections, including Thomas Howard (cat. no. 34) in 1510, Henry Guildford in 1526, William Fitzwilliam (cat. no. 29) in 1526 and Thomas Cromwell in 1537. In April 1534 he commissioned a new register for the order, which became known as the Black Book because of its black velvet cover. This book contains the statutes of the order and an account of its history and ceremonies. It was probably around the same time that Holbein produced designs for the order's insignia.

Pilgrimage of Grace

The Pilgrimage of Grace was a rising in the north of England in October 1536 against the dissolution of the monasteries. Under the leadership of the lawyer Robert Aske, Catholic landowners, craftsmen and farmers rose up in protest against the new measures taken by Thomas Cromwell and demanded the reopening of the monasteries. On behalf of Henry VIII, Thomas Howard, Duke of Norfolk, managed to restore calm by making some fine-sounding promises. When the unrest erupted again, Henry violently crushed the revolt in the spring of 1537. About 200 rebels, including Aske, were executed. After this 'success', Henry's position on the throne was stronger than ever.

Privy Chamber

The Privy Chamber did not denote merely the king's private apartment —for the Privy Chamber of Whitehall Palace, Holbein made a wall painting with the royal family— but also denoted the section of the royal household that took care of the king's personal needs. This consisted of servants, secretaries, physicians and a hairdresser, and also included nobles of varying rank. The latter had official positions such as Master of the Horse, Cupbearer, and Comptroller of the Household and were expected to keep the king company. Henry generally chose his best friends for these positions, men with whom he had spent his youth, such as Henry Guildford and William Fitzwilliam (cat. no. 29). Since they had direct access to the king, they constituted —like members of the Privy Council— an important power factor.

Privy Council

The Privy Council was the official council of the king's advisors. It was initially known as the King's Council, but this changed with Cromwell's reorganisation of government in 1536, when the number of members was fixed at nineteen. This council was a combination of nobles and other confidants of the king. It was initially led by Thomas Howard, Duke of Norfolk (cat. no. 34), as the highest-ranking noble, but from 1533 onwards Thomas Cromwell acquired more and more power. One of the clerks of the council was Thomas Elyot (cat. no. 11).

Reformation

In 1517 Martin Luther denounced the abuses of the Church in 95 theses. According to tradition, he nailed them to the doors of the Castle Church in Wittenberg in October 1517. This sparked the Reformation, the Reform movement that culminated in the Protestants leaving the Catholic Church. Although the Reformists were divided from the outset, their criticism focused on the lucrative trade in indulgences with which the Church sold believers forgiveness for their sins, the worship of images, and the display of wealth in churches. The Reformation spread rapidly, especially after Emperor Charles V gave German rulers the freedom to choose for themselves, in 1526. The Church of England was founded in 1534.

Steelyard

The Steelyard or Sta[h]lhof was the London branch of the Hanseatic League, the organisation of primarily German merchants. The actual premises of the Steelyard consisted of walled grounds with warehouses, shops, offices, dwellings, but also a church, a weighing house, an inn and a meeting hall. The premises were on the banks of the Thames, close to London Bridge, today the location of Cannon Street railway station. During Holbein's second stay in England, German merchants were among his most important clients (see cat. nos. 12, 17 and 18). The Steelyard merchants commissioned a design for a temporary triumphal arch in honour of Anne Boleyn's coronation in 1533, and for the assembly hall he painted two paintings with life-sized triumphal processions: *The triumph of riches* and *The triumph of poverty* (both now lost).

The Tudors

Henry VIII belonged to the House of Tudor, a family originating from Wales, and in 1485 he secured the throne of England. The first Tudor king was Henry's father, Henry VII, who had brought to an end the wars between the Houses of York and Lancaster, which both claimed the throne (Wars of the Roses), and who had married Elizabeth, a member of the House of York.

‹ Henry VIII's three legitimate children would all reign after him. The first was Henry's sole legitimate son, Edward VI, born in 1537 of his marriage to Jane Seymour. He reigned from 1547 until his death in 1553, when he was succeeded by Mary I, the daughter of Catherine of Aragon, born in 1516. During Mary's reign (1553–1558), Catholicism was re-established and hundreds of Protestants were burned at the stake, earning her the nickname of Bloody Mary. Elizabeth I, born in 1533 as the daughter of Anne Boleyn, then reigned for forty-five years. With her death, in 1603, the House of Tudor expired.

Whitehall Palace

Whitehall Palace stood just outside London, near Westminster on the River Thames. It was initially called York Palace, and was in the possession of the Archbishop of York, Thomas Wolsey. After this confidant of Henry VIII had fallen into disfavour, the king took over the palace around 1530 and renamed it Whitehall Palace, after the great hall that had been built there in light-coloured stone. It was a stroke of good fortune that Wolsey's palace became available at this time, since the old royal palace in Westminster had been destroyed by fire in 1512. Henry expanded Whitehall considerably, and by the end of his life it was said to be the largest palace in Europe. Besides an intricate complex of courtyards, royal residences, galleries, a chapel, service buildings, it also had tennis courts, tournament fields, and a park. Holbein made various decorations for this palace, including his most important royal commission, the wall painting of the royal family (see p. 32, fig. 3). Whitehall Palace was consumed by fire in 1698. Two parts were spared: the Banqueting House and the Holbein Gate (demolished in 1749), in which the painter may have had a studio. ER

—

Hans Holbein the Younger

Portraitist of the Renaissance

Stephanie Buck

Notes

1 On Hans Holbein the Elder see, most recently Bushart 1998 and Krause 2002 (with further bibliography). For Augsburg as a centre of art and trade see Augsburg 1980.

2 Hans Holbein the Elder's drawing techniques are examined in Landolt 1960, pp. 16-29.

3 For Holbein's links with the Netherlands see Krause 2002, pp. 66-85.

4 KdZ 2507; see C. Müller in Basel-Berlin 1997-1998, cat. no. 8.11, pp. 80-82.

5 On Holbein's life and work in general see His 1870, pp. 113-173; Woltmann 1874-1876; Chamberlain 1913; Reinhardt 1982, pp. 253-76; Rowlands 1985; Bätschmann/Griener 1997; Buck 1999. An annotated bibliography is published in Michael 1997.

6 Floerke 1906, pp. 168-193.

7 On transfer techniques see Meder 1919, pp. 521-538; Taubert 1975, pp. 387-401; Périer-D'Ieteren 1982-1983, pp. 74-94; Bambach-Cappel 1988. For the functions of Hans Holbein the Elder's drawings see Krause 2002, pp. 191-253.

8 Krause 1998, p. 111. Krause also cites Wilhelm 1983, pp. 574-579. For Burgkmair see Falk 1968 and Falk 1996, pp. 198-201 (with further bibliography).

9 On the Fugger family see Lieb 1958; trade in Augsburg is discussed in Kellenbenz 1980, vol. 1, pp. 50-71; for the Fugger chapel Bushart 1994, esp. pp. 18-29 (on the patrons), pp. 96-112 (for the still-unanswered questions regarding the designer and clerk of the works). A good introduction to the history of Augsburg is provided in Woltmann 1874-1876, vol. 1, pp. 19-40.

10 Krause 2002, pp. 91-99.

11 Strauss 1980, cat. nos. 175 and 188. On the *Ehrenpforte* see Schauerte 2001.

12 On Peutinger as an important Augsburg collector of Dürer prints in this period see Künast 2001, pp. 11-19. On the spread of Dürer's work in general see [G. Bartrum in] London 2002-2003, and in particular Koerner 2002-2003.

13 See Scheicher 1986, pp. 359-426, esp. nos. 9 and 11, pp. 377, 380. The designs were first attributed in Oberhammer 1935, p. 406.

14 Winkler 1937, pp. 142-143 and cat. nos. 483-488. For a detailed discussion of the epitaphs see Bushart 1994, pp. 115-172.

15 Metzger 2002, pp. 32-37 (in Dürer's workshop) and 43-44 (collaboration with Holbein the Elder).

16 *Erasmi Roterodami encomium moriae i.e. Stultitiae laus*, Johannes Froben, Basel, March 1515, 40, Öffentliche Kunstsammlung, Kupferstichkabinett, Basel, inv. no. 1662.141; see Schmid 1931; Michael 1986; Müller 1996, cat. nos. 10-91.

17 For Ambrosius Holbein see Foister 1996b.

18 See Karlsruhe 2001-2002.

19 See F. Hieronymus in Basel 1984, pp. III-VIII. Dürer's activities in Basel are discussed by C. Müller in Basel-Berlin 1997-1998, cat. no. 10.4, and, most recently, in Wilhelmi 2002, pp. 105-124.

20 See Lemmer 1986. Already in the first year of publication, reprints appeared, among others, in Nuremberg and Augsburg; by 1509 no fewer than five original editions had been published in Basel; in 1497 the author himself supervised a Latin edition, which made the work available to humanist scholars; and already early on translations were published in French and English. See Mähl 1980, pp. 461-462.

21 See for an English translation and introduction to this text C.H. Miller, *The Praise of Folly*, Yale University Press, New Haven and London 2003 (1979). For the Latin text (with German translation) see Erasmus ed. 1975, vol. 2. On the relationship of *In praise of Folly* to the *Ship of fools* see Baschnagel 1979.

22 See Müller 1996, p. 50. Michael 1986, pp. 19-20, note 7 for a translation of the annotation. On Myconius see Bietenholz/Deutscher 1985-1987, vol. 2, p. 475.

23 Michael 1986, no. 1, p. 51, pl. I; Müller 1996, cat. no. 10, pl. 5.

24 The drawing of two women lighting candles before an image of the Virgin (Michael 1986, no. 34, pl. XXXIV; Müller 1996, cat. no. 43, pl. 13) is also related to an illustration in Chapter 111 of the *Ship of fools* (Mähl 1980 , p. 435), where a man has laid aside his jester's cap in order to pray to a statue of the Virgin —illuminated by a candle— and other fools disturb his prayers. In the Holbein, the iconography of the Dürer model has once again been turned on its head, as Erasmus severely criticised the useless lighting of candles; it cannot be ruled out that Holbein is here ironically quoting the pictorial model in an effort to differentiate himself from his famous predecessor.

25 Michael 1986, no. 22, pl. XXII; Müller 1996, cat. no. 31, pl. 10.

26 On the likenesses of Maximilian see Von Baldass 1913-1914, pp. 247-334. Holbein the Elder appears to have met the emperor: creating an extremely intimate silverpoint portrait of him on horseback (Berlin, Staatliche Museen zu Berlin, Kupferstichkabinett, KdZ 2509); see C. Müller in Basel-Berlin 1997-1998, cat. no. 8.12, dated *c.* 1510-1515.

27 For the Latin text see Erasmus ed. 1975, pp. 82-83; The English translation by C.H. Miller (see note 21), p. 56, is as follows: 'Princes, then, for all their great happiness, still seem to me most unhappy in one respect: there is no one from whom they can hear the truth, and they are forced to take flatterers for their friends'.

28 This raises the question (not to be answered with absolute certainty) of whether Holbein could read the Latin text and Lister's commentary himself, or whether Myconius merely gave him a rough explanation of the passages to be illustrated. The drawing illustrates the content with a certain degree of freedom, and at least the illustrations appearing in the first and second third of the volume —among them the image of Maximilian— were very likely carried out under Myconius's supervision. Here, namely, Holbein used the same brown oxidised ink Myconius employed for his handwritten commentaries, whereas in the last third of the book, which is unannotated, he used black ink. Michael (1986, pp. 39-44) assumes that Holbein could read the Latin text; see also Müller 1996, p. 51.

29 Michael 1986, no. 74, pl. LXXIV; Müller 1996, cat. no. 83, pl. 23. For the Latin text see Erasmus ed. 1975, pp. 194-195. The English translation by C.H. Miller (see note 21), p. 128, is as follows: 'just as great rulers suspect and despise those who are too intelligent (as Caesar did brutus and Cassius, whereas he had no fear of the drunken Anthony , and as Nero did Seneca, and Dionysius did Plato) but are delighted with crude and simple minds, so too Christ always despises and condems those savants who rely on their own wisdom'.

30 The figures are identified in Schmidt 1941-1945, pp. 144-156, esp. 152-153; Müller 1996, p. 65; see also Krause 2002, p. 7.

31 Buck 1998.

32 Michael 1986, pp. 12-13; Müller 1996, p. 51.

33 Michael 1986, no. 64, pl. LXIV; Müller 1996, cat. no. 73, pl. 21 and p. 51.

34 Müller 1996, p. 64.

35 In contrast to most authors, Reinhardt 1981, pp. 45-46 rejects this equation, which was first proposed in Gerlo *1969* (1950), p. 46; see also E. Foucart-Walter in Paris 1985, pp. 15-16; Michael 1986, p. 148, who accepts the image as a portrait, and Müller *1996*, p. 64.

36 For the Latin text see Erasmus ed. 1975, pp. 174-175; The English translation by C.H. Miller (see note 21), p. 116, is as follows: 'But I will stop propounding apothegms lest I seem to have rifled the commentaries of my friend Erasmus'.

37 For Erasmus see Basel 1986.

38 *Portrait of Desiderius Erasmus*, Royal Collection, Hampton Court. *Portrait of Pieter Gillis (Aegidius)*, Earl of Radnor, Longford Castle; Silver 1984, cat. no. 58A,B. The portrait of Pieter Gillis was enlarged both horizontally and vertically (see Campbell *et al.* 1978). In their original state, the two portraits were the same size, thereby functioning as a pair. As they were both in the collection of Charles I, it seems likely they were the same panels once owned by Thomas More. On Gillis see Bietenholz/Deutscher 1985-1987, vol. 2, pp. 99-101.

39 Rowlands 1985, cat. no. 13; Bätschmann/Griener 1997, p. 30 and, most recently, Winner 2001, pp. 154-173; on Holbein's Erasmus portraits in general see E. Foucart-Walter in Paris 1985, pp. 9-26; Gronert 1996, pp. 74-117; Buck 1999, pp. 44-51.

40 Rowlands 1985, cat. nos. 15-16.

41 On Holbein's preparatory drawings in general see Foister 1983, p. 14.

42 Rowlands 1985, cat. no. 2. For the silverpoint drawings in the Kupferstichkabinett in Basel see Müller *1996*, cat. nos. 92-93, colour pls. 2-3.

43 Rowlands 1985, cat. no. 7; for an interpretation of the portrait see Bätschmann/Griener 1994, pp. 640-642; Bätschmann/Griener 1997, pp. 27-30; Dill 1998, pp. 245-262. For Amerbach: Bietenholz/Deutscher 1985-1987, vol. 1, pp. 42-46.

44 On Holbein's prints see Zijlma 1988; Müller 1997.

45 Allen 1906-1958, vol. *6* (1926), no. 1740: 'Qui has reddit est is qui me pinxit! eius commendatione te non grauabo, quan quam est insignis artifex. Si cupiet visere Quintinum, nec tibi vacabit hominem adducere, poteris per famulum commonstrare domum. Hic frigent artes, petit Angliam vt corradat aliquot angelatos: per eum poteris quae voles scribere'; see also Reinhardt 1981, p. 57.

46 See Dürer's journal of his travels in the Netherlands in Rupprich 1956, vol. 1, p. 151.

47 Allen 1906-1958, vol 5 (1924), no. 1452: 'Tantum idem habuit pro pictura. Et rursus nuper misi in Angliam Erasmum bis pictum ab artifice satis eleganti. Is me detulit pictum in Galliam, Rex me denuo vocat'; see also Reinhardt 1981, p. 52.

48 Allen 1906-1958, vol. 5 (1924), nos. 1400, 1403; see also Reinhardt 1981, pp. 52-53. The text written by Erasmus on the Basel portrait reads: 'In Euangelium Mar(ci) paraphras(is) per Erasmus Roterodamum autor(em) ... cunctis mortalibu(s) ius (item est)'; Klemm 1980, p. 70. Since Vögelin 1887 scholars had presumed that Holbein travelled to Lyon and Avignon in order to deliver to Bonifacius Amerbach the Erasmus portrait mentioned in the Pirckheimer letter (identified with the version in Basel); see Woltmann 1874-1876, vol. 1, p. 290; Chamberlain 1913, vol. 1, p. 174. Hartmann 1957, p. 15 however, concluded that Amerbach actually purchased the Basel Erasmus portrait only in 1542, from Holbein's wife. For this reason, E. Foucart-Walter in Paris 1985, p. 12 has suggested that Holbein took the portrait back with him to Basel. For more on this likeness see also C. Müller in Basel 1995, cat. no. 25.

49 On 7 July 1523 the king himself invited Erasmus to come to France: 'Je vous auertys que sy vous voules venyr, que vous seres le byen venu'; Allen 1906-1958, vol 5 (1924), no. 1375. Erasmus first refers to the post of treasurer on 30 March 1524 in a letter to Jean de Carondelet (see Allen 1906-1958, vol. 5 (1924), no. 1434). The subject is mentioned repeatedly in the correspondence of the following year; ibid., nos. 1439, 1446, 1471, 1484, 1487, 1488, 1529; Allen 1906-1958, vol. *6* (1926), nos. 1545, 1553.

50 See Reinhardt 1981, pp. 52-54; Ainsworth 1990, p. 174; Müller 1996, p. 11 and 100; Buck 1997, pp. 57, 305-308; Bätschmann/Griener 1997, pp. 147-148.

51 Due to the political and military situation, 1524 was a particularly poor time to be seeking favour with François I: in 1523-1524 he was struggling to put down the rebellion of the Duke of Bourbon and seeking to reconquer the Duchy of Milan. On 5 October 1524, the king crossed the Alps, where on 24 February 1525 he was defeated in the Battle of Pavia, arrested and imprisoned in Madrid; Jacquart 1997, chaps. VII-VIII, pp. 133-182. On the importance of Holbein's French journey for his work see Buck 1997, pp. 58-60, 94-100, 294-309.

52 His 1870, p. 121; Woltmann 1874-1876, vol. 1, p. 316.

53 Inv. no. 1662.126/5; Müller 1996, p. 99, cat. nos. 150-151.

54 *Portrait of Guillaume Jovenel des Ursins*, Berlin, Staatliche Museen zu Berlin, Kupferstichkabinett, KdZ 4367; S. Achenbach in Dückers 1994, pp. 307-309.

55 Zijlma 1988, vol. 14, no. 13, pp. 52-55. For a comparison of the *Utopia* with Holbein's *Ambassadors* see Zwingenberger 1999, pp. 115-117.

56 Allen 1906-1958, vol. *6* (1926), no. 1770; More speaks of Holbein as 'pictor [...] mirus est artifex'.

57 Rowlands 1985, cat. no. 24.

58 Müller 1996, cat. no. 157 (with older bibliography); for the copies see Rowlands 1985, cat. no. L.10; Lewis 1998.

59 Wilson 1996 (p. 138) thus regards the family portrait as a form of 'humanist propaganda'.

60 Rowlands 1985, cat. no. 30; E. Foucart-Walter in Paris 1985, pp. 37-48. For the identification of the handwriting see Pächt 1944, p. 138. On Kratzer see Bietenholz/Deutscher 1985-1987, vol. 2, pp. 273-274.

61 Müller 1996, pp. 107-108, see also Hinz 1991, pp. 69-96, esp. pp. 95-96.

62 For the provenance see Müller 1996, cat. no. 157; for the inventory of Amerbach's collection: ibid., pp. 281-284.

63 Allen 1906-1958, vol. 8 (1934), no. 2212; see also Reinhardt 1981, pp. 58-59. On the highly educated Margaret Roper see Bietenholz/Deutscher 1986, vol. 2, pp. 455-456.

64 This letter to Thomas More is dated 5 September 1529; see Allen 1906-1958, vol. 8 (1934), no. 2211; see also Reinhardt 1981, p. 58.

65 This is still true even if it was in fact the abstracted contour drawing in Basel that was the object of Erasmus's gratitude, rather than a now-lost small-scale colour replica of the painting, as Wilson (1996, pp. 162-163) has suggested.

66 See Allen 1906-1958, vol 5 (1924), no. 1488; on Warham as Erasmus's patron see E. Foucart-Walter in Paris 1985, pp. 27-28; Bietenholz/Deutscher 1985-1987, vol. 3, pp. 427-431.

67 Reinhardt 1981, pp. 47-48, figs. 2-3; Bätschmann/Griener 1997, p. 157.

68 Rowlands 1985, cat. no. 27; Strong 1995, no. 71 and pp. 81-84.

69 Rowlands 1985, p. 134; the original wording is found in Strong 1995, p. 81.

70 For a comparison of the portraits see the summary discussion by E. Foucart-Walter in Paris 1985, p. 34. On the interpretation see also Gronert 1996, pp. 76-86. In September 1527, Warham, acting on behalf of Henry VIII, invited Erasmus to England (see Bietenholz/Deutscher 1985-1987, vol. 3, p. 430), which underlines their close ties. Erasmus did not, however, take up the offer.

71 Bätschmann/Griener 1997, pp. 167, 169.

72 The meaning of the letter in Massys's double portrait of Erasmus and Aegidius (see note 38) is discussed in Bätschmann/Griener 1997, pp. 155-156. On the importance of letter-writing for the humanists

in general see Bätschmann/Griener 1994, pp. 643-644.

73 For the other artists working in England in this period see Chamberlain 1913, vol. 1, pp. 256-287, on Browne: ibid., pp. 258-261, and Auerbach 1954, pp. 7-8, 11-15, 54, 144; on Wright: Chamberlain 1913, vol. 1, pp. 261-262, and Auerbach 1954, pp. 13-14, 54-55, 144-145. Chamberlain emphasises the overall poor quality of the English artists.

74 On the Horenbout family see Chamberlain 1913, vol. 1, pp. 263-269; Auerbach 1954, pp. 42-45, 50-51, 68-69, 171-172; Campbell/Foister 1986, pp. 719-727; Backhouse 1991, pp. 88-93. Gerard Horenbout, Lucas's father, is listed as in Henry VIII's service from October 1528 to April 1531, but could have entered the household as early as September 1525 and remained there until February 1538, as the account books for the years in question have not been preserved; Campbell/Foister 1986, p. 720.

75 See Chamberlain 1913, vol. 1, pp. 273-287; on Volpe: Auerbach 1954, pp. 8, 12-13, 38, 140-141, 190; on Bartolommeo Penni: ibid., pp. 51, 77, 181; on Nicholas Bellin: ibid., pp. 52, 56-59, 77-78, 177-178.

76 Foister 1991, pp. 58-60; Thurley 1991, pp. 64-69; Foister 2001, pp. 109-123.

77 His 1870, p. 123.

78 His 1870, p. 126; Rowlands 1985, pp. 75-76.

79 Rowlands 1985, cat. no. 32.

80 Rowlands 1985, cat. no. 33.

81 See Palmer Wandel 1995, p. 188. For a discussion of iconoclasm in Basel and the background to the introduction of the Reformation see ibid., pp. 149-189; C. Dupeux et al. in Bern 2001, pp. 48-50.

82 See His 1879, p. 158; Reinhardt 1982, pp. 263.

83 The letter, dated 22 March and 10 April 1533 (postscript), reads: 'Sic Olpeius per te extorsit litteras in Angliam. At is resedit Antwerpiae supra mensem, diutius mansurus, si inuenisset fatuos. In Anglia decepit eos quibus fuerat commendatus'; Allen 1906-1958, vol. 10 (1941), no. 2788; see also Reinhardt 1981, pp. 65, 67.

84 The following description of these historic events is drawn from Scarisbrick 1981 and Starkey 1985. On Holbein and Henry VIII see Strong 1967; Foister 1981; London 1990-1991; Greenwich 1991; Anglo 1992; London 1995-1996; Buck 1997.

85 On the life of Thomas More: London 1977-1978, pp. 10-14; Bietenholz/Deutscher 1985-1987, vol. 2, pp. 456-459; Guy 2000.

86 Ives 1994, pp. 36-45.

87 For the Holbein-based portrait of Thomas Cromwell see Rowlands 1985, cat. no. 40. On Cromwell: Bietenholz/Deutscher 1985-1987, vol. 1, pp. 360-361.

88 Reinhardt 1981, pp. 54-56, 69. On the Apelles issue see Bätschmann/Griener 1994; Bätschmann/Griener 1997, pp. 13-34.

89 His 1870, p. 130.

90 Löcher 1985, pp. 667-86.

91 Wilson 1996, pp. 132-133.

92 Rowlands 1985, cat. no. 38; Bätschmann/Griener 1997, pp. 181-183; Buck 1999, pp. 88-91, 95.

93 Campbell 1990, p. 34.

94 Rowlands 1985, cat. no. 47; see, most recently, Bätschmann/Griener 1997, pp. 187-188; London 1997-1998 (with further bibliography); on the iconography North 2002.

95 On the relationship between drawing and painting in the workshop context, as well as the question of whether or not Holbein ran a workshop in England see Chamberlain 1913, vol. 2, p. 253; Foister 1983, p. 12; Ainsworth 1990, pp. 173-86; Foister in London 1995-1996, pp. 21-26.

96 Nicolas Bourbon, Carmen de moribus, Lyons 1536, pp. 27-29 (quoted in Rowlands 1985, p. 90, note 27). On Bourbon see Bietenholz/Deutscher 1985-1987, vol. 1, pp. 179-180.

97 Woltmann 1874-1876, vol. 2, pp. 38-41.

98 Rowlands 1985, cat. no. 61; C. Lloyd in London 1990-1991, pp. 69, 72-76 and cat. no. 29; Dülberg 1990, cat. no. 305; Lübbeke 1991, cat. no. 53 (with bibliography); Buck 1997, pp. 82-102.

99 See Hand 1993, no. 1937.1.64 (64), p. 84.

100 On the portrait as a New Year's gift see, most recently, M. Trudzinski in Hannover 2000, pp. 26-30.

101 Rowlands 1985, cat. no. 66.

102 Rowlands 1985, cat. no. 67; E. Foucart-Walter in Paris 1985, pp. 52-64; Bätschmann/Griener 1997, pp. 192-193.

103 Woltmann 1874-1876, vol. 2, pp. 36-37; Chamberlain 1912, pp. 25-30; Chamberlain 1913, vol. 2, pp. 114-154, 171-184; Reinhardt 1982, pp. 265-267.

104 Compare Rowlands 1985, pp. 116-117.

105 At the same time, Holbein also painted a portrait of Anne's sister Amalie; see Woltmann 1874-1876 (vol. 2, pp. 37-38), who cites the relevant letter from Nicholas Wotton to the king of Düren, dated 11 August 1539: 'Your Graces servante Hanze Albein has taken th'effigies of my Ladye Anne and the Ladye Amelye, and hathe expressyd theyr imaiges verye lyvelye.'

106 The historical background to Henry's marriage to Anne of Cleves and the fall of Cromwell is discussed in Scarisbrick 1981, pp. 370-383.

107 E. Foucart-Walter in Paris 1985, pp. 54-55, 59-60.

108 For a discussion of the Whitehall mural see Woltmann 1874-1876, vol. 1, pp. 418-421; Chamberlain 1913, vol. 2, pp. 93-100; Strong 1967; Rowlands 1985, cat. no. L.14; Buck 1997, pp. 103-195.

109 Rowlands 1985, cat. no. L.14a.i; London 1990-119, cat. no. 14; London 1995-1996, cat. no. 5.

110 In terms of its composition, the Whitehall mural recalls an architecturally inspired frontispiece; Buck 1997, pp. 173-178; and, more recently, M. Trudzinski in Hannover 2000, pp. 21-23.

111 Buck 1997, pp. 182-185.

112 His 1870, pp. 131-132; Reinhardt 1982, pp. 266-267.

113 Reinhardt 1982, p. 266.

114 Nicolas Bourbon, *Historiarum veteris testamenti icones ad vivum expressae*, Lugduni 1539: 'Cernere vis, hospes, simulacra simillima vivis? Hoc opus Holbinae nobile cerne manus'; Woltmann 1874-1876, vol. 2, p. 172; Floerke 1906, vol. 1, p. 193.

115 The relationship between Dürer and Holbein has been discussed repeatedly, above all in the German-language literature: Woltmann 1874-1876, vol. 1, pp. 483-488, for example, ends with a long comparison of the two artists. The most comprehensive study is Pinder 1951.

116 On Erasmus's relations with his portraitists Dürer, Holbein and Massys see Panofsky 1969, pp. 200-227, esp. pp. 205 and 223, where Panofsky examines Erasmus's reaction to Dürer's engraved portrait and quotes from letters in which the humanist refers to him as the 'new Apelles' and as an artist who deserves to be remembered forever. See also Reinhardt 1981, pp. 54-56, 69. For a discussion of Dürer as a humanist see, most recently F. Machilek in Nuremberg 2000, pp. 44-76.

—

The Darmstadt Madonna

On the genesis and development of Holbein's panel for Jakob Meyer zum Hasen

Jochen Sander

Notes

1 Many of the observations and reflections contained in this article (particularly with regards to the artistic genesis of the painting), here published for the first time, are drawn from the author's forthcoming *Hans Holbein als Tafelmaler in Basel 1515-1532*. The literature on the *Darmstadt Madonna* is extensive; the most comprehensive recent examination is O. Bätschmann and P. Griener, *Hans Holbein d. J. Die Darmstädter Madonna. Original gegen Fälschung* (Kunststück), Frankfurt am Main 1998 (Bätschmann/Griener 1998a, with references to the most important older studies).

2 For the identification of the two boys, traditionally thought to be the couple's deceased sons, see below.

3 On the possible significance of the vines see also cat. no. 7.

4 Meyer's biography and the background to his political fall are discussed in Meier 1996, pp. 236-238, and Groebner 2000, pp. 210-226.

5 Holbein also made some alterations to the figure of Dorothea Kannengießer at this time. While she was initially shown with chin-band and cap, as in the Basel portrait study, Holbein now repainted the head to give it the form we see today.

6 Riggenbach 1940, p. 477.

7 On Gerster's *Solothurn Madonna* see Bätschmann/Griener 1998b, pp. 30-34; on the first — more or less non-destructive— wave of removals of religious works in Basel, which took place in April 1528, see Roth/Dürr 1937, pp. 65-70, nos. 86-89.

8 R. Faesch, *Humanae industriae monumenta nova simul et antiqua*, 1628ff, fol. 35v, cat. no. VI (this work, which exists only in manuscript form and is now housed in Universitätsbibliothek Basel, served Patin [1676, n.p., cat.no. 25] and others as a primary source); Von Sandrart 1675, p. 252.

9 Bätschmann 1996, pp. 87-100; Bätschmann/Griener 1998a; Griener 2001, pp. 211-225.

10 Reinhardt 1954-1955, pp. 244-254.

11 Ost 1980, p. 141, note 33. For an in-depth discussion of the *Darmstadt Madonna* in relation to these images see, most recently, Bätschmann-Griener 1998, pp. 19-33.

12 Buck 1999, pp. 81-83.

13 The examination took place in the spring of 1999 at the Schloßmuseum Darmstadt, in cooperation with the Institut für angewandte Photogrammetrie und Geoinformation der Fachhochschule Oldenburg (Professor Dr Manfred Weisensee, Dipl. Ing. Ralf Jantos, and photographer Peter Meyer). A large-format camera with a line sensor with increased infrared sensitivity was used, along with normal photography lamps and an Apple-PC for the digital storage and treatment of the images. For a detailed description of this process, with regard to both theoretical and practical aspects, see Ralf Jantos's degree dissertation, *Multispektrale Aufnahmetechniken und Untersuchungen im Nahbereich*, completed in March 2001 at the Institut für angewandte Photogrammetrie und Geoinformation. I am grateful to His Royal Highness Moritz, landgrave of Hessen, for granting permission to examine the work, and to the aforementioned colleagues at Oldenburg for carrying it out.

14 The same is in principle true of the two boys as well, where the slight changes in the position of the youth's right arm and the foreshortening of the nude boy's head remain within the bounds of those normally found in Holbein's work.

15 Ainsworth/Faries 1986, pp. 25f. See also Ainsworth 1990, pp. 173-186. Holbein must have placed a kind of carbon paper between the drawing (or corresponding intermediary cartoon) and the prepared panel, which helped to transfer the lines to the wood.

16 I would like to thank Christian Müller, Basel, for allowing me to use these previously unpublished findings.

17 Meier 1996, pp. 231-248.

18 The two versions of Leonardo's *Madonna of the Rocks* are discussed in Cox/Rearick 1996, pp. 140-143, cat. nos. IV-1 (Paris), and Marani 1999, pp. 128-149 (Paris and London).

19 This link between the elder boy and St James was likewise seen by Stephanie Buck as she stated in conversation with the author. For the iconography of St James see S. Kimpel, "Jakobus der Ältere", in Braunfels 1974, pp. 23-39.

CATALOGUE ENTRIES
PROVENANCE, EXHIBITIONS
LITERATURE AND NOTES

1 Desiderius Erasmus (*c.* 1466/69–1536), *c.* 1523

PROVENANCE

Charles, Prince of Wales, from 1625 King of England, London, acquired before 1625 as a gift from Adam Newton, secretary to his brother, Prince Henry;[1] exchanged by Charles I, together with a painting by Titian, for Leonardo da Vinci's *John the Baptist* (now Paris, Musée du Louvre) from the collection of Roger, duc de Plessis de Liancourt, 'chambellan' (chamberlain) to Louis XIII, before 1637; Comte de Brienne, Paris, 1662 (possibly acquired before 1644, in all probability directly from De Liancourt); Eberhard Jabach, Paris;[2] sold by Jabach, together with 100 other paintings, to Louis XIV, 1671; Paris, Musée du Louvre, inv. no. 1345

EXHIBITIONS

London 1950-1951, no. 1; Basel 1960, no. 170; Paris 1985, no. I

LITERATURE

Rowlands 1985, pp. 58-59, 129-130, no. 15; E. Foucart-Walter in Paris 1985, pp. 9-26, 72-73, no. I; Ainsworth 1990, p. 177, note 29; Gronert 1996, pp. 92-103; Bätschmann/Griener 1997, p. 158; London 1997-1998, p. 69; Klinger/Höttler 1998, pp. 106-107, no. 16; Buck 1999, pp. 46-48

NOTES

1 On the back of the panel are the brands used by Charles I: 'CP' in ligature — an abbreviation for 'Carolus Princeps' — and the more common 'CR', 'Carolus Rex', as well as a label noting in English that the painting had been given to 'the prince' by Newton. For this and the other information on the provenance mentioned here, see Basel 1960, p. 199 and E. Foucart-Walter in Paris 1985, pp. 72-73, no. I.

2 There is a lacquer stamp with his coat of arms on the back of the panel (see E. Foucart-Walter in Paris 1985, p. 72). Da Vinci's *John the Baptist*, mentioned above, ended up back in Paris again as part of Jabach's collection.

3 For Holbein's portraits of Erasmus, see Rowlands 1985, pp. 56-59; E. Foucart-Walter in Paris 1985, pp. 9-26; Gronert 1996, pp. 74-117; Buck 1999, pp. 44-50. More specifically for the portrait in Basel, see Rowlands 1985, no. 16; Boerlin 1991, no. 31, and on the portrait in London, see Rowlands 1985, no. 13; London 1997-1998, p. 77; Winner 2001. For a superb copy after the latter painting, see Rowlands 1985, p. 128, no. 13a-III and E. Foucart-Walter in Paris 1985, p. 77, with illustration.

4 Rowlands 1985, no. 2.

5 Rowlands 1985, no. 6.

6 Rowlands 1985, no. L. 1; Buck 1999, pp. 19-20 and fig. 16.

7 Rowlands 1985, no. 7.

8 On Erasmus, see Rotterdam 1969 and Basel 1986. On Holbein and Erasmus, see Gerlo 1969; Panofsky 1969, pp. 219-220; Reinhardt 1981.

9 See Buck's essay and her note 32. In 1523 Holbein made woodcuts to illustrate Erasmus's *Precatio Dominica* [...], published in Basel (two copies in Basel, Öffentliche Kunstsammlung, Kupferstichkabinett; see Rowlands 1985, p. 60 and Müller 1997, nos. 97-98 and fig.).

10 See Buck's essay and her notes 33-34.

11 For a comparison of the two paintings, both of which were included in the 1960 exhibition *Die Malerfamilie Holbein in Basel* (Basel 1960, nos. 170-171), see E. Foucart-Walter in Paris 1985, pp. 24-25. She describes the Basel painting as a 'repetition' of the portrait described here.

12 For this book and an interpretation of the painting, see Stephanie Buck's essay and her notes 70-71.

13 Brunin 1968, p. 146 and note 4.

14 See E. Foucart-Walter in Paris 1985, pp. 18, 19, fig. 8 and p. 71, note 10. For Erasmus's cap and apparel, see also her observations on pp. 17-18 and Brunin 1968, p. 146.

15 For Holbein's second drawing in Paris, see E. Foucart-Walter in Paris 1985, pp. 22-23; Paris 1991-1992, pp. 156-157, nos. 142-143; London 1997-1998, pp. 68-69. The foreshortening of the fingers of the left hand at the top of the sheet, and the shade on them, have not been executed correctly. Holbein abandoned the hand, turned the sheet ninety degrees, and drew it again, altering the direction of the shaded section between the ring finger and the little finger. The use of different materials — silverpoint and red and black chalks — on the white prepared paper is rather uncommon. The three materials were used to achieve different effects: silverpoint for details, red chalk to render the skin convincingly, and black chalk for a fast initial attempt to sketch the writing hand (on the sheet depicted here) and the face (on the second sheet).

16 E. Foucart-Walter in Paris 1985, p. 22, fig. 12.

17 See E. Foucart-Walter in Paris 1985, pp. 22-23 and fig. 10; London 1997-1998, pp. 68-69, figs. 76 and 78.

18 According to Ainsworth (1990, p. 175, note 21), Holbein's portrait of Anne of Cleves (Rowlands 1985, no. 67) was not painted over the original drawing, but over a design based on it. This is based on the finding of pricks in the paper by the bodice (see E. Foucart-Walter in Paris 1985, pp. 57-58). The portrait of Erasmus in Basel is not the only painting in which Holbein used paper as a support (for other examples, see Ainsworth 1990, p. 175 and note 21, p. 177, notes 29-30).

19 Boerlin 1991, p. 21.

20 See Buck 1999, p. 46 and note 50 of her essay in this book.

21 See note 47 of Buck's essay.

22 E. Foucart-Walter in Paris 1985, pp. 10-11; Gronert 1996, p. 74; Buck 1999, p. 44.

23 E. Foucart-Walter in Paris 1985, pp. 11, 73; cf. also the observations in Rowlands 1985, p. 134.

24 See note 66 of Buck's essay. A second version of Holbein's portrait of Warham was sent to Erasmus (see the observations in Rowlands 1985, p. 134 and Paris 1985, under no. II).

25 See Provenance. The portrait was one of a total of 101 paintings that Eberhard Jabach sold to the king of France in 1671 (see note 2). These also included the four other Holbeins from the Louvre (see Rowlands 1985, nos. 27, 29, 30, 67 and Paris 1985, nos. I-V).

26 In the past it was therefore frequently suggested that the painting in the Louvre must have been intended for Thomas More (cat. no. 3), Erasmus's friend and correspondent in England; see E. Foucart-Walter in Paris 1985, pp. 12-13, 14 and 71, note 8.

27 See E. Foucart-Walter in Paris 1985, pp. 18-22.

28 E. Foucart-Walter (in Paris 1985, p. 16) described it as a bookmark.

29 E. Foucart-Walter in Paris 1985, p. 10.

30 Erasmus, *In evangelivm Marci paraphrasis*, Basel 1524. According to E. Foucart-Walter (in Paris 1985, pp. 9 and 17) this book appeared as early as December 1523. For the text on the painting, see Boerlin 1991, p. 21; Gronert 1996, pp. 100-102 and note 248 (as a later addition). See also note 48 of Buck's essay.

31 Rowlands 1985, no. 13 and Buck 1999, p. 48.

32 See note 64 of Buck's essay.

33 For instance, Holbein made a design for a painting on glass, since lost, that Erasmus presented to the university of Basel in 1525 (Basel, Öffentliche Kunstsammlung, Kupferstichkabinett; Rowlands 1985, p. 136; Müller 1988, no. 47 and fig.). At the heart of this image was the motto that Erasmus used from 1509 onwards, 'Concedo nulli' (I yield to no one). This motto was also written on Erasmus's memorial plaque (which has disappeared) in the Münster church, Basel and on an undated painting by Holbein that is now in Cleveland, Ohio, Cleveland Museum of Art (Rowlands 1985, no. 35).

34 'Pinxit me Durerius, sed nihil simile'; see Panofsky 1969, pp. 204-205 and note 13, p. 224; E. Foucart-Walter in Paris 1985, p. 24; Buck 1999, p. 50.

35 Buck 1999, p. 50; see also notes 115 and 116 of her essay in this book.

36 Quotation taken from Boerlin 1991, p. 21. See also Basel 1960, p. 200 and Klinger/Höttler 1998, p. 104.

37 Besides that of the tondo in Basel (fig. 1d) the attribution to Holbein of the portrait of Erasmus in New York is generally accepted (The Metropolitan Museum of Art, Robert Lehman Collection; see Ainsworth 1990, pp. 177-178, figs. 5-6 and Rowlands 1985, no. 34). The heads in both paintings appear to derive directly from the portrait now in London, on loan from the Earl of Radnor. In or before 1533, Holbein also produced a woodcut with a small, circular portrait of Erasmus in profile (Basel 1960, no. 431) and around 1538 he made a posthumous portrait of Erasmus in a woodcut (Basel, Öffentliche Kunstsammlung, Kupferstichkabinett; Müller 1997, no. 7 and fig.; see also ibid., no. 8 and illustration).

38 Basel 1960, no. 185; Rowlands 1985, no. 33; Ainsworth 1990, p. 177 and note 30; Boerlin 1991, no. 37.

39 See the catalogue of painted portraits of Erasmus after Holbein in Brunin 1968, pp. 152-157, nos. 1-38. See also Rowlands 1985, under nos. 13 and 34, Paris 1985, pp. 71-72; Ainsworth 1990, p. 177 and note 30; Klinger/Höttler 1998, pp. 101-102, 146-148. For prints after Holbein's portraits of Erasmus, see G. Luijten in Antwerp-Amsterdam 1999-2000, pp. 109-113, under no. 8.

2 The Meyer family with the Madonna, Christ and John the Baptist, known as the Darmstadt Madonna, *c.* 1525/26 *and* 1528/29

PROVENANCE

Painted for Jakob Meyer, Basel; passed by inheritance to his daughter, Anna Meyer, Basel; passed to her daughter, Ros(in)a Irmy; sold by the latter's second husband, Remigius Faesch I, burgomaster of Basel, to Iselin in 1606, for 100 gold crowns; Johann Lukas Iselin, Basel, 1606-1626; the latter's widow, Anna d'Annone, Basel, 1626-1633; sold by her in 1633 to the Amsterdam art dealer Le Blon for 1,000 imperial guilders;[1] Michel Le Blon, Amsterdam, sold to Loskaert for 3,000 Dutch guilders, in or before 1638;[2] Jacob Loskaert, Amsterdam; Jacob Woutiers, Amsterdam, 1679;[3] passed by inheritance by way of Margaretha Woutiers (Wuytiers), the wife of Jacob Cromhout, into the Cromhout family;[4] Cromhout sale, Amsterdam, 7-8 May 1709, lot 30, for 2,000 Dutch guilders;[5] dukes of Lorraine; Joseph de Lorraine, Prince of Vaudémont; Alexis Delahante, London-Paris (put up for public sale in London, 3 March 1810, lot 85, not sold; later placed with Croese art dealers, Amsterdam, 1819);[6] sold by Delahante for 2,500 *thaler* to Wilhelm, Prince of Prussia (the brother of the king of Prussia), as a gift to his wife Marianne, Princess of Hesse-Homburg, Berlin, 1822; passed by inheritance to the grand-ducal house of Von Hessen und bei Rhein, Darmstadt (exhibited in the Schloss), from 1852;[7] on loan to the Öffentliche Kunstsammlung, Kunstmuseum, Basel, 1947-1958; on loan to the Hessisches Landesmuseum, Darmstadt, 1958-1965; on permanent loan to the Schlossmuseum, Darmstadt, since 1965

EXHIBITIONS

Munich 1869; Dresden 1871, no. 193; Basel 1960, no. 177

LITERATURE

Reinhardt 1954-1955; E. Treu in Basel 1960, pp. 206-208, no. 177 (with select bibliography); Grundmann 1970; Ost 1980, p. 141, note 33; Rowlands 1985, pp. 64-66, 131-132, no. 23; Bätschmann 1996; Meier 1996; Bätschmann/Griener 1997 (German edition), pp. 8, 77, 97, 101-104, 107, 110, 112, 119, 134, 135, 145, 148, 177, 203-205; Bätschmann/Griener 1998a (with select bibliography); Bätschmann/Griener 1998b, pp. 13, 76-77, 82, 99, 101, 141, 143, 144, 180; Klinger/Höttler 1998, pp. 120-122, no. 23 (with select bibliography); Manuth 1998, p. 326; Buck 1999, pp. 76-83; M. Roskill, O. Bätschmann, T.-H. Borchert and P. Griener in Roskill/Hand 2001, pp. 13, 39, 40, 43-44, 48, 187, 211, 219, 220-221

NOTES

1 For the provenance of the painting, see e.g. Bätschmann 1996, pp. 95-97; Bätschmann/Griener 1997, pp. 203-205; Bätschmann/Griener 1998a, pp. 58-66; see also Grundmann 1970.

2 As observed in Von Sandrart 1675, pp. 249-250. See Peltzer 1925, p. 102 and Manuth 1998, p. 326.

3 See Bredius 1913, p. 205.

4 The family coat of arms was depicted on the frame of the painting that was lost in 1944. This frame is depicted in a watercolour from 1852 (Bätschmann/Griener 1998a, p. 14, fig. 8 and p. 63).

5 Manuth 1998, pp. 326, 333, notes 37-38 and Hoet/Terwesten 1752-1770, vol. I, p. 133, no. 24. The numbers in Hoet and Terwesten do not correspond to those in the sale catalogue. The works of art put up for auction on this occasion included Lucas van Leyden's famous triptych from about 1530 (Amsterdam, Rijksmuseum; Amsterdam 1986, no. 37). Holbein's painting was probably put up for sale by Jacob Cromhout (1672-1722), lord of Nieuwerkerke. His namesake Jacob Cromhout, who commissioned the famous Cromhout houses on the Herengracht canal in Amsterdam, had already died in 1669. His home at no. 366 (now in use as the Bible Museum) stayed in the family after his death.

6 On this sale, see Bätschmann/Griener 1998a, pp. 64 and 82, note 115. Sir John Murray saw the painting at Croese's gallery in Amsterdam in 1819 (see Murray 1819, p. 176).

7 See the notes in Klinger/Höttler 1998, p. 122. After the death of the last surviving member of the house of Von Hessen und bei Rhein in 1997, the painting passed by inheritance to the branch of the family in the north of Germany.

8 Basel 1960, no. 141 and Rowlands 1985, pp. 21-22, 25 and 125, no. 2.

9 The drawings and paintings all stayed together; through Meyer's granddaughter Rosa Irmy they came into the possession of the family of Faesch, burgomaster of Basel (see Faesch 1628).

10 On Meyer's life, see E. Treu in Basel 1960, p. 174; Rowlands 1985, pp. 21, 61; Meier 1996, pp. 236-238; Groebner 2000, pp. 210-226. In 1524, after he was removed from his post, Meyer again became active as the commander of a mercenary army, this time during a military campaign against France.

11 Rowlands 1985, pp. 21, 31, 51.

12 See note 18 of the essay by Sander.

13 See the essay by Sander.

14 Ost 1980, p. 141, note 33. See also Meier 1996, pp. 243-244, note 25; Bätschmann 1996, pp. 92-93, note 30; Bätschmann/Griener 1998a, pp. 19-24.

15 Bätschmann/Griener 1998a, pp. 25, 31-32, figs. 15 and 21.

16 Bätschmann/Griener 1998a, p. 25 and fig. 15.

17 See note 13.
18 On this iconographical tradition, see Bätschmann/Griener 1998a, pp. 25-33.
19 See Bätschmann/Griener 1998a, p. 25.
20 The crown, which is rendered in minute detail, probably reflects Meyer's political allegiance (see Meier 1996 and Bätschmann/Griener 1998a, pp. 34-42).
21 On this motif, see Bätschmann/Griener 1998a, pp. 42-45. See also cat. no. 7, note 1.
22 Bätschmann/Griener 1998a, p. 7.
23 In the past some authors held that upon completion the painting had been displayed in a chapel of the family's castle of Gross-Gundeldingen, just outside Basel (Reinhardt 1954-1955, pp. 249-253 and figs. 82-83). However, Meyer had already sold this building (which was demolished in 1954) in 1529 or 1530 (Bätschmann/Griener 1998a, pp. 56 and 79, note 94). See also the essay by Sander and his note 5.
24 See provenance and Basel 1960, p. 173.
25 See note 2. On Le Blon, see W.K. Zülch in Thieme/Becker, vol. 22 (1928), p. 504; De la Fontaine Verwey 1969; Bätschmann/Griener 1997, p. 203 and fig. 261. Le Blon was depicted by Van Dyck in his famous portrait series, the *Iconography* (Mauquoy-Hendriks 1991, no. 183; see also Larsen 1988, vol. II, p. 219, no. 542).
26 See the essay by Sander. See also Bätschmann 1996; Bätschmann/Griener 1998a, pp. 58-69.
27 See note 4.
28 See note 7.

3 Thomas More (1478–1535), *c.* 1527

PROVENANCE
See appendix 1; The Royal Collection, Windsor Castle, inv.no. RL 12268

EXHIBITIONS
London 1977-1978, no. 177; London 1978-1979, no. 1; New York 1983, no. 1; Houston-Hamburg-Basel-Toronto 1987-1989, no. 3; Edinburgh-Cambridge-London 1993-1994, no. 2

LITERATURE
Ganz 1911-1926, nr. XXXVI2; Parker 1945, no. 3; Foister 1983, no. 3; Ainsworth 1990, pp. 176-177

NOTES
1 On Sir Thomas More, see e.g. London 1977-1978.
2 In 1528 Holbein executed a portrait of Nicolaus Kratzer (Musée du Louvre, Paris); see Rowlands 1985, no. 30.
3 Van Mander 1604, fol. 221r; Van Mander/Miedema 1994-1999, vol. I, pp. 142-143, vol. II, pp. 114-115. See also e.g.. Rowlands 1985, p. 67; Bätschmann/Griener 1997, pp. 159-161.
4 Rowlands 1985, pp. 222-223, no. L 10. The group portrait was painted in tempera on canvas and measured 275 x 366 cm. It probably perished in a fire in Kremsier castle, Austria, in 1752. For variants and preliminary sketches, see Morison/Barker 1963, Lewi 1974 and London 1977-1978.
5 See Müller 1996, no. 157.
6 Pächt 1944, p. 138.
7 See Wilson 1996, pp. 162-163, who suggests that the gift to Erasmus was a painted variant rather than a preliminary drawing.
8 Parker 1945, nos. 1-8.
9 Parker 1945, nos. 2 and 3. Foister (1983) regards only no. 2 as a preliminary study for the group portrait, and believes that the drawing discussed here (no. 3) served as a working drawing for the painting in the Frick Collection (see below).
10 One possible exception is Holbein's portrait drawing of John Fisher, which may have been made during his first English period (see Edinburgh-Cambridge-London 1993-1994, no. 9). On the dating, see also cat. nos. 10-11.
11 On Holbein's lefthandedness, see Parker 1945.
12 With thanks to Marieke de Winkel.
13 The cartoon with Henry VIII for the lost mural in Whitehall Palace was also pounced (see London 1977-1978, pp. 60-61, fig. 61, p. 102, vol. II, note 3; see also Rowlands 1985, no. L14b), as was the cartoon for the group portrait of Henry VIII and the Guild of Barbers and Surgeons (Rowlands 1985, no. 78, fig. 119). A copy of Holbein's drawn *Portrait of Bishop John Fisher* (Parker 1945, no. 13) was also made by pouncing (see S. Foister in London 1995-1996, no. 98): tell-tale black specks of charcoal powder are visible along the contours, indicative of the use of a pattern of pricked holes. The pattern was probably pounced using a second pattern made from the original drawing in Windsor Castle, which itself displays no perforations.
14 Fahy 1968, pp. 228-233; Rowlands 1985, no. 24.
15 Ainsworth 1990, pp. 176-177; Edinburgh-Cambridge-London 1993-1994, p. 28, fig.
16 Morison/Barker, pp. 86-88; London 1977-1978, p. 31, no. 27.
17 See Ainsworth 1990, p. 177, note 28.

4 An unknown woman, *c.* 1526/28

PROVENANCE
See appendix 1; The Royal Collection, Windsor Castle, inv.no.RL 12273

EXHIBITIONS
London 1978-1979, no. 17; New York 1983, no. 14; Houston-Hamburg-Basel-Toronto 1987-1989, no. 12; Edinburgh-Cambridge-London 1993-1994, no. 7

LITERATURE
Ganz 1911-1926, nr. XVII4; Parker 1945, no. 11, Foister 1983, no. 11

NOTES
1 Cf. Panofsky 1955, plates 226 and 262; with the autograph inscription, 'Das hat albrecht dürer nach seiner hawsfrawen Conterfet zw autorff in der niderlendischen Kleidung im jor 1521...'. See Anzelewsky/Mielke 1984, pp. 109-110, nr. 106; cf. also Mandrella 1999, pp. 58-59, no. 10.
2 See London 1978-1979, p. 47. This sheet lacks a watermark, which could have provided more clarity in this respect: cf. Houston-Hamburg-Basel-Toronto 1987-1989, pp. 58, 142-144.
3 Holbein made notes of this kind on many of his portrait drawings; see e.g. cat. nos. 16, 21 and 31.
4 On Holbein's left-handedness, see Parker 1945.
5 Müller 1996, nos. 153-155.
6 Müller 1996, nos. 150 and 151.
7 Müller 1996, nos. 92 and 93.
8 On Holbein's first acquaintance with the new technique, see Bätschmann/Griener 1997, pp. 129-135 and Bätschmann 2001, pp. 37-38.

5 An unknown woman, *c.* 1526/28

PROVENANCE
See appendix 1; The Royal Collection, Windsor Castle, inv.no. RL12217

EXHIBITIONS
London 1977-1978, no. 16; New York 1983, no. 15

LITERATURE
Ganz 1911-1926, nr. XIV5; Parker 1945, no. 9, detail fig. p. 8; Foister 1983, no. 9

NOTES
1 Cf. Rowlands 1985, nos. 51 and 54. With thanks to Marieke de Winkel for her information about the costumes.
2 For the provenance of the Windsor drawings, see appendix 1.
3 Cheke probably added most of his identifications, which are in general highly reliable, after Edward VI's death in 1553 (see Foister 1983, p. 11). Cheke died in 1557.
4 Parker 1945, nos. 5, 7, 9 and 11.
5 Parker 1945, nos. 5 and 7.
6 Parker 1945, no. 8.
7 This proposition derives some support from the fact that the watermark in the sheet discussed here (Briquet 1907/1968, no.12863, see Houston-Hamburg-Basel-Toronto 1987-1989, pp. 141-144) is the same as that in four drawings of members of More's family (Parker 1945, nos. 1, 2, 7 and 8). However, it also occurs in drawings from Holbein's second English period.

6 Mary Wotton, Lady Guildford, 1527

PROVENANCE
Possibly John, 7th Lord Lumley; probably passed by inheritance to Thomas, Earl of Arundel (1585-1646); then unknown until the painting appeared at a public sale in London (Sotheby's), 14 May 1930, lot 60; purchased by the museum in 1943; The Saint Louis Art Museum, Saint Louis, Missouri, inv.no. 1:1943

EXHIBITIONS
London 2003

LITERATURE
Rowlands 1985, pp. 72, 133, no. 26; Ainsworth 1990, pp. 178-179, figs. 7-12; Bätschmann/Griener 1997, pp. 169-170; Buck 1997, pp. 158-159; Klinger/ Höttler 1998, pp. 128-129, no. 26; Buck 1999, pp. 58-61, 65; London 2003

NOTES
1 For the execution of this project, see Rowlands 1985, pp. 68-69 and Foister 2001, which also quote the sources.
2 Liverpool 2003, p. 11.
3 Foister 2001, p. 110, note 9.
4 Foister 2001, p. 111. The interpretation of the way in which the second painting was presented is partly based on speculation.
5 Foister 2001, p. 111.
6 Foister 2001, pp. 112-113. On the London Company of Painter-Stainers, see also Foister 1993.
7 Rowlands, nos. 25, 29 and 30.
8 See BNB, vol. 23 (1890), pp. 327-328.
9 Fraser 1992, p. 213.
10 See BNB, vol. 23 (1890), pp. 324-327.
11 S. Foister in London 2003. This brochure was written to commemorate the temporary reunification of the two portraits in the National Gallery, London, in the spring of 2003.
12 Ainsworth-Faries 1986; Ainsworth 1990, pp. 178-179, figs. 7-12.
13 It is not inconceivable that the decision to place the rosary and the book in Lady Guildford's hands was made at this late stage. For the considerations that may have prompted the change, see Buck 1997, pp. 158-160. The same source contains the intriguing suggestion that it was as an ironic comment on the alterations, and by way of contrast to the sitter's highly composed facial expression, that Holbein decided to depict the woman's head in the capital of the column with hair streaming and open-mouthed.

7 Lady with a squirrel and a starling, c. 1527/28

PROVENANCE
Probably Thomas Howard, Earl of Arundel and Surrey, Arundel Castle, Sussex and Arundel House, London, in Amsterdam from 1643 onward; passed by inheritance to his wife, Alatheia Howard, Antwerp and Amsterdam, 1646-1654; Jan Six, Amsterdam, c. 1658-1700; the latter's sale, Amsterdam, 6 April 1702, lot 18, for 680 guilders to Pieter Six, Amsterdam; after the latter's death in 1703 passed to his widow Ammerentia Deijmans, Amsterdam; transferred at an unknown moment in time to her brother-in-law Willem Six, Amsterdam; the latter's sale, 12 May 1734, lot 11, for 300 guilders to Pieter Six, the son of Pieter Six and Ammerentia Deijmans, Amsterdam; Govert van Slingelandt, The Hague; Sir William Hamilton, London; the latter's sale, London, 20 February 1761, lot 75, for 45 guineas to George, 3rd Earl of Cholmondeley; passed to the Marquess of Cholmondeley, Houghton Hall, Norfolk; the latter's sale, London, Christie's, 15 April 1992, lot 10 (withdrawn); purchased by the National Gallery with the support of the National Heritage Memorial Fund, the National Art Collections Fund and Mr J. Paul Getty Junior (through the American Friends of the National Gallery), April 1992; London, The National Gallery, inv. no. NG 6540

EXHIBITIONS
London 1950-1951, no. 32; London 1959, no. 12; London 1995-1996, no. 4; London 1997-1998, no. 63

LITERATURE
Rowlands 1985, pp. 72 and 134, no. 28; Roskill/Harbison 1987, p. 20; Dudok van Heel 1992, pp. 51-55; Foister 1992; Foister/Wyld/Roy 1994, pp. 6-19; S. Foister in London 1995-1996, pp. 39-40, no. 4; Foister 1996, pp. 53-54; Bätschmann/Griener 1997, p. 169; London 1997-1998, pp. 67-68, 69, 85; Klinger/Höttler 1998, p. 133, no. 28; Manuth 1998, pp. 323-324, 326; Buck 1999, pp. 59, 62-63, 65; Roy/Wyld 2001, pp. 100-101; Roskill 2001

NOTES
1 Holman 1980, pp. 148-149 and Roskill 2001, pp. 179-180, 184, note 15. See also Roskill/Harbison 1987, pp. 19-23; Bätschmann/Griener 1998a, pp. 42-45; Buck 1999, p. 59. Roskill (2001, p. 184, note 15) described the fruit under the bird's leg as a fig.
2 Buck 1999, p. 59.
3 See the observations in Foister/Wyld/Roy 1994, pp. 8, 11.
4 Parker 1945, no. 8; Hamburg-Basel 1988, no. 8. Margaret Giggs is also depicted in the group portrait drawing of the More family, now in Basel (p. 20, fig. 19); see also Müller 1996, pp. 106-108, no. 157; Müller 1998, p. 210; C. Müller in Washington 1999-2000, pp. 387-388.
5 J. Roberts in Hamburg-Basel 1988, p. 48. See also Grossmann 1951, p. 112, under no. 43; Dudok van Heel 1992, pp. 54-55; Foister 1996, p. 54 and figs. 5-6.
6 The shawl and the lady's garment, which is closed at the neck, resemble those in a portrait drawing of a lady that Holbein made in the same period (cat. no. 5); Parker 1945, no. 9.
7 S. Foister in London 1995-1996, p. 40.
8 S. Foister in London 1995-1996, p. 40.
9 Both the portrait of Robert Cheseman, the king's falconer in the realm of Henry VIII, and that of an unknown 28-year-old nobleman (cat. nos. 19 and 36) incorporate the image of a bird of prey. In a drawing in Basel, Holbein made a portrait of a small boy with his

pet monkey (p. 86, fig. 13a). He added the same creature to his sketch of about 1527 for the now lost group portrait of the More family (p. 20, fig. 19; the monkey is drawn in brown ink at lower right on the sheet, and is hard to make out).

10 The changes made to the painting are described in detail in Foister/Wyld/Roy 1994. In Holbein's *Nobleman with a hawk* from 1542, the bird was also added to the portrait at a relatively late stage (see cat. no. 36).

11 Holbein produced several independent studies of animals, including a bat and a small lamb (Basel, Öffentliche Kunstsammlung, Kunstmuseum); see Müller 1996, pp. 98-99, nos. 148-149; Müller 1998, pp. 148-151, nos. 44-45; C. Müller in Washington 1999-2000, pp. 374, 378. An infrared reflectogram of the painting discussed here revealed underdrawn lines at certain parts of the figure; Holbein probably traced a preliminary study as an aid in rendering the face (see Foister/Wyld/Roy 1994, pp. 16-17).

12 See note 10.

13 Foister/Wyld/Roy 1994, pp. 9-10.

14 Dudok van Heel 1992; Manuth 1998, pp. 323-324.

15 See Foister 1996 (with select bibliography); Manuth 1998, p. 324. For Arundel's collections, see also Weijtens 1971 and the special issue of *Apollo*, 144 (1996), no. 414 (with select bibliography).

16 See Provenance.

17 See the observations in the sale catalogue for London, Christie's, 15 April 1992, p. 20. For the Van Slingelandt collection, see Hofstede de Groot 1892, pp. 229-230; Van Riemsdijk 1892, pp. 219-224; Lunsingh Scheurleer 1967, pp. 24 and 45, note 41; Broos 1993, pp. 294-295. Holbein's painting is not mentioned in the description of the collection by Hoet/Terwesten 1752-1770, vol. II (1752), pp. 403-406; nor is it mentioned in the sale catalogue of 18 May 1768 (Lugt 1938-1987, no. 1683; copy in the Mauritshuis library). However, according to the sale catalogue for the collection of Sir William Hamilton (London, Prestage and Hobbs, 20 February 1761, no. 75; Lugt 1938-1987, no. 1138; see also Sloan 1997, p. 209) the painting came from 'Monsieur Slingeland's Collection' (see Foister 1996, p. 53). The 'Holbein' from the Van Slingelandt collection that ended up in the stadholder's collection and hence in the Mauritshuis, *Portrait of a woman from southern Germany* is no longer attributed to the artist (see Rowlands 1985, p. 228, no. R.4 and fig. 208, as Hans Holbein the Elder [sic]).

8 Thomas Godsalve (*c.* 1481-1542) and his son John Godsalve (*c.* 1510-1556), 1528

PROVENANCE

Thomas Howard, Earl of Arundel and Surrey (1585-1646), Arundel Castle, Sussex, and Arundel House, London, in Amsterdam by 1643; his wife, Alatheia Howard, Antwerp and Amsterdam, 1646-1654, inv. 1655, no. 2; purchased by Le Leu, Paris, for the Elector Palatine of Saxony, 1749 (220 *livres* and 1 *sou*, together with three other works); Gemäldegalerie Dresden since 1889, inv.no. 1889

EXHIBITIONS

Dijon 2001, no. 41

LITERATURE

Chamberlain 1913, vol. I, pp. 325-327; Fletcher/Cholmondeley Tapper 1983, pp. 91-93, fig. 9; Rowlands 1985, pp. 72, 73, 135, no. 31, fig. 61; Dresden 1992, no. 1889; Bätschmann/Griener 1997, pp. 172, 173, 177, fig. 232; Klinger/Höttler 1998, no. 31; Buck 1999, pp. 64-67, figs. 61 and 62

NOTES

1 On Thomas Godsalve, see DNB.

2 Norwich 1992, no. 4.

3 On John Godsalve, see DNB and Norwich 1992, no. 4 (and cat. no. 13).

4 Chamberlain 1913, vol. I, p. 326.

5 With thanks to Marieke de Winkel for her information on the costumes.

6 Musée du Louvre, Paris; Rowlands 1985, no. 30.

7 See Rowlands 1985, pp. 72-73.

8 See Rowlands 1985, nos. 36, 37, 38, 42, 43 and 57.

9 Musée du Louvre, Paris and Öffentliche Kunstsammlung, Basel; Rowlands 1985, nos. 15 and 16.

10 Cf. Rowlands 1985, nos. 25, 27 and 34. The piece of paper has been placed too close to John Godsalve's head, the handwriting does not seem to be Holbein's, and the effect of depth is inept (see Buck 1999, p. 67 and S. Buck in Dijon 2001, p. 172). The handwriting corresponds to that on the *cartellino* (likewise not original) on the *Portrait of William Warham* (Musée du Louvre, Paris); the sixteenth-century copy of this latter portrait in the National Portrait Gallery in London contains the same cartellino, which must therefore have been added at an early stage (with thanks to Stephanie Buck for this suggestion).

9 The Old and the New Law (the Old Testament as *Lex* and the New Testament as *Gratia*), *c.* 1530/35

PROVENANCE

Thomas Howard, Earl of Arundel and Surrey, Arundel Castle, Sussex and Arundel House, London, in Amsterdam from 1643; passed by inheritance to his wife, Alatheia Howard, Antwerp and Amsterdam, 1646-1654 (described in an inventory dating from 1655 as 'Legge Vecchio & Nove'); Henry Blundell of Ince, between 1803 and 1910; passed down in the family of Blundell and Weld, until 1981; Edinburgh, National Gallery of Scotland, inv.no. 2407

EXHIBITIONS

Liverpool 1960, no. 15; Manchester 1961, no. 89

LITERATURE

Rowlands 1985, pp. 93-94, 142-143, no. 56; Bätschmann/Griener 1997, p. 119; London 1997-1998, pp. 80-81

NOTES

1 Left, from top to bottom: LEX / Wet; MYSTERIVM IVSTIFICATIONIS / proscribed service; PECCATUM / Sin; MORS / Death; ESAYAS PROPHETA / the prophet Isaiah; ECCE VIRGO CONCIPIET FILIVM / and the Virgin shall bear a son.
Centre, from top to bottom:HOMO / Man; MISER EGO HOMO, QVIS ME ERIPIET EX HOC CORPORE MORTI OBNOXIO? RO.7 / O wretched man that I am! Who shall deliver me from the body of this death? Romans 7.
Right, from top to bottom: GRATIA / Grace; IVSTIFICATIO NOSTRA / our justification; AGNVS DEI/ Lamb of God; VICTORIA NOSTRA / our victory; IOHANNES BAPTISTA / John the Baptist; ECCE AGNVS ILLE DEI, QVI TOLLIT PECCATV MVDI.10.1 / Behold, the Lamb of God, which taketh away the sin of the world. For observations on the inscriptions in Holbein's paintings and on this painting in particular, see Buck 1997, pp. 278-280.

2 Romans 7:24.

3 Isaiah 7:14.

4 John 1:29.

5 Rowlands 1985, p. 93, note 31.
6 Rowlands 1985, pp. 93-94 and Grossmann 1961.
7 Rowlands 1985, pp. 93-94; Bätschmann/Griener 1997, p. 119.
8 Given the borrowing from Cranach and his studio, the painting was long dated to 1529 or later. On stylistic grounds, however, a more precise dating to around 1535 would seem justifiable; see also London 1997-1998, pp. 80-81.

10-11 Lady Margaret Elyot (?-1560), *c.* 1527/28 *or c.* 1532/33

Sir Thomas Elyot (*c.* 1490-1546), *c.* 1527/28 *or c.* 1532/33

PROVENANCE
See appendix 1; The Royal Collection, Windsor Castle, inv. nos. 12204 and 12203

EXHIBITIONS
London 1977-1978, no. 279 (Sir Thomas Elyot); London 1978-1979, nos. 30 and 31; New York 1983, nos. 20 and 21; Houston-Hamburg-Basel-Toronto 1987-1989, nos. 13 and 14; Edinburgh-Cambridge-London 1993-1994, nos. 10 and 11

LITERATURE
Ganz 1911-1926, nos. XV3 (Margaret Elyot) and XXV5 (Thomas Elyot); Parker 1945, nos. 14 and 15; Foister 1983, nos. 14 and 15, p. 30; Ashelford 1983, p. 32, no. 15 (Margaret Elyot)

NOTES
1 On Thomas Elyot, see Lehmberg 1960 and Major 1964.
2 Lehmberg 1960, pp. 16-17, who quotes Thomas Stapleton's *Tres Morae* from 1588 (vol. III, p. 52, Douai).
3 For a list of Thomas Elyot's publications, see Lehmberg 1960, pp. 197-198.
4 Elyot probably wrote this undated letter at the beginning of 1537. See Lehmberg 1960, pp. 153-154.
5 That Thomas Elyot is placed rather higher in the pictorial plane than his wife is probably a consequence of the fact that the sheets were cut down to size in different ways.
6 See Ashelford 1983, p. 32, no. 15.
7 Ashelford 1983, p. 33, no. 16; Rowlands 1993, p. 146, no. 319.
8 A doubtful case in this respect is Holbein's *Portrait of Bishop John Fisher* from Windsor Castle, that has a pink ground but may nonetheless have been made in Holbein's first English period. See Parker 1945, no. 13 and Edinburgh-Cambridge-London 1993-1994, no. 9.
9 Quoted by Foister 1983, p. 1.
10 Lehmberg (1960, p. 19) takes it for granted, given the historical context, that Holbein made the drawings in More's Chelsea home in 1526-1528. In the art historical literature, the drawings are always dated in 1532 or shortly afterward.

12 Hermann von Wedigh III (*c.* 1503-1560), 1532

PROVENANCE
Counts of Schönborn, Vienna, 1746; Erwin, Count of Schönborn-Buchheim, Vienna, 1871; passed by inheritance to Friedrich Karl, Count of Schönborn-Buchheim, Vienna, 1903-1923; Duveen Brothers art dealers, London, Paris and New York, 1923; Mr and Mrs Frank D. Stout, Chicago, 1923-1935 (temporarily on loan to the Art Institute of Chicago, 1924); M. Knoedler & Co art dealers, New York, 1935-1936; Edward S. Harkness, New York, 1936-1940; bequeathed by Harkness to the museum in 1940 (reserving the right of usufruct for his widow Mary Stillman Harkness until 1950); New York, The Metropolitan Museum of Art, inv.no. 50.135.4

EXHIBITIONS
Dresden 1871, no. 327; Chicago 1933, no. 20; New York 1939, no. 197; London 1950-1951, no. 9; New York 1952-1953, no. 107; New York 1956, no. 199; New York 1970, no. 234; Boston 1970, unnumbered

LITERATURE
Von Frimmel 1887, col. 379-380; Von Frimmel 1896, pp. 41-43, no. 41; Geelen 1917, pp. 178-180; Von Frimmel 1923, pp. 48-49; Wehle/Salinger 1947, pp. 214-216; Krummacher 1963, pp. 181, 184, note 10, 185-188; Markow 1978, p. 39, note 3, 40, 41; Holman 1979, pp. 139, 144, 145-146, 155-156; Löcher 1985, pp. 674, 676, 677, 679; Rowlands 1985, p. 137, no. 37; Roskill/Harbison 1987, pp. 23-24; Ainsworth 1990, p. 186; Gronert 1996, pp. 44-48; Buck 1997, pp. 30, 280; London 1997-1998, pp. 82, 83; Asmus/Grosshans 1998, p. 106; Klinger/Höttler 1998, pp. 156-157, no. 40; Buck 1999, p. 95; Roy/Wyld 2001, pp. 104, 106; Petter 2002, pp. 7, 9, 10, 15

NOTES
1 On the Hanseatic League, see Dollinger 1998; see also the bibliographical references in Holman 1979, p. 139, note 2. For a map showing the location of the Steelyard, Whitehall Palace and Holbein's first and second houses (and studios) see Liverpool 2003, p. 12, fig. 3.
2 Rowlands 1985, pp. 83-85, 223-224, nos. L. 13 A-B, fig. 192-194; Buck 1999, pp. 96-97, figs. 90-91. In 1533, Holbein designed a festive scene for a triumphal arch to celebrate the coronation in May 1533 of Anne Boleyn, Henry VIII's second wife (Löcher 1985, pp. 668-669; Buck 1999, pp. 96-97 and fig. 89).
3 For Holbein's Steelyard portraits, see Krummacher 1963; Markow 1978; Holman 1979; Löcher 1985; Rowlands 1985, pp. 81-83, 136-139, nos. 36-38, 41-45 and p. 152, no. M.14; Buck 1999, pp. 88-96; Petter 2002.
4 The portrait of Derich Berck was made in 1536 (New York, The Metropolitan Museum of Art, The Jules Bache Collection; Rowlands 1985, p. 143, no. 57); the portrait of an unknown man, perhaps another member of the Steelyard, was made in 1538 (ibid., p. 145, no. 65). See also Krummacher 1963, p. 181; Markow 1978, p. 39, note 3; Holman 1979, p. 139, note 1; Löcher 1985, p. 676; Petter 2002, p. 7.
5 Georg Gisze was initially depicted from a frontal perspective (see Rowlands 1985, p. 83).
6 Geelen 1917, pp. 178-180, with a genealogical tree of the Von Wedigh family on p. 194. The spelling of the names was not yet standardised, so that 'WID.' must indeed have been an abbreviation of the last name, which was also spelt variously as Widig[h], Wedig or Wedighe. The name may derive from the German town of Widdig.
7 Ganz 1912, p. 240. Hermann von Wedigh's membership of the Steelyard is not documented, although several indications seem to confirm it (Holman 1979, p. 145 and notes 39-40). Thus as things stand, there is no reason to exclude the portrait described here and the one in Berlin from the Steelyard portraits, as Petter (2002, pp. 9 and 10, note 17) proposes. The frontal perspective adopted in the Berlin portrait is very similar to that in other Steelyard portraits.
8 Geelen 1917, pp. 179-180 and Holman 1979, p. 145.
9 It can be seen with the naked eye that Holbein painted the gloves over the thumb and hence added them at a later stage of the composition (with thanks to Jørgen Wadum).
10 Krummacher 1963, pp. 185-187 and fig. 159; Westhoff-Krummacher 1965, pp. 37-40, 125, no. 38; Holman 1979, p. 145 and fig. 5. That Von

Wedigh's portrait was on show in Cologne at this early date is incompatible with the theory that the Steelyard portraits were intended for the merchants' meeting hall (Chamberlain 1913, vol. 2, p. 13; see also cat. no. 17).

11 Krummacher 1963, pp. 186-188. It has even been hypothesised that no elaborated preliminary study existed of this painting (Ainsworth 1990, p. 186; see also notes 9 and 26 and cat. no. 17), although the underdrawing does not exclude the possibility that one did.

12 Geelen 1917, pp. 180-182; Rowlands 1985, pp. 83, 138-139, no. 41; Asmus-Grosshans 1998, pp. 106-107. Both portraits once belonged to the collections of the Counts of Schönborn, Vienna (for this collection, see Munich 2003). Though the two panels have the same dimensions, they are certainly not counterparts, as has been assumed in the past. They differ too greatly in composition for this (Holman 1979, p. 146).

13 For the family coat of arms, see Siebmacher 1890, p. 46 and fig. 55; Von Frimmel 1887, col. 379; Geelen 1917, pp. 173, 176; Holman 1979, p. 145.

14 The first names 'Hermann Hillebrandt', first mentioned in catalogues of the Gemäldegalerie in Berlin, do not appear in the Cologne records; cf. Geelen 1917, p. 182, note 28; Holman 1979, p. 146, note 46; Petter 2002, p. 9, note 11 and p. 10, note 18.

15 See Holman 1979, pp. 152-158. The portrait of Derich Born (cat. no. 17) also bears no reference to his — in this case documented — membership of the Steelyard; see also note 7.

16 Krummacher 1963, p. 184, note 10; Holman 1979, pp. 144 and 145. This letter also occurs on a seal on the portrait of Hans of Antwerp, *c.* 1532 (London, The Royal Collection; see Von Frimmel 1896, pp. 42-43 and Rowlands 1985, pp. 136-137, no. 36). There is another portrait by Holbein with a letter possibly signifying a trade organisation inserted between the first and last names (Holman 1979, p. 156, no. 21).

17 Monti 1986, vol. 1, p. 13, line 68. See also Von Frimmel 1887, col. 380; Holman 1979, p. 145; Löcher 1985, p. 677. In the portrait of Derich Berck (see note 4) the motto can also be linked to Erasmus (Holman 1979, p. 150).

18 Gronert 1996, p. 47.

19 However, Roskill/Harbison (1987, p. 23) described it as an account-book and believed that Von Wedigh was holding not gloves but invoices; see also Woltmann 1872, p. 358 and Löcher 1985, p. 674.

20 See Holman 1979, p. 145 and note 43; Gronert 1996, pp. 46-47. See also Roskill/Harbison 1987, pp. 23-24.

21 In paintings in which Holbein used the pigment smalt for the blue background — here Holbein chose azurite — the pigment particles are often badly discoloured (see cat. no. 33). In the portrait of Cheseman from 1533 (cat. no. 19), the azurite became darker through the ageing of the medium (with thanks to Jørgen Wadum and Petria Noble).

22 London 1997-1998, p. 82.

23 Roy/Wyld 2001, p. 106.

24 In earlier portraits by Holbein, both male and female sitters generally look away from the viewer. The portrait of Benedict von Hertenstein from 1517 (New York, The Metropolitan Museum of Art; Rowlands 1985, no. 6) and that of Lady Guildford from 1527 (cat. no. 6) are exceptions to this rule.

25 Cf. the observations in Krummacher 1963, pp. 184, 192 and Markow 1978, pp. 41, 47.

26 See Ainsworth 1990, p. 186. In the underdrawing, which was not followed precisely during the painting, the left eye is situated lower in the pictorial field. There is a similar discrepancy between the underdrawn line between upper and lower lip and the painted lips, which is visible with the naked eye. With thanks to Maryan Ainsworth (The Metropolitan Museum of Art, New York), who made available unpublished infrared reflectogram assemblies of the face and hands, as well as to Petria Noble and Jørgen Wadum. In Holbein's — far later — portrait of John Chambers (cat. no. 38), the position of both eyes was changed relative to the underdrawing, as an infrared reflectogram assembly demonstrates (see Ainsworth 1990, p. 185 and fig. 26).

27 See also Asmus-Grosshans 1998, p. 106.

13 John Godsalve (*c.* 1510-1556), *c.* 1532

PROVENANCE

See appendix 1; The Royal Collection, Windsor Castle, inv.no. RL 12265

EXHIBITIONS

London 1978-1979, no. 40; New York 1983, no. 18; Houston-Hamburg-Basel-Toronto 1987-1989, no. 38; Norwich 1992, no. 4; Edinburgh-Cambridge-London 1993-1994, no. 14; London 2002, no. 349

LITERATURE

Ganz 1911-1926, no. X5; Parker 1945, no. 22; Foister 1983, no. 22

NOTES

1 One exception may be the portrait of John Fisher, which also has a pink ground; see Edinburgh-Cambridge-London 1993-1994, no. 8; cf. cat. nos. 10 and 11.

2 On John Godsalve, see DNB; Chamberlain 1913, vol. I, pp. 325-327; Norwich 1992, no. 4.

3 See Chamberlain 1913, vol. I, p. 327.

4 He was referred to there as 'John Godsalve esq. mercer' (Norwich 1992, no. 4).

5 Godsalve was made a Knight of the Carpet. Most of the identifications of Holbein's portrait drawings in Windsor Castle by John Cheke (1514-1557) were probably added after the death of Edward VI in 1553 (see Foister 1983, p. 11). On the provenance of these drawings, see appendix 1.

6 Cf. Parker 1945, nos. 6, 11 (cat. no. 4), 23 (cat. no. 30) and 57.

7 Müller 1996, no. 182.

8 The portrait of John Godsalve in Philadelphia Museum of Art (Johnson Collection), probably a copy made after a painting by Holbein that has been lost, is not based on the drawing (Rowlands 1985, no. R19, fig. 229; see also Ainsworth 1990, p. 185).

9 Some writers speculate that the drawing was intended to be pasted to a panel and then worked into a painting (Edinburgh-Cambridge-London 1993-1994, no. 14; London 2002, no. 349). Several examples of this procedure have been documented in Holbein's portraits (Rowlands 1985, nos. 5, 6, 16, 32, 45 and 67). There is no evidence at all, however, that this drawing was one such case.

14-15 William Reskimer (?-1552), *c.* 1532/33

14

PROVENANCE

See appendix 1; The Royal Collection, Windsor Castle, inv.no. RL12237

EXHIBITIONS

London 1978-1979, no. 29; New York 1983, no. 36; Houston-Hamburg-Basel-Toronto 1987-1989, no. 19; Edinburgh-Cambridge-London 1993-1994, no. 16

LITERATURE

Parker 1945, no. 31; Foister 1983, no. 31

15

PROVENANCE

Possibly Anne Trelawney-Reskimer (eldest daughter of William Reskimer) and John Trelawney (?-1568); their son Jonathan Trelawney (1568-1604) and Elizabeth Trelawney-Killigrew; gift from her father, Robert Killigrew (?-1633), to Charles I;[1] inv.no. 3019

EXHIBITIONS

London 1978-1979, no. 28

LITERATURE

Chamberlain 1913, vol. I, p. 333; Millar 1963, p. 60, no. 31; Rowlands 1985, no. 39; Klinger/Höttler 1998, no. 42; London 1997-1998, pp. 64, 65, fig. 69

NOTES

1 See L. Campbell's letter of 1 November 1985 to O. Millar, archives of the Royal Collection Trust; see also Millar 1963, p. 60.
2 See Foister 1983, Ainsworth 1990, pp. 174 ff. and Foister 1993.
3 See e.g. Ainsworth 1990, Foister 1993, Foister/Wyld/Roy 1994, pp. 6-19 and S. Foister, 'The production and reproduction of Holbein's portraits', in London 1995-1996, pp. 21-26.
4 On Holbein's working methods, see esp. Foister 1983 and the literature mentioned in the previous note.
5 On the provenance of these drawings, see appendix 1 and Foister 1983, pp. 3-12.
6 With thanks to Rachel Billinge, Rausing Research Associate, The National Gallery, London, who kindly allowed me to read the notes she made of her technical examination of the painting in 1998 (see also note 10).
7 Edinburgh-Cambridge-London 1993-1994, p. 56.
8 Another method was to cover the back of the drawing with chalk and then to trace the lines onto the panel. However, no traces of chalk are visible on the back of any of the sheets (see Foister 1983, p. 24).
9 For Vasari, see L.S. Maclehose, *Vasari on Technique*, ed. G.B. Brown, New York 1960, pp. 215, 231. On the use of preliminary drawings as aids in making portraits, see Buck 2001.
10 In the portrait of Reskimer, infrared reflectography (IRR) reveals lines of the underdrawing in the face and hands; the infrared rays cannot penetrate the background or the black clothes. Strikingly, hatching has been applied in the underdrawing of the right hand to indicate shade, something not seen in any of Holbein's other portraits (cf. e.g. Foister 1993, p. 119). The contours of the cap have been altered relative to the underdrawing. With thanks to Rachel Billinge, Rausing Research Associate, The National Gallery, London, who examined the painting with IRR in 1998. See esp. the literature mentioned in note 3.
11 Rowlands 1985, nos. 7, 25, 26, 28, 39 and 44.
12 See e.g. Markow 1978, pp. 45-47 and Holman 1979, pp. 148-149.
13 It was J. Kestell Floyer (Times Literary Supplement, 1921) who first identified the sitter as William Reskimer instead of his elder brother John. Starkey (1991, p. 75) believes that the matter is unresolved.
14 L. Campbell discovered William Reskimer's last will and testament, dated 8 April 1554 (Edinburgh-Cambridge-London 1993-1994, p. 56). Reskimer was living in Hendon, Middlesex at the time as a widower, after the death of Alice Densil, whom he had married in 1540.
15 See L. Campbell's letter to O. Millar (note 1).

16 An unknown man, *c.* 1532/34

PROVENANCE

See appendix 1; The Royal Collection, Windsor Castle, inv.no. RL12258

EXHIBITIONS

London 1978-1979, no. 38; New York 1983, no. 17; Houston-Hamburg-Basel-Toronto 1987-1989, no. 17; Edinburgh-Cambridge-London 1993-1994, no. 17

LITERATURE

Parker 1945, no. 32; Foister 1983, no. 32, p. 30; London 1997-1998, p. 70, fig. 81

NOTES

1 The suggestions given thus far for the man's identity are unconvincing (see London 1978-1979, p. 72).
2 Parthey/Pennington 1982, p. 270, no. 1547.
3 S. Foister assumes that the etching was made after the drawing (Foister 1983, p. 11; Foister 1996, p. 54). Of the Holbein paintings listed in the 1655 inventory (see note 5), either 'ritratto de homo con berettino negro' or 'ritratto d'homo con beretino negro piccolo' could possibly refer to the painted portrait (see also Edinburgh-Cambridge-London 1993-1994, p. 58).
4 On the provenance of the drawings at Windsor Castle, see appendix 1. The collection then consisted of more than ninety portrait drawings, most of which are now in Windsor Castle (see Foister 1983, pp. 3-12; Foister 1996, p. 51).
5 On the Arundel collection, see e.g. Hervey 1921, Weijtens 1971 and Apollo 144 (1996), no. 414.
6 See Cust 1911 and Hervey 1921, pp. 473-500, esp. pp. 480-483. On works by Holbein in the Arundel collection, see also Foister 1996 and Manuth 1998, p. 324. When Arundel's collection became dispersed in 1658-1659, several works by Holbein were purchased by Dutch collectors (cf. cat. nos. 7 and 33).
7 See e.g. Godfrey 1996.

17 Derich Born, (1509/10-*after* 1549), 1533

PROVENANCE

King Charles I;[1] Thomas Howard, Earl of Arundel and Surrey (1585-1646), Arundel Castle, Sussex, and Arundel House, London, in Amsterdam by 1643; his wife, Alatheia Howard, Antwerp and Amsterdam, 1646-1654; King Charles II, King's Closet, Windsor Castle (possibly sent by Sir William Temple in 1666); The Royal Collection, Windsor Castle, inv.no. OM 26 WC 64

EXHIBITIONS

London 1978-1979, no. 25

LITERATURE

Chamberlain 1913, vol. II, pp. 17-19; Millar 1963, no. 26; Krummacher 1963; Markow 1978; Holman 1979; Rowlands 1985, pp. 83, 139, no. 44; Foister/Wyld/Roy 1994, p. 19, note 30; Bätschmann/Griener 1997, p. 35; Klinger/Höttler 1998, no. 47; Buck 1999, pp. 94-96; Petter 2002, pp. 10-15, fig. 7

NOTES

1 This is clear from the letters 'CR' (Carolus Rex) branded on the back of the panel. However, there is no reference to the portrait in the inventories of Charles I; see Millar 1963, p. 57.
2 See Rowlands 1985, nos. 36, 37, 38, 41, 42, 43, 44 and 57. Only the

Portrait of Derich Berck (no. 57) dates from 1536.

3 Alte Pinakothek, Munich; Rowlands 1985, no. 45.
4 See e.g. Holman 1979, pp. 149-150.
5 Rowlands 1985, nos. R.30, M.10 and M.11.
6 See Chamberlain 1913, vol. II, p. 13.
7 Rowlands 1985, nos. L 13 A and B.
8 See Krummacher 1963 and Markow 1978, p. 40.
9 See Holman 1979, Appendix, pp. 152-158.
10 Ainsworth 1990, p. 186. She suggests that Holbein did not use preliminary drawings with contours traced for transfer in his Steelyard portraits.
11 The painting was examined in 1992 by Rachel Billinge, Rausing Research Associate in the Conservation Department of the National Gallery, London. Infrared reflectography was carried out using a Hamamatsu C2400 camera with an N2606 series infrared vidicon tube. The camera is fitted with a 36mm lens to which a Kodak 87A Wratten filter has been attached to exclude visible light.
12 For the translation and interpretation of the inscription, see Bätschmann/Griener 1997, p. 35.
13 See e.g. Rowlands 1985, p. 83 and Buck 1999, pp. 94-96. On this portrait pose, see also Raupp 1984, pp. 181-220; cf. also London-The Hague 1999-2000, nos. 53 and 54.

18 Cyriacus Kale (*c.* 1501-?), 1533

PROVENANCE

Acquired before 1737, probably by Duke Anton Ulrich; Salzdahlum Castle, 1744; Braunschweig, Herzog Anton Ulrich-Museum, inv. no. GG 18

LITERATURE

Markow 1978, p. 44; Holman 1979, pp. 146-147; Löcher 1985, p. 675; Rowlands 1985, p. 139, no. 42; Petter 2000, p. 7

NOTES

1 This merchant's mark is depicted in Holman 1979, p. 158, appendix 24.
2 A rigorous search of Braunschweig city archives has failed to discover any documents relating to Cyriacus Kale.
3 See Holman 1979, pp. 146-147 and Löcher 1985, p. 675.

19 Robert Cheseman (1485-1547), 1533

PROVENANCE

Unknown private collection, England, sixteenth century (see note 13); Charles I, London, before 1649; Charles II, London, Whitehall, 1666/1667; James II, London, Whitehall, 1685-1688; Kensington House, 1697, 1700; William III, Het Loo Palace, Apeldoorn, after 1700-1702; Johan Willem Friso, Het Loo Palace, Apeldoorn, 1702-1711 (wax stamp with his coat of arms on the back of the painting); sale Het Loo, Amsterdam, 26 July 1713, possibly lot 31 (withdrawn and sent to Friesland); palace in Leeuwarden, 1731; Het Loo Palace, Apeldoorn, 1757; Stadholder William V, The Hague, after 1770-1795; seized by the French, transferred to the Musée Napoléon (Musée du Louvre), Paris, 1795-1815; Royal Cabinet of Paintings, housed in the Gallery of William V, The Hague, 1816; transferred to the Mauritshuis, 1822; The Hague, Royal Cabinet of Paintings Mauritshuis, inv.no. 276

EXHIBITIONS

London 1950-1951, no. 26; Schaffhausen 1951, no. 43a; The Hague 1966, no. 7; New York 1979, no. 75; The Hague 1988-1989, no. III

LITERATURE

Rowlands 1985, pp. 82, 139, no. 46; Broos 1987, pp. 212-217, no. 37 (with select bibliography); Campbell 1987, p. 371; B. Broos in The Hague 1988-1989, pp. 75-77, no. III; C. Parpoil in Gien 1994, p. 170; Bätschmann/Griener 1997, pp. 181, 227, note 84; London 1997-1998, pp. 80-81; Klinger/Höttler 1998, pp. 170-171, no. 49; Buck 1999, pp. 104-105; Roy/Wyld 2001, p. 105

NOTES

1 The restoration finished in 2003 revealed that the original gold leaf inscription had been completely overpainted. Remains of the original, more refined serif letters were uncovered beneath the overpainting. On these letters, see the annual report of the Mauritshuis for 1962, p. 141; cf. also Hemelrijk 1951, pp. 47-48 and Broos 1987, p. 214). On the basis of the original, yellow remains of the mordant and traces of the original gilding, the restorer Petria Noble was able to reconstruct the text, as a result of which we now have a better approximation of Holbein's original inscription.
2 The bird was formerly described as a peregrine falcon (*Falco peregrinus*; see Broos 1987, p. 216). Recent research has shown, however, that the large bird of prey is in fact a male gyrfalcon (*Falco rusticolus*). With thanks to Daniel Butler, a falconer in Wales. For this bird, see also Van de Wall 1986, pp. 54-55.
3 For the birds used for falconry and their hunting gear, see Van de Wall 1986, pp. 47-66; see also Gien 1994.
4 Harting 1891, p. 244; Benger 1965, p. 253: 'one of the Yeoman Falconers to King Henry VIII'; Broos 1987, p. 214. In *c.* 1666-1667 Holbein's painting was described in an inventory of the English royal collections as the portrait of 'Robert Cheesman [sic] M[aste]r. Faulkon[ne]r to Hen[ry] 8' (B. Broos in The Hague 1988-1989, p. 75). Bindoff (1982, vol. I, p. 631) wrote erroneously that there was no evidence for this.
5 Chamberlain 1913, vol. II, p. 54 and Broos 1987, p. 215.
6 The biographical information on Cheseman derives from Harting 1891, pp. 243-244; Chamberlain 1913, vol. II, pp. 54-56; Benger 1965 (with genealogical tree on p. 254); Bindoff 1982, vol. I, pp. 630-631 (with select bibliography); Broos 1987, pp. 214-216. Cheseman's public offices are mentioned regularly in documents from 1523 onward.
7 Benger 1965, p. 256.
8 With thanks to Petria Noble, who examined and restored the painting in 2002-2003. During the restoration work, she observed a linear underdrawing, particularly in the face, with the aid of infrared reflectography. It can be inferred on the basis of this underdrawing that a preliminary study existed, at least of the face. The original, bluer colour of the background became visible during the restoration in lacunae in the inscription and on the right, along the contour of the cloak.
9 Rowlands 1985, pp. 138-139, no. 41. The blue colour of the background has been preserved in this painting.
10 For the sleeves in these two paintings, see London 1997-1998, pp. 80-81.
11 There is a smaller, exactly square painting by Holbein from the 1530s in the Gemäldegalerie, Berlin (*Man with lute*, panel, 43.5 x 43.5 cm; Rowlands 1985, p. 141, no. 49; Bätschmann/Griener 1997, p. 178, fig. 236). The horizontal grain of the Hague panel, which has been reduced in size by no more than 1 cm on the left and the right, is also exceptional in Holbein.
12 Buck 1999, pp. 104-105. Many years earlier, in 1515, Holbein had poked fun at gentlemen who posed with falcons, in a pen drawing he made in a copy of Erasmus's *Praise of folly* from 1515 (Basel, Öffentliche Kunstsammlung, Kupferstichkabinett). See Müller 1996, p. 57, no. 37, fig. 12 and Bätschmann/Griener 1997, p. 227, note 84.

13 On the back of Holbein's portrait, five letters and a numeral have been applied in black paint: 'W. E. P. L. C. / 46.'. These probably refer to a sixteenth-century collector. The same letters occur in another portrait by Holbein (cat. no. 37) and a portrait attributed to Willem Key in the Gemäldegalerie, Berlin (Bock *et al.* 1996, p. 60, under no. 586D; see also Chamberlain 1913, vol. II, p. 206; Broos 1987, p. 217, note 1).

20 Philipp Melanchthon (1497–1560) *and* Decorated lid, *c.* 1535

PROVENANCE
House of Hannover; transferred to Britain in 1803, preserved at Windsor Castle from 1812 onwards; Schloss Georgengarten, 1844; Fideicommiss-Galerie of the Houses of Braunschweig-Lüneberg, 1893; acquired by the Landesgalerie Hannover in 1925, inv. no. PAM. 798.

EXHIBITIONS
Hannover 2000

LITERATURE
Grossmann 1951; Reinhardt 1975, pp. 135-140; Rowlands 1985, pp. 94-95, no. 60; Düllberg 1990, pp. 41-42, 272-273, no. 269; Bätschmann/ Griener 1997, pp. 34-35, fig. 29; Buck 1999, p. 71, fig. 67; Hannover 2000, pp. 30-38, fig. 9

NOTES
1 See also cat. no. 1, fig. 1d and Rowlands no. 33.
2 Düllberg 1990, pp. 41-42, 272-273, no. 269.
3 The Phillip Melanchthon Quinquennial, website set up in 1997 to commemorate the 500th anniversary of Melanchthon's birth, ©KDG Wittenberg.
4 Reinhardt 1975 demonstrated that this meeting cannot have taken place, and was the first to highlight the correspondences between the decorations of the title page that Holbein designed for Melanchthon's Loci communes (see also note 6) and the decorations inside the lid of the small portrait discussed here. See also Rowlands 1985, pp. 143-144.
5 Ridley 1984, pp. 259-260.
6 The book was printed and published in Antwerp in 1536. For an illustration, see Hannover 2000, p. 33, fig. 10. See also Rowlands 1985, p. 94, which names Thomas Cromwell and Thomas Cranmer, Archbishop of Canterbury, as possible clients.
7 For this print, see e.g. Hamburg, Kunsthalle, Kupferstichkabinett.
8 Lucas Cranach the Elder (studio), *Portrait of Philipp Melanchthon*, Dresden, Gemäldegalerie, inv. no. 1919.
9 Foister 1981, p. 96 ff. and M. Trudzinski in Hannover 2000, pp. 30-38 discusses this possibility at length. For this, see Lehland's role in relation to inscriptions on other portraits by Holbein, cat. no. 33 and Hannover 2000, pp. 28-30, 35-36.

21-22 Richard Southwell (1503/4–1564), 1536

21

PROVENANCE
See appendix 1; The Royal Collection, Windsor Castle, inv.no. RL 12242

EXHIBITIONS
London 1978-1979, no. 23; New York 1983, no. 12; Houston-Hamburg-Basel-Toronto 1987-1989, no. 35; Edinburgh-Cambridge-London 1993-1994, no. 20

LITERATURE
Ganz 1911-1926, no. XVI2; Parker 1945, no. 38; Foister 1983, no. 38, pp. 11, 16; Buck 1999, pp. 123, 125, fig. 116

22

PROVENANCE
Thomas Howard, Earl of Arundel (1585-1646); gift to Grand Duke Cosimo II de'Medici of Tuscany, 1621; Florence, Galleria degli Uffizi, inv. no. 1087

EXHIBITIONS
Florence 1971, no. 28

LITERATURE
Gigliolo 1909; Chamberlain 1913, vol. II, p. 83; Ganz 1950, no. 88; Crinò 1960; Berti 1983, p. 168 and fig.; Howarth 1985, pp. 69-71, fig. 41; Rowlands 1985, no. 58; Edinburgh-Cambridge-London 1993-1994, p. 64 and fig.; Klinger/Höttler 1998, no. 61; Buck 1999, pp. 123, 125, fig. 117

NOTES
1 On Richard Southwell, see the DNB.
2 See Foister 1983, p. 42 and Edinburgh-Cambridge-London 1993-1994, p. 64. According to the DNB he was appointed to this position in 1538.
3 Holbein also made portraits of Richard Rich and his wife (see Parker 1945, nos. 55 and 80; Foister 1983, nos. 55 and 80, see also Rowlands 1985, no. R. 26).
4 See also London 1977-1978, pp. 109-110, no. 212.
5 For his portraits by Holbein, see Parker 1945, nos. 17 and 29, and Rowlands 1985, no. 76.
6 See Foister 1983, p. 40.
7 Both the drawing and the painting are often wrongly dated 1537, e.g. in Edinburgh-Cambridge-London 1993-1994, no. 20.
8 For other drawings that can be dated, see Parker 1945, nos. 33, 34 and 37 (all three in 1535). See also Foister 1983, nos. 33, 34 and 37.
9 With thanks to Alan Donnithorne, Royal Library, Windsor Castle.
10 To my knowledge, the painting has never been examined using infrared reflectography, so that it has not yet been possible to ascertain whether there is an underdrawing beneath the paint.
11 See Parker 1945, p. 46. It was not until the restoration in the 1970s, when the sheet was removed from the card to which it was attached, that the marks turned out to be accurate reproductions of Southwell's scars, and not blemishes on the paper.
12 See Edinburgh-Cambridge-London 1993-1994, p. 64.
13 A little sketch for a similar jewel in another portrait drawing (Parker 1945, no. 81) may possibly have been a study for this detail in the portrait of Southwell in the Uffizi (see Foister 1983, p. 18).
14 On this gift, see Giglioli 1909 and Crinò 1960.
15 EFFIGIES DOMINI RICARDI SOUTHWELLI EQUITIS AURATI CONSILIARII PRIVATI HENRICI VIII. REGIS ANGLIAE. The ebony frame may have been lost, but the four silver medallions have been preserved (see Berti 1983, p. 168). In 1913 the painting was still enclosed in its seventeenth-century frame (see Chamberlain 1913, vol. II, p. 83).
16 See Howarth 1985, p. 71.

23 Thomas le Strange (1493–1545), *c.* 1536

PROVENANCE
See appendix 1; The Royal Collection, Windsor Castle, inv.no. RL 12244

EXHIBITIONS
London 1978-1979, no. 72; New York 1983, no. 27

LITERATURE

1945, no. 43; Foister 1983, no. 43; Ainsworth 1990, pp. 183-184

NOTES

1 For biographical information on Thomas le Strange, see Rowlands 1985, under no. 59, and Foister 1983, under no. 43; www.tudor-place.com.ar/Bios.
2 She was the elder half-sister of Lord Thomas Vaux, 2nd baron of Harrowden, whose portrait was also executed by Holbein, together with his wife Elizabeth Cheney (Parker 1945, nos. 24 and 30, and no. 25, respectively).
3 With thanks to Alan Donnithorne, Royal Library, Windsor Castle.
4 Rowlands 1985, no. 59; purchased by Kimbell Art Museum, Fort Worth, 1985.
5 An examination using infrared reflectography has revealed the presence of a grid (among other things) drawn on the ground. This may have been used as an aid in the enlargement of the composition. See Ainsworth 1990, pp. 183-184, note 57.
6 See Ganz 1950, p. 246, no. 89; Klinger/Höttler 1998, p. 194, no. 63.

24-25 **Simon George**, *c.* 1536/37

24

PROVENANCE

See appendix 1; The Royal Collection, Windsor Castle, inv.no. RL 12208

EXHIBITIONS

London 1978-1979, no. 39; New York 1983, no. 30; Houston-Hamburg-Basel-Toronto 1987-1989, no. 49; Edinburgh-Cambridge-London 1993-1994, no. 19

LITERATURE

Ganz 1911-1926, no. V12; Parker 1945, no. 35; Foister 1983, no. 45; Ainsworth 1989, pp. 17-18, fig. 15; Ainsworth 1990, pp. 179-180, fig. 14; Klinger/Höttler 1998, p. 200

25

PROVENANCE

M. Birckenstock, Vienna; A. von Brentano-Birckenstock; sale Frankfurt (G.L. Kohlbacher), 4-6 April 1870, lot 113 (purchased by Moritz Gontard for Städel for Dfl. 8,500), Frankfurt, Städelsches Kunstinstitut, inv.no. 1065

LITERATURE

Chamberlain 1913, vol. II, pp. 207-208; Götz 1932; Wehlte 1932, pp. 222-23; London 1978-1979, p. 73; Rowlands 1979, p. 54; Foister 1983, pp. 36, 37; Rowlands 1985, no. 63; Ainsworth 1989, pp. 17-18, fig. 14, 16; Ainsworth 1990, pp. 179-180, fig. 13, 15, 16; Edinburgh-Cambridge-London 1993-1994, p. 62 and fig.; London 1997-1998, pp. 65-67, fig. 72, p. 82; Klinger/Höttler 1998, no. 66; Buck 1999, pp. 123-124, fig. 114

NOTES

1 See Rowlands 1985, p. 144. On the clothing, see Ashelford 1983, p. 43, no. 31.
2 Evidently the court official John Cheke, who identified the sitters in the drawings at Windsor Castle in the 1550s, did still recognise Simon George (see appendix 1).
3 On the symbolism of the carnation, which was sometimes used as a talisman, see Wolffhardt 1954.
4 Cf. also Holbein's *Portrait of a man with carnation*, in which the man is also depicted facing left (Rowlands 1985, no. 86).
5 See Ainsworth 1989, pp. 17-18, fig. 16 and Ainsworth 1990, pp. 179-180, figs. 15 and 16.
6 See Ainsworth 1990, p. 180. Infrared rays cannot penetrate the black cloak.
7 See Ainsworth 1990, fig. 16.
8 See London 1997-1998, p. 68, figs. 76 and 77.
9 See Götz 1932, fig. 86 and Wehlte 1932, pp. 222-223.
10 Götz points out the poor painterly quality of this addition and therefore questions its authenticity (Götz 1932, p. 117). These doubts would appear unjustified, however; the poor quality may be attributable to the wear in the dark paint in this section (with thanks to Bodo Brinkmann).
11 See Rowlands 1979, p. 54 and Rowlands 1985, p. 144.
12 Rowlands 1985, no. 63, suggests a dating to c. 1536-1537.
13 See Götz 1932. Wehlte describes the X-radiograph of the panel (Götz 1932, fig. 86) as rectangular (Wehlte 1932, pp. 222-223), leading one to suppose that the panel was not restored to its circular format until shortly before its publication in the *Städel-Jahrbuch* in 1932.
14 See Rowlands 1985, nos. 33, 36a and 36b, 45 (on paper), 48, 50, 51, 52, 60 (cat. no. 20), R.27-29, R.31 and R.46.
15 Cf. Rowlands 1985, nos. R.22, R.35 and R.38.

26-28 **Jane Seymour (1508/9-1537)**, *c.* 1536/37

26

PROVENANCE

Appendix 1; The Royal Collection, Windsor Castle, inv. no. RL 12267

EXHIBITIONS

London 1978-1979, no. 46; New York 1983, no. 52; Houston-Hamburg-Basel-Toronto 1987-1989, no. 26; Edinburgh-Cambridge-London 1993-1994, no. 21

LITERATURE

Ganz 1911-1926, no. XXV8; Parker 1945, no. 39; Schmid 1948, p. 373; Foister 1983, no. 39; Buck 1997, p. 72, note 229, p. 113, note 59; London 1997-1998, p. 69, fig. 79

27

PROVENANCE

Probably seen by Karel van Mander in Warmoesstraat, Amsterdam (unknown collection), before 1604;[1] Hofburg, Vienna, 1720;[2] Vienna, Kunsthistorisches Museum, inv. no. 881

LITERATURE

Chamberlain 1913, vol. II, pp. 109-113; Ganz 1950, no. 97; Rowlands 1985, p. 114, 144, no. 62; Ainsworth 1990, pp. 180-181; Edinburgh-Cambridge-London 1993-1994, p. 66; Buck 1997, p. 101; Klinger/Höttler 1998, no. 65

28 Studio of Hans Holbein the Younger
Jane Seymour (1508/9-1537), *c.* 1540

PROVENANCE

William III, London, before 1700-1702; Johan Willem Friso, Het Loo, Apeldoorn, 1701-1711; Het Loo, Apeldoorn, 1712; (?) Hof, Leeuwarden, 1757; William V, The Hague, 1774-1795; seized by the French, transferred to the Musée Napoléon (Musée du Louvre), Paris, 1795-1815; Royal Cabinet of Paintings, housed in the Picture Gallery of Prince William V, The Hague, 1816; transferred to the Mauritshuis, 1822, inv.no. 278

EXHIBITIONS

London 1950-1951, no. 19; The Hague 1988-1989, p. 39, fig. 37

LITERATURE

Ganz 1950, no. 95; Tóth-Ubbens 1968, pp. 26-28, no. 278; Rowlands 1985, no. R 23; Buck 1999, p. 109, fig. 101

NOTES

1 Van Mander 1604, fol. 223 verso; Miedema/Van Mander 1994-1999, vol. I, pp. 151-153, vol. III, p. 126.

2 The painting is identical to Holbein's portrait of Jane Seymour from the collection of Thomas Howard, Earl of Arundel (1585-1646) (Cf. Hervey 1921, p. 481, no. 167; Rowlands 1985, no. 62), of which prints were made by Wenceslaus Hollar (Parthey/Pennington 1982, no. 1427); Jane Seymour's jewellery in this circular etching differs from that in the Vienna portrait but corresponds to that in the Mauritshuis painting.

3 On Jane Seymour, see DNB; Pollard 1951, pp. 277-78, 288-89. Jane Seymour is generally believed to have been born in 1508/09, on the basis of an inscription on a portrait miniature by Nicholas Hilliard (see Reynolds 1999, pp. 74-75, no. 33).

4 Chamberlain 1913, vol. II, pp. 111-112.

5 On the Whitehall mural, see p. 32 and note 108, and on the copy by Remigius van Leemput, see ibid., note 109.

6 Rowlands 1985, no. L14b.

7 This painting was first described as a copy of the Vienna painting by Victor de Stuers (1874, p. 272). See also Woltmann 1876, p. 128, no. 161. The slight fraying along the upper and lower edges is still present: the portrait has therefore retained its original height. Ganz 1950, no. 95, describes the painting in the Mauritshuis as an original work by Holbein, which only became clear, he maintains, after the recent restoration.

8 With thanks to Marieke de Winkel for her description of Jane Seymour's apparel and headdress.

9 Cf. Ashelford 1983, p. 37, no. 23.

10 Foister 1983, p. 32.

11 Cf. London 1980-81, no. 55; Scarisbrick 1995, p. 11.

12 See London 1997-1998, p. 69. Cf. also the lapis beads 'lyke potts dressed wt golde wt a piller at thende' (the double chain hanging from her girdle?).

13 Cf. Rowlands 1993, vol. I, pp. 152-176.

14 See X. Brooke in Liverpool 2003, pp. 36-39.

15 See Rowlands 1993, pp. 149-150, no. 326; Parker 1938, pp. 133-134, no. 299.

16 See Schmid 1948, p. 373 and Buck 1997, p. 72, note 229, p. 113, note 59.

17 With thanks to Alan Donnithorne, Royal Library, Windsor Castle.

18 He refers to 'een silver laken cleedt, dat natuerlijcke silver schijnt te wesen [...] oft witte foelie onder is'. See note 1.

19 With thanks to Elke Oberthaler and Monika Strolz, Kunsthistorisches Museum, Vienna.

20 Besides the painting in the Mauritshuis, three copies are known (see Rowlands 1985, no. R 23): the one in the Duke of Bedford's collection (Woburn Abbey) corresponds closely to the painting in Vienna in the details of clothing and jewellery and the brocade pattern (see London 1980-81, no.P5; this panel (115 x 94.5 cm) is larger than the original in Vienna). The copy in the collection of the Duke of Buccleugh (Dalkeith House/Boughton House, near Kettering) and the one in the collection of Lord Sackville (Knole Castle, Kent) depict the same three-quarter length as the painting in Vienna, but their rendering of the jewellery and pearl decorations on the clothing and hood is identical to the version in the Mauritshuis. The brocade on the sleeve and undergarment in these two paintings displays a different pattern than that on the Vienna painting and the copy in Woburn Abbey. In Hollar's print after Holbein's portrait of Jane Seymour in the Arundel collection (see note 2), the same jewels and costume decorations are to be seen as in the Mauritshuis painting.

21 See Ainsworth 1990, pp. 180-81, on which the following description of the underdrawing is based.

22 The outline of the left side of the face has been drawn with metalpoint or hard chalk; the latter medium can also be used to trace a preliminary sketch for transfer (with thanks to Alan Donnithorne). It is possible that the ink lines of the face on the drawing also conceal lines drawn with metalpoint. Maryan Ainsworth (see previous note) established that the underdrawing in the Vienna portrait corresponded precisely to the drawing, which was confirmed by Monika Strolz during restoration work performed in 2002-2003. The infrared reflectogram has not yet been published.

23 Over this, two layers of grey were applied before the blue of the background was painted. The shadow in the left background was prepared, however, with dark underpainting applied over the first layer of grey paint (with thanks to Monika Strolz, Kunsthistorisches Museum, Vienna).

24 Rowlands observed that the figure in the Hague portrait appears to be sunk somewhat deeper than the background, which is characteristic of the style of a particular anonymous follower of Holbein (Rowlands 1985, p. 114). However, the same phenomenon can be seen in several portraits by Holbein himself. In the *Portrait of Jane Seymour* in the Mauritshuis, the sunken figure can be explained by the way the background has been constructed in layers, as cross-sections of the paint make clear. The pink imprimatura was applied in two layers over the white chalk ground, over which a greyish-blue layer was painted (partly decolourised smalt and white lead). Over this greyish-blue layer a thick layer of white was then applied (white lead) followed by two greenish-blue layers (azurite). It is uncertain whether the thick layer of white and the top layers of greenish-blue are original; they may have been added after the greyish-blue had faded or become damaged. At one place along the right of the neck, the flesh colour appears to have been painted directly onto the background, which could be taken as an indication that the thick white layer and the two azurite layers are in fact original. With thanks to Annelies van Loon and Petria Noble (Mauritshuis, 2003) for their technical examination and their analyses of paint samples from this painting.

25 With thanks to Jaap Boon for this observation. The print by Wenceslaus Hollar (see notes 2 and 20) and the copy from the collection of Lord Sackville (Knole Castle, Kent, see note 20) also depict the pendant attached to a pearl in this unrealistic manner.

26 For a technical description of the portrait in The Hague, see *Portraits in the Mauritshuis* (forthcoming). IRR analysis reveals an underdrawing in the face and in the hands, for instance along the left contour of the face and along the sitter's left index finger. For at these points, it deviated from the final painted surface. The IRR images were made using an AIM PtSi 640x486 camera (PtSi sensitive region 1.2-5 micron, no filter; AEG Infrarot-Module GmbH, Heilbronn, Germany) by J.R.J. van Asperen de Boer and Jaap van der Werd (FOM Institute/AMOLF, Amsterdam) 1999 and recently observed again with the Artist camera (Art Innovation, Hengelo; near Infrared 2 with a long wave pass filter 1000 nm). With thanks to Annelies van Loon and Petria Noble.

27 The examination was performed by Dr P. Klein of Hamburg University on 18 February 2002.

28 X. Brooke, in Liverpool 2003, p. 45, p. 70, note 53. Brooke also argues persuasively that Edward Seymour commissioned the two earliest copies of the portrait of Henry VIII in Whitehall Palace (Walker Art Gallery, Liverpool, en Petworth House), see ibid., pp. 64-68.

29 See e.g. Strong 1967, p. 39; Dülberg 1990, p. 285, no. 305. Copies of the portrait of the royal couple in miniature format (in a small box) were exhibited in Dresden in 1871; see Ganz 1950, p. 249, at no. 95.

30 The panel was planed down to a thickness of about 1 mm in an earlier restoration, (photograph of original back in Mauritshuis file, inv. no. 278).

31 See Buck 1997, p. 90 and note 28.

29 William Fitzwilliam, first Earl of Southampton (c. 1490–1542), c. 1536/40

PROVENANCE
See appendix 1; The Royal Collection, Windsor Castle, inv.no. RL 12206

EXHIBITIONS
London 1978-1979, no. 26; New York 1983, no. 39; Houston-Hamburg-Basel-Toronto 1987-1989, no. 39; Edinburgh-Cambridge-London 1993-1994, no. 26

LITERATURE
Parker 1945, no. 66; Foister 1983, pp. 14, 29, no. 66

NOTES
1 The biographical information on William Fitzwilliam has been taken from the DNB.
2 On the painting, see Goodison 1977, pp. 115-117, and Rowlands 1985, no. R. 32 (as having possibly been rescued from the fire at Cowdray House in 1793).
3 See London 1978-1979, p. 58. Rowlands 1979, p. 55, suggests that a copy of it perished in the fire at Cowdray House (see note 2). The collection of Thomas Howard (1585-1646), Earl of Arundel, also contained a portrait of Fitzwilliam by Holbein (Hervey 1921, pp. 481, 482). This may be the life-sized work that was auctioned from the collection of Constant Sennepart on 1 April 1704 as lot 152: 'Een conterfeytsel van den grave van Southampton, levensgroote geschildert op panel anno 1542' (see Manuth 1998, p. 326). Half-length versions of the portrait are also known (see Rowlands 1985 under R. 32, and Parker 1945, p. 54).
4 Foister 1983, p. 3.

30 James Butler, 9th Earl of Ormond (c. 1504-1546), c. 1537

PROVENANCE
See appendix 1; The Royal Collection, Windsor Castle, inv.no. RL 12263

EXHIBITIONS
London 1978-1979, no. 34; New York 1983, no. 33; Houston-Hamburg-Basel-Toronto 1987-1989, no. 32; Edinburgh-Cambridge-London 1993-1994, no. 15

LITERATURE
Ganz 1911-1926, nr. IX10; Parker 1945, no. 23; Starkey 1981; Foister 1983, no. 23, p. 30

NOTES
1 On the doubtful identification as Thomas Boleyn, see e.g. Parker 1945, p. 42, London 1978-1979, pp. 67-68 and Rowlands 1979, p. 55. For the Ormond question and the identification of the portrait as James Butler, see Starkey 1981.
2 On Piers (or Pierce) Butler, see DNB and Lord Dunboyne, *Butler Family History* (7th edition, 1991, p. 14). With thanks to John Butler.
3 On James Butler, DNB (under Piers Butler), see Starkey 1981 and Lord Dunboyne 1991 (see note 2).
4 See Starkey 1981 and Kirwan 1994.
5 With thanks to Marieke de Winkel for her information on the costumes.
6 On John Cheke (1514-1557) and his identification, see appendix 1.

31-32 Lady Elizabeth Audley (?–1564), c. 1538

31
PROVENANCE
See appendix 1; The Royal Collection, Windsor Castle, inv.no. RL 12191

EXHIBITIONS
London 1978-1979, no. 44; New York 1983, no. 47; London 1983, no. 32; Houston-Hamburg-Basel-Toronto 1987-1989, no. 40; London 1995-1996, no. 96

LITERATURE
Ganz 1911-1926, no. VIII9; Parker 1945, no. 58; Foister 1983, no. 58

32
PROVENANCE
Probably purchased by Queen Victoria;[1] The Royal Collection, Windsor Castle, inv.no. RCIN 422292

EXHIBITIONS
London 1978-1979, no. 83; London 1983, no. 31; London 1988-1989, no. 72; Edinburgh-Cambridge-London 1993-1994, no. 30; New York 1996, no. 5

LITERATURE
Chamberlain 1913, vol. II, pp. 222-223; Ganz 1950, no. 143; Strong 1983, p. 47, no. 7; Rowlands 1985, no. M. 9; Klinger/Höttler 1998, p. 283, no. HH.M.9; Reynolds 1999, no. 5

NOTES
1 See Reynolds 1999, p. 50.
2 Pächt 1944, p. 134 ff. See also Buck 1997, pp. 290-294 and Buck 1999, pp. 66-67, fig. 63.
3 See Parker 1945, frontispiece; Rowlands 1985, no. M.1; Buck 1997, pp. 253-322.
4 Strong 1983, pp. 46-50, nos. 1-14; Rowlands 1985, nos. M.2-M.14, cf. R(ejected) M.1-M.5. On the origins of portrait miniatures on vellum in the art of book illumination, see J. Backhouse in Starkey 1991, pp. 88-93. Holbein's small circular panel portraits, with a diameter of about 9 to 12 cm, are left out of consideration here (cf. cat. no. 20).
5 He eclipsed his master 'soo veel als het Sonne-licht des Manen in claerheyt overtreft'; Van Mander/Miedema 1994-1999, vol. I, p. 148, fol. 222v and vol. III, p. 120.
6 On Lucas Horenbout, see e.g. Murdoch et al. 1981, pp. 29-33; Strong 1983, pp. 12-44; Campbell/Foister 1986; Coombs 1998, pp. 21-24; London 1995-1996, no. 65; Reynolds 1999, pp. 45-49.
7 On the technique of miniature painting, see M. Tiethoff and K. Schaffers in The Hague-Apeldoorn-Nagasaki 1991-1992, pp. 13-17; see also K. Schaffers-Bodenhausen, 'Portrait miniatures and miniature portraits', in Schaffers-Bodenhausen/Tiethoff-Spliethoff 1993, pp. 11-45, esp. pp. 13-16.
8 Holbein's portrait miniature of Anne of Cleves (Victoria & Albert Museum, London) is contained in a small ivory box shaped like a Tudor rose, originating from the Tudor period. Its edges were trimmed to fit it into the box (see London 1995-1996, no. 66). Holbein's *Portrait of Philip Melanchton* (cat. no. 20) was not painted on vellum but on the wood of a box, the lid of which was also decorated by the painter.
9 Cf. cat. no. 35 and the *Portrait of Jane Small* (Victoria & Albert Museum, London); see Rowlands 1985, no. M.5 and Campbell 1987.
10 Cf. Mellen 1971; Edinburgh-Cambridge-London 1993-1994, pp. 84-85.
11 See London 1995-1996, p. 118.
12 A preliminary drawing for the portrait miniature of George Neville,

Lord Albergavenny (collection of the Duke of Buccleugh) is preserved at Wilton House (cf. Rowlands 1985, no. M.2 and Strong 1983, pp. 46, 48, figs. 39 and 40). The portrait miniature of Anne of Cleves may be based on the portrait in the Louvre, Paris, which was painted on vellum and subsequently pasted onto a panel (see Rowlands 1985, no. 67 and M.8).

13 The colour green, for instance, which is indicated in the drawing by a clover leaf, is absent from the miniature: the six precious stones on the pendant are executed in black (see London 1997-1998, p. 70, p. 102, Part II, note 16).

14 Hilliard ed. 1981, p. 69.

15 Cf. Parker 1945, p. 52.

16 See Rowlands 1985, no. 64 and Hand 1993, pp. 91-97.

17 See Parker 1945, no. 28.

18 This identification was first suggested in London 1978-1979, p. 79.

19 On Thomas Audley, see Bietenholz/Deutscher 1985-87, vol. I, pp. 75-76. Audley's Essex country house, Audley Inn, was demolished in the early seventeenth century by his descendant Thomas Howard, Earl of Arundel (1585-1646), and rebuilt as the grand Audley End. Two portraits in this house were traditionally attributed to Holbein and identified as Thomas Audley and his wife. It has been discovered that these works bear the date 1569, however, and they are now attributed to a follower of Thomas Key. A *Portrait of an unknown man* by Holbein from Audley End was sold in 1956, but English Heritage bought it back for the house in 1998 (Rowlands 1985, no. 1): the man depicted is too young to be Thomas Audley (with thanks to Gareth Hughes, English Heritage, for supplying the information on the paintings at Audley End that are mentioned here).

20 See Strong 1983, p. 47.

33 Edward (1537-1553), Prince of Wales, *c.* 1538

PROVENANCE

Probably a gift from the artist to Henry VIII, 1 January 1539; Thomas Howard, Earl of Arundel and Surrey, Arundel Castle, Sussex and Arundel House, London, *c.* 1639, in Amsterdam from 1643; passed to his wife, Alatheia Howard, Antwerp and Amsterdam, 1646-1654; probably William III, Het Loo Palace, Apeldoorn (documented there after his death, in 1711 and 1713); Ernst August, Duke of Cumberland and King of Hannover, Hannover, 1844-1851; passed to his son, George V, king of Hannover, 1851-1878 (on loan to the Welfen Museum, Hannover, from 1863 onward); passed to his son Ernst August, Duke of Cumberland and crown prince of Hannover, 1878-1923 (on loan to the Provinzialmuseum, Hannover, 1891-1924); P. and D. Colnaghi art dealers, London, 1924 or 1925; M. Knoedler & Co art dealers, London and New York, 1925; purchased by Andrew W. Mellon, Washington, July 1925; placed in the Andrew W. Mellon Educational and Charitable Trust, 30 March 1932; transferred to the museum in 1937; Washington, National Gallery of Art, inv. no. 1937.1.64

EXHIBITIONS

New York 1928, no. 6; London 1995-1996, no. 6; Hannover 2000, passim

LITERATURE

Rowlands 1985, pp. 116, 146-147, no. 70; B. Broos in The Hague 1988-1989, pp. 116-118, no. XIII (not in exhibition); Campbell 1990, pp. 69, 81, 104 and fig. 122; Hand 1993, pp. 83-91, no. 1937.1.64 (with select bibliography); S. Foister in London 1995-1996, pp. 41-42, no. 6; Bätschmann/Griener 1997, p. 189; London 1997-1998, pp. 83-84, 85, 86; Klinger/Höttler 1998, p. 217, no. 73; Manuth 1998, p. 331 and fig. 8; Buck 1999, p. 120; M. Trudzinski in Hannover 2000, passim; Roy/Wyld 2001, p. 97

NOTES

1 Rowlands 1985, pp. 146-147, no. 70; see also Hand 1993, p. 90, note 21. A good, old, copy of the painting, formerly in the collection of the Marquess of Bute, the provenance of which was confused in the past with that of the portrait discussed here (Hand 1993, p. 88 and 90, note 19; Hannover 2000, p. 39, fig. 16), was sold at auction in London, at Christie's, as lot 116, on 3-5 July 1996. There is a painted portrait of Edward VI that was formerly attributed to Holbein in The Jules Bache Collection, The Metropolitan Museum of Art, New York (see Rowlands 1985, pp. 235-236, no. R.35, fig. 243 and Ainsworth 1990, pp. 185-186).

2 Buck 1999, p. 120.

3 The English translation of the text is taken from Hand 1993, pp. 84, 86. The writer and scholar Morison was one of the ambassadors of the English court. The addition 'Car:' after his Latinised name beneath the inscription is an abbreviation of 'carminum auctor' (poet). See Hand 1993, pp. 84 and 89, note 8.

4 This mural perished by fire in 1698. Rowlands 1985, pp. 224-226, no. L. 14 and fig. 196; S. Foister in London 1995-1996, pp. 40-41, no. 5; Buck 1997, p. 125 and note 95. On texts included in Holbein's works of art, see Buck 1997, pp. 278-281.

5 Strong 1967, pp. 14, 17-18; Hand 1993, p. 88.

6 Hand 1993, p. 86. Holbein produced portrait miniatures of the prince's young classmates Charles and Henry Brandon (London, The Royal Collection; Rowlands 1985, pp. 151-152, nos. M.10-11).

7 The quotation is from the *New Year's Gift Roll*, a manuscript from 1539 in the Folger Shakespeare Library, Washington; see Hand 1993, pp. 86 and 88, note 2. For other New Year's Day gifts to the king, see Starkey 1998, p. 487.

8 Of the two portraits of Edward by Holbein that were described in inventories of the royal collections drawn up in 1542 and 1547, one was a full-length portrait painted on canvas (see Shaw 1937, p. 33, no. 47). See S. Foister in London 1995-1996, p. 41; Foister 1996, p. 52; M. Trudzinski in Hannover 2000, pp. 39-40 and figs. 16-17.

9 Rowlands 1985, pp. 115-116.

10 Rowlands 1985, p. 115; S. Foister in London 1995-1996, p. 41.

11 With at upper left the inscription 'Edward Prince.'; see Parker 1945, p. 49, no. 46; J. Roberts in Hamburg-Basel 1988, p. 86, no. 25; Ainsworth 1990, pp. 182-183. The identity of the sitter in a second sheet by Holbein in the Royal Collection bearing the inscription 'Edward Prince of Wales' —a portrait of a boy of about 5 or 6 years of age— has sometimes been questioned (see Parker 1945, pp. 55-56, no. 71, fig. 71 and Strong 1969, p. 92), although there seems little reason to doubt it. Another portrait study of Edward, also in the Royal Collection, once thought to be by Holbein, has long since been attributed to William Scrots, one of Holbein's followers (Parker 1945, p. 58, no. 85 and fig. 85; Strong 1969, pp. 92-93; Ainsworth 1990, p. 182, note 52 and pp. 185-186).
‹ Around 1538 Holbein made another portrait of Edward, in a small circular drawing, playing with a dog (Basel, Öffentliche Kunstsammlungen, Kunstmuseum); see Müller 1996, p. 134, no. 228 and fig. 68. This medallion-shaped drawing may have been intended to serve as a design for use by a goldsmith.

12 It has sometimes been assumed that this pink ground was intended to bring out the youthful tints of the prince's face (London 1997-1998, p. 84). But Holbein used a similar pink ground in other portraits, including that of Jane Seymour (cat. no. 27).

13 Hand 1993, p. 84. For the underdrawing, see J. Roberts in Hamburg-Basel 1988, p. 86, no. 25.

14 Ainsworth 1990, pp. 182-183; Hand 1993, pp. 88 and 89-90, note 17.

15 S. Foister in London 1995-1996, p. 41.

16 Hand 1993, p. 84; London 1997-1998, p. 86; Roy/Wyld 2001, p. 106.

17 The pigment used for the background is smalt, which consists of ground cobalt glass. It is not uncommon for smalt to become grey

or brown through ageing, as in the painting described here; see Hand 1993, p. 84 and London 1997-1998, pp. 84, 85.

34 Thomas Howard, third Duke of Norfolk (1473-1554), *c.* 1539/40

PROVENANCE

By inheritance to Thomas Howard, Earl of Arundel (1585-1646), the sitter's great-great-grandson; probably sold at Utrecht, 1662; sale Amsterdam, 23 April 1732; sale London, 1744, Frederick, Prince of Wales, before 1750; The Royal Collection, Windsor Castle, inv.no. 59

EXHIBITIONS

London 1977-1978, no. 207; London 1978-1979, no. 37

LITERATURE

Chamberlain 1913, vol. II, pp. 197-200; Millar 1963, pp. 59-60, no. 30; Ashelford 1983, pp. 40-41, no. 28; Rowlands 1985, no. 68; Klinger/Höttler 1998, no. 71

NOTES

1 On Thomas Howard, see e.g. DNB and Head 1995.
2 On the copies, see London 1978-1979 under no. 37 and Rowlands 1985 under no. 68. The inscription is clearly legible on the copy depicted on the cover of Head 1995.
3 On the insignia of the Order of the Garter, see e.g. Scarisbrick 1995, pp. 81-83, fig. 66.
4 See Ashelford 1983, p. 40.
5 On Edward Seymour, see X. Brooke in Liverpool 2003, pp. 43-46.
6 Foister 1983, p. 35, p. 38, note 4.
7 See Parker 1945, nos. 17 and 29 (cf. also no. 83) and Rowlands 1985, no. 76. For the portrait of Frances de Vere, see Parker 1945, no. 18.
8 See Parker 1945, nos. 16 and 19 respectively. On the identification of Lady Ratcliffe, see Foister 1983, p. 41, under no. 19.
9 See e.g. Howarth 1985, pp. 167, 164, fig. 115.
10 See Hervey 1921, pl. XXI, Howarth 1985, pp. 187-188, fig. 135 and Parthey/Pennington 1982, no. 466.

35 An unknown young man, *c.* 1540/43

PROVENANCE

Queen Sophie, The Hague; passed by inheritance to the Royal House; The Hague, The House of Orange-Nassau Historic Collections Trust, inv. no. MI/0492

EXHIBITIONS

Brussels 1882, no. 258; Brussels 1912, no. 846; Rotterdam 1910, no. 146; Delft 1966, no. 1; The Hague-Apeldoorn-Nagasaki 1991-1992, no. 33

LITERATURE

Strong 1983, p. 50, no. 11; Rowlands 1985, p. 152, no.M. 12; Schaffers-Bodenhausen/Tiethoff-Spliethoff 1993, pp. 16 and 373, no. 492 (with select bibliography); Klinger/Höttler 1998, p. 288, no. 12

NOTES

1 Strong 1983, pp. 45-53; Rowlands 1985, pp. 150-152, nos. M.2-14; Klinger/Höttler 1998, pp. 280-289, nos. M. 2-15. See also R. Strong in London 1983, pp. 45-51 and J. Roberts in London 2002-2003, pp. 116-117, nos. 40-42.
2 See Schaffers-Bodenhausen/Tiethoff-Spliethoff 1993, p. 16 and The Hague-Apeldoorn-Nagasaki 1991-1992, p. 13.
3 Strong et al. 1981, p. 36 and Schaffers-Bodenhausen/Tiethoff-Spliethoff 1993, p. 373, no. 492.
4 The present gold frame, furnished with pearls on three sides, was made in 1990. It was inspired by the frame (also non-authentic) enclosing Holbein's portrait of Jane Small (see note 8 and Campbell 1987, p. 367). Not a single one of Holbein's paintings or miniatures seems to have retained its original frame, with the exception of the circular paintings in Basel (p. 53, fig. 1d) and Hannover (cat. no. 20). The 'frame' surrounding the portrait miniature of Anne of Cleves from 1539 (London, Victoria and Albert Museum; Rowlands 1985, p. 151, no. M. 6), contained in a small ivory box with a Tudor rose, is probably not authentic, though it was made in the Tudor period (see S. Foister in London 1995-1996, p. 119, no. 66; Foister 1997, pp. 54-55 and Coombs 1998, pp. 20-21).
5 Van Mander 1604, p. 223v and Van Mander-Miedema 1994-1999, vol. I, pp. 152-153.
6 Habich 1913; Löcher 1985, p. 676; Rowlands 1985, p. 152, no.M. 14; Klinger/Höttler 1998, pp. 285-286, no. M. 14.
7 Strong (1983, p. 50, no. 11) dated the work around 1535-1540, Schaffers-Bodenhausen and Tiethoff-Spliethoff (1993, p. 373, no. 492) around 1540.
8 Formerly believed to depict Robert Pemberton's wife, it is now identified as a portrait of Jane Small, née Pemberton. See Rowlands 1985, pp. 150-151, no. M. 5; Campbell 1987 and Coombs 1998, pp. 22-23 and fig. 8.
9 Rowlands 1985, nos. M. 3-5, 10-11, 13-14. Only in one miniature, *Portrait of a 27-year-old man, believed to be Harry Maynert*, did Holbein give the sitter's initials as well as his age: 'H. M.' (Munich, Bayerisches Nationalmuseum; Rowlands 1985, no. M.13 and fig. 138).
10 Rowlands 1985, p. 152, no. M. 12. On Queen Sophie as a collector of miniatures, see Schaffers-Bodenhausen/Tiethoff-Spliethoff 1993, pp. 62-72.
11 Chamberlain (1913, vol. II, pp. 229-230) believed the young man to be a member of the Royal Household.
12 Lugt 1917, p. 9; Schaffers-Bodenhausen/Tiethoff-Spliethoff 1993, p. 373, no. 492.

36 Nobleman with a hawk, 1542

PROVENANCE

Charles I, London, before 1649; Charles II, London; James II, London; Kensington House, 1697, 1700; William III, Het Loo Palace, Apeldoorn, after 1700-1702; Johan Willem Friso, Het Loo Palace, Apeldoorn, 1702-1711; sale Het Loo, Amsterdam, 26 July 1713, lot 33 (withdrawn and sent to Friesland); palace in Leeuwarden, 1733; Het Loo Palace, Apeldoorn, 1757; Stadholder William V, The Hague, 1763-1795 (for the remaining history, see the provenance of the *Portrait of Robert Cheseman*, also in the Mauritshuis, cat. no. 19); The Hague, Royal Cabinet of Paintings Mauritshuis, inv. no. 277

EXHIBITIONS

London 1950-1951, no. 18; The Hague 1966, no. 8; The Hague 1988-1989, no. X; London 1995-1996, no. 7

LITERATURE

Rowlands 1985, pp. 120, 147, no. 75; Broos 1987, pp. 215-216; B. Broos in The Hague 1988-1989, pp. 103-105, no. X; S. Foister in London 1995-1996, p. 42, no. 7; Klinger/Höttler 1998, p. 222, no. 78

NOTES

1 The number '28' corresponds to the number in a list dating from 1713 (The Hague, Royal Archives), which was drawn up by Robert Du Val, curator of the collections of Stadholder William III. The list

provides an overview of the paintings that William III had taken to the Netherlands, including the two Holbeins that are now in the Mauritshuis. After the Stadholder's death in 1702 these paintings were claimed by Queen Anne of Great Britain. See B. Broos in The Hague 1988-1989, pp. 52 and 53, fig. 7, p. 60, fig. C 1 and p. 103.

2 With thanks to Annelies van Loon and Petria Noble of the Mauritshuis, who analysed paint samples from the background in the spring of 2003. Contrary to what is stated in Filtenborg 1994, the background consists not of ultramarine but of smalt. It is not unusual for this pigment to become discoloured with the passage of time (see also cat. no. 33, note 17).

3 With thanks to Petria Noble.

4 It is hence not, as formerly believed, a falcon. Waetzoldt (1938, p. 209) was the first author to describe the bird as a hawk.

5 B. Broos in The Hague 1988-1989, p. 103.

6 Pinder 1951, p. 86.

7 S. Foister in London 1995-1996, p. 42.

8 Waetzoldt 1938, p. 207.

9 Filtenborg 1994. It is almost impossible to infer the changes in the composition from the X-radiograph of the panel (Mauritshuis archives). On the basis of light patches at lower left on this X-radiograph, Filtenborg believed that the first version of the right hand had been painted there, before the glove was added, or even that both hands were originally in that section. It seems more likely, however, that Holbein took account of the left hand grasping the bird's hood when applying the background (with thanks to Petria Noble). The infrared reflectogram did not reveal an underdrawing.

10 Rowlands 1985, p. 147, no. 73. A man from the De Vos van Steenwijk family wears a similar hat in another portrait by Holbein, also dated 1541, which is in Berlin (Rowlands 1985, p. 147, no. 74, fig. 112).

11 The striking *craquelure* pattern of the background continues under the bird's head. In addition, it is striking that the contour of the man's right shoulder now glimmers faintly through the bird's neck.

37 Anton the Good, Duke of Lorraine (1489–1544) ?, *c.* 1543

PROVENANCE

Unknown private collection, England, sixteenth century[1]; Anthony Baker, art dealer, London; sale Sir J.E. Millais, Christie's (London), 1 May 1897; acquired by the Kaiser Friedrich Museum, Berlin; Staatliche Kunstsammlungen, Gemäldegalerie, inv.no. 586D

LITERATURE

Fischel 1926, pp. 137-140; Rowlands p. 149, 1985, no. 79; Bock *et al.* 1996, p. 60. no. 586D; Buck 1997, p. 341; Klinger/Höttler 1998, p. 230; Buck 1999, p. 131

NOTES

1 Five letters and a number have been added on the back of the portrait: 'W.E.P.L.C./46.'. These probably allude to a sixteenth-century collector. The same inscription occurs in cat. no. 19 (Robert Cheseman) and in a portrait of Willem Key; see also cat. no. 19, note 14.

2 Florence, Galleria degli Uffizi, inv. no. Ic873

3 Rowlands 1985, p. 149, no. 79.

4 Ridley 1984, p. 306; Fraser 1992, pp. 354, 357.

5 Most authors see the identification as Anton the Good as conditional upon the two men having met; see e.g. Rowlands 1985, p. 149, no. 79.

6 See Buck 1997, p. 341 and fig. 130.

38 John Chambers (1470?–1549), *c.* 1543

PROVENANCE

Thomas Howard, Earl of Arundel and Surrey, Arundel Castle, Sussex and Arundel House, London, in Amsterdam from 1643; passed by inheritance to his wife, Alatheia Howard, Antwerp and Amsterdam, 1646-1654; Leopold Wilhelm, Archduke of Austria; Vienna, Kunsthistorisches Museum, Gemäldegalerie, inv. no. 882

LITERATURE

Rowlands 1985, p. 149, no. 82; Klinger/Höttler 1998, p. 233, no. 85; Ainsworth 1990, pp. 184-185; Ferino-Pagden *et al.* 1991, p. 70, no. 882; Buck 1997, pp. 232-233; Buck 1999, pp. 129-130

NOTES

1 For a detailed discussion of the group portrait and its origins, see Buck 1997, pp. 196-252; Buck 1999, pp. 126, 128-129 and Rowlands 1985, pp. 148-149, no. 78.

2 DNB, vol. 10 (1887), pp. 30-31.

3 The portrait of Butts is in Boston, Isabella Stewart Gardner Museum (Rowlands 1985, no. 80).

4 Paper on panel, 160 x 280 cm, Royal College of Surgeons of England, London. The cartoon was completely overpainted after being transferred to the panel.

5 Ainsworth 1990, pp. 184-185; Buck 1997, pp. 232-233.

6 See Buck 1997, pp. 196-252.

7 Holbein's only other portrait displaying the letters 'SVE' instead of 'SUÆ' is the *Portrait of Lady Margaret Butts* in the Isabella Stewart Gardner Museum, Boston (Rowlands 1985, no. 81), which was made in roughly the same period.

8 It is impossible to determine, even using a microscope, IRR or X-radiography, whether any changes were made to the inscription (but see Ferino-Pagden *et al.* 1991, p. 70, no. 882). The inscription is on the original layer of paint; the later green overpainting was carefully added around the letters and figures. With thanks to the restorer Monika Strolz at the Kunsthistorisches Museum, Vienna. The print that Wenceslaus Hollar produced in 1640 after this painting — which was then in the collection of the Earl of Arundel — already exhibited the present inscription (Parthey 1853, no. 1372).

Bibliography

A

Ainsworth 1989
M.W. Ainsworth, 'Northern Renaissance Drawings and Underdrawings: A Proposed Method of Study', *Master Drawings* 27 (1989), pp. 5-38
Ainsworth 1990
M. Ainsworth, '"Paternes for phiosioneamyes": Holbein's portraiture reconsidered', *The Burlington Magazine* 132 (1990), pp. 173-186
Ainsworth 1991
M.W. Ainsworth, 'Methods of Copying in the Portraiture of Hans Holbein the Younger', *Le dessin sous-jacent dans la peinture: Colloque VIII* (1991), Leuven 1993, pp. 11-13
Ainsworth/Faries 1986
M. Ainsworth, M. Faries, 'Northern Renaissance Paintings: The Discovery of Invention', *Bulletin of the St. Louis Art Museum* 18 (1986), no. 1, pp. 23-37
Allen 1906-1958
P.S. Allen, H.M. Allen, H.W. Garrod (eds.), *Opus Epistolarum Des. Erasmi Roterodami* (12 vols.), Oxford 1906-1958
Amsterdam 1986
J.P. Filedt Kok, W. Halsema-Kubes, W.T. Kloek (eds.), *Kunst voor de beeldenstorm: Noordnederlandse kunst 1525-1580*, Amsterdam (Rijksmuseum) 1986
Anglo 1992
S. Anglo, *Images of Tudor Kingship*, London 1992
Antwerp-Amsterdam 1999-2000
C. Depauw, G. Luijten et al., *Antoon van Dyck en de prentkunst*, Antwerp (Museum Plantin-Moretus / Stedelijk Prentenkabinet), Amsterdam (Rijksmuseum, Rijksprentenkabinet) 1999-2000
Anzelewsky/Mielke 1984
F. Anzelewsky, H. Mielke, *Albrecht Dürer: Kritisches Katalog der Zeichnungen, Staatliche Museen zu Berlin, Preussischer Kulturbesitz*, Berlin 1984
Arnold 1973
J. Arnold, *A Handbook of Costume*, London 1973
Ashelford 1983
J. Ashelford, *The Sixteenth Century: A Visual History of Costume*, London 1983
Asmus/Grosshans 1998
G. Asmus, R. Grosshans (eds.), *Gemäldegalerie Berlin: 200 Meisterwerke*, Berlin 1998
Auerbach 1954
E. Auerbach, *Tudor Artists*, London 1954
Augsburg 1980
Welt im Umbruch: Augsburg zwischen Renaissance und Barock (3 vols.), Augsburg (Rathaus und Zeughaus) 1980
Augsburg 1997
B.R. Kommer (ed.), *Hans Holbein d.J. (1497/98-1543)*, Augsburg (Städtische Kunstsammlungen) 1997

B

Backhouse 1991
J. Backhouse, 'Illuminated Manuscripts and the Development of the Portrait Miniature', in *Greenwich 1991*, pp. 88-93
Bätschmann 1996
O. Bätschmann, 'Der Holbein-Streit: Eine Krise der Kunstgeschichte', *Jahrbuch der Berliner Museen* 38 (1996), pp. 87-100
Bätschmann 2001
O. Bätschmann, 'Holbein and Italian Art', in *Roskill/Hand 2001*, pp. 36-53
Bätschmann/Griener 1994
O. Bätschmann, P. Griener, 'Holbein-Apelles: Wettbewerb und Definition des Künstlers', *Zeitschrift für Kunstgeschichte* 57 (1994), pp. 626-650
Bätschmann/Griener 1997
O. Bätschmann, P. Griener, *Hans Holbein*, Cologne 1997
Bätschmann/Griener 1998a
O. Bätschmann, P. Griener, *Hans Holbein d.J. Die Darmstädter Madonna: Original gegen Fälschung*, Frankfurt am Main 1998
Bätschmann/Griener 1998b
O. Bätschmann, P. Griener, *Hans Holbein d.J. Die Solothurner Madonna: Eine Sacra Conversazione im Norden*, Basel 1998
Von Baldass 1913-1914
L. von Baldass, 'Die Bildnisse Kaiser Maximilians I.', *Jahrbuch der Kunsthistorischen Sammlungen des Allerhöchsten Kaiserhauses* 31 (1913-1914), pp. 247-334
Bambach-Cappel 1988
C. Bambach-Cappel, *The Tradition of Pouncing Drawings in the Italian Renaissance Workshops* (dissertation Yale University, 2 vols.), New Haven, Connecticut 1988
Bartrum 2002-2003
See *London 2002-2003a*
Baschnagel 1979
G. Baschnagel, '"Narrenschiff"und "Lob der Torheit": Zusammenhänge und Beziehungen', in *Europäische Hochschulschriften, Reihe I: Deutsche Literatur und Germanistik* (vol. 283), Frankfurt am Main 1979
Basel 1960
G. Schmidt, H. Reinhardt, E. Treu et al., *Die Malerfamilie Holbein in Basel*, Basel (Kunstmuseum) 1960
Basel 1984
Basler Buchillustration 1500-1545, Basel (Universitätsbibliothek) 1984
Basel 1986
Erasmus von Rotterdam: Vorkämpfer für Frieden und Toleranz. Ausstellung zum 450. Todestag des Erasmus von Rotterdam, Basel (Historisches Museum) 1986
Basel 1991
Das Amerbach Kabinett: Sammeln in der Renaissance (5 vols.), Basel (Kunstmuseum) 1991
Basel 1995
F. Nagel et al., *Bonifacius Amerbach 1495-1562: Zum 500. Geburtstag des Basler Juristen und Erben des Erasmus von Rotterdam*, Basel (Kunstmuseum) 1995
Basel 1997
Ein Schulmeister schilt vf beiden seiten gemolt: Holbeins Beitrag zur Frühgeschichte des Genrebildes, Basel (Kunstmuseum) 1997
Basel-Berlin 1997-1998
Dürer Holbein Grünewald. Meisterzeichnungen der deutschen Renaissance aus Berlin und Basel, Basel (Öffentliche Kunstsammlung, Kupferstichkabinett), Berlin (Kupferstichkabinett der Staatlichen Museen zu Berlin) 1997-1998
Benger 1965
F.B. Benger, 'Occasional Notes: Robert Cheseman, b.1485 - d.1547', *Proceedings of the Leatherhead & District Local History Society* 2 (1965), pp. 252-256
Bern 2001
C. Dupeux et al., *Bildersturm: Wahnsinn oder Gottes Wille?*, Bern (Historisches Museum) 2001
Bernhart 1922
J. Bernhart, *Hans Holbein der Jüngere*, Munich 1922
Berti 1983
L. Berti (ed.), *Galleria degli Uffizi*, Florence 1983
Bietenholz/Deutscher 1985-1987
P.G. Bietenholz, T.B. Deutscher, *Contemporaries of Erasmus: A Biographical Register of the Renaissance and Reformation* (3 vols.), Toronto-Buffalo-London 1985-1987
Bindoff 1982
S.T. Bindoff, *The History of Parliament: The House of Commons 1509-1558* (3 vols.), London 1982
Bock *et al.* 1996
H. Bock et al., *Gemäldegalerie Berlin: Gesamtverzeichnis*, Berlin 1996
Boerlin 1991
P.H. Boerlin, *Das Amerbach-Kabinett: Die Gemälde*, Basel 1991 (see *Basel 1991*)
Van der Boom 1948
A. van der Boom, *Hans Holbein de Jonge*, Naarden 1948
Boston 1970
E. Standen, *Masterpieces of Painting in The Metropolitan Museum of Art*, Boston (Museum of Fine Arts) 1970
Braunfels 1974
W. Braunfels (ed.), *Lexikon der christlichen Ikonographie* (vol. 7), Rome 1974
Bredius 1913
A. Bredius, 'Schilderijen in oude inventarissen', *Oud Holland* 31 (1913), pp. 205-206
Briquet 1907/1968
C.M. Briquet, *Les Filigranes*, Paris 1907 (reprint Amsterdam 1968)
Broos 1987
B. Broos, *Meesterwerken in het Mauritshuis*, The Hague 1987
Broos 1993
B. Broos, *Intimacies & Intrigues: History Painting in the Mauritshuis*, The Hague-Ghent 1993
Brunin 1968
H. Brunin, 'De Erasmusportretten van en naar Holbein de Jonge', *Bulletin des Musées Royaux des Beaux-Arts de Belgique* (1968), pp. 145-160
Brussels 1882
Catalogue de la Collection de Miniatures appartenant à S.A.R. Mgr. le Prince Alexandre des Pays-Bas, Prince d'Orange, Brussels (Nederlandsche Vereeniging van Weldadigheid) 1882
Brussels 1912

Exposition de la Miniature à Bruxelles en 1912, Brussels (Librairie Nationale d'Art et d'Histoire) 1912
Buck 1997
S. Buck, *Holbein am Hofe Heinrichs VIII.*, Berlin 1997
Buck 1998
S. Buck, 'Text versus Bild: Holbeins Interpretation Heinrichs VIII. am Beispiel der "Salomo Miniatur"', *Zeitschrift für Schweizerische Archäologie und Kunstgeschichte* 55 (1998), pp. 281-292
Buck 1999
S. Buck, *Hans Holbein 1497/98-1543*, Cologne 1999
Buck 2001
S. Buck, 'Comparing drawings and underdrawings: the possibilities and limitations of a method', *Le dessin sous-jacent dans la peinture: Procédé, méthodique, application, Colloque 13 (1999)*, Leuven 2001, pp. 201-212
Bushart 1987
B. Bushart, *Hans Holbein der Ältere*, Augsburg 1987
Bushart 1994
B. Bushart, *Die Fuggerkapelle bei St. Anna in Augsburg*, Munich 1994
Bushart 1998
B. Bushart, 'Hans Holbein: Vater und Sohn', *Zeitschrift für Schweizerische Archäologie und Kunstgeschichte* 55 (1998), pp. 151-168

C

Campbell 1987
L. Campbell, 'Holbein's miniature of "Mrs Pemberton": The identity of the sitter', *The Burlington Magazine* 129 (1987), pp. 366-371
Campbell 1990
L. Campbell, *Renaissance Portraits: European Portrait-Painting in the 14th, 15th and 16th Centuries*, New Haven-London 1990
Campbell *et al.* 1978
L. Campbell, M.M. Phillips, H. Schulte Herbrüggen, J.B. Trapp, 'Quentin Matsys, Desiderius Erasmus, Pieter Gillis und Thomas More', *The Burlington Magazine* 120 (1978), pp. 716-725
Campbell/Foister 1986
L. Campbell, S. Foister, 'Gerard, Lucas and Susanna Horenbout', *The Burlington Magazine* 128 (1986), pp. 719-727
Chamberlain 1912
A.B. Chamberlain, 'Holbein's Visit to "High Burgony"', *The Burlington Magazine* 21 (1912), pp. 25-30
Chamberlain 1913
A.B. Chamberlain, *Hans Holbein the Younger* (2 vols.), London 1913
Chicago 1933
A Century of Progress, Chicago (Art Institute of Chicago) 1933
Cologne 1973
K. Bund, *Hanse in Europa: Brücke zwischen den Märkten 12.-17. Jahrhundert*, Cologne (Stadtmuseum, Kunsthalle) 1973
Coombs 1998
K. Coombs, *The Portrait Miniature in England*, London 1998
Cox-Rearick 1996
J. Cox-Rearick, *The Collection of Francis I: Royal Treasures*, Antwerp-New York 1996
Crinò 1960
A.M. Crinò, 'Altri documenti sul ritratto di Southwell dello Holbein e su una statuetta di Lucrezia del Dürer', *Rivista d'arte* 35 (1960), pp. 143-151
Cust 1911
L. Cust, 'Notes on the Collection formed by Thomas Howard, Earl of Arundel and Surrey', *The Burlington Magazine* 19 (1911), pp. 278-287

D

Delft 1966
L. de Vries, *Uit Koninklijk en Rijksbezit*, Delft (Stedelijk Museum Het Prinsenhof) 1966
Dijon 2001
Dresde ou le rêve des Princes: La Galerie de peintures au XVIIIe siècle, Dijon (Musée des Beaux-Arts) 2001
Dill 1998
U. Dill, 'Der Bart des Philosophen. Holbeins Amerbach-Porträt: neu gesehen im Lichte eines bisher nicht beachteten Epigramms', *Zeitschrift für Schweizerische Archäologie und Kunstgeschichte* 55 (1998), pp. 245-262
DNB
DNB: Dictionary of National Biography (63 vols. with 3 vols. supplement, index and errata), London 1885-1904
Dollinger 1998
P. Dollinger, *Die Hanse*, Stuttgart 1998
Dresden 1871
Katalog der Holbein-Ausstellung zu Dresden, Dresden (Pavillon des Zwingers) 1871
Dresden 1992
Gemäldegalerie Alte Meister: Katalog der ausgestellten Werke, Dresden 1992
Dudok van Heel 1975
S.A.C. Dudok van Heel, 'De kunstverzamelingen Van Lennep met de Arundel-tekeningen', *Jaarboek Amstelodamum* (1975), pp. 137-148
Dudok van Heel 1992
S.A.C. Dudok van Heel, 'Een Holbein uit de collecties Six', *Maandblad Amstelodamum* 79 (1992), pp. 51-55
Dückers 1994
A. Dückers (ed.), *Das Berliner Kupferstichkabinett: Ein Handbuch zur Sammlung*, Berlin 1994
Dülberg 1990
A. Dülberg, *Privatporträts: Geschichte und Ikonologie einer Gattung im 15. und 16. Jahrhundert*, Berlin 1990

E

Edinburgh-Cambridge-London 1993-1994
J. Roberts, *Holbein and the Court of Henry VIII: Drawings and Miniatures from The Royal Library Windsor Castle*, Edinburgh (National Gallery of Scotland), Cambridge (Fitzwilliam Museum), London (National Portrait Gallery) 1993-1994
Erasmus ed. 1975
W. Welzig (ed.), *Ausgewählte Schriften, Lateinisch und Deutsch* (8 vols.), vol. 2, Darmstadt 1975
Van Everdingen 1984
L. van Everdingen, *Het Loo, de Oranjes en de jacht*, Haarlem 1984

F

Faesch 1628
R. Faesch, *Humanae industriae monumenta nova simul et antiqua*, [Basel] 1628- (Manuscript, Universitätsbibliothek Basel)
Fahy 1968
E. Fahy, *The Frick Collection: An Illustrated Catalogue, vol. I, Paintings*, New York 1968
Falk 1968
T. Falk, *Hans Burgkmair: Studien zu Leben und Werk des Augsburger Malers*, Munich 1968
Falk 1996
T. Falk, 'Hans Burgkmair I', in J. Turner (ed.), *The Dictionary of Art*, vol. 5, London 1996, pp. 198-201
Ferino-Pagden *et al.* 1991
S. Ferino-Pagden et al., *Die Gemäldegalerie des Kunsthistorischen Museums in Wien: Verzeichnis der Gemälde*, Vienna 1991
Filtenborg 1994
T. Filtenborg, 'Hans Holbein the Younger [...] Portrait of a 28-year old Falconer', *Mauritshuis in focus* 7 (1994), no. 2, pp. 24-26
Fischel 1926
O. Fischel, 'Holbeins Bildnis Herzog Antons der Guten von Lotharingen', *Jahrbuch der Preussischen Kunstsammlungen* 47 (1926), pp. 137-140
Fletcher/Cholmondeley Tapper 1983
J. Fletcher, M. Cholmondeley Tapper, 'Hans Holbein the Younger at Antwerp and in England 1526-28', *Apollo* 117 (1983), no. 252, pp. 87-93
Floerke 1906
H. Floerke (ed.), *Das Leben der niederländischen und deutschen Maler des Carel van Mander. Textabdruck nach der Ausgabe von 1617*, vol. 1, Munich-Leipzig 1906
Florence 1971
Firenze e l'Inghilterra: Rapporte artistici e culturali dal XVI al XX secolo, Florence (Palazzo Pitti) 1971
Foister 1981
S. Foister, *Holbein And His English Patrons* (dissertation University of London, Courtauld Institute of Art), London 1981
Foister 1983
S. Foister, *Drawings by Holbein from the Royal Library Windsor Castle*, New York 1983 (see also Parker 1945)
Foister 1991
S. Foister, 'Holbein as Court Painter', in *Greenwich 1991*, pp. 58-60
Foister 1992
S. Foister, 'A Lady with a Squirrel and a Starling by Holbein: Illusion and invention for an unknown sitter', *National Art Collections Fund: Annual Review* (1992), pp. 30-34
Foister 1993a
S. Foister, 'Workshop or Followers? Underdrawing in some Portraits Associated with Hans Holbein the

Younger', *Le dessin sous-jacent dans la peinture: Colloque IX (1991)*, Leuven 1993, pp. 113-124
Foister 1993b
S. Foister, 'Foreigners at Court: Holbein, Van Dyck and the London Painter-Stainers Company', in D. Howarth (ed.), *Art and Patronage at the Caroline Courts*, Cambridge 1993, pp. 32-50
Foister 1995-1996
S. Foister, 'The Production and Reproduction of Holbein's Portraits', in *London 1995-1996*, pp. 21-28
Foister 1996a
S. Foister, '"My foolish curiosity": Holbein in the collection of the Earl of Arundel', *Apollo* 144 (1996), no. 414, pp. 51-56
Foister 1996b
S. Foister, 'Ambrosius Holbein', in J. Turner (ed.), *The Dictionary of Art*, vol. 14, London 1996, pp. 665-666
Foister 1997
S. Foister, 'Holbein in England: Ein Höhepunkt der Portraitmalerei', *Belvedere: Zeitschrift für bildende Kunst* 3 (1997), no. 2, pp. 42-59
Foister 2001
S. Foister, 'Holbein's Paintings on Canvas: The Greenwich Festivities of 1527', in *Roskill/Hand 2001*, pp. 109-123
Foister/Wyld/Roy 1994
S. Foister, M. Wyld, A. Roy, 'Hans Holbein's *'A Lady with a Squirrel and a Starling'*, *National Gallery Technical Bulletin* 15 (1994), pp. 7-19
De la Fontaine Verwey 1969
H. de la Fontaine Verwey, 'Michel le Blon: Graveur, Kunsthandelaar, Diplomaat', *Jaarboek Amstelodamum* 61 (1969), pp. 103-125
Foucart-Walter 1985
See *Paris 1985*
Fraser 1992
A. Fraser, *The Six Wives of Henry VIII*, London 1992
Friedländer 1942
M.J. Friedländer, *On Art and Connoisseurship*, London [1942]
Von Frimmel 1887
T. von Frimmel, 'Kunsthistorisches: Zwei Bildnisse von Hans Holbein d.J.', *Kunstchronik: Beiblat zur Zeitschrift für bildende Kunst* 22 (1887), col. 379-380
Von Frimmel 1896
T. von Frimmel, *Kleine Galeriestudien. Neue Folge. III. Lieferung: Die Gräflich Schönborn-Buchheim'sche Gemäldesammlung in Wien*, Leipzig 1896
Von Frimmel 1923
T. von Frimmel, 'Das Wedigh-Bildnis von Hans Holbein dem Jüngeren in der Wiener Galerie Schönbrun-Puchheim', in *Von alter und Neuer Kunst (Ausgewählte Kunstgeschichtliche Aufsätze)*, Vienna [1923], pp. 48-49 (previously published in *Wiener Galerien*)

G

Ganz 1911-1926
P. Ganz, *Die Handzeichnungen Hans Holbein d.J. in 50 Lieferungen und kritisches Katalog*, Berlin 1911-1926
Ganz 1912
P. Ganz, *Hans Holbein d.J. Des Meisters Gemälde in 252 Abbildungen*, Stuttgart-Leipzig 1912
Ganz 1923
P. Ganz, *Handzeichnungen von Hans Holbein d.J.*, Berlin 1923
Ganz 1937
P. Ganz, *Die Handzeichnungen Hans Holbeins d.J.: Kritischer Katalog*, Berlin 1937
Ganz 1950
P. Ganz, *The Paintings of Hans Holbein: First Complete Edition*, London 1950
Geelen 1917
W. Geelen, 'Mitteilungen über Porträts des Kölner Patriciergeslechts von Wedigh und Unterlagen zur Bestimmung derselben', *Beiträge zur Kölnischen Geschichte / Sprache / Eigenart* (1917), nos. 10-11, pp. 171-195
Gerlo 1969
A. Gerlo, *Erasme et ses portraitistes: Metsijs, Dürer, Holbein* (2nd edition), Nieuwkoop 1969 (1st edition: 1950)
Gien 1994
C. Parpoil, T. Vincent (eds.), *La chasse au vol au fil des temps*, Gien (Musée International de la Chasse) 1994
Giglioli 1909
O. Giglioli in *Rivista d'Arte* 6 (1909), pp. 333-337
Glaser 1924
C. Glaser, *Hans Holbein d.J. Zeichnungen*, Basel 1924
Godfrey 1996
R. Godfrey, 'Hollar's prints for the Earl or Arundel: Copies of lost works from the Arundel Collection', *Apollo* 144 (1996), no. 414, pp. 36-38
Götz 1932
O. Götz, 'Holbeins Bildnis des Simon George of Quocoute', *Städel Jahrbuch* 8 (1932), pp. 116-148
Goodison 1977
J.W. Goodison, *Catalogue of Paintings in the Fitzwilliam Museum, Cambridge, vol. III: British School*, Cambridge 1977
Greenwich 1991
D. Starkey (ed.), *Henry VIII: A European Court in England*, Greenwich (National Maritime Museum) 1991
Griener 2001
P. Griener, 'Alfred Woltmann and the Holbein dispute, 1863-1871', in *Roskill/Hand 2001*, pp. 211-225
Groebner 2000
V. Groebner, *Gefährliche Geschenke: Ritual, Politik und die Sprache der Korruption in der Eidgenossenschaft im späten Mittelalter und am Beginn der Neuzeit*, Konstanz 2000
Grohn 1955
H.W. Grohn, *Hans Holbein d.J. als Maler*, Leipzig 1955
Gronert 1996
S. Gronert, *Bild-Individualität: Die "Erasmus"-Bildnisse von Hans Holbein dem Jüngeren*, Basel 1996
Grossmann 1951
F. Grossmann, 'Holbein Studies - II', *The Burlington Magazine* 93 (1951), pp. 111-114
Grossmann 1961
F. Grossmann, 'A Religious Allegory by Hans Holbein the Younger', *The Burlington Magazine* 103 (1961) pp. 491-494
Grundmann 1970
G. Grundmann, *The Darmstadt Madonna*, Darmstadt 1970
Guy 1985
J. Guy, *Tudor England*, Oxford 1985
Guy 2000
J. Guy, *Thomas More*, London 2000

H

Habich 1913
G. Habich, 'Ein Miniaturbildnis von Hans Holbein in Danzig', *Zeitschrift für bildende Kunst* 24 (1913), pp. 194-196
The Hague 1966
150 jaar Koninklijk Kabinet van Schilderijen, Koninklijke Bibliotheek, Koninklijk Penningkabinet, The Hague (Mauritshuis) 1966
The Hague 1988-1989
B. Brenninkmeyer-de Rooij, B. Broos, E. de Heer & B. Slot, *Paintings from England: William III and the Royal Collections*, The Hague (Mauritshuis) 1988-1989
The Hague-Apeldoorn-Nagasaki 1991-1992
M. Tiethoff, K. Schaffers, *Portretten in miniatuur: Portretminiaturen uit de stadhouderlijke en koninklijke verzamelingen*, The Hague (Mauritshuis), Apeldoorn (Nationaal Museum Paleis Het Loo), Nagasaki (Palace Huis ten Bosch Museum) 1991-1992
Hamburg-Basel 1988
J. Roberts, *Holbein: Zeichnungen vom Hoff Heinrichs VIII. Fünfzig Zeichnungen aus der Sammlung Ihrer Majestät Queen Elizabeth II, Windsor Castle*, Hamburg (Kunsthalle), Basel (Kunstmuseum) 1988 (see also *Houston-Hamburg-Basel-Toronto 1987-1989*)
Hand 1993
O. Hand, with S.E. Mansfield, *German Paintings of the Fifteenth through Seventeenth Centuries* (The Collections of the National Gallery of Art: Systematic Catalogue), Washington-New Haven 1993
Hannover 2000
M. Trudzinski, *Edward VI. als Kind: Ein Wiedersehen* (Meisterwerke zu Gast in der Niedersächsischen Landesgalerie Hannover, vol. V), Hannover (Niedersächsisches Landesmuseum) 2000
Harting 1891
J.E. Harting, *A Catalogue of Books, Ancient and Modern, Relating to Falconry with Notes, Glossary, and Vocabulary*, London 1891
Hartmann 1957
A. Hartmann, 'Bonifacius Amerbach als Verwalter der Erasmusstiftung', *Basler Jahrbuch* (1957)
Head 1995
D.M. Head, *The Ebbs and Flows of Fortune: The Life of Thomas Howard, Third Duke of Norfolk*, Athene-London 1995
Hemelrijk 1951
J.M. Hemelrijk, 'Latijn op schilderijen', *Hermeneus: Maandblad voor de Antieke Cultuur* 23 (1951), pp. 46-48
Hervey 1900
M.F.S. Hervery, *Holbein's "Ambassadors": The Picture and the Men*, London 1900
Hervey 1921
M. Hervey, *The Life, Correspondence and Collections of Thomas Howard, Earl of Arundel*, Cambridge 1921
Hilliard ed. 1981
R.K.R. Thornton, T.G.S. Cain, *A Treatise Concerning the*

Arte of Limning by Nicholas Hilliard, Manchester 1981
Hinz 1991
B. Hinz, 'Holbeins "Schola Thomae Mori" von 1527', in H. Wunder, C. Vanja (eds.), *Wandel der Geschlechterbeziehungen zu Beginn der Neuzeit*, Frankfurt am Main 1991, pp. 69-96
His 1870
E. His, 'Die Basler Archive über Hans Holbein den Jüngeren, seine Familie und einige zu ihm in Beziehung stehende Zeitgenossen', in A. von Zahn (ed.), *Jahrbücher für Kunstwissenschaft* 3 (1870), pp. 113-173
His 1879
E. His, 'Holbeins Verhältniss zur Basler Reformation', *Repertorium für Kunstwissenschaft* 2 (1879), pp. 156-159
Hoet/Terwesten 1752–1770
G. Hoet, P. Terwesten, *Catalogus of naamlyst van schilderyen, met derzelver pryzen* (3 vols.), The Hague 1752–1770
Hofstede de Groot 1892
C. Hofstede de Groot, 'Schilderijenverzamelingen van het Geslacht Slingelandt [...]', *Oud Holland* 10 (1892), pp. 229-237
Holman 1979
T.S. Holman, 'Holbein's Portraits of the Steelyard Merchants: An Investigation', *Metropolitan Museum Journal* 14 (1979), pp. 139-158
Houston-Hamburg-Basel-Toronto 1987–1989
J. Roberts, *Drawings by Holbein from the Court of Henry VIII: Fifty Drawings from the Collection of Her Majesty the Queen, Windsor Castle*, Houston (The Museum of Fine Arts), Hamburg (Hamburger Kunsthalle), Basel (Kunstmuseum), Toronto (Art Gallery of Toronto) 1987-1989 (see *Hamburg-Basel 1988*)
Howarth 1985
D. Howarth, *Lord Arundel and his Circle*, London-New Haven 1985
Hulftegger 1950
A. Hulftegger, *Les dessins de Holbein*, Paris 1950

I

Ives 1994
E.W. Ives, 'The Queen and the painters: Anne Boleyn, Holbein and Tudor Royal Portraits', *Apollo* 140 (1994), no. 389, pp. 36-45

J

Jacquart 1997
J. Jacquart, *François Ier*, Paris 1997
James 1998
S.E. James, '"Lady Margaret Douglas" and "Sir Thomas Seymour" by Holbein: Two miniatures re-identified', *Apollo* 147 (1998), no. 435, pp. 15-20

K

Karlsruhe 2001–2002
Spätmittelalter am Oberrhein: Maler und Werkstätten 1450–1525, Karlsruhe (Staatliche Kunsthalle Karlsruhe) 2001-2002
Kellenbenz 1980
H. Kellenbenz, 'Augsburger Wirtschaft 1530-1620', in *Augsburg 1980*, vol. 1, pp. 50-71
Kimpel 1974
S. Kimpel, 'Jakobus der Ältere', in W. Braunfels (ed.), *Lexikon der christlichen Ikonographie*, vol. 7, Rome 1974, pp. 23-39
Kirwan 1994
J. Kirwan, 'A Portrait of James Butler, 9th Earl of Ormond', *Butler Society* 3 (1994), no. 4, pp. 512-513
Klemm 1980
C. Klemm, *Hans Holbein d.J. im Kunstmuseum Basel*, Basel 1980
Klinger/Höttler 1998
D.M. Klinger, A. Höttler, *Holbein: Die Malerbrüder Ambrosius und Hans d.J., Werkverzeichnis: Gemälde und Miniaturen*, Nuremberg 1998
Knackfuss 1896
H. Knackfuss, *Holbein der jüngere*, Bielefeld-Leipzig 1896
Koerner 2002–2003
J. Koerner, 'Albrecht Dürer: A Sixteenth-Century Influenza', in *London 2002-2003*, pp. 18-38
Krause 1998
K. Krause, 'Hans Holbein d.Ä. und Hans Burgkmair: Alternativen in der Augsburger Malerei um 1500', *Zeitschrift für Schweizerische Archäologie und Kunstgeschichte* 55 (1998), p. 111
Krause 2002
K. Krause, *Hans Holbein der Ältere*, Munich-Berlin 2002
Krummacher 1963
H. Krummacher, 'Zu Holbeins Bildnissen Rheinischer Kaufleute', *Wallraf-Richartz Jahrbuch* 25 (1963), pp. 181-192
Künast 2001
H.-J. Künast, 'Die Graphiksammlung des Augsburger Stadtschreibers Konrad Peutinger', in J. Roger Paas (ed.), *Augsburg, die Bilderfabrik Europas: Essays zur Augsburger Druckgraphik der Frühen Neuzeit*, Augsburg 2001, pp. 11-19

L

Landolt 1960
H. Landolt, *Das Skizzenbuch Hans Holbeins des Älteren im Kupferstichkabinett Basel*, Olten-Lausanne-Freiburg 1960
Lehmberg 1960
S.E. Lehmberg, *Sir Thomas Elyot: Tudor Humanist*, Austin, Texas 1960
Lemmer 1986
M. Lemmer (ed.), *Sebastian Brant, Das Narrenschiff: Nach der Erstausgabe (Basel 1494) mit den Zusätzen der Ausgaben von 1495 und 1499 sowie den Holzschnitten der deutschen Originalausgaben* (3rd edition), Tübingen 1986 (1st edition: 1962)
Lewi 1974
A. Lewi, *The Thomas More Family Group*, London 1974
Lewis 1998
L. Lewis, *The Thomas More group portrait after Holbein*, Leominster 1998
Lieb 1958
N. Lieb, *Die Fugger und die Kunst im Zeitalter der hohen Renaissance*, Munich 1958
Liverpool 1960
Pictures from Ince Blundell Hall, Liverpool (Walker Art Gallery) 1960
Liverpool 2003
X. Brooke, D. Crombie, *Henry VIII Revealed: Holbein's Portrait and its Legacy*, Liverpool (National Museums & Galleries on Merseyside, The Walker) 2003
Löcher 1985
K. Löcher, 'Der Londoner Stahlhof und Hans Holbein', in C. Meckseper (ed.), in *Stadt und Wandel: Kunst und Kultur des Bürgertums in Norddeutschland 1150-1650*, vol. 3, Niedersachsen (Landesausstellung) 1985, pp. 667-686
London 1950–1951
Catalogue of the exhibition of works by Holbein & other masters of the 16th and 17th centuries, London (Royal Academy of Arts) 1950-1951
London 1959
The Houghton Pictures, London (Agnew's) 1959
London 1977–1978
J.B. Trapp, H. Schulte Herbrüggen, *'The King's Good Servant': Sir Thomas More*, London (National Portrait Gallery) 1977-1978
London 1978–1979
Holbein and the Court of Henry VIII, London (The Queen's Gallery, Buckingham Palace) 1978-1979 (see also *Rowlands 1979*)
London 1980–1981
Princely Magnificence: Court Jewels of the Renaissance, 1500-1630, London (Victoria and Albert Museum) 1980-1981
London 1983
R. Strong, *Artists of the Tudor Court: The Portrait Miniature Rediscovered 1520–1620*, London (Victoria and Albert Museum) 1983
London 1988–1989
Treasures from the Royal Collection, London (The Queen's Gallery, Buckingham Palace) 1988-1989
London 1990–1991
C. Lloyd, S. Thurley, *Henry VIII: Images of a Tudor King*, London (Hampton Court Palace) 1990-1991
London 1995–1996
K. Hearn (ed.), *Dynasties: Painting in Tudor and Jacobean England 1530–1630*, London (The Tate Gallery) 1995-1996
London 1997–1998
S. Foister, A. Roy, M. Wyld, *Making & Meaning: Holbein's Ambassadors*, London (The National Gallery) 1997-1998
London 2002–2003a
G. Bartrum et al., *Albrecht Dürer and his Legacy: The Graphic Work of a Renaissance Artist*, London (The British Museum) 2002-2003
London 2002–2003b
J. Roberts, *Royal Treasures: A Golden Jubilee Celebration*, London (The Queen's Gallery, Buckingham Palace) 2002-2003
London 2003
[S. Foister], *Holbein: Portraits of Sir Henry and Lady Guildford*, London (The National Gallery) 2003 (brochure)

London-The Hague 1999–2000
C. White, Q. Buvelot (eds.), *Rembrandt by himself*, London (The National Gallery), The Hague (Mauritshuis) 1999-2000
Lübbeke 1991
I. Lübbeke, *The Thyssen-Bornemisza Collection: Early German Paintings 1350–1550*, London 1991
Lugt 1917
F. Lugt, *Le portrait-miniature illustré par la collection de S. M. la Reine des Pays-Bas*, Amsterdam-Leipzig 1917
Lugt 1938–1987
F. Lugt et al., *Répertoire des catalogues de ventes publiques intéressant l'art ou la curiosité* (4 vols.), The Hague-Paris 1938-1987
Lunsingh Scheurleer 1967
T.H. Lunsingh Scheurleer, 'De stadhouderlijke verzamelingen', in *150 jaar Koninklijk Kabinet van Schilderijen, Koninklijke Bibliotheek, Koninklijk Penningkabinet*, The Hague 1967, pp. 11-50

M

Machilek 2000
F. Machilek, 'Albrecht Dürer und der Humanismus in Nürnberg', in *Nuremberg 2000*, pp. 44-76
Maclehose 1960
L.S. Maclehose, *Vasari on Technique*, New York 1960
Mähl 1980
H.-J. Mähl (ed.), *Sebastian Brant: Das Narrenschiff übertragen von Hermann A. Junghans*, Stuttgart 1980
Major 1964
J.M. Major, *Sir Thomas Elyot and Tudor Humanism*, Lincoln, Nebraska 1964
Malibu-New York 1982–1983
Holbein and the Court of Henry VIII: Drawings from the Collection of H.M. Queen Elizabeth II, Windsor Castle, Malibu (The J. Paul Getty Museum), New York (The Pierpont Morgan Library) 1982-1983
Manchester 1961
German Art 1400–1800, Manchester (City Art Gallery) 1961
Van Mander 1604
K. van Mander, *Het Schilder-boeck*, Haarlem 1604
Van Mander/Miedema 1994–1999
K. van Mander, *The lives of the illustrious Netherlandish and German Painters*, edited by H. Miedema (6 vols.), Doornspijk 1994-1999
Mandrella 1999
D. Mandrella, *Dessins allemands et flamands du Musée Condé à Chantilly: De Dürer à Rubens*, Chantilly 1999
Manuth 1998
V. Manuth, 'Zum Nachleben der Werke Hans Holbeins d.J. in der holländischen Malerei und Graphik des 17. Jahrhunderts', *Zeitschrift für Schweizerische Archäologie und Kunstgeschichte* 55 (1998), pp. 323-336 (reprinted in *Senn 1999*, pp. 323-336)
Marani 1999
P.C. Marani, *Leonardo da Vinci: The Complete Paintings*, New York 1999
Markow 1978
D. Markow, 'Hans Holbein's Steelyard Portraits, reconsidered', *Wallraf-Richartz Jahrbuch* 40 (1978), pp. 39-47
Mauquoy-Hendrikx 1991
M. Mauquoy-Hendrikx, *L'Iconographie d'Antoine van Dyck: Catalogue Raisonné* (2 vols.), Brussels 1991
Meder 1919
J. Meder, *Die Handzeichnung*, Vienna 1919
Meier 1996
N. Meier, 'Zeitgeschehen und Heilserwartung: Die Krone der "Darmstädter Madonna" von Hans Holbein', *Zeitschrift für Schweizerische Archäologie und Kunstgeschichte* 53 (1996), pp. 231-247
Mellen 1971
P. Mellen, *Jean Clouet: Complete Edition of the Drawings, Miniatures and Paintings*, London-New York 1971
Metzger 2002
C. Metzger, *Hans Schäufelin als Maler*, Berlin 2002
Michael 1986
E. Michael, *The Drawings by Hans Holbein the Younger for Erasmus' 'Praise of Folly'* (dissertation), New York-London 1986
Michael 1997
E. Michael, *Hans Holbein the Younger: A Guide to Research*, New York-London 1997
Millar 1963
O. Millar, *The Tudor, Stuart and Early Georgian Pictures in the Collection of Her Majesty the Queen* (2 vols.), London 1963
Monti 1986
R.C. Monti, *Terence: Andria (Bryn Mawr Latin Commentaries*, 2 vols.), Bryn Mawr 1986
Morison/Barker 1963
S. Morison, N. Barker, *The Likeness of Thomas More*, London 1963
Müller 1988
C. Müller, *Hans Holbein d.J. Zeichnungen aus dem Kupferstichkabinett der Öffentliche Kunstsammlung Basel*, Basel 1988
Müller 1996
C. Müller, *Öffentliche Kunstsammlung Basel, Kupferstichkabinett. Katalog der Zeichnungen des 15. und 16. Jahrhunderts. Teil 2A. Die Zeichnungen von Hans Holbein dem Jüngeren und Ambrosius Holbein*, Basel 1996
Müller 1997
C. Müller, *Hans Holbein d.J. Die Druckgraphik im Kupferstichkabinett Basel*, Basel 1997
Munich 1869
Ausstellung alter Bilder, Munich (location unknown) 1869
Munich 2003
B. Fassbinder, H. Asenbaum, M. Kersting, *Barocke Sammellust: Die Sammlung Schönborn-Buchheim*, Munich (Haus der Kunst) 2003
Murdoch *et al.* **1981**
J. Murdoch, J. Murrell, D.J. Noon, R. Strong, *The English Miniature*, New Haven-London 1981
Murray 1819
J. Murray, *Tour in Holland in the year MDCCCXIX*, London [1819]

N

New York 1928
A Loan Exhibition of Twelve Masterpieces of Painting, New York (M. Knoedler & Co) 1928
New York 1939
Masterpieces of Art, New York (New York World's Fair) 1939
New York 1952–1953
Art Treasures of the Metropolitan, New York (The Metropolitan Museum of Art) 1952-1953
New York 1956
German Drawings, New York (The Metropolitan Museum of Art) 1956
New York 1970
Masterpieces of Fifty Centuries, New York (The Metropolitan Museum of Art) 1970
New York 1979
William & Mary and their House, New York (The Pierpont Morgan Library) 1979
New York 1983
Holbein and the Court of Henry VIII: Drawings from the Collection of Her Majesty Queen Elizabeth II, New York (The Pierpont Morgan Library) 1983
New York 1996–1997
C. Lloyd, V. Remington, *Masterpieces in little: Portrait Miniatures from the Collection of Her Majesty Queen Elizabeth II*, New York (The Metropolitan Museum of Art) 1996-1997
North 2002
J. North, *The ambassadors' secret*, London 2002
Norwich 1992
A. Moore, C. Crawley, *Family and Friends: A Regional Survey of British Portraiture*, Norwich (Norwich Castle Museum) 1992
Nuremberg 2000
M. Mende et al., *Albrecht Dürer: Ein Künstler in seiner Stadt*, Nuremberg (Stadtmuseum Fembohaus) 2000

O

Oberhammer 1935
V. Oberhammer, *Die Bronzestandbilder des Maximilian-Grabmales in der Hofkirche zu Innsbruck*, Innsbruck 1935
Ost 1980
H. Ost, 'Ein italo-flämisches Hochzeitsbild und Überlegungen zur ikonographischen Struktur des Gruppenporträts im 16. Jahrhundert', *Wallraf-Richartz-Jahrbuch* 41 (1980), pp. 133-142

P

Pächt 1944
O. Pächt, 'Holbein and Kratzer as Collaborators', *The Burlington Magazine* 84 (1944), pp. 134-139
Palmer Wandel 1995
L. Palmer Wandel, *Voracious idols and violent hands: Iconoclasm in Reformation Zurich, Strasbourg, and Basel*, Cambridge 1995
Panofsky 1955
E. Panofsky, *The Life and Art of Albrecht Dürer*, Princeton 1955
Panofsky 1969
E. Panofsky, 'Erasmus and the Visual Arts', *Journal of*

the Warburg and Courtauld Institutes 32 (1969), pp. 200-227

Paris 1985
E. Foucart-Walter, with P. Klein, *Les peintures de Hans Holbein le Jeune au Louvre (Les dossiers du Département des Peintures*, vol. 29), Paris (Musée du Louvre) 1985

Paris 1991-1992
Dessins de Dürer et de la Renaissance germanique dans les collections publiques parisiennes, Paris (Musée du Louvre, Cabinet des Dessins) 1991-1992

Parker 1938
K.T. Parker, *Catalogue of the Collection of Drawings in the Ashmolean Museum: Netherlandish, German, French and Spanish Schools*, Oxford 1938

Parker 1945
K.T. Parker, *The Drawings of Hans Holbein in the Collection of His Majesty the King at Windsor Castle*, Oxford-London 1945 (see also Foister 1983)

Parthey 1853
G. Parthey, *Wenzel Hollar*, Berlin 1853

Parthey/Pennington 1982
R. Pennington (ed.), *A Descriptive Catalogue of the Etched Work of Wenceslaus Hollar* (revised edition of Parthey 1853), Cambridge 1982

Patin 1676
[C. Patin], 'Index Operum Joh. Holbeinii', in [*Moriae Enconium*]. *Stultitiae laus. Des. Erasmi Rot. declamatio, Cum commentariis Ger. Listrii, & figuris Jo. Holbeinii. E codice Academiae Basiliensis*, Basel 1676

Peltzer 1925
A.R. Peltzer (ed.), *Joachim von Sandrarts Academie der Bau-, Bild- und Mahlerey-Kunste von 1675: Leben der berühmten Maler, Bildhauer und Baumeister*, Munich 1925

Périer-D'Ieteren 1982-1983
C. Périer-D'Ieteren, 'Dessin au poncif et dessin perforé: Leur utilisation dans les anciens Pays-Bas au XVe siècle', *Bulletin van het Koninklijk Instituut voor het Kunstpatrimonium* 19 (1982-1983), pp. 74-94

Petter 2002
K. Petter, '"Wenn du die Stimme hinzufügst, ist hier Derich selbst,...": Eine Spurensuche zu den Stalhof-Portraits von Hans Holbein d.J.', *Belvedere: Zeitschrift für bildende Kunst* 8 (2002), no. 1, pp. 4-17 (with an English translation on pp. 74-80)

Pinder 1951
W. Pinder, *Holbein der Jüngere und das Ende der Altdeutschen Kunst*, Cologne 1951

Pollard 1951
A.F. Pollard, *Henry VIII*, London-New York-Toronto 1985

R

Raupp 1984
H.-J. Raupp, *Untersuchungen zu Künstlerbildnis und Künstlerdarstellung in den Niederlanden im 17. Jahrhundert*, Hildesheim-Zürich-New York 1984

Reinhardt 1954-1955
H. Reinhardt, 'Die Madonna des Bürgermeisters Meyer von Hans Holbein d. J.: Nachforschungen zur Entstehungsgeschichte und Aufstellung des Gemäldes', *Zeitschrift für Schweizerische Archäologie und Kunstgeschichte* 15 (1954-1955), pp. 244-254

Reinhardt 1975
H. Reinhardt, 'Ein unbekannter Holzschnitt Hans Holbeins d. J. von 1536 und Holbeins Melanchthon Bildnis', *Zeitschrift für Schweizerische Archäologie und Kunstgeschichte* 32 (1975), pp. 135-140

Reinhardt 1981
H. Reinhardt, 'Erasmus und Holbein', *Basler Zeitschrift für Geschichte und Altertumskunde* 81 (1981), pp. 41-70

Reinhardt 1982
H. Reinhardt, 'Nachrichten über das Leben Hans Holbeins des Jüngeren', *Zeitschrift für Schweizerische Archäologie und Kunstgeschichte* 39 (1982), pp. 253-276

Reynolds 1988
G. Reynolds, *English Portrait Miniatures* (revised edition), Cambridge 1988

Reynolds 1999
G. Reynolds, *The Sixteenth and Seventeenth-Century Miniatures in the Collection of Her Majesty the Queen*, London 1999

Ridley 1984
J. Ridley, *Henry VIII*, London 1984

Van Riemsdijk 1892
B.W.F. van Riemsdijk, 'Schilderijenkabinetten in de XVIIIe eeuw', *Oud Holland* 10 (1892), pp. 219-228

Riggenbach 1944
R. Riggenbach, 'Die Besitzungen der Walliser in Basel', *Blätter aus der Walliser Geschichte* 9 (1944), pp. 473-502

Roberts 1979
J. Roberts, *Holbein*, London 1979

Roskill 2001
M. Roskill, '*Lady with a Squirrel and a Starling* by Holbein: Incursions of the Figurative in His Portraits', in Roskill/Hand 2001, pp. 174-185

Roskill/Hand 2001
M. Roskill, J.O. Hand (eds.), *Hans Holbein: Paintings, Prints, and Reception* (*Studies in the History of Art*, vol. 60), Washington 2001

Roskill/Harbison 1987
M. Roskill, C. Harbison, 'On the nature of Holbein's portraits', *Word and Image* 3 (1987), no. 1, pp. 1-26

Roth/Dürr 1937
P. Roth, E. Dürr (eds.), *Aktensammlung zur Geschichte der Basler Reformation in den Jahren 1519 bis Anfang 1534*, vol. 3, Basel 1937

Rotterdam 1910
Catalogus der Tentoonstelling van Portretminiaturen, Rotterdam (Rotterdamsche Kunstkring) 1910

Rotterdam 1969
Erasmus en zijn tijd, Rotterdam (Museum Boijmans Van Beuningen) 1969

Rowlands 1979
J. Rowlands, 'Review: Holbein and the Court of Henry VIII', *Master Drawings* 17 (1979), pp. 53-56

Rowlands 1985
J. Rowlands, *Holbein: The Paintings of Hans Holbein the Younger. Complete Edition*, Oxford 1985

Rowlands 1993
J. Rowlands, with G. Bartrum, *Drawings by German Artists and Artists from German-Speaking Regions of Europe in the Department of Prints and Drawings in the British Museum: The Fifteenth Century, and the Sixteenth Century by Artists Born before 1530* (2 vols.), London 1993

Roy/Wyld 2001
A. Roy, M. Wyld, '*The Ambassadors* and Holbein's Techniques for Painting on Panel', in Roskill/Hand 2001, pp. 96-107

Rupprich 1956
H. Rupprich (ed.), *Dürer: Schriftlicher Nachlass* (3 vols.), Berlin 1956

S

Von Sandrart 1675
J. von Sandrart, *L'Academia Todesca della Architectura, Scultura & Pittura: Oder Teutsche Academie der Edlen Bau- Bild- und Mahlerey-Kuenste* [...], Nuremberg-Frankfurt am Main 1675

Scarisbrick 1981
J.J. Scarisbrick, *Henry VIII*, London 1981

Scarisbrick 1995
D. Scarisbrick, *Tudor and Jacobean Jewellery*, London 1995

Schaffers-Bodenhausen/Tiethoff-Spliethoff 1993
K. Schaffers-Bodenhausen, M. Tiethoff-Spliethoff, *The Portrait Miniatures in the Collections of the House of Orange-Nassau*, The Hague-Zwolle 1993

Schaffhausen 1951
Meisterwerke flämische Malerei, Schaffhausen (Museum zu Allerheiligen) 1951

Schauerte 2001
T.U. Schauerte, *Die Ehrenpforte für Kaiser Maximilian I. Dürer und Altdorfer im Dienst des Herrschers*, Munich-Berlin 2001

Scheicher 1986
E. Scheicher, 'Das Grabmal Kaiser Maximilians I. in der Hofkirche', in *Die Kunstdenkmäler der Stadt Innsbruck, Die Hofbauten* (*Österreichische Kunsttopographie*, vol. 47), Vienna 1986, pp. 359-426

Schmid 1931
H. A. Schmid, *Erasmi Roterodami Encomium Moriae, i.e. Stultitiae Laus Lob der Torheit* (2 vols.), Basel 1931

Schmid 1948
H.A. Schmid, *Hans Holbein der Jüngere: Sein Aufsteig zur Meisterschaft und sein englischer Stil* (3 vols.), Basel 1948

Schmidt 1941-1945
G. Schmidt, 'Ein Selbstbildnis Hans Holbein des Jüngeren unter den Randzeichnungen zum "Lob der Torheit"?', *Öffentliche Kunstsammlung Basel: Jahresberichte 1941-1945*, pp. 144-156

Senn 1999
M. Senn (ed.), *Hans Holbein der Jüngere: Akten des Internationalen Symposiums Basel, 26.-28. Juni 1997*, Basel 1999

Shaw 1937
W.A. Shaw (ed.), *Three inventories of the years 1542, 1547 and 1549-50 of pictures in the collections of Henry VIII and Eduard VI*, London 1937

Siebmacher 1890
G.A. Seyler (ed.), *J. Siebmacher's grosses und allgemeines Wappenbuch in einer neuen, vollständig geordneten und reich vermehrten Auflage mit heraldischen und historisch-*

genealogischen Erläuterungen. Fünften Bandes vierte Abtheilung. Zweitausend bürgerliche Wappen, Nuremberg 1890
Silver 1984
L. Silver, *The Paintings of Quinten Massys with Catalogue Raisonné*, Oxford 1984
Sloan 1997
K. Sloan, 'Sir William Hamilton's "Insuperable Taste for Painting"', *Journal of the History of Collections* 9 (1997), pp. 205-227
Starkey 1981
D. Starkey, 'Holbein's Irish Sitter?', *The Burlington Magazine* 123 (1981), pp. 300-303
Starkey 1985
D. Starkey, *The Reign of Henry VIII: Personalities and Politics*, London 1985
Starkey 1987
D. Starkey et al., *The English Court: From the Wars of the Roses to the Civil War*, London 1987
Starkey 1998
D. Starkey (ed.), P. Ward, A. Hawkyard, *The Inventory of King Henry VIII: Society of Antiquaries MS 129 and British Library MS Harley 1419*, London 1998
Strauss 1980
W.L. Strauss, *Albrecht Dürer: Woodcuts and Woodblock*, New York 1980
Strong 1967
R. Strong, *Holbein and Henry VIII*, London-New York 1967
Strong 1969
R. Strong, *National Portrait Gallery: Tudor and Jacobean Portraits*, London 1969
Strong 1983
R. Strong, *The English Renaissance Miniature*, London 1983
Strong 1995
R. Strong, *The Tudor and Stuart Monachy: Pageantry, Painting, Iconography, I. Tudor*, Woodbridge 1995
Strong *et al.* 1981
R. Strong et al., *The English Miniature*, New Haven-London 1981
De Stuers 1874
V. de Stuers, *Notice historique et descriptive des tableaux et des sculptures exposés dans le musée royal de La Haye*, The Hague 1874

T

Taubert 1975
J. Taubert, 'Pauspunkte in Tafelbildern des 15. und 16. Jahrhunderts', *Bulletin de l'Institut Royale du Patrimoine Artistique* 15 (1975), pp. 387-401
Thieme/Becker 1907-1950
U. Thieme, F. Becker, *Allgemeines Lexicon der bildenden Künstler von der Antike bis zur Gegenwart* (37 vols.), Leipzig 1907-1950
Thurley 1991
S. Thurley, 'The Banqueting and Disguising Houses of 1527', in *Greenwich 1991*, pp. 64-69
Thurley 1993
S. Thurley, *The Royal Palaces of Tudor England*, New Haven-London 1993
Tóth-Ubbens 1968
M. Tóth-Ubbens, *Schilderijen en beeldhouwwerken 15e en 16e eeuw: Catalogus 1*, The Hague 1968
Trapp/Herbrüggen 1977-1978
See London 1977-1978
Trudzinski 2000
M. Trudzinski, *Hans Holbein Edward VI. als Kind: Ein Wiedersehen*, Hannover 2000 (see *Hannover 2000*)

V

Vögelin 1887
S. Vögelin, 'Wer hat Holbein die Kenntnis des classischen Altertums vermittelt?', *Repertorium für Kunstwissenschaft* 10 (1887), pp. 345-371

W

Waetzoldt 1938
W. Waetzoldt, *Hans Holbein der Jüngere: Werk und Welt*, Berlin 1938
Van de Wall 1986
J.W.M. van de Wall, *De valkerij op Het Loo: The Royal Loo Hawking Club 1839-1855*, Haarlem 1986
Washington 1999-2000
C. Müller et al., *From Schongauer to Holbein: Master Drawings from Basel and Berlin*, Washington (National Gallery of Art) 1999-2000
Wehle/Salinger 1947
H.B. Wehle, M. Salinger, *The Metropolitan Museum of Art: A Catalogue of Early Flemish, Dutch and German Paintings*, New York 1947
Wehlte 1932
K. Wehlte, 'Röntgenologische Gemäldeuntersuchungen im Städelschen Kunstinstitut', *Städel Jahrbuch* (1932), pp. 220-227
Weijtens 1971
F.H.C. Weijtens, *De Arundel-collectie: Commencement de la fin, Amersfoort 1655*, Utrecht 1971
Wescher 1941
P. Wescher, *Grosskaufleute der Renaissance: In Biographien und Bildnissen*, Frankfurt am Main 1941
Westhoff-Krummacher 1965
H. Westhoff-Krummacher, *Barthel Bruyn der Ältere als Bildnismaler*, Munich-Berlin 1965
Wilhelm 1983
J. Wilhelm, *Augsburger Wandmalerei 1368-1530: Künstler, Handwerker und Zunft*, Augsburg 1983
Wilhelmi 2002
T. Wilhelmi, 'Zur Entstehung des "Narrenschiffs" und der illustrierten Terenz-Ausgabe', in T. Wilhelmi (ed.), *Sebastian Brant: Forschungsbeiträge zu seinem Leben, zum "Narrenschiff" und zum übrigen Werk*, Basel 2002
Wilson 1996
D. Wilson, *Hans Holbein: Portrait of an Unknown Man*, London 1996
Winkler 1937
F. Winkler, *Die Zeichnungen Albrecht Dürers* (2 vols.), Berlin 1937
Winner 2001
M. Winner, 'Holbein's Portrait of Erasmus with a Renaissance Pilaster', in *Roskill/Hand 2001*, pp. 154-173
Wolffhardt 1954
E. Wolffhardt, 'Beiträge zur Pflanzensymbolik: Über die Pflanzen des Frankfurter "Paradiesgärtleins"', *Zeitschrift für Kunstwissenschaft* 8 (1954), pp. 177-196
Woltmann 1872
A. Woltmann, *Holbein and His Time*, 1872
Woltmann 1874-1876
A. Woltmann, *Holbein und seine Zeit: Des Künstlers Familie, Leben und Schaffen* (2 vols.), Leipzig 1874-1876

Z

Zijlma 1988
R. Zijlma, 'Ambrosius to Hans Holbein the Younger', in T. Falk (ed.), *Hollstein's German Engravings, Etchings and Woodcuts 1400-1700* (vols. 14, 14a, 14B), Roosendaal 1988
Zwingenberger 1999a
J. Zwingenberger, *Holbein der Jüngere: Der Schatten des Todes*, Bournemouth 1999
Zwingenberger 1999b
J. Zwingenberger, *The Shadow of death in the Work of Hans Holbein the Younger*, London

Index

Page numbers in *italic* refer to illustrations